The Chinese Path Series

China's Financial System Development and Reform

Chen Jiangsheng, Liu Lei, Zhang Tao
Translated by Liu Huaiyu et al.
Proofread by Wang Yanshu

Paths International Ltd

中国财经出版传媒集团
经济科学出版社
Economic Science Press

Preface

The Chinese path refers to the path of socialism with distinctive Chinese characteristics. As Chinese President Xi Jinping points out, it is not an easy path. We are able to embark on this path thanks to the great endeavors of reform and opening up over the past 30 years and more, and the continuous quest made in the 60-plus years since the founding of the People's Republic of China (PRC). It is based on a thorough review of the evolution of the Chinese nation over more than 170 years since modern times and carrying forward the 5,000-year-long Chinese civilization. This path is deeply rooted in history and broadly based on China's present realities.

A right path leads to a bright future. The Chinese path is not only access to China's development and prosperity, but also a path of hope and promise to the rejuvenation of the Chinese nation. Only by forging the confidence in the path, theory, institution and culture can we advance along this path of socialism with Chinese characteristics. With this focus, *The Chinese Path Series* presents to readers an overview in practice, achievements and experiences as well as the past, present and future of the Chinese path.

The Chinese Path Series is divided into ten volumes with one hundred books on different topics. The main topics of the volumes are as follows: economic development, political advancement, cultural progress, social development, ecological conservation, national defense and armed forces building, diplomacy and international policies, the Party's leadership and building, localization of Marxism in China and views from other countries on the Chinese path. Each volume on a particular topic consists of several books which respectively throw light on exploration in practice, reform process, achievements, experiences and theoretical innovations of the Chinese path. Focusing on the practice in reform and opening up with the continuous exploration since the founding of the PRC, these books summarize on the development and inheritance of China's glorious civilization, which not only display a strong sense of the times, but also have profound historical appeal and future-oriented impact.

The series is conceived in its entirety and assigned to different authors. In terms of the writing, special attention has been paid to the combination of history and reality, as well as theory and practice at home and abroad. It gives a realistic and innovative interpretation of the practice, experience, process and theory of the Chinese path. Efforts are made on the distinctive and convincing expression in a global context. It helps to cast light on the "Chinese wisdom" and the "Chinese approach" that the Chinese path has contributed to the modernization of developing countries and solutions to human problems.

On the basis of the great achievements in China's development since the founding of the PRC, particularly since the reform and opening up, the Chinese nation, which had endured so much and for so long since the modern times, has achieved tremendous growth—it has stood up, become prosperous and grown in strength. The socialism with distinctive Chinese characteristics has shown great vitality and entered a new stage. This path has been expanded and is now at a new historical starting point. At this vital stage of development, the Economic Science Press of China Finance & Economy Media Group has designed and organized the compilation of *The Chinese Path Series*, which is of great significance in theory and practice.

The program of *The Chinese Path Series* was launched in 2015, and the first publications came out in 2017. The Series was listed in a couple of national key publication programs, the "90 kinds of selected publications in celebration of the 19th CPC National Congress", and National Publication Foundation.

Editorial Board of *The Chinese Path Series*

Contents

Chapter 1
China's Financial System Prior to Reform and Opening Up

China's long and continuous financial history twists its way in the process of integrating into vicissitudes of Chinese society, it has experienced endless despair and yielding points, featuring a wave-like advance and spiral ascent. In this chapter, we will divide China's financial developments before reform and opening up into three phases:

(1) Ancient China's financial system has seen significant developments on currency, credit and financial institutions during the millennium evolution.

(2) Republic of China's finance such as the monetary reform, developments of the banking as well as insurance industry pressed forward with indomitable will during the period of upheaval.

(3) Establishment of the unified financial system after the founding of the People's Republic of China in 1949.

1.1 Changes of ancient China's financial system

The evolution of ancient China's currency can be presented in the process of from barter system to the shells as general fixed equivalents, and later the material currency to cast currencies until the officially recognized silver as legal tender. Moreover, the credit business grew continuously with the monetary development accordingly, thus ancient China's financial industry and financial system have witnessed their prosperity through the traditional financial institutions, e.g. the recorded monetary evolution in the Book of Rites of Zhou, the pawnage transactions of Treasure Bowl (long-lasting warehouse) in the Southern and Northern Dynasties (420-589), government-owned loaning in Sui Dynasty (581-618), mortgage agency in the Song Dynasty, pawnshops as well as private banks in the Ming Dynasty (1368-1644), the exchange and draft banks in the Qing Dynasty (1644-1912).

1.1.1 The evolution of currency in ancient China

China, as one of the pioneering countries in the world to use currency, its history of using currency can be traced back to 4,000 or 5,000 years ago. The Ping Zhun Shu of Records of the Historian compiled by Sima Qian mentioned that medium of trade in agriculture, industry and commerce leads to the prevalent of tortoise shells, gold, knife and shovel-shaped coins which are used as currencies, that's too long before the ancient Gaoxin Times to be recorded. Yet the extensive use of currency gradually began to emerge with the social division of labor which enhanced the production and exchange of commodity. There were bound to be large-scale exchange of commodity with the continuous detailed division of labor in society. Thus, there must be a certain commodity and medium of exchange which can serve as a general equivalent for facilitating the transaction in the process of exchanging commodity, as opposed to merely relying on barter trade. Many materials, which served as general fixed equivalent like shells, jade, knife, salt and leather, etc., all played the role of exchanging medium in different times and regions in ancient China. In the long-lasting exchanging process, the general fixed equivalents gradually fell on a certain commodity and evolved into currency. As of its birth, currency has undergone multiple monetary reforms and evolution from shell coins, cast bronze coins to gold and silver currencies, integrating itself into the course of history.

(1) *Shell-money*

According to ancient documents, inscription on bronzes and archaeological excavations, shell coins as the earliest currency in China, emerged in about 2000 BC. As one of the most original currencies in ancient China, natural shells are also the most common and longest lasting primitive currency. Shell coins in circulation increased accordingly with the popular of commodity exchange. Because of the limited supply of natural shells, artificial shells appeared on the scene to meet people's increasing needs. Among the earliest artificial shells were stone shells, bone shells, ceramics shells and cast bronze coins which were widely into circulation in the late Shang Dynasty as the earliest metal coins in ancient China. The appearance of bronze coins led the ancient currency into a new stage, which is a significant evolution from natural currency to artificial ones.

(2) *Bronze coins*

The bronze coins were firstly used among the aristocrats and merchants after they emerged in late Shang Dynasty. The bronze developed greatly in the Western Zhou Dynasty (1046 BC-AD 771) and appeared in various shapes of bronze shells, bronze pieces, bronze compacts, fragments of bronzeware, together with the primitive shovel-shaped bronze coins. The widely used iron tools in the Spring and Autumn Period promoted the social productivity unprecedentedly. On the basis of specialized and geographically divided handicraft industry and commerce being a part of the whole society, bronze coins started to be produced massively. Yet the bronze coins of every vassal state differs greatly from one another on the shapes and currency unit due to the feudal separatist rule and the imbalance of economic development, four major monetary systems with characteristics of each vassal state gradually began to form, i.e. the shovel-shapes coins, the knife-shaped coins, the round coins and bronze coins of Chu. The shovel-shaped coin was named for its shovel-like shape which was mainly circulated among the Central Plains. Knife-shaped coin was the general expression for all the knife-shaped coins including the shapes of pointed knife and sharp knife which were cast during the Spring and Autumn Period and Warring States Period. Round coins as a kind of advanced currency, they are also called round gold or ring-shaped coins, mainly used respectively in Qin and Chu State during the Warring States Period. Bronze coins of Chu which are also named as ant's nose (Yibi) or ghost face (Guilian) coins, are bronze coins cast in State of Chu where circulated widely as major currency for its simple production process, being valued by piece and easy to carry and trade.

Nevertheless, each vassal state used its own currency caused by the imbalanced economic development, the different culture and disrupted political rule. Take the State of Qin for example, its bronze coins were cast to round shape with square hole and inscribed the characters of "Half Tael". In addition, the gold and cloth were also legal currency. China's first Monetary Law "*The Unified Currency of Qin across the Country*" was enacted in 210 BC after First Emperor of the Qin Dynasty unified China. It prescribed the nationwide circulation of the Half Tael coins which are round shaped with square hole. The nationwide circulation of Half Tael coins put an end toward the confusing circumstances incurred by various shapes and discrepancies in weight of ancient Chinese coins, presenting a major evolution in ancient China's monetary history from the messy shapes to normal ones. The Half Tael's pattern of round shape with square hole, which was officially designated, lasted until the early Republic of China.

(3) *Gold and silver currency*

Copper was associated with money for a long time by Chinese for its circulation history of more than 2000 years. If someone concerns too much about money, he or she will be derided as "smell of copper". Although there are archaeologically excavated cast gold and silver coins, no records of widely used gold and silver coins in circulation before the circulation of silver dollars. Because of its large-scale circulation in the Song Dynasty, silver has been serving as metage coin with measurement unit of Tael, therefore "Silver Tael" is frequently mentioned. There was possible much flow of imported silver dollars in the Ming Dynasty when they were handled as silver tael. The wide circulation of silver dollars started from the Opium War and the mostly used among them were Mexico Eagle dollars. The late Qing government began to mint its own silver dollars for the reason of making circulation more convenient. The first one among them are the "Dragon Dollars" on which are patterns of dragon. The silver dollar was set as official currency in 1910. The silver dollars with Yuan Shih-kai's portrait were minted by Beiyang government, while the ones with Sun Yat-Sen's by the Kuomintang government. Silver dollar is the typical form of precious minted coins in western countries. The appearance of gold and silver minted coins in western countries can be traced back to very long time ago, with consistent characteristics of imporous, round-shaped as well as the ruler's portrait on them.

The silver had all the monetary functions in the Song Dynasty and became much wider circulated with the economic developments in the Mid-Ming Dynasty. In 1436, the ban on silver was lifted by Emperor Yingzong of the Ming Dynasty who virtually gave legal permission to use silver, thus the opener and more popular silver was used by both the government and the public, and then the silver became the official currency with its basic functions of value scale and circulation means. The government also regulated the exchange rate between silver and copper coins during Emperor Jiajing of the Ming Dynasty period (1522-1566). Moreover, regulations prescribed that transactions concerning large sum of money to be charged with silver, while those with small ones with copper coins, thus silver was granted as the legal currency. Inherited from the Ming Dynasty, the monetary system which was dominated by silver in the Qing Dynasty still consisted of silver and copper coins, and the currency used in handling of transactions was similar to that of the Ming Dynasty. Measurement unit of silver remained unchanged, silver was customarily combined with "tael" by the Qing Dynasty, thus silver tael became the measurement unit of silver as the major official currency.

(4) *The paper currency*

Marco Polo once told the westerners about something unusual in China in his *The Travels of Marco Polo*: "Wherever the businessmen of Khan deal with others or purchase, they use the banknotes whose function is the same as pure gold". In the Northern Song Dynasty, iron coins were minted on a large scale by government across some regions with the purpose of making up the lack of copper coins due to the shortage of copper supply. It was recorded in the History of the Song Dynasty that one Guan of iron coins minted in Sichuan region weighs 25.8 jin (a unit of weight). A piece of Luo fabric would cost iron coins weighing 130 jin. Iron coins' being too cumbersome to carry as well as the economic developments, resulted in the birth of a kind of banknote which is called Jiaozi in Sichuan region. Jiaozi was originally jointly issued by tradesmen of Sichuan region, circulating across Sichuan region and was easily to exchange at any time. Yet later the issuing of Jiaozi shifted from the tradesmen to special institutions set up by the government due to the tradesmen's bankruptcy. Being the major official currency, the banknote Jiaozi's circulation has been expanded to everywhere besides Sichuan with the co-circulating of silver and copper coins. In addition, the Song government was forced to keep a massive army for protection against the threats and invasions from the northern states of Liao, Xia and Jin. As a result, the Song government relied on issuing the banknote to cover the huge deficit incurred by the heavy military expenditure and extreme tight budget, accordingly furthered the development of banknotes. The birth of Jiaozi marks a significant evolution from metal currencies to paper money. It is the first paper money both in China and the whole world.

The currencies tended to be unified by the time of the Yuan Dynasty. In 1276, Kublai Khan launched a monetary reform through withdrawing the banknotes circulated in southern China, including the banknotes of Guanzi, Huizi. Copper coins were also banned, and the Zhongtong banknotes were printed by copperplate printers instead of the former woodblock ones. Thus, the nationwide currency unification appeared. The early stage of the Yuan Dynasty has experienced the transition from exchangeable silver credit certificate to the non-exchangeable paper money. Integrated regulation on banknote management was promulgated in the beginning of the Yuan Dynasty. *The Circulating Regulation of Zhiyuan Baochao banknote*, which was issued by the Yuan government in 1287, is the first and the most complete regulation in China.

Yet the "Daming Baochao" banknote issued during the Ming Dynasty, was non-exchangeable. The circulation of copper coins at the beginning of the Ming Dynasty was transferred to the Daming Baochao banknote due to the insufficient supply of the copper coins. Daming Baochao banknote were printed by the Ministry of Revenue, while the local governments were not granted the permission to print. Daming Baochao banknote was the only paper money issued over 200 years of the Ming Dynasty Period. Nothing but the Reign Title of the Hongwu Emperor was printed on the banknote. The highest denomination is one Guan, no more banknotes with higher denomination were printed ever since despite the later inflation. The Daming Baochao banknote did not wear well for the poor quality of the paper at that time. Meanwhile, the Ming government simply issued the banknote without withdrawing, resulted in the accumulated banknotes flooding the market. Therefore it was discarded by the public for its rapid depreciation following the inflation. The Baochao banknote was actually abolished during the Reign Year of Emperor Zhengde and no more paper money was issued during the Ming Dynasty ever since. The Chinese paper money which started from the Song Dynasty, gradually faded out of the arena of economic life.

(5) *Major monetary reform*

First, the currency unified by First Emperor of the Qin Dynasty, known in Chinese as Qin Shi Huang. After the unification of China in 221 BC, the First Emperor of the Qin Dynasty took a series of measures, among them was the unification of currency, to consolidate the feudal centralization of authority. Unified currency included gold and copper coins, which was circulated all over the nation. The gold was recognized as the first-class currency, with the measurement unit of Yi, while the copper coins were the second-class currency and counted by pieces. Chinese characters of "Half Tael" were inscribed on the coins, indicating the weight of each coin which was historically mentioned as Half Tael. All the other valuable materials were strictly prohibited as currency from circulating. The unification of currency by First Emperor of the Qin Dynasty was an important measure to consolidate the centralization of authority policy, benefiting greatly the exchange of goods and materials as well as the trading developments.

Second, the monetary reform issued by Emperor Wu of the Han Dynasty. The changeable monetary system in the beginning of the Han Dynasty caused a chaotic state of the currency due to the unofficially minted copper coins. In 113 BC, the Emperor Wu of the Han Dynasty started to readjust the monetary system. The first step was to reserve the coinage; ShangLinSanGuan which belonged to central government was responsible to mint Wuzhu coin. Prefectures were forbidden to mint coins and their previously minted coins were all destroyed, in addition to send all the copper product to Shanglin Sanguan. Secondly, to promote a nationwide use of Wuzhu coins, excluding all the other coins from entering the circulation. The Emperor Wu of the Han Dynasty reserved the coinage and distribution rights through the reform of monetary system, which is beneficial to the unification and stability of currency as well as the economic developments and the consolidation of political power. Meanwhile, the promoted Wuzhu coins had formed a new monetary system which was fit for the social economic developments. Wuzhu coin inherited the pattern of Half Tael coin, and its finalized weight was suitable for both using and circulating which was established after decades of years. It was the idealist medium of commodity exchange, and the major ancient Chinese currency by going through the periods of the Three Kingdoms, the Jin Dynasties, the Northern and Southern Dynasties, the Sui Dynasty and the beginning of the Tang Dynasty with its spanning over 700 years.

Third, the monetary reform by Wang Mang in Western Han Dynasty. During his regency and the New Dynasty ruling period, Wang Mang launched four major monetary reforms over merely ten years for the purposes of weakening the old clans' power and their plundering on the public's wealth, on the pretext of reform based on the ancient practice. The confusing varieties of currency seriously obstructed the unofficial trading process. Moreover, the coins shrank and the price rose continuously, which was actually the exploitation of common people's wealth. The ultimate failure of monetary reform was one of the reasons why the New Dynasty died out rapidly.

Fourth, the monetary reform by Emperor Gaozu. In 621, a major monetary reform was launched by Emperor Gaozu to abolish Wuzhu coin and mint Tongbao coin. Ever since then, the Zhu and Tael currencies, which have lasted for several hundred years, were cancelled and evolved into the phases of Tongbao coin. This reform acted as a summary of coin pattern in the past 1,000 years. Firstly, the copper coin's round shape with square hole pattern and its five-Zhu weight were once more officially recognized. The reform set a benchmark of mintage for the following-up dynasties by regulating the size and purity of the coins. Secondly, the complete separation between the coin's name and weight marked a significant evolution in Chinese monetary history. Finally, the Chinese currency has entered into a new stage of coin with Emperors' reign titles on it since then.

Fifth, the birth of Chinese banknotes. Chinese banknotes are the earliest paper money in the world. From the Jiaozi of the Song Dynasty to the Zhiyuan Baochao banknotes of the Yuan Dynasty and Daming Baochao banknotes of the Ming Dynasty, all the above-mentioned keep a marked record in global monetary history. The developed Chinese commodity economy and technology, especially the improved printing skills, made the birth of banknote a matter of necessity. While the banknotes were too advanced for the social political economy in those days, therefore its doomed ending was destined.

1.1.2 The development of credit in ancient China

(1) *The creation of credit*

The early credit appeared in physical form and currency. Credit emerged at the end of the primitive society. The birth of credit is under two premises: one is the existence of private assets; the other is the social polarization. The credit occurred when the poor borrowed money from the rich. Thus, it can be concluded that the credit existed before the birth of currency and it didn't rely on the premise of the existence of currency.

The initial loaning is the physical one, mainly including the food and farming tools, etc., which are the necessity of life and manufacture. There were lots of limitations in the physical loaning, like creditors, variety of physical materials, time and places. The credit of currency broke the limitation of entity credit. For the debtors, one can purchase goods in need, and for the creditors, they can use currencies either as reserved wealth or for purchasing other goods. Thus, the debit and credit enlarged after the birth of currency and currency loaning has made up another part of the early credit.

At the early stage of feudal society, governmental institutes, aristocrats and big landlords constituted the majority of lender. Since the borrower had varying degrees of personal bondage with the lenders, it was difficult for them to dodge the debts. Thus, credit loaning mainly made up the loaning business and with comparatively higher rate of interest. Lending money and acquiring interest were very common during the Warring States Period. Usurers who were mentioned as Ziqian persons, appeared in the Qin and Han Dynasty. Some usurers, who obtained abundant capital, went to such an extent that sometimes even the government took out loan from them for military expenditure. During the Northern and Southern Dynasties there were financial institutes called Temple which specialized in loaning. Buddhism was accredited as the national religion by the ruling class, and the Buddhist temples scattered across the country during that period. The temples were granted exemption from corvee and tax. Large sum of land and money were donated to temples from both the emperors and civilians. As a result, the wealthy temples issued loaning with its abundant capital for usurious profits. Bureaucratic landlords and dignitaries also put their personal savings in temples and entrusted them for profits. Thus, temples of that time were the places that managed usury business.

(2) *The birth of remittance*

The business was flourishing during the Tang Dynasty. Merchants who often carried cash to trade found it neither convenient nor safe. Therefore some of them entrusted their money to shops for deposit service, and some of them put their money in pharmacies or Persian shops managed by foreigners, which were the initial business of saving and deposit. With the developments of business, remittance emerged at the requirement of increasing demand for currency, while the currency was shortage and not allowed to be taken out of the country. Remittance business, which was named as Feiqian or Bianhuan during Tang Dynasty, is the earliest check in the world. It was the notice letter sent by the depositor on which indicated with the sum of money, name of payee, name of remitter and the remitting date. The local governments of all regions established their liaison offices in the city of capital during the Tang Dynasty. The military and envoy also set their own agencies to contact with central government. If merchants were unable or unwilling to bring the cash home after they had sold their goods, they could hand over their money to the agency of their own hometown and were offered a receipt which was hold half piece by either party. The merchant of receipt holder brought the half of receipt to the relevant institute to claim his money when he went back home. So long there was no discrepancy between the two halved pieces, he can retrieve his money in cash, thus the remittance business came into shape.

(3) *The development of pawnbroking*

Pawnbroking business is commonly called "pawnshop". It was also called "Dianzhi" in Northern and Southern Dynasties and was called "Jieku" and "Zhiku" in the Song Dynasty, those among them which were operated by the Buddhist temples were called "Changshengku", and they were called "Jiedianku" or "Jieku" during the Yuan Dynasty. Apart from the mortgage loan, the pawnshops in the Yuan Dynasty also managed the credit loan business. In addition to the privately-owned pawnshops, the government also started to set up institutions of pawnbroking, e.g. the Zhidianku, which was also called "Liuquan", was set up by the Jin Dynasty government. The Yuan government established state-owned pawnbroking called "Guanghuiku". Since the Song Dynasty, the exchange business developed rapidly with the increased variety of currencies. There were the gold and silver shops and the silver shops who both managed exchange business. Jiaoyinpu in the Song Dynasty managed all the exchange business as well as bought and sold various sales licenses. The remittance business was gradually on the wane with the prevalence of currencies.

Financial industry, especially the pawnbroking business, had gained significant development during the Ming and Qing Dynasties and pawnshops were everywhere across the country. Statistics showed that there were more than 20,000 pawnshops throughout the whole country in 1644 and 600 or 700 pawnshops in Beijing alone by 1744. Some pawnshops possessed capital of tens of thousands or hundreds of thousands taels.[1] The pawnshop owners consisted mainly of the businessmen, the landlords, bureaucrats and even the governments who invested in pawnbroking industry. The ones owned by governments were called "official pawnshop". The pawnshops conducted business of loaning, as well as deposit and exchange.

The Qing Dynasty experienced an increasing booming of pawnbroking industry. There were over 20,000 pawnshops of different sizes across the country in 1664 (the 3rd year in the reign of Emperor Kangxi), among which 4,695 in Shanxi province and 2,688 in Guangdong province.[2] The business has been extended from the mortgage loans to the credit loans, taking deposits and currencies exchange. Moreover, the large pawnshops could issue banknotes. Privately-owned pawnshops coexisted with the state-owned ones and there were pawnshops invested by local government for purpose of making profits.

(4) *The rise of money shops*

New financial institutes such as money shops, old-style chinese private bank and exchange shops also emerged during the Ming and Qing Dynasties. Money shops could trace back to the Mid-Ming Dynasty which was for meeting the need of exchanging gold, silver, coins and banknotes by mainly conducting the exchange business. By the end of Ming Dynasty, money shops have become important credit institutions and they not only handled the above-mentioned currencies exchange, but also conducted deposits, loans and remittance business. Old-style Chinese private

[1] Qu Yanbin, "The revival of Chinese pawn auction industry", *Encyclopedic Knowledge*, 1996(12), p.29-30.

[2] Ye Chenyi, *Corporate Credit Management*, Shanghai: Fudan University Press, 2011, p.47.

banks originated in the beginning of Qing Dynasty and its business was similar to those of money shops. They both issued banknotes and silver notes which can be redeemed for copper coins and silver. Banknotes and silver notes have gained a wide circulation with the money shops and old-style Chinese private banks established throughout the whole country during the Reign of Emperor Qianlong. Exchange shops functioned as the major financial institutes in the Qing Dynasty and it mainly engaged in remittance which were also known as Exchange Shops of Shanxi, for it was initiated by merchants from Shanxi. The exchange shops' business was extended from the original service of remittance for merchants to remitting, deposits and loans of the public money from both the governments and government officials. In addition to the privately-owned financial institutes, there were also the Bank of Official Fund which were established by the Qing Government, conducting all the financial business.

Credit forms have changed greatly with the social vicissitude in the late Qing Dynasty. On one hand, western-style financial institutes were established under the western invaders' protection in the process of western allied powers' invasion into China. The Qing Government, despite of its financial constraints, established its first domestic bank in Shanghai in 1897—Imperial Bank of China. Later, the state-owned and privately-owned banks gradually grew into the pioneering power in financial industry. On the other hand, the traditional local financial institutes diverged markedly under the influence from both abroad and home. Inspired by the short-term loans business from the foreign invested banks, the local money shops gained development and became one of the three major powers in modern Chinese financial market. Yet the exchange shops were on the wane for failing to adapt to the new situation.[1]

1.1.3 Features of ancient Chinese finance

There are shared characteristics between the Chinese finance and that of the world. However, finance differs from countries, cultures and times. Now let us discuss about it from two perspectives of currency and credit.

(1) *Characteristics of ancient Chinese currency*

Through the evolution of ancient Chinese currencies, we can conclude the main features of ancient Chinese currencies as follows: The first one is consistency. China is one of the first currency-using countries and only China remains using currencies from

[1]Ba Shusong, "The focus and direction of China's financial reform", *Business Weekly*, 2012(21), pp.57-67.

the past thousands of years. The second one is that dominated currency is the coin with the round-shape and square hole. This kind of currency existed in China for at least 2,000 years. This creative design is not only for easy carrying and reducing waste, but also for easy producing and calculating. The excellent calligraphy inscribed on it also adds mystical color to the Chinese culture and offers full of endless reverie. The third one is that China is the earliest country to have banknotes. Thanks to the extraordinary development of ancient Chinese commodity economy, Chinese banknotes are the earliest banknotes all over the world. Yet, at the earlier stage of banknotes which was frequently used as a tool of covering the financial deficits by the rulers, it was gradually discarded by the society. The fourth one is that the central government monopolized the coinage. The Qin State established the political system of centralization upon the unification of ancient China. From the perspective of coinage, the central government monopolized the coinage right. The setting up of relevant institutions, the implementation of monetary policy, the issuing and managing of currencies were all under the unified implementation of the central government. In China's ancient history, weakened centralization, fragmented self-governing local authorities and social chaos occasionally happened, and messy mintage, devaluated currency and sharp rise of price would follow, which would cause significant adverse influence on economic development and people's livelihood.

(2) *Features of credit in ancient China*

We can conclude the following characteristics of credit in ancient China from the history of credit's development: The first one is diversification of credit. There were varieties of credits including loans, remittance, mortgage, money shops and all of them enriched credits in ancient China. The second one is the huge role played by the government. The imperial court as the representative of ruling class, operated the financial institutions with authority power directly and indirectly, which made itself the significant role in the development of ancient China's finance. The third one is the developed business credit. Business credit exists in the process of social reproduction and it plays a major role in commodity and circulation. The earliest recorded business credit in ancient China was in the Rites of Zhou about the transactions on credit. There were also transactions on credit between the border soldiers and local civilians in the writing bamboo slips of the Han Dynasty. By the time of the Tang and Song Dynasties, the birth of Feiqian and Jiaoyin greatly promoted the business activities at that time. Yet the abnormal development of business credit and the increasingly strengthened government credit brought not only the continual strengthened central tyranny but also the hyperinflation as well as the financial bubbles, which caused serious damages to the political economy and people's livelihood at that time.

1.2 Financial system of Republic of China period

The Republic of China period, which started from 1912, is the final stage of modern history of China. Moreover, it is also a major transition of Chinese society from feudal society to the modern one.[1] The founding of Republic of China marked a new era of Chinese society from traditional one to modern one. Chinese society presented a dual economy situation in the field of economy, and in the field of finance it also presented a dual financial structure; that is the coexistence of the traditional financial institutions and the modern financial institutions. The economic and social development were damagingly affected by chaotic warlords and instable society during the Republic of China period. Thus there was direct impact from the financial reform on the common people and society of China.

1.2.1 Monetary reform during the Republic of China period

At the end of the Qing Dynasty, there were various kinds of currencies and they appeared in a mess. The coexistence of silver dollars, copper coins, foreign silver dollars and many other banknotes had brought a lot of inconvenience to social and economic development. The chaotic state of currencies was exacerbated rather than being improved after the establishment of Republic of China. Republic of China has experienced three major monetary reforms: The first one is the substitution of dollar for tael, which played a positive role in the unification of currency. The second one is the abolition of silver standard as currency reform, which was with positive effect on the unification of currency, getting rid of the impact from the fluctuation in silver prices, stabilizing the finance as well as recovering and developing economy. The last one is issuing the banknote of Gold Yuan, which ultimately resulted in currency depreciation and led the whole national economy into hyperinflation.

(1) *The substitution of dollar for tael*

From the founding of Republic of China till the 1930s, with the fractional copper dollars and copper coins, the silver dollars and silver taels remained the dominant currencies circulating in Chinese society, and there were banknotes with extreme low

[1] Li Chunyan, "Explore the history of financial reform in the Republic of China period", *Lantai World*, 2012 (19).

value and heavy depreciation issued by numerous banks across the country. The various banknotes in circulation reflected the chaotic state of the finance at that time. There were over 100 forms of silver as the dominant currency, e.g. fragmented silver, silver ingot, silver cake, and shoe-shaped silver ingot, etc.[1] The government of Qing's long-term neglect of the standard silver mintage led to much difference of numerous silver currencies in shapes, purity and weight. Therefore, the silver currencies holders were forced to weigh the currencies, appraise the purity and check the exchange rate. The silver dollar alone appeared in about 20 forms, e.g. the Yuan silver dollar which was commonly named as "Yuan Big Head" dollar, the Sun silver dollar on which the portrait of Dr.Sun Yat-Sen as well as the imported silver dollars from Japan, Spain, etc. Much inconvenience was caused by the messy currencies to the economic and business activities during the Republic of China period. For example, the silver dollars, which were taken as the measurement of commodity value, was convenient in the daily transactions and the people's livelihood. Yet the silver tael was the standard currency regulated by the government for taxation. Therefore repeated converting calculations were required in circulation. The divorce between the transaction and currency standard and the large-scale financial black markets exhausted wealth of both the country and the public.

The Substitution of Dollar for Tael is virtually a monetary reform through cancelling the circulation of silver tael and employing the silver dollars as a means of payment. On Mar.1,1933, the Ministry of Finance of Kuomintang government promulgated Law of Substitution of Dollar for Tael and pronounced the initial execution in Shanghai. The law prescribed that the latest exchange rate of the new silver dollar against the former silver taels in circulation in Shanghai: 0.715 (the former used silver tael or coin): 1(the new issued silver dollar), and this law took effect on Mar.10, 1933.[2] Another "Mintage Regulation of Silver Currency" was issued by the Ministry of Finance on Mar.8 which prescribed that the exclusive mintage right belonged to the Central Mint, and dollar was the unit of standard silver currency which weighs 26.6971 grams with a silver content of 88%, copper 12% and that is a pure silver content of 23.493448 grams. On the obverse of the newly-issued silver dollar is the bust portrait of Dr. Sun Yat-Sen, and the pattern of a sailing boat on

[1] Li Chunyan, "Explore the history of financial reform in the Republic of China period", *Lantai World*, 2012 (19).

[2] Hou Jianxin, "Review on the financial industry of the national government from 1927 to 1937", *Journal of Inner Mongolia Normal University* (*Philosophy and Social Sciences Edition*), 2014(3).

the reverse.[1] The Ministry of Finance issued another "Notice of Substitution of Dollar for Tael" which prescribed that the nationwide cancellation of silver tael for dollar started on Apr.6 and from then on, the transactions on silver tael would be illegal. By the end of 1933, abolishing the silver tael across the country achieved success basically. The silver standard system, which lasted for thousands of years in China, was withdrawn from the history arena.

"Substitution of dollar for silver tael" can be a powerful decision of integrating the currencies and it conformed to the objective needs of commodity development, led a positive step of the Chinese monetary system towards the modernization. Nevertheless, at that time China was the silver-consuming country and was unable to get rid of the control from foreign countries on the coinage right. Other countries and the silver-yielding ones had the ability to impact the economy of the countries who use silver standard by manipulating the price of silver. From the point of global view, the western countries of that time successively abandoned the gold standard, while China was just establishing its silver standard. China had missed the world trend despite catching up with the final stage of silver standard. Therefore the silver standard was destined to be short-lived.

(2) *Reform of the legal tender*

Although the silver dollars have substituted the silver tael, there remained numerous circulating silver dollars in various forms. In addition to the local silver dollars, there were also the silver dollars from aboard as well as the silver dimes, silver cents and copper coins, etc. Therefore the currency circulation system was still in a state of chaos. The capitalist countries including the UK and the US abandoned the gold standard in succession after the economic crisis from 1929 to 1933. During the period from December of 1933 to May of 1934, the US prescribed "The Silver Purchase Act" and the "Silver Bill" and prepared to purchase 24.42 million ounces of silver annually within 4 years with the intention of raising the price of silver. Meanwhile the US banned the silver export and issued silver certificates as well as nationalized the silver, resulting in a massive silver outflow in China. The Ministry of Finance of Republic of China estimated that the aggregate of silver smuggling was more than 200 million yuan. The most immediate impact on China which was on the silver standard, were the deflation and fiscal exhaustion, as well as the following

---

1 Cheng Shengshu and Jin Zujun, "Inflation during the Period of the Republic of China: three changes in the currency system", *Journal of Jiangxi University of Finance and Economics*, 2011(4).

financial depression and reversed economy. The Republic of China government was forced to abandon the silver standard and set up a new financial and monetary system.

Apart from the various widely circulated silver dollars, the banknotes issued by numerous banks also played an important role in the complicated monetary system of that time. The rights of issuing paper currency were separated to multiple banks, and there were dozens of banks which were granted the issuing rights of paper currency during the Beiyang Government period. On the eve of the establishment of Nanjing government, there were still over 30 issuing banks. And there were 16 remained before the reform of legal tender. The Kuomintang Government prescribed the Regulation of Fiscal Reform on Nov. 3,1935 and started to implement the reform of legal tender. It was regulated that the banknotes issued by three banks which included the Central Bank, the Bank of China and the Bank of Communications (the Farmers Bank of China was later included on Jan. 20,1936) were officially recognized as the legal tender, and other banks were granted the issuing rights no more. Other banknotes that were still in circulation were withdrawn gradually and were not put into circulation again.

The silver was nationalized, and the silver standard was abandoned after the legal tenders were officially in circulation. Ever since then the silver was allowed neither be purchased nor circulated, which completely divorced the legal tenders from silver. Implementing the legal tenders cut off the direct links between currencies and silver. Therefore the thousands of years' Chinese monetary history of taking the precious metals as the circulating currencies was at an end. The chaotic state of modern China's monetary system tended to be integrated and the separated issuing rights were monopolized by the four state-owned banks, which indicated the start of integrated circulation of currency. Although it was an enormous progress in Chinese monetary history, there were certain drawbacks of issuing and circulating the legal tender which eventually broke out. For example, the imperious way of nationalizing the silver was essentially an indirectly exploitation of the people's wealth. The public's anger was therefore aroused. In addition, the legal tender acted as a certain banknote and its amount of issuing was under control of the Central Government. However, the lack of effective supervision has foreshadowed the hyperinflation incurred by the unlimited circulation of banknotes in the future.

(3) *Issuing the gold yuan banknote*

The short-term integration of currency through issuing and circulating the legal tender helped China get rid of the deflation situation. However, the serious inflation occurred following the uncontrolled circulating of the legal tender. Since its first issue in 1935, the total circulation amount of legal tender issued by the Kuomintang Central Government's designated issuing banks soared from 1.4 billion yuan to 7.8 billion yuan in 1940 and exceeded 1,000 billion yuan in 1945 and was in the aggregate of the staggering 663 trillion yuan in 1948. From1935 to 1948, the total amount of legal tender in circulation has increased by 470 thousand times[1] and due to lack of actual increase of the governmental gold reserve and foreign currencies, there was hyperinflation and China's economy was on the verge of total collapse. For details, please see Table 1–1.

Table 1–1 Issue amount of legal tender banknote and additional issue index

Date	Circulation (100 million yuan)	Additional money index (Jun., 1937=1)
Jun., 1937	14.10	1.00
Dec., 1937	16.40	1.16
Dec., 1938	23.10	1.64
Dec., 1939	42.90	3.04
Dec., 1940	78.70	5.58
Dec., 1941	151.00	10.71
Dec., 1942	344.00	24.40
Dec., 1943	754.00	53.46
Dec., 1944	1,895.00	134.36
Aug., 1945	5,569.00	394.84

Source: Wu Gang, *Historical resource of inflation in old China*, Beijing: People's Publishing House, 1958, pp.92-95. Cited from Hong Jiaguan, *Chinese financial history*, Chengdu: Southwestern University of Finance and Economics Press, 1993, p.352.

Aiming to solve the flooding of legal tenders in circulation and to save the collapsing national economy from the hyperinflation, the Kuomintang Government issued "Financial and Economic Emergency Disposition Order" on Aug.19, 1948 that determined to implement the Gold Dollar Standard and the legal tender must be withdrawn within the set period. The Gold Dollar banknotes contain pure gold of 0.22217 grams legally, and the exchange rate between Legal Tender and Gold Dollar banknote was: 3,000,000 : 1, and the exchange rate between Circulating Banknote of Northwestern Regions and Gold Dollar banknote was: 300,000 : 1. The amount of

[1] Li Chunyan, "Explore the history of financial reform in the Republic of China period", *Lantai World*, 2012 (19).

Gold Dollar Banknote launched by the Central Bank to the market was 2 billion yuan. Moreover, it also declared a mandatory and complete replacement for all other currencies including Legal Tender, gold, silver and the foreign currencies on Aug.19, 1948.

Shortly after the issuing of Gold Dollar Banknote, it began to devalue much faster than that of the Legal Tender for the shortage of gold reserve and unlimited printing, so the public used Gold Dollar Banknote to purchase as a hedge against inflation and soon there was a panic purchase. With intention to manage the collapsing economy and currency value, the Kuomintang Government declared a depreciation of 80% on Gold Dollar Banknote. Meanwhile, the government kept increasing the issuing of Gold Dollar Banknote to cover the wartime deficit. The total amount of issued Gold Dollar Banknote has accumulated to 1.2 billion yuan by the end of September and to 8.1 billion yuan by the end of December, which was 4 times of the planned amount of circulation. And eventually the amount soared to 130 trillion yuan which is 240 thousand times of the initial issue 10 months ago[1]. As the Gold Dollar Banknote increasingly devalued, soon there emerged the Gold Dollar Banknote with denomination for 5 million. As the Kuomintang government collapsed in all aspects, there was no way for it to manage the difficult situations of nationwide military, political and economic crises. The Gold Dollar Banknote reform has experienced a total bankruptcy. The rarely-seen catastrophe in monetary history did not end until it was withdrawn by the People's Bank of China at negotiated price.

In summary, whether succeeded or failed, the several monetary reforms during the Republic of China period have marked significantly in the process of modern Chinese financial history. Those practices that comply with the objective financial laws deserve affirmation, while those that only serve feudal political power other than the public are not only lessons but also should be condemned by history.

1.2.2 The development of banking in the Republic of China

From the establishment of China's first bank in 1897, Imperial Bank of China, till the outbreak of the Revolution of 1911, only few banks actually set up and survived. After the founding of Republic of China, due to the changes from home and aboard and especially the favorable opportunities came along the First World War, there was a golden age in China's banking industry. 14 banks were set up in 1912 alone. The

[1] Li Chunyan, "Explore the history of financial reform in the Republic of China period", *Lantai World*, 2012 (19).

number of banks increased to 58 in 1928 and added up to 164 in 1937. Among which were 4 state-owned banks, 26 provincial and municipal banks as well as 134 commercial banks[1]. The rapid development of China's banking business in this stage established the basic framework of Chinese banking industry and those commercial banks which later exerted great influence on China's economy were all established during this period and gained developments.

1.2.2.1 The national banks

(1) *The Central Bank*

SunYat-Sen established the National Bank of the National Revolutionary Government in Guangzhou in 1924. And the Central Bank was set up by the Northern Expeditionary Army in Wuhan in 1926. Both of the banks neither lasted for a long time nor actually performed the basic functions of Central Bank. The Nanjing Government enacted the Ordinance of Central Bank for the purposes of monopolizing the finance and financing for the treasury after the establishment of the Nanjing National Government in 1927. The Central Bank was set up and directly administered by the Nanjing Government. The dominant state-owned Central Bank, with the most financial power aimed mainly at integrating the national currency and treasury, adjusting the domestic finance. Thus, it was called "the bank of banks". Later after the multiple reconstruction, its business scope spread from the initial 7 items of business to 13 which contained the business of taking deposits, managing legal reserve and treasury securities of other banks, rediscounting trade bill, buying and selling checks and treasury bonds, etc. From the establishment of Central Bank in 1928 to 1936, the capital of the Central Bank increased by about 25 times, deposits increased by about 48 times, the issuing number of banknotes increased by 28 times and the net profit increased by about 70 times[2]. All these wealth laid the foundation for the Nanjing Government's controlling and monopolizing China's finance.

(2) *Bank of China*

The Bank of China evolved from the former The Ta-Ching Government Bank. In 1913, the Ministry of Finance of Beiyang Government issued the Regulations of Bank of China which clearly stipulated that the Bank of China adopted the shareholding system with a total share of 60 million yuan and the government and private capitalist

---

1 Zhang Peng and Li Kechuan, "Research on Chinese commercial banks function evolution", *Journal of Financial Development Research*, 2011 (2).

2 Ma Changwei and Yao Huiyuan, "The voucher system in the issuance of banknotes during the Republic of China and its enlightenment", *Studies of International Finance*, 2014 (6).

held half of the share respectively. The bank had one president and one vice-president who were appointed by government via the Ministry of Finance and the whole banking business was under the government's supervision. The Bank of China became the government's money vault and tools of fundraising due to the excessive money it had provided for the government. In 1917, the Bank of China began to reorganize and the president and vice-president were held concurrently by the chairman of board instead of being appointed by the government, which greatly limited the power of government, and the management direction of the Bank of China gradually turned into commercialization. As a result, there was not much share which belonged to the government by 1923. After its reorganization, the Bank of China gained great developments by proactively taking the professional steps as an international bank of remittance. By the end of 1934, its total asset reached 975.65 million yuan, and its deposits reached 546.69 million yuan which accounted for 20% of the whole country's bank deposits and became the core of China's banking business.[1] To strengthen the control over the Bank of China, the Nanjing Government mandatorily increased the share capital by taking advantage of the economic crisis which started in 1934. It regulated that the total share of the Bank of China was 400 million yuan and the government and private capitalists held half of the shares respectively. Meanwhile, the government brought the Bank of China under its complete control by appointing Soong Tse-ven as the chairman of board.

(3) *Bank of Communications*

The Bank of Communications was established in 1907 and was jointly managed by the government and private capitalists with the rated capital of 10 million of silver taels, the government held 40% of the shares. It had the dual nature of ordinary bank and chartered bank. After the Revolution of 1911, it was granted to manage the treasury and issue the exchange certificate. The Bank of Communications eventually became the fundraising tool of the Beiyang Government. The excessive sum of political borrowing exhausted the cash reserve, damaged its credit, and incurred two suspended withdrawal crises on the Bank of Communications. In 1922, the Bank of Communications constantly increased stock shares, and enacted the business policies of getting rid of the warlord, reforming the issue, placing emphasis on industrial and commercial enterprises. Thus, the Bank of Communications gradually embarked on a

[1]Hou Jianxin, "Review on the financial industry of the National Government from 1927 to 1937", *Journal of Inner Mongolia Normal University* (*Philosophy and Social Sciences Edition*), 2014 (3).

path to healthy development. By 1935, its total saving deposits has accumulated to 470.63 million yuan and loans has accumulated to 344.35 million yuan. For the purpose of strengthening control over the Bank of Communications, the Government revised "Regulations of Bank of Communications" to raise the quota of directors sent by the government as well as the chairman of board, the general manager shall be appointed by the Ministry of Finance. The Government also gathered funds for uniform distribution, extended more service to industrial and commercial enterprises and managed the loan-deposit business. Thus, the Bank of Communications has turned into a financial institute of bureaucratic capital.

(4) *The Farmers Bank of China*

The Farmers Bank of China was established on the basis of the reconstruction of four provinces' farmers bank in 1935. Kong Xiangxi was the first chairman of board, and later was replaced by self-appointed Chiang Kai-Shek. On the beginning of its establishment, it proclaimed its mission was to provide funds for peasants to revitalize the rural economy, which essentially managed the fundraising for military expenditure. The Farmers Bank of China was the monopolistic financial institute in rural areas managed by the Four Families[1], featuring the nature of feudalism and military. With the support of the Nanjing Government, all the above-mentioned four big banks had evolved into bureaucratic capital.

(5) *The Postal Remittances and Savings Bank*

The Nanjing Government set up the General Office of Postal Remittances and Savings Bank in Shanghai in 1930, which was directly under the Ministry of Transportation. The business of taking-deposits and remittance which were formerly managed by post offices were incorporated within the General Office of Postal Remittances and Savings Bank in accordance with international practice and the post offices held the sole responsibility of posting service since then. The General Office set up its divisions in Shanghai, Nanjing and Hankou respectively in 1931. With the whole country's postal revenue as a guarantee, the General Office of Postal Remittances and Savings Bank had capital assets of merely 10 million yuan and accumulated to 50 million yuan in 1935 and it managed the business of fixed deposits, bank books, cheque for deposits, deposits in installments, withdrawing in lump sum as well as the banknote issuing and other general businesses. On Mar.1, 1935, the

[1] The Four Families, refer to the families controlling of China's political, economic lifeblood in the first half of the 20th century, namely the Chiang Kai-shek family, Soong Tse-ven family, Kong Xiangxi family and Chen Guofu, Chen Lifu family.

Nanjing Government enacted the Organization Laws of Postal Remittances and Savings Bank and reconstructed the General Office of that to relevant bureau and put it directly under the General Office of Postal Bureau to manage the business of nationwide remittance and savings deposits. The above-mentioned institute was equivalent to state-owned bank of savings deposits. With advantage of having branches in urban and rural areas across the country, it managed the taking-deposits business through extending its influence upon the remote and isolated regions.

(6) *The establishment of the Head Office of Four Banks Association*

The Head Office of Four Banks Association[1] was set up in Aug., 1937 and became the supreme monopolized financial institute of the Nanjing Government, among which were the Central Trust of China, Bureau of Postal Remittances and Savings and Central Cooperative Bank. The Head Office was set up to meet the requirements of the financial economic management in wartime. All the economic financial strategies were within its broad business scope and the fundraising for all the other departments. The establishment of the Head Office has laid the foundations for the consolidation of Central Bank of China. The Nanjing Government made much use of the war to foster the Central Bank of China with political power, made it to be the financial core with supremacy by outmatching any other financial institutes, thus achieved target of totally ruling the financial industry.

1.2.2.2 National capital banks

Confronted with the complex situation of home and abroad, the national capital banks of China had gained rapid developments during the Republic of China period, among which the typical ones were "The Three Banks in South" and "The Four Banks in North" (See Table1–2). "The Three Banks in South" is the combined reference to Zhejiang Commercial Bank, Zhejiang Industrial Bank and Shanghai Commercial Savings Bank. All the bankers of the three banks were from Jiangsu and Zhejiang provinces. They supported each other and managed the business in unison and all the three banks chose Shanghai as their base. Although there was no external manifestation of the associated group, they essentially resulted in the effective jointly-operation. "The Four Banks in North" was the joint name of the four banks as follows: Yanye, Jincheng, Dalu, Zhongnan. The three banks of Yanye, Jincheng and Zhongnan established the joint venture and included the Bank of Dalu the ensuing year in the

---

[1] The Head Office of Four Banks Association is the shortened form of the Central Bank, Bank of China, Bank of Communications and the Farmers Bank of China.

union. That was the origin of the name of "the Four Banks in North". The management targets were to raise abundant capital funds, to share business information and therefore to make developments of business. Although that was a rather low-level mode of joint venture, as well as a narrowed business scope, it remained the first and unique jointly-operated group.

Both the Four Banks in North and the Three Banks in South were in extensive connections with national industry and commerce. Among the funds operation of the above banks, there was a substantial portion of loans for industrial and commercial items, so they were very well-deserved the title of Chinese commercial banks' backbone. It should be noted that the national financial capital group could fairly exert influence over the society. Numerous strong partners of the Four Banks in North were warlords and bureaucrats and gained the governmental support for them. So they obtained the controlling power on financial business in northern China, which was only next to that of Bank of China and Bank of Communications. While the majority of the partners who was in control of the Three Banks in South were financial tycoons from Jiangsu and Zhejiang provinces, who were the financial supporters of the Chiang Kai-shek-led southern China political power and provided the Nanjing Government with funds for huge military expenditure.

Table 1–2 Brief of "the Three Banks in South" and "the Four Banks in North" during the Republic of China period

Type	Name of bank	Founding time	Location of head office	Invested by	Business features
The Three Banks in South	Zhejiang Commercial Bank	1907	Hangzhou (Later moved to Shanghai)	Zhejiang Railway Corporation	Running the real estate
	Zhejiang Industrial Bank	1909	Hangzhou	Joint venture by Local government of Zhejiang and merchant	Abundant in foreign currencies
	Shanghai Commercial Savings Bank	1915	Shanghai	Privately-owned	Excellent service, rapid development
The Four Banks in North	Bank of Yanye	1915	Beijing (Later moved to Shanghai)	Planned public-privately joint venture, later shifted to privately-owned	Abundant in savings deposits
	Bank of Jincheng	1917	Tianjin (Later moved to Shanghai)	Privately-owned	Numerous branches with industry-prone loans

(continued)

Type	Name of bank	Founding time	Location of head office	Invested by	Business features
The Four Banks in North	Bank of Dalu	1919	Tianjin (later moved to Shanghai)	Privately-owned	Focused on general taking deposits and extending loans
	Bank of Zhongnan	1921	Shanghai	Invested by returned overseas Chinese	Abundant in initial capital, authorized rights to issue banknotes, industry-prone loans

Source: Xi Hui, 60 *years of Finance in New China*, Beijing: China Financial Publishing House, 2010, pp.6-8.

There also existed the title of Five Banks in South, which was the combined name for the "three Banks in South" and Bank of China together with Bank of Communications, referring mainly to the means taken by the two banks for purposes of shaking off the governmental control on them and evolved into the commercialized banks as well as made a shift of management emphasis to Shanghai. Moreover, the private investors from the south were promoted into the management. So the two banks were operated as commercial banks in fact. However, the Nanjing Government held the monopolized financial policy to strengthen the control over the commercial banks. The Bank of China and Bank of Communications were reconstructed into the banks of bureaucratic capital, and were interrupted in the process of commercialization. And the Four Banks in North and the Three Banks in South were also delayed their sustainable development[1].

1.2.2.3 Foreign banks

Foreign banks in China refers to the ones set in China shortly after the Opium War, the first one among which was the British Oriental Bank set in Hong Kong in 1845. Then foreign banks emerged in quantities in China after it. After the founding of Republic of China, although the British financial power still prevailed over its international peers, impaired by the First World War, it was on the decline. And the United States of America as well as Japan, both took the opportunities brought by the First World War and spared no efforts to expand their financial influence in China, and eventually resulted in the co-existence of the three powers of UK–US–Japan (see Table 1–3).

[1] Pan Liangui, "The Four banks in north and the three banks in south", *China Finance*, 2003 (1).

Table 1–3 Brief of foreign banks during the Republic of China period

Country	Typical bank	Branches	Developments
The UK	HSBC	Headquarter in Hong Kong, Branch Office in Shanghai	Powerful front-runner of foreign banks in China, operated Qing government's indemnities loans, mastered China's tariff and management rights of salt tax
The US	Citibank	Based in Shanghai, set up numerous branches	With the support of American sector and government, gained rapid development
Japan	Yokohama Specie Bank, Bank of Taiwan, Bank of Chosen	Rapid expansion of numerous branches	The most active among all the foreign invasion powers, gained the fastest development of financial influence

Source: Hong Jiaguan, *Chinese Financial History*, Chengdu: Southwestern University of Finance and Economics Press, 1993, pp.189-195; John King Fairbank, *The Cambridge History of China: Republican China (1912-1949, Part* 1), Beijing: China Social Sciences Press, 2006, pp.220-222.

After the Anti-Japanese War, all the banks of defeated Japan, Germany and Italy were taken over by the "Four Banks-Two Bureaus" of the Nanjing Government. Yet the banks of the US, the UK and France, thanks to the privileges they enjoyed, were in dominant position in competing with local Chinese commercial banks. Such situations did not end until the founding of the People' s Republic of China in 1949.

1.2.3 The non-bank financial institutes during the Republic of China period

The new modern financial institutes all over the late Qing Dynasty made great progress with its advanced regulations and management as well as the abundant capital, eventually established the local and national financial system covering all levels and fields including insurance and credits cooperation.

(1) *Insurance market*

Insurance industry emerged with the increasing risks incurred by overseas trading in western countries. Triggered by commodity economy and ocean transportation trade, the modern western insurance industry was gradually perfected and kept expanding overseas since 18th century. In 1805, foreign merchant set up Canton Insurance Society which was the first insurance company in China. Ever since then the Chinese insurance market was monopolized for almost 60 years. The Shanghai Yihe Insurance company, which was China's first domestic-based insurance company, was set up on May 25,1865. It marked the birth of modern national insurance industry. Ever since then China's national insurance institutes began to boom. In 1907 the Qing Government drafted its first modern insurance decree Draft Articles of Insurance

Industry. There were already more than 30 insurance companies that were run by Chinese national capitalists by 1920s[1]. Insurance industry has gained its initial development in Beiyang Government period. The setup of insurance institutes has extended from the costal port cities to hinterland. The insurance business scope has expanded from the traditional river transportation risk and warehouse fire risk to life insurance, automobile risk and mail risk, etc. During the Nanjing Government period, the funds which were increasingly invested by banking industry have greatly strengthened the domestic insurance industry; so the insurance institutes gained further development both in quantity and quality. There was wider coverage including the additional glass risk, elevator risk and theft risk, etc. The insurance business scope expanded overseas, presenting an unprecedent prosperity. According to Yearbook of Chinese Insurance of 1937, there were 40 insurance companies across the country, 60% among which were Shanghai-based, and made it the core of Chinese insurance industry. Yet after the outbreak of the Anti-Japanese war, the insurance business began to shrink rapidly.

(2) *Securities market*

The first Chinese securities market traced back to the end of the Qing Dynasty. The stocks which were issued by Li Hongzhang-led China Merchants Steamship Navigation Company and Ministry of Revenue of the Qing Government, are the first stocks ever in Chinese history. The Shanghai Public Shares Corporation and the Shanghai Stock Exchange, which were organized by agents from Shanghai were the earliest stock exchange in China. Yet influenced by multi factors and the backward financial awareness at that time, both of the two stock exchanges contributed little to the economic developments.

The stock market was booming again with the craze for the rubber stocks during the Republic of China period, yet the stocks exchange remained as a kind of complement to the market. The Beiyang Government enacted The Stocks Exchange Law on Dec.29, 1914, presenting the first regulations and law of stocks market management in Chinese history. Due to high profits, there was a great upsurge in setting up stock exchange. And there were 70 stocks exchange in Shanghai alone by the September of 1921, causing the profiteering speculation, and ultimately led to another serious financial storm in Shanghai after the rubber stocks crisis, which was

[1] Zhu Huaxiong and Kong Jie, "Research on insurance thought during the Republic of China (1912-1949) — A survey of industries based on national insurance", *Economic Perspectives*, 2011 (11).

known as the "Crisis incurred by Trust and Exchange in 1921"[1]. After this crisis, the reputation of stocks exchange completely went bankruptcy everywhere. The bonds issued by the Nanjing Government began to substitute for the stocks in financial market and became the main trade object. After the outbreak of the Anti-Japanese War, securities markets saw its brief final craze under the background of price soaring, and then began to decline.

(3) *The trust business*

The trust business in China rose in 1920s. A large number of trust companies and exchanges were set up in Shanghai in 1921; however, most of which went bankruptcy for failing in the profiteering speculation. The major banks began to set up the trust department after 1928, by which way the trust business began to develop again and many new trust companies were set up. Please see Table 1–4.

Table 1–4 Brief of trust companies around 1930

Name	Founding time	Total asset	Address of head office
TongYi Trust Company	1921	Nominal 2.5 million yuan, actual amount 0.5 million yuan	Shanghai
Central Trust Company	1921	3 million yuan	Shanghai
HeKun Trust Company	1930	0.5 million yuan	Shanghai
Shanghai Trust Company	1930	0.2 million yuan, increased to 1 million yuan in 1934	Shanghai
HengShun Trust Company	1930	0.75 million yuan	Shanghai
TongHui Trust Company	1931	1 million yuan, actual amount 0.5 million yuan	Shanghai
GuoAn Trust Company	1928	0.5 million yuan	Shanghai
Southeast Trust Company	1931	1 million, actual amount 0.5 million yuan	Shanghai
Shanghai XingYe Trust Commune	1933	1.5 million yuan	Shanghai
SiHang Trust Department	1937	—	Shanghai

Source: *National Bank Yearbook* (related years), cited from the book's compilation group, *Financial History of China*, Chengdu: Southwestern University of Finance and Economics Press, 1993, p.286.

To monopoly the trust business, the Nanjing National Government started to plan for the Bureau of Central Trust in June of 1934, and 10 million yuan was granted to it by The Central Bank as capital funds. It was officially opened on Oct.1, 1935 in Shanghai. Three businesses including trust, savings deposit and purchasing materials, with specially the Central Savings Society and insurance division which managed the

[1] Sun Jianhua, "Analysis of fragility of Chinese stock exchanges and its causes in modem times", *Economic Management Journal*, 2014 (1).

post and insurance business for government employees and military personnel. The business of purchasing was actually for purchasing the aviation equipment, arsenal, etc., which served directly the expanding army and preparation for wars, thus the division was referred to as the governmental munitions purchase department. Upon its foundation, the division monopolized the trust business, disrupted and excluded other trust companies and trust divisions attached to all the banks' trust department, thus became the Nanjing National Government's important tool of monopolizing international trades and exerting the comprador business activities. It played a leading role in the bureaucratic capitalist financial system.

1.2.4 The financial developments under the leadership of the Communist Party of China (CPC)

1.2.4.1 Finance in the revolutionary base areas

After the failure of the Revolution in 1927, the CPC began to lead the Chinese revolution independently and set up the revolutionary bases in Jinggangshan, Hailufeng and provinces of Hubei, Henan, Anhui in succession. The finance began to be developed accordingly with the economic construction in these bases.

(1) *Currencies in revolutionary base areas*

In the beginning stage of the bases, there were various currencies including silver coins, copper coins and banknotes, and banknotes consisted of credit certificates, silver bills and copper bills, etc. Currencies of the revolutionary base areas must be integrated for meeting the requirements of stabilizing the areas' financial markets and holding responsibility of the people's interest. Thus, the mints and banknotes printing plants were established in almost all the Soviet-controlled areas. Statistics showed that there were more than 60 banknotes issuing institutes with over 200 kinds of currencies issued by the Soviet banks and in the name of other economic institutes attached to Soviet government[1]. To raise the banknotes' credits, all the banknotes issued by Soviet banks and its branches were negotiable. For example, the one-yuan banknote was printed "promise to pay bearer one yuan on demand with this note". The Soviet government's understanding on banknote issuing was deepening with the practice.

(2) *The financial institutes in revolutionary base areas*

Each revolutionary base area set up its own independent financial division because the bases were isolated from each other. The major ones among them were

[1] Zhu Ping and Jiang Hongye, "Soviet currency during the agrarian revolutionary war (iii)", *China Finance*, 1982 (1).

Bank of Liudong Civilian, Bank of Donggu, Industrial and Agricultural Bank of Jiangxi Province, Industrial and Agricultural Bank of Western Fujian, Soviet Bank of Shaanxi, Gansu and Shanxi. In 1931, the Central revolutionary base founded the Chinese provisional government of Soviet in Ruijin, Jiangxi province, established the National Bank of Soviet in the following year, and enacted meanwhile the Interim Regulations of National Bank of Chinese Soviet Republic with a rated capital assets of 1.4 million yuan and started operation after having 200 thousand yuan. The National Bank consisted of the Head Office, Branches and Sub-branches, and took over the treasury from the Ministry of Finance and started currency issue in 1934. The National Bank of Soviet handled individuals' savings deposits and issued bonds to support the revolution as well as meet the requirements of economic development in the base areas.

Moreover, the bases attached great importance to the development of credit cooperatives. The credit cooperatives in Soviet-controlled areas gradually became great assistants of the banks by handing over some of their money to the banks as shares to enrich the bank capital, acting on personal deposits, extending loans to peasants, acting on exchange certificate and public bonds issuing; all of which eventually made up the deficiencies of the national banks' shortage of branches.

1.2.4.2 Finance in the anti-Japanese base areas

After the outbreak of Anti-Japanese War, the Anti-Japanese base areas set up their own financial industries one after another to support the long-term war and kept developing with the developments of the base areas.

(1) *Currencies circulated in the Anti-Japanese base areas*

There was an extremely chaotic circulation in Japanese-occupied areas after the outbreak of the war because the legal tender banknotes, the local circulation bills and the certificates issued by banks in Japanese-occupied areas coexisted. Therefore, the currencies in base areas must be issued for purposes of ensuring the army supplies and stabilizing prices.

Several different stages of the currency issuing in Shaanxi-Gansu-Ningxia border regions:

a. The circulation of Guanghua certificates. According to the agreement that signed by Kuomintang and CPC after the outbreak of Anti-Japanese War, no currency was allowed to be issued except for the legal tender banknotes in circulation. Yet the banknotes used by the Eighth Route Army were only in denomination of 5 yuan and

10 yuan, so the lack of fractional currencies caused inconvenience in circulation[1]. In 1938, Guanghua stores were set up to issue Guanghua certificates as token which were mainly the fractional currency with small denominations and they were equivalent to the legal tender banknotes for meeting the requirements of producing and circulating in board areas.

b. Issuing the border areas currency. After the Southern Anhui Incident, economic blockade was exerted by National Government and in order to develop economy and ensure the supplies, the border regional banks started to issue the banknotes for circulation in border regions in 1941, which gradually withdrew the Guanghua certificates and the legal tender banknotes were prohibited from circulation.

c. Issuing the circulation certificates. In 1944, the Bank of Border Regions issued the commercial circulation certificate for trading companies in border areas to stabilize the prices. However, restricted by the situations at that time, it failed to achieve the set goal due to the co-existence of the circulation certificates and border region currency.

It should be noted that currency credit systems in different anti-Japanese base areas across the country were scattered and all the base areas issued their own currency in accordance with their different currency credit system. Yet there was a uniform policy of currency credit system. The financial activities taken in the Anti-Japanese base areas played a significant role in the Anti-Japanese war in ensuring producing and supplying the army.

(2) *Financial institutes in the Anti-Japanese base areas*

During the Anti-Japanese War, more than ten banks were set up successively in the CPC-led the Anti-Japanese base areas and their fundamental tasks were to implement the economic policies made by the government, issue currencies, protect people's wealth, stabilize prices, support finance and develop production, thus they could consolidate the Anti-Japanese base areas and support the Anti-Japanese War. The major banks of that time were Bank of Shaanxi-Gansu-Ningxia border Regions, Bank of Shanxi-Chahar-Hebei Border Regions, Bank of Southern Hebei, Farmers Bank of Northwest, Bank of Beihai, Bank of Jianghuai and Bank of Dajiang.

1.2.4.3 Finance during the new democracy period

(1) *Establishment of the People's Bank of China and integration of currencies*

At the early stage of War of Liberation, the liberated areas were blocked,

[1] Zhang Minhui and Li Jianchun, "The enhancement of our party's cognition of currency in the bank currency issuance of Shaanxi–Gansu–Ningxia border region", *Journal of Shandong Academy of Governance*, 2012 (1).

encircled and separated. So they have to keep the economic system of "separately managing under the integrated leadership" maintained during the Anti-Japanese War and to issue their own currencies independently. With the enlargement of the liberated areas, the issue and circulation of currencies gradually evolved from separation to integration. In Northeastern China, the provincial banks were established one after another to issue the northeastern currency which circulated in the whole northeastern China. In inner Mongolia, the Autonomous Association of Inner Mongolia set up the Bank of Eastern Mongolia to issue the circulation certificates which are equivalent to northeastern currency. In central China, the Bank of Central China was established in the Anti-Japanese base of central China to issue the currency of Central China. Moreover, various currencies including the banknote of Zhongzhou, banknote of Xinong, banknote of border regions of Shanxi–Chahar–Hebei were issued in other liberated areas. With the deepening of liberating progress, the central government established the People's Bank of China to issue renminbi (RMB) as standard currency and to withdraw and exchange the numerous currencies issued by local authorities, which gradually formed the integrated market across the country. In this process, the CPC effectively consolidated the status of renminbi, stabilized the prices and gained the public's supports by taking multiply means of expanding using scope of renminbi, consolidating its credits and improving its purchasing power.

(2) *The setup of new financial system*

When the People's Liberation Army (PLA) achieved the nationwide military victory, the new democratic financial system in embryonic form also gradually developed across the country. The new financial system involved the national bank, specialized banks, banks of public-private operation, private banks and credit cooperatives.

The national bank is the People's Bank of China which is the main and leading part of the financial system, bearing the socialist nature. The People's Bank of China showed its strong vitality upon its establishment by making a quick clearance on the financial market which served the imperialism, feudalism and bureaucratic capitalism and establishing independent and integrated financial market as well as currency system which serve the production and commodity circulation. The People's Bank of China also made great contribution to developing the new democratic financial system, raising and accumulating funds, supporting the nationwide liberation as well as industry and agriculture production, strengthening the socialist economic leadership, activating and stabilizing the market, all of which created conditions for the recovery and development of the national economy.

1.3 The financial system after the founding of the People's Republic of China

Chinese financial system was set up and developed after the establishment of the People's Bank of China on Dec.1,1948. The founding of People's Republic of China led Chinese financial industry to turn to a new page. At the beginning stage of the People's Republic of China, the CPC was confronted a harsh situation of economic finance, of which were the extremely low national economic aggregate, the chaotic state of economic order as well as the hyperinflation. Main measures included taking over and reconstructing the banks on bureaucratic capital, transforming the private banks, establishing non-banking financial institutes one after another, setting up sub-branches of People's Bank of China all over the country and strengthening leadership as well as adjusting all kinds of financial institutes. The planned economic system was set up in 1953, the financial system of People's Republic of China which was under the unified leadership of People's Bank of China that consisted of banks, insurance industries and credit unions, initially formed.

1.3.1 Establishment of the People's Republic of China's financial system

(1) *The development of the People's Bank of China*

The Chinese People's Political Consultative Conference (CPPCC) enacted Organization Law of the Central People's Government of PRC in September, 1949. The People's Bank of China was incorporated into the units which were directly under the Government Administration Council and was entitled to function as a national bank. The People's Bank of China performed the basic functions including establishing an independent and integrated currency system, forming the national financial system, managing the national finance and supporting the production recovery as well as developing economy.

(2) *Transformation of the bureaucratic and national capital financial institutes*

At the beginning stage of the People's Republic of China, the financial institutes of Kuomintang bureaucratic capital were confiscated and taken over, and the special privileges for foreign banks set in China were abolished. The Central Bank of

Kuomintang and other financial institutes including the "Four Banks-Two Bureau-One Vault"[1] and the other official financial institutes were taken over by People's Bank of China, and the Bank of Communications and Bank of China were transformed respectively into the long-term investment bank and national bank which specialized in foreign currency. By 1952, the Bank of China and the Bureau of Overseas Business of the People's Bank of China had jointly operated, and the Bank of Communications was under the leadership of the Ministry of Finance.

The privately-owned financial institutes on national capital were reshaped, some of which were ordered to suspend business and the rest of them were transformed to public-private partnership. Banks of national capital and old-style Chinese private banks were permitted to be remained under the strict supervision and management of the government, and they were gradually on the transformation to socialism. In December of 1952, by the means of transitional forms, all the private banks made up the uniform public-private partnership and a general administration was established in Beijing, thus the socialist transformation of private finance completed. In 1955, the public-private partnerships were turned into specialized banks for savings deposits and were merged into the relevant institutes of the People's Bank of China respectively.

(3) *Establishment of the integrated and independent currency system of renminbi*

The currency of renminbi which was issued upon the founding of the People's Bank of China (PBOC) marked the beginning of the currency system of the PRC, yet it had not turned to be the nationwide currency by then. Apart from the uniform renminbi issued in the three major liberated zones including Northern China, Eastern China and Northwestern China, the currencies were still separately issued in the rest of the liberated zones. The unlimited printing of Gold Yuan banknote inflicted hyperinflation upon the Kuomintang-ruled zones, gold and silver, even the foreign currencies were employed as major currencies. After the founding of the PRC, the newly-established government confronted an urgent task of establishing an integrated and independent currency system through occupying the nationwide financial market with renminbi. The government took resolute means to abolish the Gold Yuan banknotes as well as all the other paper money and exchange bills issued by the Kuomintang government and local authorities. The speculation of gold and silver as well as the circulation of foreign currencies were prohibited by the government through tightening the supervision

[1] Four Banks-Two Bureau-One Vault refers to The Central Bank, Bank of China, Bank of Communications, The Farmers Bank of China, Central Trust of China, Postal Remittance and Savings Bureau and Central Cooperative Bank.

on gold and silver and tightening the circulation of gold and silver on negotiated price, together with making regulations on foreign currencies, with additional means of price comparison, exchange within the deadline. It took the People's Republic of China only one year to establish its own independent and integrated currency system.

(4) *Insurance and credit cooperatives*

The establishment of financial system also includes establishing and developing non-bank financial institutes like rural credit cooperatives and People's Insurance Company of China, etc.

Chinese rural credit cooperatives had a long history of developments. There were still over 800 credit cooperatives before the founding of the PRC, yet most of which tended to be terminated because of currency inflation. A majority of regions in countryside remained the arenas of usury due to the old China's backward economy and too little influence on the rural areas exerted from the new banks. In order to support financial services in the countryside, the special cooperative organizations of peasants, which named as the Rural Credit Cooperatives, were set up across the country in 1952. The credit cooperative organizations once adopted several forms of Mutual Support Groups, Credit Departments of Supply and Marketing Cooperative and Credit Cooperatives, among which the Credit Cooperatives were the advanced ones. By the second half of 1955, Credit Cooperatives almost existed in every rural area all over the country and their business include taking-deposits, lending money, transferring and settlement of accounts, all of which made the credit cooperatives the powerful assistants of national bank.

On Oct.20, 1949, the People's Insurance Company of China(PICC) was founded and its branches were set up across the country one after another. It was initially the subsidiary to the People's Bank of China and was incorporated into the Ministry of Finance in 1952.[1]

1.3.2 The establishment of the overall unified financial system

With the gradual forming of the planned economic system of the PRC during the "First Five-year Plan" period, the Chinese financial system began to reform in accordance with the planned economy pattern and eventually formed the unified financial system with the People's Bank of China as the unique financial institute.

---

[1] Sun Naiyan and Jin Xizai, "Overview of the development of China's insurance industry since the reform and opening up", *Modern Management Science*, 2012 (6).

In 1952, the Bank of China started to jointly operate with the Bureau of Overseas Business attached to People's Bank of China. The Bank of Communications and PICC began to be directed by the Ministry of Finance. The Agricultural Cooperative Bank was withdrawn, and the general office of public and private partnership was established. In 1954, the central government determined to abolish the region level administration, and the regional branches of People's Bank of China were also cancelled, which eventually formed the vertical management system and strengthened the uniform leadship and management of the PBOC's head office upon the nationwide financial activities. In October of 1954, the People's Construction Bank of China, which was under the Ministry of Finance's direction, was founded and functioned as a state-owned bank specialized in managing the fixed assets investment, and was withdrawn in 1958. In 1955, 14 cities' public and private partnership banks started to cooperate with the local saving deposits department of PBOC. In 1956, the general administration of the public private partnership bank jointly operated with the Bureau of Private Business of the Head Office of the People's Bank of China, which means the banks of public-private partnership were incorporated into the People's Banks of China. In 1955, The State Council granted the establishment of the Agricultural Bank of China which was rescinded in 1957 and then established a rural financial authority in the People's Bank of China to manage the financial business in the nationwide countryside.[1]

Various kinds of banks and other financial institutes were cancelled in successive and were put into the People's Bank of China. The operation of credit funds, either the source or application, were under the uniform control of the head office of the People's Bank of China and the financial services were also centralized to the People's Bank of China. Commercial banks and stock market were withdrawn. By then, the unified Chinese financial system had been established. The People's Bank of China became the center of credit, settlement and cash allocation, which nearly monopolized all the financial business across the country. The People's Bank of China served as both the issue bank and commercial bank, and exercised the functions of the two kinds of banks.[2]

---

[1] Liu Xiaoping, "Learning Deng Xiaoping's Financial Theory to Speed Up the construction of modern financial enterprises", *Financial Reference*, 2004 (12).

[2] Li Li, "China's Financial Revolution during 1979-2006", *Business Times*, 2007 (11).

1.3.3 The uncertain financial system during the "Great Leap Forward" and the "Cultural Revolution" period

During the "Great Leap Forward" period (1958-1960), adversely affected by the "leftism", China experienced an excessive increase in the heavy industry and the agriculture and the light industry was ignored, which resulted in a serious imbalance of agriculture and industry in the national economic proportion (see Table 1–5). Some mistakes were also made in financial institutes, which led to the losing control on credit loaning and issuing large-scale additional currencies and both of them aggravated the imbalance in the national economy.

During that period, the domestic insurance business was suspended, and the People's Construction Bank of China was withdrawn. In 1960, aiming to rapidly improve the extreme difficult situations of the national economy at that time, the central government determined to take a series of measures according to the policy of "adjusment, consolidation, enrichment and improvement". Opinions of adjusting and improving the banking credit business were given by the central government and it released the Decisions on Strengthening the Uniform Work on Banking and Strictly Controlling Currency Issue, Notice of Altering the Position of the People's Bank of China in National Organization. In addition, the central government resumed and built relevant necessary regulations and all of these measures enhanced the banks' position in economy. The People's Construction Bank of China was restored again in 1962 and its functions were further clarified and its rank was upgraded from the vice-ministerial level to the ministerial one. The Agricultural Bank of China was restored in 1963 and its institutions from the higher levels to the grass roots have been established.

Table 1–5 The growth rate and proportion of agriculture and industry during the "Great Leap Forward" period

Year	Gross output index of industry and agriculture (take the last year as 100)			Percentage of gross output (%)	
	Agriculture	Industry	Industry and agriculture	Agriculture	Industry
1957	103.6	111.5	107.9	43.3	56.7
1958	102.4	154.8	132.2	34.3	65.7
1959	86.4	136.1	119.5	25.1	74.9
1960	87.4	111.2	105.4	21.8	78.2

Source: *China Statistical Yearbook* (*1983*), Beijing: China Statistics Press, 1983, pp.18-20.

The outbreak of "the Cultural Revolution" in 1966 seriously undermined the

Chinese financial system and its banking business was practically in stagnation. The two above-mentioned banks which were just restored were respectively incorporated into The People's Bank of China and the Ministry of Finance. Later, all the bureaus within the Head Office of the People's Bank of China were withdrawn apart from departments of the political work and business and theses two departments maintained the daily work with great efforts. In 1969, the Head Office of the People's Bank of China was incorporated into the Ministry of Finance and only reserved its signboard externally. The branch offices of the People's Bank of China were either merged into the financial department to form the Bureau of Finance or incorporated into the Bureau of Finance and as one of its business teams. The management system was seriously weakened due to the separated organization and relevant policies as well as regulations were difficult to implemented. The financial institutes essentially acted as the accountant and cashier of the finance. Until 1978, the People's Bank of China separated from the Ministry of Finance and started a new era of Chinese financial system reform.

1.3.4 Characteristics of the unified financial system

(1) *The single institute*

The whole country's credit activities were concentrated in the People's Bank of China for purposes of distributing and managing. The People's Bank of China was the only bank then and the Bank of China was one of its subordinate unit. The rural credit cooperatives actioned as the basic institutes of the People's Bank of China for a long time. The regional banks, stock-holding banks, foreign banks and non-bank financial institutes were all strictly prohibited from setting up. The People's Bank of China not only functioned as the nation's central bank, but also conducted businesses such as taking-deposits, extending loans and carrying out settlement.

(2) *The centralized credit*

With the banks' centralization and unification, the credit funds management tended to be centralized and excluded the roles of funds market. The People's Bank of China made the plans of credit receipts and payments in accordance with the production orders for enterprises from the government as well as the financial budget. In addition, the People's Bank of China made the currency issue plans based on the labor wage and the agricultural purchase plan to manage the credit funds in the form of "unified deposing and loaning, unified raising and distributing". All the saving deposits, which taken by the institutes of all levels of People's Bank of China, must be handed over to the head office for unified allocation and these institutes had no permissions to arrange the money at their discretion. The loan origination by the banks of all levels must be operated after the assessment of the head office and they were only allowed to extend the loans within the quota limits.

(3) *No boundary between the government and enterprises*

Banks are financial enterprises which manage the currencies and take credit business. However, the banks' status and functions were distorted to be the administrative institutes attached to finance departments as their accountant and cashier, so the banks couldn't operate and seek balance independently. Banks acted as the tools of governments of all levels for economic expanding and the means of achieving the financial balance.

(4) *Closed itself from the outer world*

Chinese financial institutes had neither contacts with international financial institutes such as the International Monetary Fund (IMF) and the Asian Development Bank (ADB) nor the business connections with foreign banks and they had no financial branches overseas. There were few branches of other foreign banks in China and the few remained branches of foreign banks like HSBC in Shanghai had no actual business in China. There were no specialized and independent banks that operated foreign exchange service. The Bank of China actually was bureau of foreign business of the People's Bank of China with little business and slow development.

Under the special highly centralized framework of the planned economy, the unified financial system was conducive to deliver polices and control the overall economy, which nonetheless sacrificed the efficiency of the distribution of resource and led to many problems in economy. With the implementation of Chinese economic system reform, the financial system reform was also of historical necessity.

Chapter 2
The Starting of China's Financial System Reform

From the history, the year 1979 was the starting of China's economic system reform, as well as the starting of China's financial system reform. In the 30 years from 1949 to 1978, China's financial system was a grand unification. China's finance was typically under repression and closed state, and there was no real financial market. On the Third Plenary Session of the eleventh CPC Central Committee that was held in the December of 1978, the strategy of shifting work focus onto economic construction started the reform of economic system. On Jan.4, 1979, the symposium of the first secretary of the CPC committee of provinces, municipalities and autonomous regions, Deng Xiaoping said that banks do not only function as accounting, but also should function as the lever to promote the development of economy and the innovation of technology. This is the real meaning of banks.[1] Under this perspective, China started a new period of planned and organized reform of financial system. [2] China's financial system reform started formally and developed with Chinese characteristics.

2.1 The start of banking system reform

With the rapid spread of the economic system reform, consequences happened as follow: monetization of economy increased; significant adjustment appeared in the national income; sharp increase in the ratio of social fund flowing into banks by credit channel; financial service started quickly; the demand of capital of every national economic department increased. The former highly concentrated state banking system which People's Bank of China played both roles of central bank and commercial bank

---

1 Shang Ming, Chen Li and Wang Chengming, *Financial Memorabilia of the People's Republic of China*, Beijing: China Financial Publishing House, 1993.

2 Hu Anquan, "The internal logic of the evolution of the CPC reform thought", *Review of Economic Research*, 2012 (72).

could not able to meet the demand of the objective circumstances with decentralization of economic administration, diversification of economic entity and horizontal economic ties. Therefore, highlighting the financial management function of PBOC, establishing modern central banking system, restoring state professional bank, and reforming the administrative system of bank credit had brought up to the agenda.

2.1.1 The preparation of establishing central banking system

During "the cultural revolution", the Head Office of PBOC was merged into the ministry of finance, and only maintained its named as the People's Bank of China in the foreign affairs. On Oct.7, 1976, the People's Bank of China held a national bank meeting in Shenyang. Three principles were proposed and must be followed when exploring the administrative system of bank credit was in process. Firstly, the right to issue paper money is belonged to the central bank. Secondly, there must be a unified and balanced plan throughout the country. Thirdly, fiscal and credit fund must be under separate control. In order to ensure the three principles mentioned above, in the November of 1977, the State Council promulgated a regulation named "Several Regulation about Reorganizing and Reinforcing the Function of Banks". It emphasized that banks should fully play their function by insisting centralized and unified banking business and establishing flexible and practicable banking system. On Dec.31, 1977, the State Council decided to separate the Head Office of PBOC from the Ministry of Finance, and it became the first class ministry and commission directly under the State Council. The decision had been valid since Jan.1, 1978. Bank institutions in every province, municipality and autonomous region should also follow the regulation. People's Bank of China implements its management under both local government and the headquarters, and the headquarters plays a major role. In order to reinforce the centralization and unification of the command system of financial administration and bank business, they practiced unified policies, planning, regulation, fund procurement and issuance of paper money. Meanwhile, to open up a new situation for People's Bank of China, when the banks establish branches, they should enrich the leading group by bringing in and training more talents who understand policies and business.

Previously, the government and business functions are mixed together, and both financial management and credit operation were controlled by PBOC. As the development of socialist commodity economy and reform of planned economic system were in process, the former organization format did not meet the need of new developing trend anymore. In the February of 1979, the State Council endorsed the minutes of meeting of PBOC, it emphasized that banks should be quickly included in socialist modernization, and the function of banks must be well understood. It also stated that banks were more flexible and effective than administrative means as it was the hinge of fund and connection of economy in the country. In the January of 1981, the State Council issued Decision on Reinforcing Credit Management and Strictly Control the Issuance of Paper Money. The decision emphasized that PBOC shall faithfully implement its function as the central bank. In the July of 1982, the State Council authorized PBOC to function as the central bank in order to reinforce the financial management. Meanwhile, the professional banks were asked to play their role more sufficiently. In the September of 1983, the State Council formally issued "Decision on PBOC Specializes Its Function as Central Bank". It stated that PBOC specializes its function as central bank, and no longer conduct industrial and commercial credit and deposit service. In 1984, Industrial and Commercial Bank of China (ICBC) was established. It took over the function of industrial and commercial enterprises deposit, loan, settlement service and the deposit service of urban resident from PBOC. So far, the preparation was made to independently function as the central bank and further meet the new central bank system.[1] The financial system at that time is described in Figure 2–1.

2.1.2 Restore and establish professional bank

(1) *Restore Agricultural Bank of China (ABC)*

In the December of 1978, to meet the need of reform and development of rural economic system, reinforce the management of rural fund, and support the development to rural economy, "Decision (draft) on fasten the development of agriculture by CPC" was issued on the Third Plenary Session of the Eleventh CPC Central Committee. The restoration of Agricultural Bank of China (ABC) and the development of rural credit service had become a significant decision of developing agriculture. Establishment of professional banks in China's reform and opening up started.

In the February of 1979, the State Council issued "Notification on the Restoration of Agriculture Bank of China". In the notification, it stated that ABC was under the

[1] Chang Jian and Rao Changlin, "Historical investigation and analysis of characteristics of legal system of China's central bank", *Journal of China University of Mining & Technology* (*Social Science*), 2014(3).

direct leadership of the State Council, and it was escrowed by PBOC. The headquarters of ABC started work on the 30th of March in 1979. Within this year, every province, municipality and autonomous region set up its branches. ABC carried out its administration under the control of the headquarters and province, municipality and autonomous region. This was the forth restorations of ABC since it merged with PBOC in 1965 for the third time. The main missions were to unify the management of agricultural fund, centralize rural credit, lead rural cooperative, and develop rural financial service. After the restoration of ABC, the cooperative rural financial system had been formed. The system was under control of ABC, and collaborated by rural credit cooperative.[1]

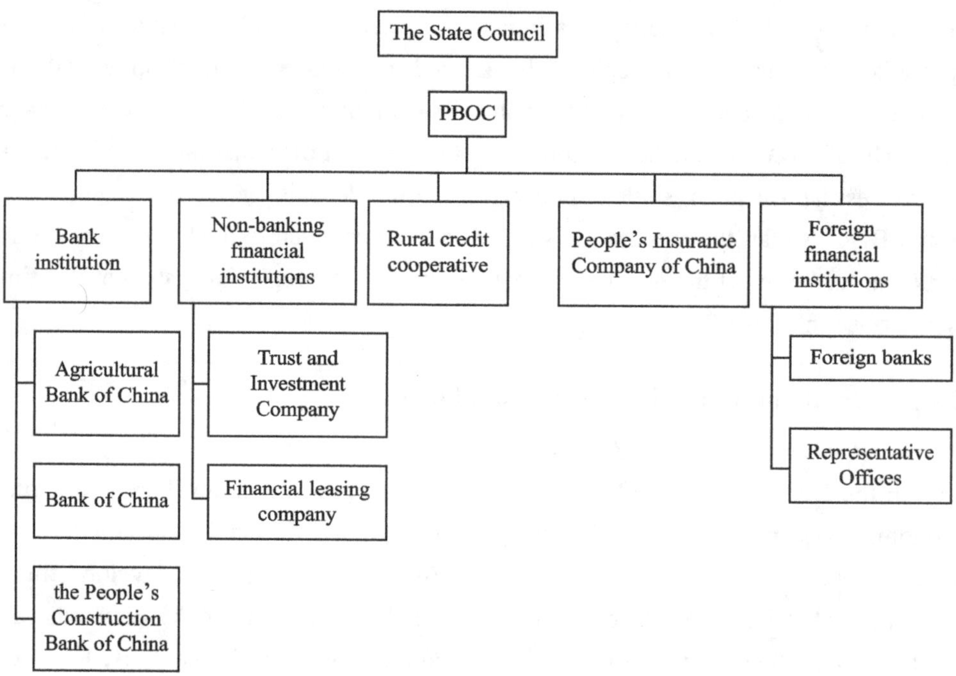

Figure 2–1 The financial system of China before the establishment of central bank (1983)

Source: Wei Benhua, *The New Financial Framework of China*, Beijing: China Machine Press, 2010, p. 80.

(2) *Restore Bank of China (BOC)*

International settlement became heavier gradually as more international trade and connection happened. In order to play its role effectively in the new era, the State

[1] Su Huaiping, "Review rural finance development from the ABC's history", *The Chinese Banker*, 2012 (11).

Council agreed and endorsed the "Report on the System Reform of Bank of China" on Mar.13, 1979. In the report, it was said that extensive authority could be given to BOC appropriately; State Administration of Foreign Exchange was established; separated BOC from PBOC; it was under direct control of the State Council, and was still escrowed by PBOC. BOC and State Administration of Foreign Exchange were different departments, but same group of leaders, and it was authorized with the administration of state foreign exchange, it thus was a state organ. Since most of business of BOC was corporate, all levels of BOC administration should follow the corporate administration system and independent accounting.[1] BOC was reshuffled from Hubu Bank in 1912, and the general administration division moved to Beijing from Shanghai in 1950. In 1952, it was merged by PBOC, but still called BOC when it was dealing with international affairs, and it set up the Administration of Foreign Business. The separation in 1979 was actually the restoration of the system of Bank of China. As the professional bank in foreign exchange, it played an important role in operating foreign exchange trading, holding foreign trading credit, raising and using foreign fund, fostering exporting product and international settlements, carrying out and increasing overseas remittance, etc.

(3) *Restore People's Construction Bank of China (PCBC)*[2]

Since 1950s, PCBC had been subordinate to the Ministry of Finance. Its mission was to fund capital construction and supervised the use of fund. It did not function its role as a bank. In 1978, PCBC was approved to be a direct department of the State Council. For reinforcing the appropriation and supervision of the fund, branches were set up in the whole country. In the August of 1979, the State Council decided to separate PCBC from the Ministry of Finance, it became an independent bank. PCBC was a professional bank in managing investment in the fixed assets, and continued to carry out supervision of the state appropriation of investment fund. In 1980, besides changing allocation of funds into loans, it also allocated loan on capital construction by absorbing deposit. The loan mainly supported excavation and renovation project for products in short supply, city comprehensive development and construction of commercial buildings.[3] Instead of dealing with fiscal service only, PCBC gradually

---

[1] Xu Shiyuan, "The evolution of the livelihood view since China started reform and opening up", *Journal of Zhejiang Ocean University (Humanities Sciences)*, 2011 (5).

[2] The People's Construction Bank of China was renamed as China Construction Bank on Mar.26, 1996.

[3] Gu Xiaojing and Wang Dingxiang, "China's financial development and urbanization process", *Financial Theory & Practice*, 2011 (9).

included more financial business, and the ratio of financial business was increasing.

(4) *Establish Industrial and Commercial Bank of China* (*ICBC*)

On Sep.17, 1983, the State Council formally issued "Decision on PBOC Specializes Its Function as Central Bank". It stated that PBOC specializes its function as central bank, and no longer conduct industrial and commercial credit and deposit service. ICBC was formally established on Jan.1, 1984. As the direct bureau-level economic firm under the State council, ICBC took over the function of industrial and commercial enterprises deposit, loan, settlement service and the deposit service of urban resident from PBOC. ICBC became a professional bank in managing urban finance, providing financial service for urban industrial and commercial enterprise and the residents. ICBC was focusing at: raising and using fund according to the state polices; supporting the development of industry and extension of commodity circulation; supporting collective and individual industry and business and tertiary industry; promoting urban economy; enhancing fund management; adjusting currency circulation in the market; dealing with currency clearing; maintaining currency value and price stability; managing and fastening the fund circulation of state owned and collective enterprises; improving economic benefit.[1]

The state professional banks were carrying out their business within certain stipulated circumstances, but they were not real bank. When they were supporting the development of national economy and driving the reform of economic system, it still faced the problem of "public financing" and "longterm" in using credits. It was necessary to deal with the relationship between policy-related bank loans and commercial credit, in order to become independent economic subject in the market and meet the need of national economic development.

2.1.3 Administrative system reform of bank credit

Since the reform and opening-up policy, the country started to focus more on how law of value affects economy. It started to support economic development and adjust the economic circulation by using financial means. The management system of bank credit thus became important part of the financial system reform.

In order to aim at the abuse of managing system of centralized "unified deposit and loan", and to adapt economic system reform and meet the demand of credit loan for national economic development, in 1979, the reform of credit system started. In

[1] Jiang Lichang, "The birth of industrial and commercial bank of China", *China Urban Finance*, 2012 (1).

this year, PBOC started its pilot program in 6 provinces, such as Shanghai, Jiangsu, Shaanxi to carry out "unified plan, classified management, connecting deposit and loan, balance controlling". In 1981, PBOC promoted "unified planning, classified management, connecting deposit and loan, and differential contracting-out" in the whole country. "Unified planning" means that the headquarters of PBOC made credit "differential responsibility" plan according to the regulation, the balance was checked and ratified by PBOC and the balance was for the branches of PBOC and other specialized banks. "Level to level administration" means clarified responsibility and the limit of authorities of PBOC and its branches and specialized banks under the circumstance of credit fund differential contracting-out and the state plan. "Deposit and loan link" means those banks which undertake differential contracting-out, must link its deposit and loan together in direct ratio. "Differential contracting-out" states the usage of approved credit fund. In order to keep the seriousness of the credit plan, "deposit balance" needs to be achieved and "debit balance" must not be surpassed. In this context, "deposit balance" means the balance when the resource of credit fund is larger than application credit fund. "Debit balance" means the balance when application credit fund is larger than the resource of credit fund.

This is a new attempt after the reform and opening up. The main idea of the system is that instead of using credit target as a indicator to control the total amount of currency supply, credit balance is used. The advantages are stated below: (1) Differential contracting-out minimizes the management power over the fund plan, motivates the bank institutions to absorb deposit and expands their autonomous authority in operating. (2) Differential contracting-out system brought attention and gained support from the government on the issue of fund raising and application, thus promoted local economy. (3) It improved the management level of banks, this is because differential contracting-out required them to keep balance between the deposit and loan, thus increased their awareness and responsibility in fund management.[1] In conclusion, differential contracting-out showed unified plan on the macro level and motivation on the micro level.

The reform motivated the government and banks to manage credit fund in whole. As the reform of financial system and the foundation of diversified financial markets, it broke the boundaries of fund flow between different regions, departments and

---

[1] Liu Dong, "Developing finance and deepening the reform of China's financial system", *New Thinking*, 2012 (10).

ownership systems. The fund started to cross flow, thus the financial business shifted from "grand unification" to separate operation. However differential contacting-out also had obvious drawback. For example, the management was built on planned economic system, whatever the PBOC or the other specialized banks still need to follow economic instructions and plans, thus they were still "eating from the same pot" (getting an equal share regardless of the work done). The PBOC easily lost its control on the scale of social credit under the principle of "more deposit more loan". Therefore, differential contraction-out is essentially "eating from the same pot", and could only be the period of transition.

2.2 Restore and develop insurance market

Social security is named as "the damper of the society", it is an important condition to keep the society stable. As commercial insurance is an crucial constituent part of social security, it plays an important role in promoting social security system. Meanwhile, Insurance is a form of economic compensation and economic compensation system organized in the whole society. It is also a main source of fund raising and crucial part of Chinese financial market. Therefore, the restoration and development of insurance market became an important mission of Chinese financial reform after the reform and opening up.

2.2.1 Restore domestic insurance business of People's insurance company of China

The People's Insurance Company of China (PICC) which was found in 1949 was initially subordinate to PBOC, and since 1952, it was allocated under the Ministry of Finance according to the system of Soviet Union. However PICC stopped its domestic business in 1959 after the highly concentrated planned economic system. It was then handed over to the Overseas Business Office of PBOC and operated a small amount of overseas business. It was still named as PICC, but it was actually not an independent insurance company.[1]

With the reform of economic system and financial system, in order to promote state fund raising and provide economic compensation for state and collective property,

[1] Liu Yingshuang, "The course of Chinese financial reform: based on the recount of financial institution, financial market, financial regulation", *Social Sciences in Nanjing*, 2011 (4).

a decision that was made on PBOC National Branch President Meeting in February of 1979 stressed the restoration of domestic insurance business by setting up experimental unit. It is aimed to serve the production and the people under the principle of free will. In April 1979, with the approval of the state council, the PBOC issued the "Notice Concerning the Resumption of Domestic Insurance Business and the Strengthening of Insurance Institutions", and decided to re-establish insurance institutions and resume domestic insurance business. In 1980, the PICC was formally operated as an economic entity directly under the state council. By the end of 1980, PICC had restored branches in 28 provinces, autonomous regions and municipalities across the country except Tibet. The main tasks of the PICC were to raise and establish insurance funds, allocate economic compensation, prevent disastrous losses, enhance social welfare and serve the "Four Modernization" construction.

2.2.2 Initial development of domestic insurance market

Since the PICC resumed its domestic insurance business in 1980, businesses such as enterprise property insurance, family property insurance and motor vehicle insurance have been recovered and developed rapidly across the country. From 1980 to 1988, the premium income of PICC increased from RMB0.46 billion to RMB10.92 billion, with an average annual growth rate of 48%, as shown in Table 2–1.

Table 2–1 Premium income of PICC (1980-1988) Unit: RMB100 million

Item	1980	1981	1982	1983	1984	1985	1986	1987	1988
premium income	4.6	7.7	9.9	12.3	19.8	33.1	52.6	79.1	109.2
premium income on property	2.9	5.3	7.5	10.0	14.3	21.6	31.0	42.1	57.3

Source: Statistics of the People's Insurance Company of China.

Enterprise property insurance is the first kind of insurance that recovers after restoring the domestic insurance. From 1980 to 1984, a total of RMB2.9 billion was collected from enterprise property insurance premiums. At the same time, it provided economic compensation for enterprises suffering from accidental disasters and strongly supported the development of enterprise production. Next, PICC started its cargo insurance and vehicle insurance business. From 1980 to 1984, a total of RMB55.78 million was collected for cargo transportation insurance and RMB0.893 billion for motor vehicles. In addition, it also gradually opened family property insurance, rural insurance and life insurance. It greatly enriched the insurance market.

2.2.3 Development of foreign insurance business

The overseas insurance business of PICC was severely damaged in "the cultural revolution". Except for a few export businesses, all the overseas and international reinsurance business stopped. After 1979, with the recovery of domestic insurance business, overseas insurance business has been rapidly developed. In addition to restoring and continuing to develop foreign-related insurance businesses such as import and export cargo transportation insurance, Marine insurance for ocean-going voyages, aircraft insurance for international air routes and international reinsurance, PICC also started some new types of insurance in 1979, such as the "three-plus-one" trading-mix[1] insurance. It meets the needs of foreign trade, so that foreign trade enterprises can not only safeguard their own economic interests in China, but also strive for non-trade foreign exchange income for the country. In order to support the introduction of foreign investment and adapt to the needs of merchants, in 1979, we also launched insurance against investment risk (political risk), which attracted the interest of Hong Kong and overseas investors and the attention of international insurance market. In 1982, Hong Kong Min'an Insurance Company set up a branch in Shenzhen, which was the first foreign insurance company to enter the mainland market after China's reform and opening up.

As the number of new types of insurance continues to increase, the service sector expands constantly, and the insurance premium income of foreign-related insurance increases constantly, it has a great effect on compensating the loss of foreign exchange funds of China's industry, transportation, trade and other industries, safeguarding national economic interests and promoting foreign economic exchanges.

With the deepening of China's reform and opening up, and continuous development of economic and trade relations with foreign countries, PICC has also developed extensive business ties with foreign insurance institutions and strengthened cooperation with the international insurance sector. PICC widely entrusts the agent of claim settlement and average inspection abroad, in order to provide services for the inspection of insurance materials and ships in foreign countries. By 1986, PICC had entrusted more than 300 agents to serve the insurance business in more than 100 countries and regions. At the same time, PICC has also accepted the commission of 111 foreign insurance companies to provide the foreign insurance industry with the

[1] "Three-plus-one" trading-mix refers to the processing of supplied materials, processing of samples, assembly of supplied parts and compensation trade, which were the forms of foreign trade at that time.

services of agency of claims settlement and average inspection in China. In addition, PICC has joined some international insurance organizations. It joined the Asia Pacific insurance company in 1979; In 1980, it set up the joint venture with American International Underwriters (AIU) and opened a Sino-Us insurance company in Bermuda, specializing in the worldwide reinsurance business as well as the insurance business related to North America and China's trade; in 1982 an insurance liaison office was established in London, England, and a Chinese reinsurance company was established in Hong Kong, China. All these show that China's insurance institutions and insurance business have entered the international insurance market, and the relationship with the world insurance industry is increasingly close.

2.3 The start of capital market of People's Republic of China

Since the reform and opening up, China's economy has transformed from a planned system to a market system. In the process of transformation, the reform of state-owned enterprises has gradually deepened and China's economy has continued to develop. Therefore, in order to meet the demand of promoting ownership reform and resource allocation, the financial system is needed to be set up to adapt to it.

2.3.1 Reform of stock-holding system and the emergence of stocks

Since 1978, the household contract responsibility system has appeared in rural China. In some areas, peasants have set up a batch of joint stock township enterprises by means of "substitute funds for labor, substitute labor for funds", which has become the earliest prototype of shareholding economy after the reform and opening up.

In the early 1980s, some small state-owned and collective enterprises in the city also began to carry out a variety of joint stock system attempts, and initial stocks began to appear. For example, in 1980, PBOC acted as agent for Fushun Red Brick Factory to issue 2.8 million shares to enterprises; In 1980, Chengdu Industrial Exhibition Trust Corporation issued 2,000 shares to all people and collective ownership at a par value which was RMB10 thousand per share. It actually raised RMB14 million by 1983, and this was the first recorded joint-stock company established by fund raising since the founding of the People's Republic of China; In July 1983, Baoan Joint Investment Corporation in Guangdong province published a prospectus in

Shenzhen Special Zone Daily, with the county finance as the guarantee, to raise RMB13 million in stock issuance to the society. This was the first company offering for subscription through the press. In October 1984, China established the direction of reform of the city and the entire economic system, and proposed to further liberalize the urban collective enterprises and the small state-owned enterprises. From 1984 to 1986, Beijing, Guangzhou, Shanghai and other cities selected a few enterprises to carry out joint stock system as experimental cities. In 1984, for example, Beijing Tianqiao Department Store Corporation, the first state-owned enterprise to undertake joint-stock reform, publicly offered shares for three years. In December 1986, "Regulations of the State Council on Deepening Enterprise Reform and Enhancing Enterprise Vitality" pointed out that cities could select a few qualified large and medium-sized state-owned enterprises to carry out the joint stock system. Under the leadership of these companies, there have also been activities in the form of recruiting share and raising funds by stocks to run enterprises. At the same time, more and more enterprises, including some large state-owned enterprises, were carrying out share-holding pilot programs by semi-publicly or publicly issuing stock. The primary stocks market emerged.[1]

In fact, the joint-stock companies in this period were all non-listed companies, thus none of the corporate stocks could be freely traded or circulated. In addition, the stocks were due to repay and often issued be par value, and they kept the principal, interest and dividend, they thus had the characteristics of a bond. The object of issue is mostly internal staff and local public. It was not a standard stock, because it was mostly self-issued without underwriters.[2]

2.3.2 The reemergence of treasuries and corporate bonds

The government stopped issuing bonds in 1958. Not until July 1981 did the state council decide to issue bonds once a year in response to the national fiscal deficit. The allotted time of national debt issued from 1981 to 1984 was 10 years. Starting from the 6th year after the issuance, and drawing by lot to repay 5 times in 5 years, the principal and interest had to be paid off completely in the 10th year. At that time, the issuance of national debt adopted administrative distribution method. After 1990, with the gradual formation of national debt trading market, it was freely subscribed by urban

[1] Li De, "Reform and development of China's securities market", *Financial Perspectives Journal*, 2011 (4).

[2] Liu Hongru, "The development and prospect of China's capital market", *Financial Science*, 1999 (2).

and rural residents. In 1991, the state changed the mode of issuing government bonds to treasuries underwriter that was constituted by financial institutions. The marketization was initially started. The treasury bonds issued in the beginning should be prohibited from circulation and transfer. The treasury issuance scale from 1981 to 1991 is shown in Table 2–2.

Table 2–2 The treasury issuance scale from 1981 to 1991

Year	Issuance (100 million)	Balance (100 million)	Balance/GDP (%)
1981	48.66	—	—
1982	43.83	92.49	—
1983	41.58	134.07	2.32
1984	42.53	176.60	2.46
1985	60.61	237.21	2.65
1986	62.51	293.07	2.87
1987	116.87	391.53	3.27
1988	188.77	558.64	3.74
1989	223.91	769.33	4.55
1990	197.23	890.34	4.80
1991	281.25	1,059.99	4.90

Source: PBOC.

With the development of reform and opening up, bank credit was gradually unable to meet the needs of enterprise production. Started from 1982, a small amount of enterprises spontaneously raised fund and paid interest to the public and its internal staffs by means of "substitute funds for labor and substitute labor for funds". The enterprise bonds emerged. In 1982, China International Trust and Investment Corporation issued foreign financial bonds on the Tokyo stock exchange of Japan. This was the first time that China issued foreign financial bonds in the international market. In 1984, China implemented a tight monetary policy to control severe inflation. In this macro context, some construction projects financed by bank loans were short of funds, and Banks started to issue financial bonds to support the completion of these projects. The interest rate of financial bonds was generally higher than deposit interest. Financial debt became a regular financing tool for banks.

2.3.3 The emergence of securities circulation market and intermediary institutions

With the increase of the issuance of securities and the gradual expansion of the investor team, the demand for securities circulation is increasingly strong, and the counter trading of stocks and bonds has gradually appeared all over the country. In August 1986, Shenyang Trust and Investment Corporation took the lead in trading stocks and bonds on behalf of customers, as well as fund raising business of enterprise by mortgaging bond. In September of the same year, Jing'an Securities Business Department of ICBC Shanghai Trust and Investment Company took the lead in carrying out counter trading for the stocks of Feilo Acoustics Company and Yanzhong Industrial Company, marking the emergence of the initial form of secondary stock market.

From April 1988, the state approved seven cities, including Shenyang, Shanghai and Shenzhen, to carry out transfer business of personal treasury bonds; in June, the national debt transfer market extended to 54 large and medium-sized cities in 28 provinces, autonomous regions and municipalities. By the end of 1988, treasury transfer market appeared in the whole country. The treasury transfer market by counter trading is the starting of the secondary bond market.

With the formation of the primary and secondary markets, securities operating institutions began to emerge. In September 1987, Shenzhen Special Zone Securities Corporation, the first professional securities company in China, was established. In 1988, the PBOC set up 33 securities companies in each province to adapt to the nationwide promotion of national debt transfer. At the same time, the financial departments also set up a number of securities companies. These institutions are China's earliest securities companies, and their main business was to engage in the management of national debt.

2.3.4 The bill market recovered gradually

After the reform and opening up in 1979, the restoration of commercial credit became the inherent requirement of economic operation. Then the commercial bill as commercial credit certificate also entered the financial field again. In 1980, Shanghai began to test the practice of accepting and discounting commercial bills by professional Banks. In February 1981, the bank offices in the Yangpu District and Huangpu District in Shanghai cooperated to test the first discount of the commercial acceptance bill within the same city. Then Xuhui District Office of the PBOC Shanghai Branch and the Tianchang County Branch of Anhui Province jointly cooperated to try out the discount of the first non-local bank acceptance bill. In May 1982, PBOC confirmed Shanghai's practice and experience in the bill business trial, and decided to conduct the bill business trial in Chongqing, Hebei and Shenyang. In December 1984, PBOC issued the "Provisional Measures for Acceptance and Discount of Commercial Bills" on the basis of summarizing the experience of trial commercial bill acceptance and discount in Shanghai, Chongqing and other places. It was decided to carry out this business throughout the country from April 1985, and "The Rediscount Methods of People's Bank of China" was issued in April 1986. It opened the bill rediscount business of the central bank to professional banks.[1]

With the support of the PBOC, China's bill market developed greatly from 1982 to 1987. According to incomplete statistics, by November 1986, more than 140 cities in China had established the above businesses, and handled 3,637 acceptances of commercial bills with amount of RMB0.56 billion in total. There was 12,820 transactions of banks acceptance with total amount of RMB3.32 billion. It included 15,310 transactions with amount of RMB3.56 billion from the specialized banks and 4,155 transactions with amount of RMB1.7 billion from PBOC. However, due to the long-term lack of commercial credit in China and the lack of experience of Banks in the discount operation and management of bills, the irregularities and false bills in the bill market were quite serious. By 1988, the bill business was closed, and the bill market in China entered a standstill stage.

2.4 The rise of opening up in finance

It is the consistent proposition of the Chinese government to develop international cooperation with other countries on the basis of equality and mutual benefit. However, limited by the international political and economic situation, China's international financial exchanges truly fully started only after 1979. Since the reform and opening up, PBOC has returned to the International Monetary Fund (IMF) and the World Bank (WB) on behalf of the government of the People's Republic of China. It has also joined inter-governmental financial institutions such as the Asian Development Bank, the African Development Bank and the Bank for International Settlements, and has established friendly relations with the central banks of many countries and non-bank financial institutions such as insurance companies. It has broadened the channels of financing for the country and actively participated in relevant international financial cooperation.

---

[1] Wu Xiaoqiu, "China's 'three-dimensional' financial reform", *Capital Markets*, 2014 (1).

2.4.1 Fully restore and develop cooperation with international financial organizations

After the Third Plenary Session of the 11th CPC Central Committee, financial opening up, as an important part of opening up, was also strengthened rapidly. The large-scale development of exchanges and cooperation with international financial organizations was the most powerful opening step, which makes China's international financial relationship achieve a breakthrough all-round development in international financial relations.

2.4.1.1 Restoration of seats at IMF and the World Bank

China is a founding member of IMF and World Bank. In 1971, when it resumed its legitimate seat in the United Nations (UN), it began preparations for the reinstatement of the professional institutions under UN. On Mar.25, 1980, having been invited by the Bank of China(BOC), the IMF sent a delegation to Beijing for consultations on the reinstatement of Chinese government's legitimate seat in the organization. On Apr.17, 1980, the IMF formally adopted a resolution to restore China's legal seat. In September, the board of governors of IMF adopted a resolution that listed the People's Republic of China as a separate constituency with an executive director.[1] On behalf of the Chinese government, PBOC participated in the council, the organization's highest authority, and appointed the president of PBOC to be the member of the council.

On Apr.10, 1980, the World Bank delegation held consultations on the restoration of China's legitimate representation in the World Bank. Through the efforts of both sides and with the support of many friendly countries, the agreement was reached through the first negotiation. On May 15, 1980, the executive board of the World Bank decided to restore China's representation in the World Bank and its subsidiary, the International Development Association (IDA) and the International Finance Corporation (IFC).

Since China resumed its membership in the World Bank in 1980, the Chinese government has been considering the establishment of an investment bank as an intermediary financial institution for the World Bank's small and medium-sized industrial projects, and has gradually established it as a professional bank to raise funds from abroad for investment and credit. After a period of preparation, the China

[1] Li Hongjiang, "The development and future of Chinese foreign direct investment", *Commercial Research*, 2004 (5).

Investment Bank (CIB) was formally established on Dec.23, 1981. The highest authority of CIB was the board of directors, and there was a managing board of directors under the board of directors, which was responsible for handling matters authorized by the board of directors and other major issues in daily work. Under the general guidelines for national construction and economic plan, the CIB should, in accordance with the unified financial policies of the state and the various business systems of the bank, issue investment loans and handle foreign exchange investment and other business. The main task of CIB was to accept loans from international financial institutions, raise capital from abroad through other channels and methods, provide foreign exchange and renminbi investment credit to Chinese enterprises, and serve to promote China's socialist modernization. The establishment of CIB further accelerated the pace of China's opening up in finance.

2.4.1.2 Participating in various international financial organizations

(1) *Joining Asian Development Bank* (*ADB*)

The ADB, which headquartered in Manila, the capital of the Philippine, is a regional inter-governmental financial organization funded by most developing countries and major developed countries in the Asian region. Since 1983, China has held several negotiations with the Asian development bank on the main focus on the Taiwan question. In February 1983, the Chinese government formally asked to join the ADB. On Feb.17, 1986, the council of the ABD formally adopted a resolution admitting Chinese government to be a member.

(2) *Joining African Development Bank* (*AFDB*)

Most countries in Africa have long-term cooperative relations with China. Before 1979, China's economic assistance to Africa was mainly non-reimbursable. As the international situation changes, and joining the African development bank was a realistic option as more standardized and effective forms of assistance that is needed to be found. The PBOC applied to the AFDB and the African Development Fund (AFDF) in November 1984. In May of the following year, the AFDB formally accepted the application of the People's Republic of China to the AFDB and its AFDF during the 21st annual conference held in Brazzaville, capital of the Congo.

(3) *Joining the Bank for International Settlements* (*BIS*)

The PBOC has formally established a business relationship with the BIS since December 1984 and attended its annual meeting as an observer. China then filed a formal entry application and became its formal member in 1996. Since then, the

PBOC has sent staff to attend the monthly meetings of the BIS and participated in the study of the "Agreement on Basel International Banking Regulatory".

In addition, the PBOC has established cooperative relations with 50 central Banks of all developed and major developing countries in the world. Through bilateral exchanges, it provides a useful reference for China to establish a central banking system with its own characteristics.

2.4.2 International financial activities have become increasingly frequent

(1) *"Going global" and bringing in of financial institutions*

With the development of reform and opening up, China's financial institutions began to try the overseas financial market. Chinese financial institutions, including the BOC, have set up branches not only in Hong Kong, Singapore, Tokyo, London and New York, but also in southeast Asia and Africa. The PICC broadly entrusts the agent of claim settlement and average inspection abroad, and provides overseas services for the inspection of China's insurance materials and ships. By 1986, the PICC had entrusted more than 300 agents to serve the insurance business in more than 100 countries and regions. In addition, PICC joined a number of international insurance organizations.

It shows more sincerity and courage of China's reform and opening up that China gave foreign financial institutions permission to enter the Chinese market. The entry of foreign financial institutions into China also brought opportunities for them to explore a wider market and obtain more lucrative returns. From 1979 to 1981, 31 foreign financial institutions set up representative offices in China. In July 1981, the headquarter of the PBOC approved the establishment of the Shenzhen branch of Nanyang Commercial Bank, which was the first foreign bank introduced after the founding of the People's Republic of China. In 1983 and 1985, China successively promulgated and implemented the "Regulations of the People's Bank of China on the Establishment of Permanent Representative Offices in China for Overseas Chinese and Foreign-funded Financial Institutions" and the "Regulations on the Administration of Foreign-funded Banks and Sino-foreign Joint Venture Banks in Special Economic Zones of the People's Republic of China". The regulations provided legitimate guarantee for foreign financial institutions to set up business branches in China.

(2) *Foreign exchange deposits and credit grew rapidly*

Before 1982, the foreign exchange deposit business was only operated by BOC. There was only single type of foreign currency deposit. It mainly absorbed remittances, foreign banknotes, currency bills of individuals, enterprises, groups and foreign agencies in China from foreign countries or Hong Kong and Macao regions. Since 1982, foreign banks have been permitted to set up commercial financial institutions in China to set up foreign exchange business.[1]

In the past, the amount of foreign exchange funds absorbed by Chinese Banks at home and abroad were less and mainly transferred to overseas banks. At the end of 1979, only US$3.9 billion was transferred. On Aug.30, 1980, the State Council issued the "Regulations on Short-term Foreign Exchange Loan of Bank of China", which stated the achievements and functions of the foreign exchange loan. In the late 1980s, national professional banks began to cross-operate foreign exchange business and a number of new commercial banks, non-banking financial institutions and foreign banks had also started to engage in foreign exchange credit business. Such a situation was formed where foreign exchange credit operations were managed by a number of banks; the types, coverage and amount of loans were increasing.

2.4.3 Positive outcomes of financial opening up

(1) *Bring in large amount of foreign exchange resources*

The first achievement of financial opening up was the large-scale amount of foreign exchange resources, it raised a huge amount of funds for China's economic construction. On Apr.30, 1980, China and Japan signed an agreement in Beijing regarding the loan, amount of 50 billions yen, provided by Japan in 1979. It was clearly stated in the "Instructions on Strengthening the Use of Foreign Capital", issued by the CPC central committee and the state council in September 1983, that foreign capital was a long-term economy policy. Since then, China had raised a large amount of funds by loans form international financial organizations (mainly from the World Bank), foreign governments, spot exchange and buyer's credit of foreign banks and external international bonds and bills.

(2) *Draw on the advanced management experience of foreign financial institutions*

Foreign financial institutions, especially foreign banks, are highly internationalized and have their own characteristics in operation and management. Chinese Banks have benefited greatly as foreign financial institutions conducted business in China, and brought advanced management experience to China, such as strict and effective

[1] Liu Jing, "Foreign banks in China: business development and regulatory status", *Contemporary Economics*, 2011 (4).

organizational structure, accounting control system, independent business division, clear responsibilities and strict authorization approval procedures. In addition, it provided valuable experience for the operation and management of Chinese Banks such as the independent, reasonable and orderly internal audit system and scientific and efficient staff management mode.

(3) *Improve the level of foreign financial management in China*

In the practice of raising foreign debts, China has formed a foreign debt management mechanism with Chinese characteristics. The mechanism consists of three levels: first, it was the planning decision-making body which is responsible for making the general policies and general plans for country's foreign debt management; the second thing was the management and control mechanism, which is responsible for the scale and cost of the overall national debt; third, the executing agency of the loan, including the financing agency and the spending department, was responsible for the raising, allocating and repaying of the loan. The three levels were combined organically to form the foreign debt management system on the basis of external statistic monitoring; with the characteristic of "double windows", with the core of planning.[1] However, the foreign exchange guarantee issued by China's domestic institutions was not under management. In March 1981, the "Provisional Regulations of the People's Republic of China on Foreign Exchange Management" was promulgated and implemented, stipulating that no financial institution other than the Bank of China shall operate foreign exchange business without the approval of the State Administration of Foreign Exchange. On Feb.5, 1987, the PBOC promulgated the "Provisional Regulations on Providing Foreign Exchange Guarantee by Domestic Institutions". This was a major step for China to improve its legal system, use legal means to adjust and manage foreign capital relations and protect the interests of each country.

2.5 The start of the reform of foreign exchange management system

After the founding of the People's Republic of China, China has adopted the method of unified collection and allocation of foreign exchange, and different methods of linking foreign exchange receipt of proceeds. Such a system greatly benefited the

[1] Wang Renfei, "Discussion on the current situation and mode of China's foreign debt management under the new situation", *Journal of Financial Development Research*, 2013 (8).

concentration of foreign exchange and the enhancement of the comprehensive utilization of the country's foreign exchange resources. However, it was difficult to mobilize the initiative of enterprise in earning foreign exchange. In addition, for a long time, China's foreign exchange was under the unified management of the Bank of China. Such a management system was not conducive to develop international financial exchanges, attract foreign capital, improve economic efficiency, and carry out opening-up policy.

2.5.1 Carry out the system of foreign exchange retention

On Aug.13, 1979, the State Council issued the "Regulations on Developing Foreign Trade and Increasing Foreign Exchange Income", and decided to implement the foreign exchange retention system. The foreign exchange was under centralized management. Besides keeping it for the important area, the country would allocate a certain amount of foreign exchange to enterprises that earned foreign exchange. After these enterprise sold the foreign exchange to the state, the state allowed it to retain a certain proportion of the right to use foreign exchange. Only when foreign exchange was needed in actual foreign economic transactions can foreign exchange earning enterprises apply to the foreign exchange management department for the use of the quota, and the quota was matched with the corresponding renminbi to the bank to be converted into cash at the exchange rate. All local and central contracting department shall first complete the task of the turning in foreign exchange to the central government in full amount according to the regulations, and the rest of the foreign exchange retained shall be redistributed. The proportion of the retention of general merchandise is 25%, of which the local government keep 12.5% and the manufacturing enterprise keep 12.5%. The proportion of retention of non-trade foreign exchange is generally 30% to 40%. With the deepening of the reform of the foreign trade system, export subsidies were abolished, and the retained proportion of foreign trade was changed to be determined according to the categories of commodities. The local government and export enterprise keep 80% of the exporting receipts of the general merchandise, and 100% for electron-mechanical product and certain technological product. At the same time, the central government purchases 30% of the retained foreign exchange from export suppliers and foreign exchange enterprises at the price of foreign exchange swap. During this period, foreign exchange retained mainly work for foreign trade enterprises.[1]

As a supplementary allocation method for the planned allocation of foreign exchange, foreign exchange retention has played a positive role in rewarding export, resolving export losses, arousing the initiative of foreign exchange earning in all aspects and developing industrial and agricultural production. In 1979, the total amount of foreign exchange retention in China was US$1 billion, accounting for 5.4% of the total foreign exchange income in that year, and RMB9.36 billion in 1985, accounting for 31.1% of the total foreign exchange income in that year. However, there were some problems in the implementation of the foreign exchange retention system, such as the separation of foreign exchange quota and foreign exchange entity, and it caused excess allocation of foreign exchange resources. In 1985, the country's balance of foreign exchange declined sharply, and the country had to control it by using and allocating the retained foreign exchange quota. In 1988, the balance of foreign exchange retained amount exceeded the amount of the state foreign exchange balance, and the state had to adopt the method of recording the balance of foreign exchange retained amount to freeze the amount of foreign exchange retained amount.

2.5.2 Carry out foreign exchange swap

China's foreign exchange funds have been vertically distributed for many years. There was no foreign exchange market. After the implementation of the foreign exchange retention system in 1979, various regions, departments and enterprises have foreign exchange income that they can allocate. However, there was an imbalance between the demand and supply of foreign exchange. For example, some enterprises who had foreign exchange retention did not have the demand in foreign exchange, whereas some enterprises that need to import technique and equipment did not have the foreign exchange retention. In order to promote the horizontal financing of foreign exchange funds, balance the surplus and deficiency and improve the efficiency of utilization, in October 1980, the State Administration of Foreign Exchange and the Bank of China started to manage foreign exchange by issuing a notice on foreign exchange, and formulating the "Regulations on the Allocation of Foreign Exchange Quotas". In the starting period, only cash transactions are allowed, sell quota thus was needed to be transferred into cash first. After August 1981, the foreign exchange quota

[1] Li Yang, *Research on the 30 Years of China's Financial Reform and Opening up*, Beijing: Economy & Management Publishing House, 2008.

was allowed to be allocated with compensation. At that time, the proportion of foreign exchange retention was small, and the amount of allocation was limited, and it was mainly carried out among state-owned enterprises. From 1980 to 1985, the accumulative turnover of foreign exchange allocation was US$1 billion. The price of foreign exchange allocation was strictly limited, and it was stipulated that the price of foreign exchange allocation could be increased by 5% to 10% on the basis of the settlement price within the foreign exchange of trade (US$1 = RMB2.8). As a result, the exchange rate of the allocation market is relatively stable. However, overvaluation occurred in the exchange rate. Moreover, there was an unreasonable difference in the price regulation between trade and non-trade foreign exchange retention, which makes the source of foreign exchange in the market greatly be restricted, as well as the scale, effect and range of the market.

2.5.3 Issuing foreign exchange certificate (FEC)

After China adopted the opening-up policy, the tourism industry developed rapidly. There was an increase in the use of foreign currency to purchase goods, as the number of foreigners, overseas Chinese and compatriots from Hong Kong, Macao and Taiwan who come to China's mainland for tourism, visits, and business has increased greatly. In order to expand business and collect more foreign exchange, some domestic departments directly mark up commodities in foreign currency and accepted foreign exchange, foreign exchange was thus circulated in some coastal cities. However, the supply of goods to foreign guests could not be guaranteed, as Chinese residents and families of overseas Chinese also purchased these scarce commodities in those stores that were specially set up for foreign guests which are sold in renminbi. In order to prevent foreign exchange arbitrage and purchase of scarce product, and to avoid the circulation of foreign exchange in the Chinese market, China issued foreign exchange coupons from Apr.1, 1980. Foreign visitors, overseas Chinese, compatriots from Hong Kong and Macao, foreign consulates and delegations could obtain FEC from banks with their foreign exchange to pay for consumption in hotels, restaurants, airports and designated shops. When leaving the country, the unused FEC could be taken abroad and be brought into the country next time. They might also be exchanged into foreign exchange and taken out of the country within the limit of 50% of the original exchange amount.[1] The issuance of foreign exchange certificates facilitates the

[1] Tang Liu and Wang Xuxiang, "Exchange Management: Review and Forecast", *The Chinese Banker*, 2013 (4).

consumption of some foreigners in foreign country and achieves the expected purpose. However, the circulation of FEC in China also brought some problems. The circulation range and object of FEC gradually expanded, and the simultaneous circulation of renminbi and FEC in some regions affected the credit of renminbi. In some areas, lawbreakers created problems by selling foreign exchange coupons, buying supplies and conducting black-market transactions. Therefore, China stopped issuing FEC from January 1993.

2.5.4 Actively utilize foreign capital and accelerate the development of a foreign exchange management system

After the reform and opening up, China began to use foreign capital. As the opening up continued to expand, foreign capital was used in more and more forms and on a larger scale. In order to encourage foreign investment in China, China has formulated the foreign exchange management methods for overseas-funded enterprises which were different from domestic ones. In August 1983, the state administration of foreign exchange promulgated the "Regulations for the Implementation of Foreign Exchange Management in Overseas Chinese-funded Enterprises, Foreign-funded Enterprises and Sino-foreign Joint Ventures". It allowed them to retain foreign exchange income, required foreign investment enterprises to balance their foreign exchange receipts and expenditure and open foreign exchange accounts in banks; it allowed them to borrow and repay loans from domestic and foreign banks without prior approval; it allowed them to buy and sell foreign exchange through the exchange swap centres. This played an important role in the introduction and utilization of foreign capital.

At the same time, in order to meet the requirements of opening up and the reform of foreign trade system, China also set up institutions and formulated laws and regulations on strengthening and improving macro-control of foreign exchange and activating foreign exchange management. In February 1979, the State Administration of Foreign Exchange was approved to be established and its duty was to manage foreign exchange nationwide. In July 1979, the "Law on Sino-foreign Joint Ventures" was enacted, and at the end of 1980, the "Regulations on Foreign Exchange Management" was promulgated.

At the end of 1979, China International Trust and Investment Corporation, a state-owned financial enterprise under the direct leadership of the state council, was established. Starting from Financial institutions such as specialized banks in special economic zones, foreign-funded banks and sino-foreign joint venture banks, which have been established in succession, other banks were allowed to handle part of foreign exchange business as well. As foreign exchange business was successively carried out by other commercial banks, in order to conduct unified management, in August 1982, the state council decided to merge the State Administration of Foreign Exchange into the PBOC.[1]

During this period, a large number of bank and non-bank financial institutions were established successively; it gradually changed the credit funds supply system, expanded the amount and range of loans, and changed the method of allocating loans according to plan only. By the end of 1983, there were 106,957 financial institutions in China, including 49,687 national banks, 1,317 insurance companies and 5,595 urban credit cooperatives.[2] Although great changes took place in the financial system at this stage, the reform of the financial system at this stage was not actually substantial. Financial institutions were set up within the original institutional framework and financial business was developed in accordance with the changes in economic development. In other words, the financial system reform at this stage was subordinate to the development of financial business, and it did not really reconstruct the financial order in the system base on the requirements of the mechanism of socialist market economy. Therefore, the reform of the financial system needs to be promoted as a matter of course, and it is also a necessity for further deepening reform and opening up.

---

[1] Dai Juan, "On the reform and development of the financial system", *China Science and Technology Review*, 2014 (19).

[2] *China Finance Yearbook 1991*, Beijing: China Finance Press, 1991. Quoted in Jiang Shiyin, 30 *Years of Rational Thinking on the Reform of China's Financial System*, Beijing: Jinghua Press, 2009, pp. 120-121.

Chapter 3
The Exploration Stage of China's Financial System Reform

On Oct.20, 1984, "Decision on Economic Structural Reform" had been approved via the third Plenary Session of the 12th CPC Central Committee, in which it proposed to expand the economic reform from the rural area to urban area and targeted to establish a socialist economics institution with Chinese characteristics, full of life and vitality. To implement the planned commodity economy based on the state ownership was clearly put forward. And the government should improve the tax system, and reform the fiscal and financial institution, within the meantime to reform the pricing system. Deng Xiaoping had gave a highly appraised view that the documents of this economic institutional reform was good to explain the socialist. It did the first draft of political economy combining the basic principle of Marxism with Chinese socialist practice.[1]

In Oct. 1987, the 13th CPC Central Committee proposed further to "a socialist economics institution should integrate planning and marketization. The reformed economic operation mechanism, in general, should be the national regulated market, and the enterprises will be market-oriented". This proposal theoretically confirmed the dominated position of marketization, pointed out the path for further deepening reform, and built the theoretical foundation, which initiated the comprehensive exploring for economic reforming.

Under the spirit guidance of the 3rd Plenary Session of the 12th CPC Central Committee and the 13th CPC Central Committee, the key point of China economics reform switched from rural area to urban area since 1984 until 1993. The urban reforming included not only industry, commerce, but also technology, education and all works of life. These urban reforms have significantly changed economics operation mechanism in China. In this duration, the market-oriented adjustment of economic

[1] *Selected Works of Deng Xiaoping*, Vol.III, Beijing: People's Publishing House, 1993, p.91, p.83.

activities has greatly enhanced, and the economy situation had great improvement. In order to provide the sufficient fund support for economic development, the Central Government began to implement the financial institutional reform.

Decision of the CPC Central Committee on Economic Institutional Reform of the 3rd Plenary Session of the 12th CPC Central Committee in 1984 clearly stated that in the meantime of pricing reform, we should further improve the tax system, and reform the fiscal and financial institution.[1] The seventh Five-year Plan for the National Economic and Social Development, which was approved by the CPC national congress in Sep. 1985, put forward the guidance and requirements of financial reform. On Dec.19, 1986, when the CPC central committee was debriefed the contemporary economic situation and reform designation of the following year, Deng Xiaoping called for the pace of financial reform to be bigger, and once again emphasized "make the real bank".[2] In this context, the People's Bank of China (PBOC) systematically raised 4 goals to establish the new financial institutional reform: the first one is to establish the powerful, flexible, hierarchical macro-financial control and regulation system; the second one is to establish the multi-channels, multi-forms, multi credit instruments and fund accommodation credit system subject to bank credit; the third one is to establish a variety of financial institutions coexisting and collaborated socialist financial organizations system subject to national banks leaded by central bank; the fourth one is to establish the modern management system of financial institutions.

To achieve these four goals, the PBOC head office proposed a series of financial reform measures. The first is to set up the central bank system, the PBOC independently act as the central bank, and no longer to take the commercial banking business; the second is to break through the traditional order-based financial regulatory model, and switch to economic-and-administrative-combined bidirectional regulatory transformation; the third is to further play the role of banking through the commercialization and enterprise-orientation of the specialized banks; the last is to form a diversified and hierarchical financial institutions' system via the development of non-banking financial institutions, such as trust and investment companies, financial companies, leasing companies, and securities intermediaries. Meanwhile, the government had set up the Shenzhen and Shanghai stock exchanges and a number of securities companies to develop the capital market rapidly, and reform the foreign currency

---

[1] *Decision of the CPC Central Committee on Economic Structural Reform*, Beijing: People's Publishing House, 1984.

[2] *Selected works of Deng Xiaoping*, Vol.III, Beijing: People's Publishing House, 1993, p.193.

management system and speed-up the financial opening. By 1992, China has preliminarily established a multi-level, multi-form and multifunctional Chinese-characteristics socialist financial system with the co-existing of other commercial bank and non-bank financial institutions subject to national banks led by central bank.

3.1 Establishment of the central bank system

Since the reform and opening up, via the establishment of professional banks and other financial institutions, China has preliminarily changed the pattern of the monopoly of PBOC, and single bank financial system, which is undoubtedly a breakthrough and innovation in China financial system. The issues arose when financial institutions began to be diversified and competition gradually formed, there was no established central banking system. The PBOC assumed the dual functions of central bank and Commercial Bank, and after the resumption and separation of Agricultural Bank of China and Bank of China, the PBOC still took the urban commercial credit business, which was vividly described as both a referee and an athlete, and the central bank function cannot be performed effectively.[1] Without the self-restraint mechanism, the benefit driven of the professional banks resulted in the runaway credit with the disordered competition. In view of the realities of the time and the practice of economic and financial development, China urgently needed to establish a real central banking system.

In 1981, to deal with fiscal deficit in consecutive years, the bank issued many currencies. As the consequence, the market liquidity was excess, and the inflation rate raised up rapidly. The State Council had to launch the "Decision on the effective strengthening of credit management and strict control of currency supply". There were eight provisions to request the resolute measures to control the currencies supply, stabilize the market prices, and ensure the smooth conduct of economic adjustment, in which clearly stated the PBOC should conscientiously implement the responsibilities of the central bank.

On Sep.17, 1983, the State Council issued the "Decision on the sole central bank function of PBOC", which in turn announced the establishment of central banking system and stipulated the PBOC was the government organization under the State Council to regulate the national financial business, and no longer to deal with the

---

[1] Liu Hongru, "The formation of China's central banking system", *China Finance*, 2013 (23).

commercial financial business.

In January 1984, the Industrial and Commercial Bank of China(ICBC) was established to undertake the industrial and commercial credit and savings business, which was originally handled by the PBOC. The establishment of ICBC has enabled the PBOC to get rid of specific banking business and is a sign that China's financial system has basically been built.

In June 1985, the PBOC head office decided to restore the affiliated agencies in all counties and cities below the prefecture level to form a national-wide system covering from the central government to the provinces and counties. The independence of the PBOC highlights the central government's awareness of macroeconomic regulation and control.[1] On Jan.7, 1986, the "Provisional Regulations on Banking Management of the PBOC" promulgated by the State Council was the first comprehensive banking regulation since the founding of the PBOC. Although the nature and status, duties and institutions of the Central Bank, and the establishment of the central bank has made clear provisions on a series of issues such as the socialist financial system at the center, and the provisions on the functions of the central bank also include "unified management of the liquidity of state-owned enterprises" on behalf of the state, which indicates that the primary functions of the central bank at that time were in the exploratory stage.

The establishment of the central bank system in 1983 was an important reform and a revolutionary breakthrough in the field of financial system reform. After 1983, with the deepening of reform and opening up and financial system reform, and the improvement of public understanding, the central bank was gradually moving toward the market economy system. For instance, recognizing and establishing several commercial banks to allow competition, the four major professional banks have also changed to commercial banks, and no longer emphasized the specialized function; abolished the capital mobility and special loan tasks of the central bank branches, and the profits-driven examination of the branches. The assessment method has made the PBOC truly become a detached central bank without profits examination. In the implementation of monetary policy, the PBOC also uses economic means, such as deposit-loan ratio management and open-market operations, to gradually weaken the use of administrative means. However, the PBOC also has some unsatisfactory aspects in acting as the central bank. For example, the PBOC is still responsible for managing

[1] Chen Ganlin, "China's political restructuring since the reform and opening up", *Developing*, 2011 (10).

the liquidity of state-owned enterprises and special loans to non-financial institutions; in terms of macroeconomic regulation and control, many of the PBOC's control measures are difficult to play a practical role, and monetary credit is difficult to control; in aspect of financial supervision, the functions and authorization relationship of head office and branches of PBOC are unclear and mixed up, which leads to the widespread localism of branches. From 1992 to 1993, under the complicated circumstances of overheated economy and chaotic financial order, the two major functions of the PBOC's macro-control and financial supervision failed to play their due role. The defects of the original central bank system were obviously exposed. Further clarifying and strengthening the functions of the central bank has become an important part of the next financial system reform.

3.2 Breaking through the traditional financial macro–control mode

Generally speaking, there are three modes of financial macro-control: First is the indirect regulation mode adopted by the market economy countries, and the central bank mainly regulates financial institutions and financial markets through various indirect economic levers instead of direct administrative orders to intervene in economic activities; second is the planned economies use the direct regulation to formulate and implement comprehensive credit plans and credit policies by the competent authorities of the national monetary policy, and to directly regulate the circulation of money using the directive indicators with administrative authority. The reform of the China regulatory system is initiated by this direct regulation system; the third is the bidirectional regulation mode, which refers to the combination of the direct and indirect regulation system, the complex financial regulation mode with two sets of policy instruments and the regulatory objectives. The central bank comprehensively applies this mode to implement planed control, refinancing, deposit reserve ratio and interest rate adjustment to achieve monetary policy objectives.

Since the early 1980s, as China's traditional planned economic system is gradually shifting to a socialist market economic system, the market is playing an increasingly important role in economic life. In line with this, the direct regulation method based on administrative measures, which has been formed for many years, has been gradually being transformed into an indirect regulation mode with the economy as the main body. In the financial system reform plan formulated by the PBOC in 1984, it was clarified that the primary goal of the financial system reform was to establish a strong macro-control, flexible and hierarchical financial control and regulation system featured with indirect regulation. In order to promote the effective collection and use of social funds, maintain the basic balance between total social demand and supply, and keep the basic stability of the currency to push forward the coordinated development of the economy and the rationalization of the economic structure, we must break through a series of traditional concepts and regulatory models.

3.2.1 Implementing "real loan and deposit" credit management

After the PBOC specifically exercised the functions of the central bank, in response to the shortcomings of the "balanced payment responsibility" management method for credit funds, in April 1985, the State Council requested that the loan and currency issuance should be controlled under the national plan. And from the beginning of the year, the credit funds were regulated by the "real loan and deposit" management system, that is, "unified plans, division of funds, real loan and deposit, and mutual financing", to solve the problem of irregularities of credit funds using.

The management system of "real loan and deposit" adapts to the needs of planned commodity economy development, and is a system that combines direct and indirect regulation and based on planed management. Meanwhile, the management method of "real loan and deposit" also adapted to the objective needs of the financial system in which the central bank was the core, professional banks and various financial institutions coexisted, in turn the relationship between the PBC and the professional banks was shifted from the planned quota distribution relationship to the debtor-creditor relationship, which has basically changed the situation of China's long-term unified and irregular credit funds. It has positively resulted in strengthening macro-control and invigorating capital circulation and promoting the process of implementing indirect financial regulation of central bank.

The "real loan and deposit" approach laid the foundation for the deepening of China's banking system reform. However, due to the insufficient depth and breadth of the economic system reform at that time, there are still some imperfections: Firstly, the management of central bank liabilities, especially the deposits and statutory deposit reserves, mainly focuses on pooling funds. The supply of sufficient funds will guarantee the implementation of macro-control of professional banks by the central bank. Therefore, the central bank has a large concentration of deposits, and the statutory deposit reserve ratio has a single structure. Secondly, due to the lack of clear provisions on the excess reserve level of professional banks, the professional banks institutionally rely on the central bank for the adjustment of the capital position; the third is to implement the planed borrowing management for the professional banks to borrow from the central bank, and actually hand over the basic currency control rights in the borrowing plan to the professional banks; fourthly, the professional bank loans from central bank are divided into planned loans and temporary loans, and low interest rates are offered to the planned loans. This has the effect of restricting the temporary loans of professional banks, but also motivates the professional banks to try to obtain borrowing plans and expand the basis of borrowing; fifthly, due to the lack of relevant provisions of non-banking financial institutions lending and financial management, for which the credit outside the banking credit expansion caused by the rise of other financial institutions to provide institutional opportunity. And, for regional economic development, the local PBOC branches at all levels will limit the regional braches to lend funds out of the region and affect the horizontal integration of funds.

3.2.2 Trial of using indirect means to regulate money supply

Under the traditional system, professional banks must guarantee the supply of funds if they have a plan. In the mid-to-late 1980s, the PBOC tried to regulate the money supply by reforming the credit fund management system and adjusting the statutory deposit reserve ratio.

(1) *Reforming the credit fund management system*

The first is to change the way credit plans are prepared and issued. In 1986, when the PBOC formulated the national comprehensive credit plan, it insisted in determining the resource of credit funds according to the amplification of the narrowly defined money supply M1 (deposit + cash) based on the reasonable economic growth rate, the price increase rate and the currency circulation speed, and accordingly to determine the size of the loan to constrain the demand for funds with money supply. At the meantime, based on the composition of long-term and short-term funding sources, PBOC can determine the proportion of long-term and short-term capital using, and in accordance with the order of production and post-infrastructure, arrange the working capital loans first, and then fixed-asset loans to ensure the rationalization of the money supply structure. The second is to adopt a quota management method for credit funds of financial institutions. Every year, the PBOC head office allocates and issues the loan quota to all state-owned banks' head offices, and so do these head offices to their branches. It is dual-controlled by the professional banks' head offices and the PBOC branches and is mainly operated by professional banks to carry out so-called "annually bottoms up, quarterly monitoring, monthly assessment, and timely adjustment" management. Thirdly, the PBOC withdrew the credit scale control rights from the provincial banks and round up the credit scale allocation and re-lending rights, the benchmark interest rate regulation, and the currency issuance rights to the head office of PBOC, which reduced the control of credit scale. The branches of the PBOC can only refinance the professional banks within the credit line according to the economic development and the tightness of the money.

(2) *Adjusting the statutory deposit reserve ratio*

In 1985, the "real loan and deposit" credit reform requested professional banks to deposit their required deposit reserve to the PBOC at a certain rate. This ratio is the required deposit reserve ratio. Adjusting the required deposit reserve ratio is a powerful policy tool for monetary authorities to control the money supply. The PBOC also tried to control the money supply by controlling the ability of professional banks to create demand deposits by adjusting the required deposit reserve ratio. In October 1987, in order to reduce the scale of money and credit that has been expanding since March 1986, the PBOC raised the deposit reserve ratio of professional banks, non-bank financial institutions and rural credit cooperatives from 10% to 12%. This step not only enabled the PBOC to concentrate RMB10 billion for the production capital needs of the year, but also controlled the credit and monetary aggregates of the year effectively.

3.2.3 Establish a bidirectional control system with direct control as the main and indirect regulation as the supplement

After a brief attempt from 1986 to 1987, due to the indirect regulation and control measures that could not control the double expansion of money and credit caused by the economic overheating that began in 1988, the PBOC was forced to adopt more and frequent controlling of the money supply by directly limiting the total size of credit together with the indirect controlling measures. This direct control of the loan limit has dominated the regulation of money supply. Even though, the PBOC has not given up the indirect regulation to monitor the money supply. This forms a bidirectional control system with direct control as the main and indirect regulation as the supplement.

After 1988, China financial macro-control model adopted a method of controlling both the total scale of loans and money supply. Within the scale of the loan, professional banks can lend as more as deposit; beyond this scale, they can not lend more even with more deposit. According to the national credit plan, the PBOC conducts loan quota management to professional banks on the one hand; on the other hand, it uses the central bank refinancing to regulate the funds supply of the entire country, that is, the bidirectional regulation of loan scale and credit funds.

In order to adapt the financial regulation mechanism to the development of the market economy, the central bank has been looking for the best approach of financial macro-control, and never gave up using indirect means, such as central bank refinancing, deposit reserve, interest rate, etc. However, being restrained by the conditions of the time, what really works in monetary policy was the loan limit. The PBOC has exerted a huge influence on the growth of the national economy and the stability of the price level through the control of the loan limit, the "main gate" for regulating the money supply, and the transmission of monetary policy.

However, with the improvement of China's economic marketization, the commodities exchanged with the currency, whether it is consumer goods or capital goods, begin to flow according to the principles of market economy, while the currency itself flows based on the planning method of the loan quota in different levels. It obviously cannot adapt to the needs of economic development, and resulted in various contradictions and conflicts, and the progressive decline in the effectiveness of loan scale control. The central bank gradually turned to the control of the base currency issuance, thereby establishing a financial macro-control system with direct and indirect regulation.

It is important to note that since 1988, although the People's Bank of China has adopted the double-track method of direct regulation and indirect regulation, the several means of indirect regulation have been distorted because the bank system and operation system are not sound, the relationships between the bank and the government, banks and enterprises, the central bank and specialized banks are not normal. For example, the role that the required reserve might play is offset by the central bank's reloan; the management system of state-owned enterprises has not been adjusted in time, and both sides of capital are not sensitive enough to the change of credit cost caused by the change of interest rate, which leads to the adjustment effect of interest rate cannot be effectively exerted; the open market business can hardly play the role of regulating money supply because the market system and market mechanism of national debt have not been formed. It has broken through the old direct control mode, but how to establish and improve the financial macro-control mode that meets the needs of the development of socialist market economy still needs further exploration.

3.3 Enterprise reform of professional banks

Since the reform and opening up in 1978, the Chinese economy has switched from a product economy to a commodity economy. The "great unity" banking system has not been suitable to the development of the commodity economy, and the reform of commercial banks is imperative. The 3rd Plenary Session of the Twelfth CPC Central Committee held in 1984 clearly stated that "in addition to price reform, we must further improve the taxation system and reform the fiscal and financial institution". It can be said that it is the deepening of the economic system that has pushed China's financial industry to "operate a real bank" as the goal of commercial bank reform and carry out comprehensive reform of the financial industry. In Sep. 1985, the recommendations of the Twelfth National Congress on the Seventh Five-year Plan emphasized that professional banks should adhere to the entrepreneurial reform. To this end, the PBOC and the relevant state departments formulated financial system reform plans, which clearly stated that banks should become independent legal financial enterprises, with the goal of maximizing profits, commercialization, self-operating, self-financing, self-retention risks, self development.[1] China's professional banks have started a long-term entrepreneurial reform since then.

The establishment of a professional banking system in the early 1980s was only the first step in rationalizing China's banking institutions. In order to promote the commercialization of professional banks, China began to implement commercial accounting for these banks in 1980 and began to explore ways for professional banks to switch to commercial banks, allowing professional banks to develop in the direction of integrated operations. After more than ten years of exploration and hard work, by 1993, "making the PBOC a real central bank and turning professional banks into real commercial banks" have gradually become the consensus and basic idea of China's financial system reform.[2]

3.3.1 Deficiencies in the Administration of Traditional Professional Banks

Since the reform and opening up, in order to adapt to the economic and financial

---

[1] Tao Shigui, *The Internal Logic and Path Choice of China's Banking System Change*, Beijing: People's Publishing House, 2014, p.58.

[2] Hu Hai'ou, *Reform and Development of China's Financial System*, Shanghai: Fudan University Press, 2004, p.86.

needs of China's rapid development, China has gradually broken down the "great unity" financial system since 1978, and restored and established the Agricultural Bank of China (ABC), the Bank of China (BOC), the China Construction Bank (CCB), and the Industrial and Commercial Bank of China (ICBC) and other professional banks to promote the diversified development of China's financial institution system. However, for a long time, in the old mode of product economy with single plan management and excessive concentration of power, China's distribution of materials is basically carried out in accordance with the plan of unified purchase and marketing, and banks that operate currency and credit are regarded as state organs. The banks were not recognized as the relatively independent economic entities and not allowed to operate independently as a state-owned financial enterprise. Banks issue loans according to national plans, and bad debt funds are written off bad debts, and they cannot be held accountable. Since the professional bank of the time was born out of the "great unity" financial system, it has strong administrative management characters from the beginning with many drawbacks.

Firstly, the egalitarianism and "eating from the same pot" is widespread in professional banks, and it cannot reflect the principle of socialist distribution according to workload. Banks are special enterprises that operate monetary credit business. To improve the efficiency of credit funds, objectively require banks to choose loan investment and loan scale according to the law of value and the law of credit funds movement on the premise of implementing national financial policies. However, using administrative means and methods to operate monetary funds will inevitably lead to administrative intervention and "power loans". In addition, the separation of operational benefits and self-interests, the separation of responsibilities, rights and interests of professional banks at all levels, and the absorption of deposits, the turnover of funds, and the efficiency has no direct interest to the bank itself, and it is impossible to stimulate the banks at all levels to do a good job in business management. This kind of fund management system makes the basic-level financial enterprises having no pressure, no motivation, lack of vitality, suppresses the enthusiasm of the employees, and makes the financial enterprises losing self-accumulation, self-development, self-reform and self-improvement, and cannot match the needs of the development of the commodity economy.

Secondly, the development of enterprises requires the support of the bank's supporting funds. The banks that adopt the administrative management method and the credit fund supply system determined by this have distorted the relationship between enterprises and banks, making enterprises rely too much on banks and only focus on doing good relationships with banks, thereby to obtain credit funds, without paying attention to how to improve the efficiency of credit funds using. While strengthening cross-regional horizontal economic integration has become an important section of economic system reform, the "big pot" system in which credit funds are over-concentrated and vertically managed has been unable to meet the requirements of horizontal financing of funds, and contradictions are increasingly exposed. As the main channel of financing, professional banks are the main body of financial markets. However, the banking system adopting administrative management methods can only bring about the vertical distribution of funds, and it is impossible to use the market mechanism to carry out horizontal financing of funds. The funds of various professional banks are basically the vertical management system from top to bottom, and the funds cannot be used effectively. The funds of the grassroots banks of various professions are in the state of "well water does not make river water", lack of flexibility in fund management, and without necessary autonomy. All of them are obeyed by the deployment of superior banks, and they have no initiative to operate funds. Instead, they have fostered dependence. Many grassroots banks do not understand how much the financial system reform related to themselves. The superior is ever-changing, and the grassroots are still the same. It is difficult to play its due role for supporting and promoting horizontal economic integration.

Thirdly, macroeconomic regulation and control relies on professional banks consciously and effectively accepting the adjustment signals and instructions from the central bank. However, professional banks that implement administrative management systems are prone to fall into the passive situation with out-of-control expansion, or austerity in rigid uniformity, because of the lack of corresponding interest and restraint mechanisms. When the central bank uses economic means for macro management, professional banks, as the conductors of these economic means, are difficult to make the sensitive response since they are not real enterprises. Since the absent of a good transmission intermediary, macroeconomic regulation certainly cannot be flexible and effective.

The enterprise reform of professional banks is an inevitable result of the recognition of "funds are special commodities" under the conditions of establishing a socialist commodity economy and is an important part of the financial system reform during this period.

3.3.2 The main measures for the entrepreneurial professional banks

In Sep. 1985, the CPC Central Committee clearly stated in the Seventh Five-year Plan proposal: Professional banks should adhere to the direction of entrepreneurial reform. In Jan. 1986, the State Council promulgated the "Provisional Regulations on Bank Administration of the People's Republic of China", which stipulated: The professional bank is an economic entity with independent accounting. In accordance with the provisions of national laws and administrative regulations, it exercises its powers independently and conducts business activities. In Mar. 1987, the Government Working Report adopted by the Fifth Session of the Sixth National People's Congress further pointed out: Conditionally implements the enterprise-oriented transform of financial institutions such as professional banks and insurance companies below the provincial level, and gradually achieves independent operation and self-supporting.

Enterprization is to make professional banks become self-employed, self-supporting, and relatively independent economic entities, and become socialist legal entity with self-reform and self-development capabilities and certain rights and obligations.[1] To this end, within the scope of various national economic and financial regulations, the bank shall have the autonomy of deposits, lending, foreign exchanges, human, financial and materials, and the bank's operating results should be linked to the interests of the employees. The banks with the above rights and interests should take the risks of the loan. When the business is not good and fails to pay, the bank should be reorganized or bankrupt. In this way, we can truly combine responsibility and rights. The professional bank entrepreneurial reform mainly concentrated in two aspects: one is the transition from institutional management to enterprise management, with the aim of comprehensively promoting responsibility, power, and all conditions under the premise that various external conditions and internal management systems are basically unchanged. The combination of enterprise management reform, breaking "eating from the same pot" of distribution, mobilizing the enthusiasm of grassroots banks, and improving the vitality of the financial system; the other one is to break the "eating from the same pot" of funds allocation, gradually strengthening the financial constraints of professional banks, and breaking inter-bank business restrictions, expanding the scope of business, and making professional banks transition from "quasi-business" to real enterprises. The reform measures of this period mainly include:

[1] Wu Xiaoling, "The core and significance of bank corporatization", *Journal of Financial Research*, 1986(10).

The first is to introduce the cross-cutting business and industrial competition. The economy development objectively requires enterprises to provide comprehensive services of local and foreign currency, and long-term and short-term funds. While maintaining the business characteristics, all professional banks have opened urban and rural currency exchange business, and there has been the competition situation of "BOA go ashore, agricultural banks enter the city, ICBC go to the countryside and CBC enter the factories";[1] banks and enterprises can also mutually choose each other independently. A company can obtain services from several banks at the same time, and the bank no longer assumes the obligation to provide loans to a group of fixed customers. Through the cross-cutting business, the monopoly has been broken, and the professional banks have been given the pressure of market competition, which has improved the management level, service level and commercial benefits of the bank.

The second is to enter the financial market for horizontal financing. With the progressive establishment of the interbank borrowing, the discounting bill, the foreign exchange swap and other currency markets nationwide, the professional banks use the time difference, regional difference and inter-bank difference in the credit capital turnover process to do the interbank borrowing business in the financial market, and balance the temporary shortfall of the capital position to improve the efficiency of the use of funds.

The third is to accelerate the transformation of internal operating mechanisms. In the internal management mechanism of the reform, professional banks have implemented various forms of internal business responsibility systems, such as the target operating responsibility system, the president's responsibility system, and various contract responsibility systems, in the basic units and business organizations at all levels of professional banks to combine business performance with the vital interests of bank officers and staff. In the mean time, the labor and personnel management system were reformed, and the middle-level cadre employment system, the term responsibility system, and the cadre quantitative assessment system were implemented. The institutional management of professional banks has gradually turned to enterprise management. The reform measures of state-owned banks during this period are shown in Table 3–1.

In addition, A national comprehensive bank, the Communication Bank of China,

---

[1] Xie Ping and Xu Guoping, *Path selection: Financial Supervision System Reform and Central Bank Functions*, China Financial Publishing House, 2004, p.89.

was re-established in Jul. 1986. As the pioneer institutional innovation in the banking industry, it was the first joint-stock commercial bank in China, and the earliest market-oriented banking institution. Subsequently, several comprehensive banks and commercial banks were established, such as CITIC Industrial Bank, Shenzhen Development Bank, Hua Xia Bank, Shanghai Pudong Development Bank, and other national or regional commercial banks. This has played a significant role to further introduce market competition mechanism and improve the overall strength and service level of the industry and accumulate valuable experience for exploring the commercialization of China's banks.[1]

Table 3–1 The related measures of state-owned bank reform (1985-1994)

Reform Goal	The transformation of four major state-owned banks from specialized operations to enterprise management.
Business model	Since 1985, professional banking business can be properly crossed, moderate competition, mutual selection of banks and enterprises, allowing access to financial markets for horizontal financing.
Fund management	Since 1985, the implementation of the "unified plan, divided funds, the real deposit of loans, mutual financing", and "limit management, deposit and loan" management methods, lead the transfer of funds between the central bank and professional banks from plan allocation to market-oriented credit relationship.
Financial system	Profit retention, full responsibility of revenue and expenditures.
Internal management	President's responsibility and target management system.
Reform measures for separating the banks in different natures	In the second half of 1992, the national professional bank was officially proposed to change to a state-owned sole liability company, three policy banks were established in 1994.

Source: Tao Shigui, *The Internal Logic and Path Choice of China's Banking System Change*, Beijing: People's Publishing House, 2014, p.58.

3.3.3 Achievements and difficulties of professional bank enterprise reform

The exploration of professional bank entrepreneurial reform is not plain sailing. But overall, it has achieved a lot of successful results, mainly reflected in the following aspects: First, it promoted the enthusiasm of professional banks to organize funds, and accumulated a large amount of funds for the development of the national economy; second, it has expanded its credit capacity and changed the pattern of "big finances and small banks" in the past; third, it has enhanced the ability of professional banks to self-accumulate and self-development, and also increased the income of the state finances; fourth, it promoted the improvement of the status and role of

[1] Ding Yifan, "Reform and development of China's financial system", *Marxism & Reality*, 2013(2), pp. 15-21.

professional banks, and changed the role of accountants and cashiers of these banks in the past, and made banks getting to be an important lever for the state to regulate economic life.

Through several years of reform practice, it was proved that the professional banks' entrepreneurial reform still has certain difficulties under the circumstances of that era. Firstly, there was still an inconsistency in the understanding of the professional banks' entrepreneurial reform. For example, those who are skeptical about the corporatization of professional banks worried that there is a contradiction between the corporatization of professional banks and the management functions of banks, contradictions with financial macro-control, and contradictions with social and economic benefits, and those who agree to the corporatization of specialized banks are enterprise-oriented have a variety of different understandings of corporatization and the objects of corporatization. Secondly, professional banks have long been in an absolute advantage and a high degree of monopoly in China's financial industry, which brought more monopoly benefits to professional banks. On the other hand, it is difficult to quickly form normatively and equally competitive environment in the entrepreneurial reform. As the consequence, this has greatly affected the process of entrepreneurial reform in professional banks. Thirdly, the proportion of non-performing assets loans in professional banks is relatively high, which has become a heavy burden that is difficult to get rid of in the entrepreneurial reform of professional banks. In the past, due to the mismatch of government functions and the characteristics of the planned economy, professional banks have undertaken many functions that should be borne by the financial sector, resulting in many non-performing assets. In this situation, to solve the old non-performing assets is the premise to prevent the new non-performing assets, to maintain the good liquidity, safety and efficiency of professional banks. Thus, the professional banks will not be able to transform to the profit-maximization commercial banks. Finally, the internal management of professional banks is not good, the risk awareness and market concept are weak, the quality of personnel is not high, and the structure of institutions and personnel is bloated and inefficient. It also brings many difficulties to the entrepreneurial reform of professional banks.

The entrepreneurial reform of professional banks is an exploration of the nature and developmental direction of professional banks. This kind of exploration provides a basis for establishing the reform goals of professional banks transforming to commercial banks, and prepares for this transformation.

3.4 Development of non–bank financial institutions

With the deepening of reform and opening up, China's non-bank financial institutions have also been restored and rapidly developed while establishing a central bank system and reforming the bank's credit system.

3.4.1 Several pilot reform institutions of insurance

Since the 3rd Plenary Session of the 11th CPC Central Committee, with the approval of the State Council, it has decided to re-establish insurance institutions and resume domestic insurance business. The People's Insurance Company of China (PICC) has restored and established branches in various provinces, municipalities and autonomous regions across the country, which constitutes the main body of China's insurance market supply. However, in 1985, with the needs of social and economic construction and development, the PICC monopolized all the insurance businesses in the country and could not adapt to the market needs of the situation. The issue of whether to handle insurance for many enterprises has aroused the attention and theory exploration of the society. The PICC is the administrative department of the insurance industry. The PICC has started an organized pilot project since 1986. "Interim Regulations on the Administration of Insurance Firms" announced on Mar.3, 1985 clarified that new insurance companies with independent legal status may be established in accordance with relevant regulations, and the establishment of insurance companies, the nature of the PICC and the scope of business operations, the solvency of insurance enterprises, insurance reserves and reinsurance have been made normative regulations, perfected China's insurance legal system, and promoted the development of China's insurance industry.

On Jul.15, 1986, the PBOC approved the establishment of the Xinjiang Production and Construction Corps Agriculture and Animal Husbandry Insurance Company, which mainly engaged in the agriculture and animal husbandry insurance business within the Xinjiang Production and Construction Corps. This was the second insurance company established beside the PICC in New China. The company's registered capital was RMB20 million at the beginning, funded independently by the Xinjiang Production and Construction Corps, and the capital gradually increased to RMB70 million. Although the company's business area and business volume were still small, as the main body of the insurance market, its emergence indicated that the era of competition in China's insurance market has been coming.

In Mar. 1988, with the approval of the State Council, Shenzhen Ping An Insurance Company (Ping An) was established on the basis of the former Shekou Social Insurance Company of China Merchants, and officially opened on Apr.27, 1988. Ping An is a regional joint-stock company formed by the joint venture between Shekou Industrial Zone of China Merchants and Shenzhen Trust and Investment Co. of ICBC with a registered capital of RMB30 million and HK$30 million. With the relatively flexible business mode, in the year of establishment, it was recorded a premium of RMB6 million. Its business scope was mainly in the Shenzhen Special Economic Zone, and after it began to spread into important inland cities, opening a gap in the monopoly of the PICC.

On Feb.20, 1988, the Insurance Department of CBC Shanghai Branch opened. On Mar.25, the Insurance Department of CBC Dalian Branch was also allowed to open. Due to the large number of branches of the CBC, and many branches opened insurance business, the insurance business of CBC has expanded rapidly. However, the insurance departments of the CBC branches are not independent legal entities. It was not naturally the real insurance company, just the pilot model for competitive insurance market. In May 1991, the CBC Insurance Department was isolated from the CBC and approved by the PBOC, to establish the China Pacific Insurance Company (CPIC). As China's second national, vertical and horizontal insurance company, its establishment has marked breakage of the monopoly of the PICC for decades, and the Chinese insurance market has entered an era of diversified competition.

In Mar. 1988, Ping An Insurance Company was established in the Shenzhen Special Economic Zone. This was the first joint-stock insurance company in the history of the People's Republic of China. Its establishment marks the formation of a three-legged situation in the insurance market. In the next few years, the PBOC has approved the establishment of several joint-stock insurance companies such as Tianan Insurance Co., Ltd., Dazhong Insurance Co., Ltd. and Xinhua Life Insurance Co., Ltd., and the domestic insurance market showed unprecedented prosperity.[1]

With the increase of insurance entities, the insurance business has also become more diversified, the scope of insurance funds has been broadened, and the methods and means of application have been further diversified. The loan-based capital

---

[1] Shang Ming, *50 Years of Finance in New China*, Beijing: China Financial & Economic Publishing House, 2000.

operation model has thus been changed, and the proportion of securities investment has increased. On institutional level, PICC has also established the fund institutions such as the Capital Utilization Department. At the beginning of 1993, the PICC established the wholly-owned subsidiaries, PICC Trust and Investment Company and Shenzhen Sunshine Fund Management Company, which created a new form of capital operation organization and formulated the "Interim Measures for the Use of Funds in PICC" and strengthened management of capital operations.

Regarding to the supervision of the insurance industry, "Interim Provisions on the Administration of Insurance Enterprises" promulgated by the State Council in 1985 clarified that the PBOC is the national insurance authority. While the PBOC exercises the duties of the insurance authority department, the State Planning Commission also exercises the function of formulating the national insurance industry development plan, and the Ministry of Finance is responsible for supervising the financial accounting system of the insurance industry. With the development of the insurance industry, the PBOC has continuously strengthened its insurance supervision function. In 1988, the PBOC announced "Notice on Strengthening the People's Bank of China to Exercise the Duties of the State Insurance Administration". In 1989, the General Office of the State Council announced, "Notice on Strengthening the Management of Insurance Enterprises", reaffirming and further clarifying the insurance supervision function of the PBOC. Until 1998, the China Insurance Regulatory Commission was established to supervise and manage the national insurance market.[1]

The policy-supported insurance business reform also made great progress during this period. China's policy-supported insurance mainly includes agricultural insurance and export credit insurance. Agricultural insurance was once one of the major insurances in China's insurance business in the 1950s. Since the PICC resumed trials of agricultural insurance companies in 1982, the business has achieved great development. From 1982 to 1995, the agricultural insurance premium income was RMB3.77 billion, and the payment of compensation reached RMB3.9 billion. Agricultural insurance has made important contributions to the steady development of agricultural production in China.[2] Export credit insurance refers to a credit institution that provides a security mechanism for exporting receivables of goods, services,

---

[1] He Dexu, *Research on China's Financial Innovation and Development*, Beijing: Economic Science Press, 2001, p.71.

[2] Shang Ming, *50 Years of Finance in New China*, Beijing: China Financial & Economic Publishing House,2000, pp. 230-231.

technology and capital that are insured by enterprises. China established the export credit insurance system in 1988, and the PICC established the Export Credit Insurance Department, which is responsible for the promotion and management of export credit insurance. In 1994, the Export-Import Bank of China was established, and its business also included export credit insurance business.

3.4.2 Recovery and reform of the postal savings system

Postal financial business refers to the financial services handled by the postal department using postal infrastructure, mainly including savings, remittance and other agency business and capital-related asset business. China's postal remittance business began in the Qing Dynasty since 1898, and the savings business began in 1919. In 1930, based on the operation of the original savings and remittance business of the post office, the National Government established the Postal Savings and Storage Industry Administration in Shanghai, parallel to the General Post Office and under the management of the Ministry of Communications. Postal finance business occupied an important position in the old Chinese financial system. After the founding of the People's Republic of China, the postal savings business was suspended in 1953.

After the reform and opening up, in order to give full play to the advantages of the resourceful postal system, provide basic financial services to the masses, accumulate social funds, and develop the national economy, and in accordance with the instructions of the State Council, the Ministry of Posts and Telecommunications and the PBOC jointly issued the "Regulations on Printing and Distributing Postal Savings". The Joint Notice of the Agreement stipulates that the postal savings business will be officially opened on Apr.1, 1986 at post offices throughout the country.[1] This business has developed rapidly in China. By the end of Mar. 1991, the fifth anniversary of the establishment of postal savings, the postal savings balance had exceeded RMB20 billion, equivalent to the total balance of savings deposits of urban and rural residents nationwide until 1978. The number of post offices doing the postal savings business in the country has reached 17,305, with an average annual increase of 57%. The postal savings network is ranking third in the country after the ICBC and ABC with more than 40,000 full-time and part-time employees engaged in postal savings. With the increasing variety of postal savings business, the postal savings rules

---

[1] Tan Yao, "Study on the Development of Chinese Postal Savings Banks", *Journal of Regional Financial Research*, 2012(2), pp. 55-61.

and regulations have been continuously improved. By the end of 1988, 25 provinces, municipalities and autonomous regions had established postal savings and remittance bureaus, basically forming a national postal savings management system. The Ministry of Posts and Telecommunications has successively formulated rules and regulations such as the "Postal Savings Charter", the "Postal Savings Business Rules", the "Postal Savings Accounting Method", and the "Interim Measures for the Administration of Postal Savings Funds".

However, for a long time, due to various reasons such as the institutional issue, postal savings has implemented "only deposit and no loan" in the way of operation, and all the funds absorbed by the county and below are turned over to the PBOC. Due to the long-term integration of government administration with enterprise, there is risk-free spread income in the operation, the postal savings business lacks the motivations for the long-term, the service level could not go up, and the internal control loopholes of the grassroots are hidden. The "pumping machine" effect of the outflow of funds from rural area has also been widely criticized. The "pumping machine" effect of the outflow of funds from rural outlets has also been widely criticized. At the same time, the demand for postal savings funds to return to the rural area is great, but the risk control and guarantee mechanisms are difficult to be effectively solved, and the risk pricing of funds is difficult to match the actual affordability of rural areas. The next step of the postal savings reform is to learn from the international advanced experience and set up a savings bank to let it operate independently and assume its own profits and losses. At the same time, it will solve the problem of returning postal savings funds to the rural market.

3.4.3 The rise of pawnshop

In the 1950s, the Chinese pawn industry, which had risen and fallen for more than thousand years, entered into a public-private partnership in the whole industry with the socialist transformation movement of capitalist industry and commerce.[1] After the reform and opening up, the pawn industry began to recover in China. By no means accidental, the pawnshops have resumed after 30 years of demise in our country. Under the new situation, we will persist in reform and opening up, developing the market economy, and providing policy guarantee and living space for the survival of

[1] Fang Chunqin, "Discussion on the ownership of pawn industry in China", *Theory Research*, 2013(23), pp. 112-113.

pawnshops.

At that time, our country faced serious contradiction between supply and demand of funds. The national bank's credit channel was insufficient for loans and the form of loans was single. It was difficult to meet the credit needs of small and medium-sized enterprises (SMEs) such as collective and individual SMEs, especially to meet the social needs of diversification of small funds, such as personal demand for funds, emergency funding needs and other issues. The pawn industry followed the trend of China's reform and opening up and the development of market economy and mitigated the demand for funds in the social sphere. At the same time, the pawn industry itself has the characteristics of low risk, small amount, fast turnover, simple procedures and high profit, which lead it to restore in China and develop rapidly. The first pawn shop in China to resume business was the Yongtaichang pawn shop in Shaoyang City, Hunan Province, which opened on Nov.15, 1987. According to incomplete statistics, by the end of October 1988, there were 21 provinces, municipalities and autonomous regions in the country with a total of 168 pawn institutions, mainly distributed in areas where the individual and private economy developed earlier in loose governance, such as Wenzhou in Zhejiang Province, Guangdong Province, Liaoning Province and other places.[1] In the two years after Deng Xiaoping's "Southern Talks" in 1992, a total of one or two thousand pawn shops were opened nationwide. The rise of the pawnshop industry has played a certain role in facilitating the lives of the masses, stabilizing the individual economy, and guiding private lending. At the same time, it has also played a positive role in supporting local economic development, thus arousing the society's greater demand for it, specifically embodied in:

First, the pawnshop is a helpful supplement to China's current financing channels. Since the reform and opening up, China has basically ended the simplification of financial institutions. There are many types of financial institutions, but these financial institutions are mainly oriented to corporate legal entities in the use of funds. Although urban and rural credit cooperatives also provide credit for individuals, they tend to be small, multi-conditional, and complicate to meet personal needs. The pawnshop has made up for the shortcomings of the existing financing channels by its simple procedures, small amount and fast turnover.

Second, the pawnshop is an important force to effectively suppress the Chinese

---

[1] Hu Yanlong, *New China's Financial History*, Kunming: Yunnan University Press, 1993, p.357.

private usury. Beginning in the mid-to-late 1980s, due to the lack of national credit channels, the demand of funds for economic development was relatively large, making private lending rates generally as high as 20% per month, and often even more than 30% per month. The recovery of the pawnshop has greatly cracked down and suppressed the private usury. The recovery of the pawnshop has turned the financing direction of some debtors from the private loan shark to the pawnshop. The pawnshop has carried out the statutory interest rate, which is much lower than the private usury, and makes the private usury in competitive disadvantage. And the pawnshop cooperates with banks and credit cooperatives to jointly tackle with the private usury.

Third, it can support production and facilitate the masses. Under the impact of the tide of the socialist market economy, some pawnshops are able to solve the worries of these enterprises due to the fierce competition, poor marketing, and the difficulties of bank credit pressure. At the same time, lending to urban residents was an important task of pawnshops at that time. Benefit and convenience have become the business objectives of pawnshops.

However, there were some issues in the development of the pawn industry at the time: First, the examination and approval institutions were chaotic. Among the 168 pawnshops opened in 1988, less than 60 were approved by the PBOC, and the rest were approved by the public security departments, the taxation departments, the municipal civil administration departments, the planning commissions, the economic commissions, and other government departments. Second, the interest rate is generally higher. At that time, most pawnshops stipulated that the monthly interest rate was 6% to 9%, which is equivalent to 6 to 10 times of the bank's working capital loan interest rate. Third, there is less working capital. The working capital of the pawn industry is limited to the amount of its own capital. However, the free funds of many pawnbrokers are seriously insufficient to meet the needs of the pawn industry. The fourth is beyond business scope. Some have absorbed deposits from the society, concurrently engaged in the consignment of goods and the acquisition of waste materials; some have issued credit loans to collective industrial and commercial enterprises, which are obviously beyond the scope of business of the pawn industry. In addition, the qualifications of the staffs are mixed and uneven, lacking the expertise of the identification of the object, which leads to the subjective and random nature of the evaluation of the pawn.[1]

[1] Hu Yanlong, *New China's Financial History*, Kunming: Yunnan University Press, 1993, p.358.

From 1987 to 1996, the national pawnshop industry showed a situation of multiple management, disordered development, and chaotic management. In 1995, the Ministry of Public Security issued the "Measures for the Administration of Public Security in the Pawnshop". In 1996, with the approval of the State Council, the national pawnshop industry was supervised by the PBOC, and the PBOC issued the "Interim Measures for the Administration of Pawnshops", which cleaned up the national pawnshops. In 2000, according to the requirement of the financial institutional reform, with the approval of the State Council, the pawn industry was handed over to the State Economic and Trade Commission for unified management. From then on, pawnshops were disqualified from financial institutions and classified as "special industrial and commercial enterprises". After the withdrawal of the State Economic and Trade Commission in 2003, the market access and daily supervision work of the pawnbroking industry was handed over to the Ministry of Commerce. In 2005, after the Ministry of Commerce and the Ministry of Public Security jointly promulgated the "Pawn Management Measures", the national pawnshop industry re-entered the rapid and healthy development stage, the number of pawnshops increased, the industry strength was further enhanced, the business scale continued to expand, and the business structure was continuously adjusted with economic development. The industry's service function for social and economic development and the financing function of providing "short and fast" for SMEs are increasingly apparent.

3.4.4 The emergence and development of financial companies

Enterprise Group Finance Company, referred to as Finance Company, is a non-bank financial institution established by large enterprise groups and serving members of enterprise group. It is the product of China's economic and financial system reform, and the objective necessity of the enterprise groups development. Since the emergence of the first financial company in 1987, the team of financial companies has strongly grown up with the development of enterprise groups. Its role in promoting the development of enterprise groups has been fully reflected and has become an important part of China's financial system.[1]

In the mid-1980s, with the deepening of China's economic system reform, the

[1] Zhou Xun and Liu Xin, "Problems in the development process of finance company in enterprise group and suggestions for improvement", *Finance & Accounting*, 2011(10), pp. 35-37.

horizontal economic integration among enterprises was rapidly developed. As a result, the various types of enterprise groups with products or funds as the link have been set up, the total amount of capital flow among the enterprises began to increase. With the reform of the corporate financial system, the former special-purpose fund system has been changed, and the funds that enterprises can freely control have begun to increase. Although in general, China is still a country with shortage of funds, corporate funds are always in shortage. However, from the perspective of a large group of companies, due to the large number of subsidiaries, the production cycle of each enterprise is not consistent, and the timing of funds using is different, which leads to the large amount of funds borrowed from banks on the one hand, while some funds are temporarily idle in banks with low-interest, resulting in an increase in the overall capital cost of the group and a decline in efficiency. With the enhancement of business sense, making the best allocation of production factors to centralize the scattered temporary idle among many enterprises applying to the enterprises that need funds urgently within the group become an inherent requirement for the development of enterprise groups. Under this circumstance, some large-scale enterprises or enterprise groups have successively set up internal banks or settlement centers to handle centralized distribution and compensate used of corporate funds within the group and have formally proposed to establish financial institutions. To this end, the PBOC formally proposed the concept of a finance company at the end of 1986, targeting non-bank financial institutions that operate part of the banking business and part of the trust business. The scope of services is limited to non-bank financial services within the group head quarter and its affiliates. In May 1987, the PBOC formally approved the establishment of the financial company within the first large enterprise in China, namely Dongfeng Motor Finance Company. Since the birth of Dongfeng Finance Company, by the end of 1998, the PBOC has approved the establishment of 71 financial companies with an asset size of RMB193.1 billion, as shown in Table 3–2.

Table 3–2 Financial company history

Item	1990	1991	1992	1993	1994	1995	1996	1997	1998
Number of institutions	17	19	27	39	56	65	67	71	71
Asset (RMB billion)	10.2	13.0	18.2	24.0	44.1	79.1	132.2	175.4	193.1

Source: Shang Ming, *50 Years of Finance in New China*, Beijing: China Financial & Economic Publishing House, 2000, p.200.

At the beginning of the establishment of the finance company, it mainly engaged in some traditional financial services such as settlement, deposit and loan, etc., with relatively single varieties and small asset scale. Due to the lack of clear management regulations, the PBOC has adopted a case-by-case approach to the management of financial companies. Except for the business scope limited to the enterprise group, the characteristics of the financial company are not reflected in the design of the business variety. In 1991, in order to promote the concentrated development of the industry, the State Council approved the "Notice on the Selection of a Group of Large-scale Enterprise Groups to Carry Out Pilot Projects" of the State Planning Commission, the Commission for Economic Reform and the State Council Production Office, which clarified that large enterprises should develop in the direction of grouping. A pilot enterprise group with conditions can establish a finance company with the approval of the PBOC. In 1992, the PBOC and the three commissions of the pilot enterprise group jointly issued the "Notice on the Establishment of Financial Companies by National Pilot Enterprise Groups", which standardized the conditions and business management of the establishment of financial companies in the pilot group and made clear the non-pilot enterprise group finance company should refer accordingly to implement. Since then, the finance company has entered a stage of rapid development. The development of financial companies has played a certain role in promoting the financial support and financial services of enterprise groups and supporting the development of enterprise groups. These mainly reflect in:

First, it has promoted the transformation of enterprise groups from production to management. Through the financial company, the group company strengthened the unified dispatching and management of funds. The subordinate member units further strengthened the intensive management of funds due to the compensated use of funds within the group, completely changing the past accustomed to reaching out to the funds, and rarely consider the cost of capital.

Second, it has accelerated internal capital turnover, reduced financial expenses, and improved the benefit of the Group's funds. The financial company's internal settlement and loan issuance function has played a positive role in accelerating capital turnover and reducing triangular debt between enterprises. In addition, through the unified management and use of the deposit funds of the enterprise group, it not only enhances the capital control ability of the enterprise group, but also reduces the overall capital cost of the enterprise group, thereby improving the overall capital use efficiency of the enterprise group.

Third, it has alleviated the shortage of funds for some subsidiaries, especially in solving the urgent need for funds, which has made up for the shortcomings of the bank's credit system and played a remarkable role. As the financial company's funding sources are greatly restricted, its financial support to the enterprise group is still relatively limited, and the fund financed only about 10% of the group's total liabilities. However, because the financial company has a better understanding of the internal enterprises of the group, it is often able to solve the urgent needs of the capital needs of key enterprises in a timely manner. Moreover, the finance company has a better understanding of the business benefits and solvent ability of the internal enterprises, so that the financial company can play a greater role for some enterprises that have a greater risk from the perspective of the bank and have actual development potential and solvent ability.

However, financial companies also face some problems in their development, mainly in the following aspects: First, the scale of assets is limited, and the support for the development of enterprise groups is insufficient. In the 1990s, the finance company's financing accounted for only about 10% of the group's total liabilities, indicating that the financial company is still far from meeting the large demand for funds in the development of the enterprise group. Second, the variety of business is relatively simple, unable to meet the needs of the diversification of financial services in the development of enterprise groups. Due to the relatively narrow scope of business of financial companies, most companies are mainly engaged in traditional deposit and loan business. The supply of financial services is still far from the development requirements of enterprise groups. Compared with commercial banks, the advantages are not remarkable. Third, it is greatly affected by the situation of the group, and a few companies have a certain degree of operational risk. Overall, due to the dual supervision of the PBOC and the enterprise group, most of the financial companies are in good operating condition and there is no systematic or industrial risk. However, since the financial company's business scope is mainly within the group, the business situation of the enterprise group is bound to have a conclusive influence on the financial company.[1]

There are many reasons for the above issues of financial companies. The most important one is that the problem of financial company's function positioning has not

[1] Wen Feng, "A brief discussion on the problems and countermeasures faced by China's financial companies in the development process", *Journal of Hunan College of Financial and Economic*, 2005, 21(2), pp. 23-25.

been solved well. As a new type of financial institution, financial companies face enormous development potential, and it is also necessary to further clarify the direction of development and promote a healthy and normalized development.

3.4.5 The emergence and development of financial leasing companies

The financial leasing company is a non-bank financial institution established with the approval of the PBOC and focusing on financial leasing. Although the scale of China's financial leasing companies is relatively small compared with other financial institutions, the introduction of modern financial leasing business has opened new channels for corporate financing in China and has taken a new path in equipment investment.

The first financial leasing company established in China to engage in modern financial leasing business is the Chinese Leasing Company. It was established in 1981 by China International Trust and Investment Corporation. In 1984, it was approved by the PBOC to obtain a financial license, officially as a non-bank financial institution began to operate. From 1986 to 1987, the financial leasing team expanded rapidly. The PBOC also noticed the trend of financial leasing and began to intervene in the management and authorization of financial leasing companies. State-owned financial leasing companies began to declare as non-bank financial institutions. Banks and trust investment companies also began to operate the financial leasing business.[1] In 1988, the leasing industry reached its first peak. In the second half of the year, due to the tightened money supply in overheated economy, the penetration rate of leasing began to decline for the first time. By 1990-1992, the leasing amount gradually increased, especially after Deng Xiaoping visiting Shenzhen in 1992, and China entered another period of overheating, and the lease amount and lease penetration rate both reached historic highs. The financial leasing industry was getting to be distorted under the impact of the bubble as shown in Table 3–3.

Table 3–3 Financial leasing companies history

Item	1990	1991	1992	1993	1994	1995	1996	1997	1998
Number of institutions	9	9	11	13	14	16	16	16	16
Assets (RMB billion)	4.89	5.31	7.27	6.44	10.40	13.40	16.80	18.90	18.60

Source: Shang Ming, *50 Years of Finance in New China*, Beijing: China Financial & Economic Publishing House, 2000, p.200.

[1] Huang Lei, "Analysis on the development process and countermeasures of financial leasing in China, *Market Weekly*, 2011 (6), pp. 3-4.

Due to the small scale of assets, financial leasing companies account for a small proportion in the financial system and have a limited role in promoting economic growth. However, because of their unique financing methods, they also play a positive role in product sales and equipment investment. In terms of financial leasing, China still has problems such as imperfect laws and regulations, unclear functional positioning, imperfect capital market, multiple management, and multiple governance. It needs to be resolved in the next step of reform and development to boost the health development of the financial leasing industry and fully to play its unique role to further promote the development of the national economy.

3.5 Financial market reform and up-to-date development

In the early days of reform and opening up, it was generally believed that financial markets were the product of capitalist economy and finance. There should be no financial market and capital market existing in the socialist economy, let alone capital market. Places for capital market speculation, such as stock exchanges, are incompatible with the socialist system. Since 1985, with the development of commodity economy, the investment entities are diversified, the various forms of spontaneously financing activities are more and more. The finance source on investment can not rely solely on fiscal system. Relying on the vertical allocation of funds by banks, the commodity market is difficult to develop. Therefore, gradually liberalizing the financial market has become an important part of the financial system reform after the reform and opening up. In the "Proposal of the CPC Central Committee on Formulating the Seventh Five-Year Plan for National Economic and Social Development" adopted in 1985, it was clearly stated that "with the guidance and management of the PBOC, use the various financial instruments to actively develop horizontal financial resources, promote the gradual formation of the capital market". Since then, the reform of China's financial market has kicked off.

3.5.1 The formation and development of the money market

(1) *The development of the interbank borrowing market*

Prior to 1984, the financing activities were mainly implemented by the PBOC in the intrasystem vertical planning and dispatching. The financing activities were not operated through the market, and there was no financial interbank borrowing market. In 1984, the PBOC started to act solely as the central bank, and the financial system was initially formed, and dominated by the central bank, with professional banks as the main body and other coexisted financial institutions. The demand for mutual financing raised among the financial institutions. In Oct. 1984, the PBOC established a credit fund management system of "unified plans, divided funds, real deposit and loan, and mutual financing". At that time, it was clear that "mutual financing" was a horizontal adjustment of funds, mainly operated in the way of interbank borrowing in various regions.[1] As a result, financial institutions in some regions initiated interbank borrowing activities, but the amount of borrowing was small and didn't form a scale market.

In 1986, the interbank borrowing market in China had substantially being operated. The "Provisional Regulations on Bank Administration of the PBOC" promulgated by the State Council on Jan.7, 1986 made provisions for "professional banks can borrow from each other, and interest rates among the professional banks are negotiated by both borrowers and lenders", which provides a legal basis for domestic interbank lending market development. In the same year, the PBOC issued the "Notice on Promoting Interbank Lending Operations for Financial Institutions", which further carried forward interbank lending among financial institutions, and the short-term capital borrowing market became quite lively.

In 1986, the first capital borrowing market for urban credit cooperatives after the reform of China's economic system was officially opened in Wuhan, Hubei. In the same year, China successively established interbank lending broker institutions in some large and medium sized cities such as Guangzhou and Shanghai. Based on this, China has gradually formed a cross-regional and cross-system interbank lending market based on central cities or economically developed cities. In the same year, the amount of interbank lending funds reached more than RMB30 billion. After 1987, a nationwide interbank lending market was gradually formed. The lending business developed rapidly throughout the country, and the interbank lending transaction volume increased significantly to RMB230 billion, and so did in the following years stably.

In 1990, the PBOC promulgated the "Trial Measures for Interbank Lending

[1] National Cadre Training Textbook Compilation and Review Steering Committee, *Financial Development and Risk Prevention*, Beijing: People's Publishing House, 2011, p.145.

Management", which was the first time that standardized the interbank lending business and proportion requirements and stipulated that cities with relatively developed economies and relatively large financing volumes could be re-established on the basis of the former capital market. In the financial market, a member fund is established to provide cross-regional interbank lending business for financial institutions, and market information and consulting services. So far, a multi-channel interbank lending market financing framework in the form of financial markets, capital markets, and short-term financing companies has basically taken shape.

After the second half of 1992, the Chinese economy experienced a new round of overheating. The interbank borrowing market also began its second rapid development period, and there was also a phenomenon of illegal borrowing of funds. The huge amount of borrowing funds was borrowed out of the banking system in various means, and the interest rate was also raised to an unreasonable level, which boosted the expansion of fixed asset investment and caused huge inflationary pressure. In order to suppress illegal borrowing, in the second half of 1993, the PBOC successively promulgated a series of "Notice on Adhering to the Work of Clearing and Disposing of Unlawful Lending Funds" and the "Policy Regulations on Continued Correction of Symptoms of Unlawful Lending". Policies and regulations, rectify and standardize the interest rate, duration, use of funds, intermediary agencies, etc., to limit the scale of financial institutions' offer and bid. After more than a year of rectification, China's interbank lending market has entered a more standardized stage, forming a loose and intangible lending market dominated by the PBOC financing center, and making the interbank lending market a practical solution to the settlement of bills. These temporarily finance the underfunded position market before the clearing center finally set up. By 1995, the PBOC revoked the interbank lending institution established by commercial banks and established a national unified interbank lending market led by the PBOC. The establishment and operation of the national interbank lending market has promoted the management of the asset-liability ratio of financial institutions and has become an important market for commercial banks to effectively allocate funds and conduct liquidity management and has created conditions for the deepening of the interest rate system reform.

(2) *The establishment and development of the commercial notes market*

The commercial notes market is one of the oldest markets in the money market and is a market for commercial notes acceptance, discounting and rediscounting. A commercial note is an unsecured promissory note issued by a company that promises to be cashed to the holder on a specified date.[1] Since 1979, with the liberalization and expansion of commercial credit, commercial notes have been used to replace credits, and commercial paper credits have been vigorously promoted. The development of bank notes acceptance discount business has been emphasized to incorporate commercial credit into the bank credit system. China's notes discount market thus be set up as the consequence. In 1980, the PBOC Shanghai Branch took the lead in piloting offices in two districts of Yangpu and Huangpu, and in 1981, it commissioned the discount of the first commercial acceptance bill in the same city. Subsequently, the Xuhui District Office of the PBOC Shanghai Branch and the Tianchang County Branch of Anhui Province jointly cooperated to try out the discount of the first non-local bank acceptance bill. In May 1982, the PBOC head office approved the "Request for Instructions on Restoration of Bill Acceptance and Discounting Services" proposed by the Shanghai Branch, and tried it in Chongqing, Shenyang and Wuhan. In December 1984, on the basis of summing up the pilot experience, the People's Bank of China issued the Interim Measures for the Acceptance and Discount of Commercial Bills of Exchange and decided to conduct commercial paper acceptance and discounting business nationwide from April 1985. In 1986, "The PBOC Rediscounted Trial Measures" was promulgated, and officially opened a rediscounting business for professional banks to push forward the promotion of commercial paper and the development of discounting business.

In the early 1990s, the mutual arrears between Chinese companies, namely the "chain debts", became increasingly serious, which greatly hindered the development of China's economy. In response to this situation, in 1991 the PBOC promulgated the "Notice on Strengthening the Management of Commercial Bills of Exchange" to further regulate the use of commercial bills and the behavior of bank bills in the discounted market. In 1992, the "Interim Measures of PBOC on the Management of Financial Institutions Management" divided into two different ways for loan distributions to financial institutions from PBOC as credit loans and rediscounting, stipulated in the specific operations the rediscounting business can be done with lower interest rates, so that the commercial drafts of the acceptance and discount market have a better development foundation. In 1994, in order to facilitate state-owned large and medium-sized enterprises to timely recover the account receivable, clean up and

---

[1] Shang Ming, *50 Years of Finance in New China*, Beijing: China Financial & Economic Publishing House, 2000, p.276.

prevent arrears, improve the efficiency of capital use, and promote the development of national commercial bill acceptance, discounting and rediscounting business, on Jul.7, the PBOC issued the "Notice on the Implementation of Commercial Bills of Exchange Settlement in the Coal, Power, Metallurgy, Chemical and Railway Industries", and the issuance of the "Methods of Commercial Bill of Exchange" and "Rediscounting Measures" to support the discounting and rediscounting of five industry bills. Since then, the commercial bill discounting and rediscounting business has experienced fresh and faster development. In 1995, the "Law of Bills of the People's Republic of China" was promulgated, and the principle of the bills and related legal responsibilities was made. After 1995, the Chinese bill market, which was dominated by commercial bills, achieved steady development on the basis of norms. Commercial bills of exchange not only became an important financing channel for enterprises, but also became an important credit tool and monetary policy operation for the PBOC to regulate the economic structure. The rapid development of commercial bills effectively regulates corporate credit behavior, prevents enterprises from defaulting on payment, improves the quality of bank credit assets, and strengthens the macro-control role of the central bank.

3.5.2 Development of securities market

3.5.2.1 The cultivation and development of the bond market

China's bonds mainly include government bonds and corporate bonds. Government bonds are primarily national debt issued by the central government to raise financial funds. Corporate bonds are the means by which enterprises raise funds.[1]

(1) *National debt issuance market*

In the early days of the founding of the People's Republic of China and the First Five-year Plan period, China had issued discounted public debts and national economic construction bonds, and they were suspended soon after for some reasons. After the Third Plenary Session of the 11th CPC Central Committee, the state began a large-scale economic construction, and the fiscal revenue and expenditure showed a deficit. In order to overcome the country's financial difficulties and raise funds for key construction, the State Council decided to issue a national debt once a year in 1981 to restore the national debt issuance market. The national debt issued in 1981-1984 was

[1] Hu Hai'ou and Wu Guoxiang, *The theory and practice of China's financial reform*, Shanghai: Fudan University Press, 2000, p.312.

10 years. The period of the national debt issued from 1985 to 1987 was adjusted to five years, and the principal and interest payments were paid once after five years. The period of issuance since 1988 has been shortened to four years. After 1992, it was changed to two times a year. The term is divided into three years, five years, and two years, one year, and six months. Before 1990, the issuance of China's national debt was basically based on a combination of political mobilization and administrative distribution. In fact, it was apportioned to domestic enterprises, financial institutions and residents on a voluntary basis. With the development of the economy and the increase of residents' income, the public's awareness of investment has increased, laying a foundation for the formation of the national debt issuance market. From 1991 to 1995, the Ministry of Finance began to use the underwriting method to sell some government bonds to residents through the Ministry of Finance and bank outlets. This is the beginning of breaking the administrative allocation method and marking the initial formation of China's national debt issuance market. In 1994, through the electronic network system of the Shanghai Stock Exchange, semi-annual and one-year physical Treasury bills were successfully issued on a larger scale. With the downward adjustment of the bank deposit interest rate, the inflation rate has been falling therefore. All the issuance of treasury bonds since 1996 has adopted a bidding method, which has formed a more reasonable price decision mechanism, accelerated the process of interest rate reform, and improved the efficiency of treasury bond issuance, decreased the cost of issuing treasury bonds; at the same time, it also reflects the principles of fairness, equitableness and openness, increases the transparency of the market, and lays the foundation for the standardized development of treasury bond issuance and circulation market.

(2) *Treasury bond trading market*

In 1981, when the issuance of government bonds was resumed, the national debts stipulated by the state were not transferable. Some speculators took advantage of it and bought it at a low price, reselling it and making huge profits. All sectors of the community have suggested opening up the government bond trading market. In 1985, the bank opened discount business on the treasury bills that individuals subscribed for. On Aug.5, 1986, Shenyang Trust and Investment Corporation was approved by the PBOC Shenyang Branch to open counters for securities such as treasury bills and corporate bonds. The transfer of business marks the starting of the stock exchange market. Since then, Shanghai, Wuhan, Guangzhou and other cities have also held a non-standardized securities transfer trading market. In Apr. 1988, with the approval of the State Council, the pilot projects to open the treasury bond transfer market were officially launched, and Shenyang, Shanghai, Chongqing, Wuhan, Guangzhou, Harbin and Shenzhen became the first pilot cities. In Jun. 1988, another 54 cities were approved to carry out the pilot projects of the treasury bond transfer market, and the treasury bills issued in 1985 and 1986 were officially listed and transferable. The transaction was very active, which fundamentally changed the situation of "no market" in the national debt market. In 1990, the state decided to fully liberalize the treasury bond trading market, allowed all types of treasury bonds to enter the market, and formed a national unified treasury bond trading network. In the form of market organization, with the establishment of Shanghai and Shenzhen stock exchanges and the securities trading centers of some cities, China has formed a national debt circulation market dominated by centralized transactions, decentralized over-the-counter transactions and curb exchanges. In addition, the state has also established a central government bond registration and settlement company to undertake the unified custody and settlement of national treasury bonds, and provide good services for the issuance, circulation, redemption and market monitoring of treasury bonds. After 1994, China's national debt issuance and market trading volume have increased rapidly.

(3) *Key corporate bonds and capital construction bonds*

In China, corporate bonds are classified into bonds issued by state professional investment companies and local enterprises in provinces, municipalities and autonomous regions according to the issuers. National investment company bonds also include key corporate bonds and capital construction bonds. Key corporate bonds are bonds issued by key enterprises to raise construction funds. In 1987, before the establishment of national professional investment companies including energy investment companies, raw material investment companies, transportation investment companies, and electromechanical textile investment companies, key corporate bonds were issued by key enterprises in the power, metallurgy, non-ferrous metals, petrochemical and other industries. After 1988, it was switched to a national professional investment company. From 1987 to 1992, a total of six key issues were issued for key corporate bonds, with a closing balance of RMB15.611 billion. The capital construction bonds are jointly printed and issued by the State Professional Investment Corporation, China National Petroleum Corporation and the Ministry of Railways and bear economic responsibility and legal responsibility according to the proportion of bond funds. It was issued once respectively in 1988, 1989 and 1991. Since they are basically issued by means of administrative purchases and deadlines, and their issuers are also national professional investment companies, they have the nature of quasi-state bonds, not corporate bonds in the typical sense.[1]

(4) *Corporate bonds*

Since 1984, due to the inability of bank credit to meet the needs, various fund-raising methods have emerged. Many township and village enterprises took the lead in adopting the "fund-labor" and "labor-funding" methods to raise funds from employees in the factory. At that time, the internal fund-raising momentum of the enterprise was very popular, and the management work was lagging, and there was no rule to follow. Some internal fund-raising has no evidence; some bonds are of unknown nature, the term is unknown, and the interest rate is high; some are forced to apportion, and some are used to transfer enterprise-specific funds to internal bonds to employees. By the end of 1986, the total amount of such corporate bonds without regulations was about RMB10 billion, and the circulation of such bonds was extremely irregular.[2] In order to standardize the issuance of corporate bonds, in March 1987, the State Council promulgated the "Provisional Regulations on the Administration of Corporate Bonds", which stipulates that the issuance of corporate bonds must be approved by the PBOC, and the PBOC, together with the State Planning Commission and the Ministry of Finance, should establish annual quota of the total amount of corporate bond issuance. On Mar.5, 1989, the State Council issued the "Notice on Strengthening the Management of Internal Bonds in Enterprises" to make the management of internal corporate bonds in the country unified and standardized. According to statistics, the total amount of corporate bonds issued nationwide in 1987 was RMB3 billion. By 1992, the total amount of corporate bonds issued in the same year increased to nearly RMB70 billion, a record high.[3] However, with the emergence of economic overheating, some enterprises have experienced the indiscriminate fund-raising, chaotic investment, and chaotic speculation. Since the second half of 1993, some corporate bonds have not been repaid in time, and the government has to organize the bank to advance for payment of the maturity bonds. The confidence of corporate bonds is getting worse and worse, and the bond market is seriously shrinking. After Year 1993, the issuance of corporate bonds entered a long downturn period as shown in Table 3–4.

---

[1] Yao Sui, *History of China Finance*, Beijing: Higher Education Press, 2007, pp.526-527.

[2] Yao Sui, *History of China Finance*, Beijing: Higher Education Press, 2007, p.527.

[3] CSRC, *China Capital Markets Development Report*, Beijing: China Financial Publishing House, 2008, p.5.

Table 3–4 Corporate bond issuance, redemption and balance Unit: billion

Year	Issuance	Redemption	Ending
1986	10.000	1.623	8.377
1987	3.000	2.742	8.635
1988	7.541	4.672	11.504
1989	7.526	4.394	14.636
1990	12.637	7.729	19.544
1991	24.996	11.431	33.109
1992	68.371	19.276	82.204
1993	23.584	25.548	80.240
1994	16.175	28.204	68.211
1995	30.000	33.630	64.661
1996	26.892	31.780	59.773
1997	25.523	21.981	52.102

Source: CSRC, *China Securities and Futures Statistical Yearbook*, Beijing: China Financial & Economic Publishing House, 1998, pp.10-11.

3.5.2.2 The establishment and development of the stock market

(1) *Stock issuance*

Since the reform and opening up, China's national economy has developed greatly. That stimulated the capital needs of the state and enterprises, surpassing the sum of the financial allocation and bank credit capacity at that time; on the other hand, the disposable income of residents increased significantly, and they began to consciously look for investment directions. This has created conditions for the transformation of the shareholding system of China's enterprises and the establishment and development of the stock market. While banks use market mechanisms to invigorate funds, direct financing activities among enterprises, and between enterprises and individuals, have emerged. Since 1981, some enterprises in China have started to raise funds by issuing stocks. Since Sep. 1984, the pilot work of the shareholding system has started in Beijing, Shanghai, Guangzhou, and Shenyang. In Jan. 1986, trials of financial system reforms began in Shenyang, Guangzhou, Chongqing, and Changzhou, allowing some financial institutions to handle the issuance and transfer of stocks. In Sep. 1986, the business department of Jing'an District of ICBC Shanghai branch set up a securities counter trading point, Jing'an Securities Business Department, and became the first stock trading counter in the country. Feilo and Yanzhong stocks began to be listed and traded, creating the history in the People's Republic of China, and promoting the development of the Chinese shareholding system. In Mar. 1987, the State Council promulgated the "Notice of the State Council on Strengthening the Management of Stocks and Bonds". In the same year, Shanghai formulated the "Interim Provisions on Securities Counter Trading", and the municipal government officially promulgated the "Interim Measures for the Administration of Shanghai Stocks". More detailed regulations have been made on the stock issuance market and the circulation market.

(2) *Stock exchange market*

By 1990, the shareholding system reforms of enterprises in Shanghai and Shenzhen were processed smoothly. There were 4 industrial enterprises, 4 commercial enterprises, 2 financial enterprises, and 1 real estate enterprise in Shanghai participating in this pilot project. This project has a total share capital of RMB0.887 billion, of which 7 have issued individual shares to the society; Shenzhen has 5 companies issued stocks to the society to raise funds, with a total of RMB0.27 billion. During this period, stock exchange transactions have been also expanded, and stock prices have risen rapidly. But in general, because the stock transferring was limited to over-the-counter transactions, the trading venues were scattered, the information transmission was not working effectively, the trading methods are relatively backward, and it is not easy to manage. As a result, the black market is rampant, and the trading order is extremely chaotic.[1] In 1990, the 8th Five-year Plan adopted by the Seventh Plenary Session of the 13th CPC Central Committee proposed: "Progressively expand the issuance of bonds and stocks, and strictly strengthen management. Establish and improve stock exchanges in large cities with conditions".[2] On Dec.19, 1990, the first stock exchange in China, the Shanghai Stock Exchange, was formally established. On Jul. 3, 1991, the Shenzhen Stock Exchange was formally established and opened, marking the official formation of the Chinese stock market. Since then, the off-site decentralized transaction has entered the on-site centralized trading, and the trading means has realized computer pairing and paperless operation. Several companies have been listed in the two stock exchanges. So far, the Chinese stock market has taken an important step toward internationalization and standardization. On Nov.30, 1991, the first B-share of the People's Republic of China, Shanghai Vacuum Electronic Devices Co.,

---

1 Yao Sui, *History of China Finance*, Beijing: Higher Education Press, 2007, pp.528-529.

2 *Suggestions of the Central Committee of the Communist Party of China on Formulating the Ten-Year Plan for National Economic and Social Development and the 8th Five-Year Plan*, Beijing: People's Publishing House, 1991.

Ltd. was first issued overseas by Shanghai Shenyin Securities Co., Ltd., with an amount of RMB100 million. On Feb.21 of the following year, Vacuum B shares were officially listed on the Shanghai Stock Exchange. In 1994, six Chinese companies directly issued H shares in Hong Kong, and two other companies issued N shares in the United States to raise funds overseas through stock markets. Raising funds through international and domestic stock markets has effectively promoted the reform of China's state-owned enterprises and the adjustment of economic structure.

As an integral part of the financial market, the stock market plays an increasingly important role in expanding corporate financing channels, reforming operational mechanisms, raising public awareness of investment, and achieving rational allocation and full utilization of funds. It has greatly promoted the development of China's economy and laid the foundation for the establishment of China's market economic system.

(3) *Securities management*

China's securities market was originally managed by the PBOC, but with the market development, this situation has also changed accordingly. In Oct. 1992, the State Council decided to establish the Securities Commission of the State Council as the main institution for the unified macro management of the national securities market. It is responsible for formulating major policies concerning the development of the securities market and formulating relevant management regulations. At the meantime, the China Securities Regulatory Commission was established as the executive body for the supervision and management of the securities industry and the securities market. It was under the guidance, supervision, inspection and centralized management of the Securities Commission of the State Council. This marks the beginning of a unified regulatory system in China's securities market. After the establishment of the Securities Commission of the State Council and the China Securities Regulatory Commission, its terms of reference gradually expanded with the development of the market. In Nov. 1993, the State Council decided to transfer the pilot work of the futures market to the Securities Commission of the State Council, and the China Securities Regulatory Commission implemented it. In Mar. 1995, the State Council formally approved the "China Securities Regulatory Commission's Institutional Preparation Plan" and determined that the China Securities Regulatory Commission is a sub-departmental institution directly under the State Council. It is the regulatory executive department of the Securities Commission of the State Council, to regulate the futures market in accordance with laws and regulations.

3.5.2.3 The establishment and development of the securities investment fund market

An investment fund is an investment method that aggregates small amounts of socially dispersed funds and entrusts specialized institutions (investment fund companies) to manage and diversify investment risks and share investment profits. The operation is mainly for investors to issue shares or beneficiary voucher to raise funds. The investment fund company will diversify the concentrated funds into stocks, bonds and money market, or industrial projects, in a combination manner according to the best income target and the minimum risk of investment. The profit, if any, will be redistributed to investors or partially used for company accumulation and distribution according to the articles of incorporation.

With the rise of China's second wave of reforms, in order to open new financial varieties, some financial institutions in China have started investment fund business and tentatively set up some investment funds. In 1987, Bank of China, China International Trust and Investment Corporation and some foreign institutions set up investment funds for overseas investors, but the scale was small and had little impact. With the rapid development of China's securities market, domestic investment funds have made substantial breakthroughs with relatively rapid development. In Oct. 1991, the PBOC Wuhan Branch approved the establishment of the "Wuhan Securities Investment Fund" with a scale of RMB10 million, which is the first fund after China's reform and opening up. Since then, many funds have been set up in China, and the scale of investment funds during 1992 to the first half of 1993 has expanded rapidly. At the end of 1992, the State Council clearly stipulated that investment fund securities were examined and approved by the PBOC, which concentrated on the authority for examination and approval, and advocated to actively organize the pilot projects of investment fund securities. By the end of 1996, a total of 75 investment funds had been established nationwide, with a total approved size of RMB5.822 billion and an actual fundraising of RMB5.707 billion.[1]

The establishment and reform of the financial market has effectively promoted the deepening of China's economic reform and the development of China's economic construction.

The first is to promote the shareholding system reform of Chinese enterprises.

[1] Yang Xitian, *The 6th Volume of China's Financial History: the Period of the People's Republic of China (1949-1996)*, Beijing: China Financial Publishing House, 2002, p.441.

The establishment of financial markets has greatly changed the composition of corporate funding sources. The issuance of bonds and stocks closely links the interests of enterprises, employees and investors, prompting enterprises to maximize the use of funds, giving good-performing enterprises a chance to stand out from the crowd, and forcing companies with poor business performance to withdraw from the market. In addition, the development of the notes market has also changed the way of companies' fund-raising, and the borrowing and fund-raising of enterprises has shifted from credit to billing. The development of the capital market has greatly promoted the shareholding reform of state-controlled commercial banks. Bank of China, Industrial and Commercial Bank of China and China Construction Bank have successively listed on the Shanghai and Hong Kong Stock Exchanges, successfully completed the shareholding system transformation and increased the capital adequacy ratio.

The second is to promote the soundness and standardization of the commercial banking system. China's professional banks have already stepped out of the unified banking system. From the index loans of superior banks, they have gradually moved towards the loan system of depositing and depositing more loans and depositing real loans. This change determines that China's professional banks can autonomously determine the use of funds and it also requires rational allocation of affluent funds. The establishment of financial markets not only provides them with such opportunities and possibilities, but also stimulates their need to adjust the lack of funds. For example, it is possible to balance the capital position by trading in the market and the bill market, and it is also possible to adjust the remaining funds through the purchase and sale of government bonds. In addition, the central bank issued special treasury bonds through the national debt market, and in accordance with the requirements of the Basel Accord, offset the capital of commercial banks, prompting China's commercial banks to take a big step toward standardization.

The third is to cultivate residents' awareness of venture capital. In the planned economy, China's residents have almost desire to preserve their value, and there was no willingness to invest. This has become the social atmosphere in which Chinese enterprises, commercial banks and central banks operate in a planned economy. In the market economy, almost all economic operations are based on the public investment speculation demand. The concept of Chinese residents investing in stock bonds promotes the transition of Chinese enterprises and banks. The maturity of this concept will also make the public the party of the game and that has become the basis for the macro-control of the central bank and has promoted the maturity of the central bank's macro-control measures.

The fourth is to promote the transition of the central bank's macro-control measures. The establishment and development of the financial market has increased the use of the central bank's monetary policy tools and enriched the central bank's control measures. The central bank buys and sells treasury bonds and central bank bills through the financial market, conducts open market operations in a timely manner, regulates the money supply, and achieves the purpose of using market means to regulate economic development.

3.6 Reform of foreign exchange management system

In Oct. 1980, China began to handle foreign exchange adjustment business, marking the beginning of the emergence of the foreign exchange market. In 1986, the foreign exchange adjustment business was handed over by the Bank of China to the State Administration of Foreign Exchange (SAFE), which opened a foreign exchange adjustment business between foreign-invested enterprises and a quota adjustment business for foreign exchange between domestic enterprises. After 1988, all provinces have set up foreign exchange adjustment centers to further expand the scope of foreign exchange adjustments.[1]

China's exchange rate reform has undergone a tortuous process. In 1993, a new major turning point began. On Jan.1, 1994, the official exchange rate announcement was stopped, and the exchange rate of the foreign exchange adjustment center has been the only Chinese currency exchange rate. A single managed floating exchange rate system was established. In 1996, current account convertibility was realized, and a new round of foreign exchange reform was initiated.

3.6.1 Reform of foreign exchange administration

At the beginning of the founding of the People's Republic of China, China's foreign exchange administration was the PBOC, and foreign exchange was uniformly distributed by the State Council's Finance and Economic Committee. After the national economy enters the planned economic construction, the Financial and Economic Committee was revoked, and the State Planning Commission, the Ministry of Finance, the Ministry of Foreign Trade, and the PBOC respectively assume certain

[1] Ding Yifan, "Reform and development of China's financial system", *Marxism & Reality*, 2013(2), pp. 15-21.

responsibilities for foreign exchange management. This multi-headed foreign exchange management system was not suitable to the new situation of opening-up. To this end, in Mar. 1979, the State Council approved the "Report of the People's Bank of China on Reforming the Banking System of China" and the establishment of the State Administration of Foreign Exchange and gave it the function of managing the national foreign exchange. In Aug. 1982, the SAFE was separated from the Bank of China, and placed under the leadership of the PBOC. In Sep. 1983, the State Council approved the PBOC to exclusively exercise the functions of the central bank to uniformly manage state foreign exchange. The State Administration of Foreign Exchange exercised foreign exchange management functions under the leadership of the Central Bank. In Jun. 1988, the State Council decided that the SAFE is a bureau-level institution directly under the State Council and is managed by the PBOC. In Dec. 1989, the SAFE was upgraded to the vice-ministerial level and was still managed by the PBOC.

The establishment of the SAFE and the level upgrading reflects the specialization of foreign exchange management and the importance of foreign exchange management in the administration of the entire national economy and provides a solid institutional foundation and organizational assurance for the continuous deepening and improvement of foreign exchange system reform and foreign exchange management.

3.6.2 Foreign exchange management system reform

From the early days of the founding of the People's Republic of China to 1979, China implemented a highly centralized foreign exchange management system. This foreign exchange management system was adapted to the needs of the mandatory planning management system and the state monopoly foreign trade management system. However, with the deepening of economic reform, this kind of system has become increasingly suppression of the enthusiasm of enterprises and institutions for earning foreign exchange. After 1979, with the expansion of opening up to the outside world, the amount of foreign capital used has gradually increased. In order to meet the needs of the new situation, the state decided to introduce a competition mechanism in the foreign exchange business by allowing the national professional banking business to cross. Beside the Chinese banks, other financial institutions, including commercial banks and foreign-funded financial institutions, after examination and approval by the SAFE, were awarded the "Permit of Foreign Exchange Business" and become designated foreign exchange banks to operate foreign exchange business. In this way, China's foreign exchange management system has evolved from the exclusive operation of the foreign exchange business of the Bank of China to all the state-owned commercial banks and other commercial banks, and the domestic banks and foreign banks jointly operating in foreign exchange systems.

3.6.3 The development of the foreign exchange adjustment market

Since Oct. 1980, the Bank of China has begun trials of foreign exchange adjustments and has set up foreign exchange adjustment centers in major provinces and major coastal cities to handle the retention of foreign exchange and self-owned foreign exchange adjustment business of local, departmental, state-owned and collective enterprises, and foreign invested enterprises. The Bank of China adjusts the foreign exchange surplus between foreign exchange demand and supply side, so that the limited foreign exchange funds can be more fully utilized, marking the starting up of China's foreign exchange adjustment market.

With the overheating of China's economy in the mid-1980s, the scale of investment continued to expand, the demand for imports soared, and the supply of foreign exchange was insufficient. The price of over-the-counter foreign exchange transactions greatly exceeded the price of foreign exchange adjustments. The foreign exchange adjustment business had no market and was tending to stop. Since 1985, the state has begun to reform the foreign exchange adjustment business, and the foreign exchange adjustment business was handed over to the SAFE for approval. In Nov. 1985, the Shenzhen Special Economic Zone took the lead in setting up a foreign exchange adjustment center led by the Shenzhen Municipal Government. Since Mar. 1988, foreign exchange adjustment centers have been established in various places. However, due to the different proportions of foreign exchange in regions and departments, there was a lack of horizontal interchanges, basically one price per share, forming multiple exchange rates. In Mar. 1988, the exchange rate was released, and the buyers and sellers agreed on the status of foreign exchange. The PBOC moderately intervened in the market and guided the use of foreign exchange (or foreign exchange market access) through the formulation of the "Foreign Exchange Adjustment Guideline". The importance of market regulation was increasing. In the first half of 1993, due to the overheating of the domestic economy, the Chinese currency faced a large depreciation pressure, and the country re-limited the foreign exchange market, but this move led to the spread of over-the-counter transactions. In the second half of the year, in line with the state's macroeconomic regulation and control, the implementation of moderately tight fiscal and monetary policies and the elimination of price limits, the PBOC intervened for the first time by selling foreign exchange reserves, and gradually stabilized the exchange rate to around RMB8.7 for US$1. The level laid the foundation for the exchange rate in early 1994. From 1986 to 1993, the transaction volume of the national foreign exchange adjustment market was US$102.9 billion, which effectively guaranteed the use of foreign exchange in various departments, eased the tension of Chinese currency funds held by foreign exchange enterprises, promoted the development of export-oriented commodity economy, and improved foreign investment environment. See Table 3–5.

Table 3–5 National transaction scale of foreign exchange adjustment market

Unit: US$100 million

Item	1986	1987	1988	1989	1990	1991	1992	1993
Amount	24.0	42.5	62.5	85.7	131.6	204.5	251.0	227.6

Source: SAFE.

3.6.4 Exchange rate system reform

From 1981 to 1984, the exchange rate system in which the internal settlement price of trade and the non-trade official price were coexisted. In 1981, China set an internal settlement price of foreign exchange, which was calculated based on the average foreign exchange cost of export commodities at the time plus 10% profit, and was set at US$1 to RMB2.8, which is applicable to the settlement of import and export trade. At the meantime, the official exchange rate was continuing to be announced at US$1 to RMB1.5, and the original "package currency" calculation and adjustment would be used for the settlement of non-trade foreign exchange. This doubletrack exchange rates system have played a role in encouraging exports and benefiting the non-trade interests, but there has been confusion in the scope of application, which has brought many complicated problems to foreign exchange accounting and management. With the rise of the US dollar exchange rate in the international market, China gradually lowered the official Chinese currency exchange rate in response to this change. By the end of 1984, the official exchange rate had approached the internal settlement price of internal trade foreign exchange.

A unified pegged exchange rate system was introduced from 1985 to 1990. On

Jan. 1, 1985, the internal settlement price was cancelled, and the official exchange rate was re-altered. The exchange rate was US$1 to RMB2.8. In order to eliminate the overvaluation of the exchange rate, the renminbi exchange rate is adapted to the changes in prices, and it plays a role in regulating the balance of payments. During the period, China adjusted the exchange rate several times according to changes in domestic prices, and gradually adjusted to US$1 to RMB5.22 on Nov.17, 1990. In these years, the downward adjustment of the renminbi exchange rate is mainly based on the change in the average export exchange cost of the country. The downward adjustment of the exchange rate lags behind the increase in domestic prices.

A managed floating exchange rate system was introduced from 1991 to 1993. Since Apr.9, 1991, the adjustment of the official exchange rate has been changed from a large-scale, one-time adjustment to a gradual slow adjustment, that is, a management float has been implemented. By the end of 1993, it was adjusted to US$1 to RMB5.72, which was dropped 9% as of Nov.17, 1990.

3.6.5 Relaxation of foreign exchange controls for domestic residents

In the early days of reform and opening up, China allowed domestic residents to hold foreign exchange, but it was not allowed to be used domestically. Foreign currency can only be sold to designated national banks to be converted into Chinese currency, and foreign currency deposit accounts are not allowed to be opened in banks. After the reform and opening up, many overseas Chinese returned to China to visit relatives or make remittance to China, and personal overseas communicating gradually increased, which also increased the sources of national foreign exchange. The original management method is not conducive to encourage remittances and individuals to earn foreign currency. To this end, China has gradually relaxed its foreign exchange controls on individuals. Since 1985, the state has approved the Bank of China to open personal foreign exchange deposits. This confirms that personal foreign exchange can be retained in the form of foreign exchange deposits, and no longer requires mandatory foreign exchange settlement to be sold to the state. Since 1988, some developed areas and overseas Chinese have opened personal foreign exchange adjustment business, allowing individuals to sell their foreign exchange at the adjusted price. Since Nov. 1991, with the approval of the State Council, the SAFE promulgated the "Interim Measures for Foreign Residents of Domestic Residents and Domestic Residents to Participate in the Adjustment of Private Uses of Foreign Exchange", which further relaxed the management of foreign exchange for domestic residents and allowed residents to sale the foreign currency with the foreign exchange adjustment price through banks. In the same year, the PBOC decided that the head offices of various professional banks and their branches could open foreign exchange business, allowing the professional banking business to cross over.

3.6.6 Establishment of the foreign debt management system

Since the reform and opening up, China has actively encouraged foreign investors to invest directly in China. Since 1979, China has successively promulgated a series of foreign-funded and foreign-debt management regulations, including the "Law of the People's Republic of China on Sino-Foreign Equity Joint Ventures", the "Law of the People's Republic of China on Foreign-invested Enterprises" and so on, and the foreign exchange management of foreign-funded enterprises were different from that of domestic enterprises. In Aug. 1983, the SAFE promulgated the "Implementation Rules on Foreign Exchange Administration of Overseas Chinese Enterprises, Foreign-funded Enterprises, and Sino-foreign Joint Ventures". In principle, foreign-invested enterprises are required to balance foreign exchange earnings, allowing them to retain foreign currency earnings and open foreign currency accounts in banks for their own usage; allowing them to lend to domestic and foreign banks in "borrow and repay themselves" means without approval in advance; and allowing them to buy and sell foreign exchange through the foreign exchange adjustment center. This has played an important role in drawing into and using of foreign capital.

In terms of borrowing foreign debts, to ensure that the scale of borrowing is controlled within the capacity of the state, and use foreign debts for projects that are urgently needed in the country to achieve good economic benefits, China has established plan management and window management for external borrowing, the loan approval system, the external debt statistics monitoring system, and the external debt guarantee system. It is stipulated that domestic institutional borrowings must be included in the national plan for the use of foreign capital and be approved step by step. These measures have improved the effectiveness of China's use of foreign capital and solved the problem of insufficient funds in economic construction.

On Nov.14, 1993, the "Decision of the Central Committee on Some Issues Concerning the Establishment of a Socialist Market Economic System" adopted by the Third Plenary Session of the 14th CPC Central Committee clearly stated: "Reform the foreign exchange management system and establish a managed floating exchange rate management system and a unified and standardized foreign exchange market in supply and demand basis to gradually make the Chinese currency as a convertible currency",[1] which clearly made the direction for the reform of the foreign exchange management system.

[1]*Decision of the Central Committee of the Communist Party of China on Some Issues Concerning the Establishment of a Socialist Market Economic System*, Beijing: People's Publishing House, 1993.

Chapter 4
Deepening Stage of China's Financial System Reform

In 1993, the "Decision of the Central Committee on Some Issues Concerning the Establishment of a Socialist Market Economic System" adopted by the 3rd Plenary Session of the 14th CPC Central Committee clearly stated that "the goal of China's economic system reform is to establish a socialist market economic system",[1] and it is required to accelerate the economic reforms to build this new system.

With the rapid advancement of economic reforms, the financial system reform has been further deepened. On Dec.25, 1993, the State Council issued the "Decision on Financial System Reform" and the "Notice on Further Reforming the Foreign Exchange Management System" at the request of the 3rd Plenary Session of the 14th CPC Central Committee, clearly stating the four objectives of the financial system reform: First, establish a strong macro-control system for central banks; second, implement a separation between policy-based finance and commercial finance, and establish a financial organization system with state-owned commercial banks as the main body and multiple financial institutions coexisting; third, establish a unified opening financial market with orderly competition and strict management; fourth, reform the foreign exchange management system and coordinate foreign exchange policy and monetary policy[2]. The financial system reforms focusing on the above objectives began to be implemented step by step in 1994, which set off a new upsurge in China's financial system reform, and China's financial system reform entered a deepening stage.

---

[1] *Decision of the Central Committee of the Communist Party of China on Some Issues Concerning the Establishment of a Socialist Market Economic System*, Beijing: People's Publishing House, 1993.

[2] Wang Guangqian, *China's New Stage of Economic Growth and Financial Development*, Beijing: China Development Press, 2004, p.75.

4.1 Central bank system reform

In Dec. 1993, the State Council promulgated the "Decision on Financial System Reform", pointing out that it is necessary to strengthen the macro-financial control capacity of the PBOC and turn it into a real central bank. The main function of the PBOC is to formulate and implement monetary policy to maintain the stability of the currency, implement strict supervision and management of financial institutions, and ensure the safe operation of the financial system.[1] Since 1994, the PBOC has accelerated the reform and the functional transformation.

4.1.1 Promulgation and implementation of the "Law of the People's Republic of China on the People's Bank of China"

On Mar.18, 1995, the 3rd Session of the 8th National People's Congress passed the "Law of the People's Republic of China on the People's Bank of China" (hereinafter referred to as "the Law"), which clarified the nature and status of the People's Bank of China as a central bank in the form of law and guaranteed the leadership of the PBOC to fully carry out the duties of a real central bank under the State Council's supervision. The Law not only established the status of the PBOC as a central bank for the first time in the form of national legislation, but also established "separate operation and separate supervision" as the basic regulatory thinking in financial industry in three divisions of banking, securities and insurance. The promulgation and implementation of the Law provides legal guarantee for the PBOC to better perform its functions of formulating and implementing monetary policy, stabilizing currency value, strengthening financial supervision, and ensuring the secured and effective operation of the financial system.

The Law is China's Central Bank Law and the first financial law in 46 years since the founding of the People's Republic of China. Its promulgation and implementation are important achievements of China's financial system reform and milestone in China's financial legal system construction. It marks that China's financial industry has entered the track of legalization and standardization. First, the Law clarifies the role and authority of the PBOC as a central bank in financial

[1] The State Council, "Decision of the State Council on the reform of the financial system", *Gazette of the State Council of the People's Republic of China,* 1993(3).

macro-control, and legally guarantees the authority of the PBOC to formulate and implement monetary policy. Article 2 of the Law stipulates: The People's Bank of China shall, under the leadership of the State Council, formulate and implement monetary policy and implement supervision and management of the financial industry. Second, the Law regulates the monetary policy framework. It has clearly defined the direction for the macro-control of the PBOC and provided organizational and technical guarantees. The Law stipulates the monetary policy objectives, that is, maintaining the stability of the currency's currency value and promoting economic growth; stipulating the institutional setup of the Monetary Policy Committee; and specifying the central bank's tools for implementing monetary policy.

According to the provisions of the Law, the PBOC has three basic functions: First, the service function. As the bank of the government and the bank of the bank, the PBOC provides financial services such as fund services, clearing and settlement, and agency services to government, commercial banks and other financial institutions. The second is the regulatory function. The PBOC uses its financial means to regulate and control the money supply and credit scale to achieve the expected monetary and macroeconomic policy objectives. The third is the supervision function. As the highest authority in financial management, the PBOC inspects and supervises the establishment, withdrawal and business operations of banks and other financial institutions and implements necessary management controls on financial markets to maintain the stability and soundness of the financial organizational system.

4.1.2 Organizational reform of PBOC

For a long time, the organizations of the PBOC has always implemented a general-branch system, that is, a single structure system. The head office is in Beijing, and the subordinate institutions are consistent with the administrative divisions of China. With the gradual improvement of the socialist market economic system, the drawbacks of PBOC's national administrative divisions gradually emerged. Under the influence of the interests of all parties, the administrative intervention from the local governments to the financial supervision of the PBOC branches is very serious. Under the influence of local protectionism and departmental intervention, the independence and professional level of central bank supervision is not fairly enough.

In order to strengthen the independence, professionalism and authority of the central bank, further rationalize the relationship between the central bank and the government and various government departments, and avoid local government intervention in the PBOC, the National Financial Work Conference held at the end of 1997 clearly stated it is necessary to close the provincial branches in a planned and step-by-step manner and change the situation according to the administrative divisions. In 1999, the PBOC officially implemented provincial-level institutional reforms: the provincial branches of the PBOC were revoked, and branches were established in 9 central cities as the dispatched institutions of the PBOC according to regional relevance, economic and financial aggregates, and financial supervision requirements, and delineate the areas under its jurisdiction.

After the provincial branch of the PBOC is revoked, its original duties are borne by the branch of the jurisdiction and the provincial capital city branch. After the PBOC Beijing Branch and Chongqing Branch were revoked, their respective responsibilities were assumed by the head office of the PBOC.

Establish a financial supervision office. In order to assist branches to implement financial supervision independently, impartially and effectively, financial supervision offices were set up in cities without branches where the governments of provinces, autonomous regions and municipalities directly under the central government are located. Their main responsibilities are: according to the authorization of the branches, to conduct on-site inspections to the financial institutions of provinces, autonomous regions and municipalities directly under the central government; to investigate and deal with financial violations of law and regulations handed over by branches; to conduct special investigations on discipline inspection and supervision; and to promptly penalize the financial institutions and relevant responsible persons with the violations of law and regulations on behalf of branches.

Enrich the functions of the provincial capital city branch. PBOC set up the central subbranches in the provincial capital cities without branches and the Shenzhen Special Economic Zone. In addition to continuing to perform the duties assumed by the original branch, the above-mentioned central subbranches will in charge of the management summary of the original provincial branches in the treasury management, payment clearing, cash issuance and financial statistics.

4.1.3 Reform of supervision function of the PBOC

With the continuous adjustment of the functions of the PBOC, the supervision function of the PBOC on the financial industry has also undergone a process of shifting from centralized and unified supervision to multiple supervision. The PBOC's supervisory duties on the securities industry, insurance industry and banking industry are gradually transferred to relevant institutions, thereby ensuring that the PBOC truly performs the role of the central bank and carries out the duties of the central bank's monetary policy formulation, financial security and financial macro-control.

The monetary policy function of the PBOC is separated from the financial supervision function. In Oct. 1992, the Securities Commission of the State Council and the China Securities Regulatory Commission were proclaimed to set up, marking the beginning of a unified regulatory system for the Chinese securities market. The Securities Commission of the State Council is the competent authority for the unified macro-management of the securities market by the state. The China Securities Regulatory Commission is the regulatory enforcement agency of the Securities Commission of the State Council, which regulates the securities market in accordance with laws and regulations.[1]

In Mar. 1995, the State Council formally approved the "China Securities Regulatory Commission's Institutional Establishment Plan" and determined that the China Securities Regulatory Commission is a sub-departmental institution directly under the State Council. It is the regulatory enforcement agency of the Securities Commission of the State Council. The futures market is regulated in accordance with laws and regulations. In Apr. 1998, according to the institutional reform plan of the State Council, it was decided to merge the Securities Commission of the State Council and the China Securities Regulatory Commission together to form a state-level institution directly under the State Council.[2]

On Apr.15, 1997, the State Council formulated the "Regulations of the Monetary Policy Committee of the People's Bank of China" in accordance with the Law. The Regulations stipulate that the "Monetary Policy Committee is the advisory agency for the PBOC to formulate monetary policy". And in Jul. 1997, the Monetary Policy Committee was then set up.

On May 16, 1998, the CPC Central Committee Financial Working Committee was formally established. On Aug.3, 1998, the PBOC issued the "Notice on the Supervision of the Foreign Exchange Business of Financial Institutions of the State Administration of Foreign Exchange into the People's Bank of China". From then on, the approval of business market access for the foreign exchange and the quality and

---

[1] Fan Fangzhi, "The forecast and review of our country's central bank organizational reform to the 30th anniversary of China's opening up and reform policy", *Journal of Central University of Finance & Economics*, 2009(2), pp. 20-24.

[2] Ma Qingquan and Liu Zhao, *A brief history of Chinese securities*, Taiyuan: Shanxi Economic Press, 2015, p.418.

risk supervision of foreign currency assets for financial institutions undertaken by the SAFE, have been transferred to the relevant departments respectively of the PBOC according to the categories of financial institutions, and those for insurance companies and securities companies were still handled by the SAFE.

The China Insurance Regulatory Commission was established on Nov.18, 1998 as the competent department of commercial insurance throughout the country. It is a state-owned institution directly under the State Council. It performs its administrative functions in accordance with the authorization of the State Council and uniformly supervises and manages the insurance market in accordance with the relevant laws and regulations.

On Mar. 2003, in accordance with the "Opinions on Deepening the Administrative System and Institutional Reform" reviewed and approved by the 2nd Plenary Session of the 16th CPC Central Committee and the State Council's institutional reform plan approved by the 1st Session of the 10th National People's Congress, the regulatory function to banks, financial asset management firms, trust and investment companies and other deposit-taking financial institutions of PBOC will be separated from the PBOC and integrated with the relevant functions of the Central Financial Working Committee to establish the China Banking Regulatory Commission. Thereafter, together with the China Securities Regulatory Commission and the China Insurance Regulatory Commission, which were established in 1992 and 1998 respectively, these institutions have formed a separate supervision structure for China's financial industry. Thus, the "unified" era of PBOC since 1949, which was integrated all functions of banking, policy making, currency control, and supervision, has also come to an end.

On Dec.27, 2003, the 6th Session of the Standing Committee of the 10th National People's Congress deliberated and adopted the "Law of the People's Republic of China on the People's Bank of China (Amendment)", clearly defining: "The PBOC is a department of the State Council and is the Central Bank of the People's Republic China, and is a macro-control department that formulates and implements monetary policies, maintains financial stability, and provides financial services under the leadership of the State Council." Then, the monetary policy function of the Central Bank of China has been completely separated from the financial supervision function.

4.2 Commercial bank system reform

4.2.1 Professional bank converted to commercial bank

When the top four state-owned banks resumed or established, they were engaged in credit business in the prescribed fields, so they were called the four-major state-owned professional banks. With the development of the economy and the deepening of the economic system reform, state-owned enterprises have gradually shifted to relatively independent commodity producers and operators. The professional division of labor of banks has been unable to meet the needs of corporate financing. Therefore, the division of labor of these specialized banks has been broken and raised conditional crossover in business. The crossover has brought competition, which has caused many issues. The four-major state-owned professional banks have some problems such as unclear positioning, inflexible operating mechanism, and excessive proportion of non-performing assets. Apart from their own reasons, this is also related to their large number of policy-oriented businesses. Since the professional banks at that moment were not commercial banks, they also assumed a large number of administrative tasks and issued various policy loans. The central bank could directly release the loans scale to them, stipulate deposit and loan interest rates, or even directly determine the enterprises projects and amounts that must be loaned, and institutions are set up according to administrative divisions. It is difficult to get rid of local government intervention. The professional bank of this period is a functional two-in-one in pursuit of profits and policy tasks. They played an important role in the financial network, collected 90% of the credit funds in the entire banking system, and assumed more than 75% of the deposit business nationwide. The institutional outlets cover almost all of China's urban and rural areas. [1] If the functions of these banks do not change, the financial market system will be difficult to form in this situation. Therefore, it is necessary to transform professional banks into state-owned commercial banks, and it is an inevitable requirement of complying with the reform of the financial system.

In Nov. 1993, the 3rd Plenary Session of the 14th CPC Central Committee proposed a decision to accelerate the reform of the financial system. Subsequently, the

[1] Editorial committee, *Financial Institution Personnel Management Practice*, Vol.1, Beijing: Contemporary China Publishing House, 1999, p.151.

State Council made the "Decision on Financial System Reform" and proposed to make state-owned professional banks into real commercial banks. The state has adopted a series of reform measures, including the establishment of three policy banks to separate the policy finance business of professional banks, the establishment of asset management companies to solve the problem of bad assets of professional banks, and the improvement of unified legal person system, internal control system and internal governance structure. And other reform measures to promote the conversion of professional banks to commercial banks. In May 1995, the "Commercial Banking Law" was promulgated and implemented, and the equal status of the four major national professional banks and the nature of commercial banks were established in the form of law. Since then, China's four major professional banks have become state-owned commercial banks, and become independent legal entity of "self-operated, self-sustaining, self-financing, self-discipline". Under the guidance of the Commercial Bank Law, the four state-owned commercial banks are the main subjects of the Chinese financial system, with the constant reform.

4.2.1.1 The adjustment of the operation and management of the state-owned commercial banks

(1) *Further rationalize the relationship between state-owned commercial banks and the central bank*

All business activities of state-owned commercial banks must strictly abide by the state's relevant financial laws and regulations, and consciously accepted the supervision of the central bank. This fundamentally solved the relationship between state-owned commercial banks and the central bank and laid a solid foundation for future regulatory work.

(2) *Emphasize the status of an independent legal person of a state-owned commercial bank*

The head office of the state-owned commercial banks strengthened central management and improved the ability to uniformly allocate funds. The Bank conducted unified accounting. Market transactions were not allowed between branches, and the operating principles of "self-operated, self-sustaining, self-financing, self-discipline" were implemented. Branches and sub-branches of state-owned commercial banks no longer had independent foreign investment rights. Generally, only the head office of a state-owned commercial bank could be financed by the central bank, and the head office of the state-owned commercial bank was fully responsible for the liquidity and ability to pay of the bank assets. State-owned commercial banks could break the business scope of each professional bank to crossly operate and compete.

(3) *Standardize the investment behavior of state-owned commercial banks according to the principle of divided operations*

In 1993, the State Council required commercial banks not to invest in non-financial enterprises. The amount of investment by state-owned commercial banks in the insurance, trust and securities industries should not exceed a certain percentage of their capital and should be deducted from their capital on calculating the adequacy ratio. State-owned commercial banks must be separated from the insurance, trust and securities industries in terms of human resource, finances, and materials, and divided operations should be implemented.

4.2.1.2 Separate policy finance

In order to solve the issue of state-owned commercial banks pursuing profits while also undertaking a large number of policy-based financial services, in 1994, China established three policy banks, namely the China Development Bank, the Exim Bank of China and Agricultural Development Bank of China, to clarify the policy banks should be managed reinforcely, and adhere to the principle of self-responsibility, capital preservation, and non-compete clause with commercial financial institutions. The establishment of policy banks to separate policy-based financial services from state-owned commercial banks will help to improve the autonomy of commercial banks and facilitate the further reform of state-owned commercial banks. In the meantime, it also helps to cut off the direct link between policy loans and the base currency and ensure that the central bank controls the initiative of the base currency. The specific situation regarding the establishment and development of policy banks will be discussed in the next section.

4.2.1.3 Cancellation of the loans scale and implementation of asset- liability ratio management

With the deepening of financial reforms and the increasing of financial institutions, the proportion of state-owned commercial banks' loans to the use of assets of all financial institutions has dropped from nearly 90% at the end of 1993 to around 75% at the end of 1996; the proportion of the broad money (M2) fell from around 90% at the end of 1993 to around 60% at the end of 1996. In the case of the remarkable decline in the proportion of loans to state-owned banks, even if the scale of state-owned banks loans was constrained, it was still difficult to control the total amount of loans national wide, which made the central bank's controlling over the scale of state-owned bank credits greatly weakened in the past years. To this end, since 1994, the PBOC has gradually narrowed the scope of control over the scale of state-owned banks' credit, and gradually implemented asset-liability ratio management. Since 1998, the PBOC has completely abolished the control of the loan quota of state-owned commercial banks and began to implement the management system of "planning guidance, self-balancing, proportional management, and indirect regulation". In the meantime, state-owned commercial banks were required to act as legal entities to manage the source of funds and the use of funds. The cancellation of loan scale constraints and the implementation of asset-liability ratio management have given state-owned commercial banks the autonomy to operate as an independent legal entity, which is another important step for state-owned commercial banks to move toward commercial operation.

4.2.1.4 Issuance of special government bonds to supplement the capital of state-owned commercial banks

According to reports from four state-owned commercial banks, at the end of June 1997, the net capital of Industrial and Commercial Bank of China, Agricultural Bank of China, Bank of China and China Construction Bank were RMB94.6 billion, RMB37.4 billion, RMB113.7 billion and RMB49.7 billion respectively. However, in fact, because the banks did not adopt a prudent accounting system at the time, the provision for bad debts was seriously insufficient, and the capital of state-owned commercial banks was seriously insufficient, and there was a high systemic risk. In Nov. 1998, the Ministry of Finance issued a special treasury bond of RMB270 billion, which was specifically used to supplement the capital of four state-owned commercial banks. According to the calculation at the time, the average capital adequacy ratio of the four state-owned commercial banks after the supplementary capital could be more than 8%. This national capital injection has alleviated the contradiction of insufficient capital of state-owned commercial banks to a certain extent, but this policy has certain limitations. After the completion of capital injection, state-owned commercial banks have not established dynamic capital replenishment mechanism, and expansion speed of commercial bank assets was under-estimated, the capital was insufficient to fulfill these demands.

4.2.1.5 Establishment of asset management company and divestment of non-performing loans

From the situation at the time, although the four state-owned commercial banks have done a lot of work in establishing a modern enterprise system and strengthening credit management, due to changes in the economic environment, inadequate financial legal system, weak financial supervision, weak social credit concepts, etc., the scale of non-performing loans accumulated by commercial banks was growing. According to the low-level accounting standards at that time, the non-performing asset ratio of China's banking industry was 30% in the late 1990s. Some economists deemed that China's banking industry was technically bankrupt.[1] To build public confidence in the financial industry and initiate reform of state-owned banks, it is necessary to solve the problem of bad assets in the banking industry. In 1999, China Cinda Asset Management Co., China Orient Asset Management Co., China Huarong Asset Management Co., Ltd. and China Great Wall Asset Management Co., Ltd. were established to purchase or host the non-performance loans of China Construction Bank, Bank of China, Industrial and Commercial Bank of China and Agricultural Bank of China. The Chinese government has injected more than RMB270 billion, divested the non-performing assets of the four state-owned commercial banks of RMB1,400 billion, reduced the proportion of non-performing loans, improved the asset structure, and the capital adequacy ratio, which made them approach to the international standardized commercial banks quickly and avoided the impacts of the financial crisis to our economy. The establishment of asset management companies is a key arrangement in the process of market-oriented reform of state-owned banks and is a helpful attempt in the process of market-oriented reform of the entire financial and even economic system.[2]

4.2.2 Establishment of the new type commercial banks

(1) *Joint-stock commercial banks*

In April 1987, China's two joint-stock commercial banks, Bank of Communications and China Merchants Bank, opened successively, which pulled open the prelude to the reform and development of China's joint-stock commercial banks. With the deepening of reform and opening up and the reform of the financial system, the joint-stock

[1] Yi Gang, *On the Financial Reform of China*, Beijing: The Commercial Press, 2009, p.289.

[2] Yi Gang, *On the Financial Reform of China*, Beijing: The Commercial Press, 2009. p.291.

commercial banks established on the basis of new institutions and new mechanisms have developed rapidly, the institutions and businesses have expanded rapidly, and the overall strength has grown steadily. The management has shown its unique vitality and fresh power.

Since the State Council approved the re-establishment of Bank of Communications in September 1986, more than a dozen joint-stock commercial banks including Shanghai Pudong Development Bank, Hainan Development Bank[1], Hua Xia Bank and China Minsheng Bank have been established. After more than ten years of development, the role of joint-stock commercial banks in the Chinese financial system has been continuously strengthened. On the one hand, the establishment and development of joint-stock commercial banks has expanded the competition entities, broke the monopoly of the banking industry, promoted the formation of the competition mechanism of the banking system and the improvement of the competitive level, and promoted the comprehensive application of innovative financial instruments by providing diversified service to customers, and the significant improvement of the service level of state-owned commercial banks. This gradually formed a new pattern of multi-level and multi-type financial institution organization system that meets the requirements of the socialist market economy, which is conducive to the establishment of a division of labor and cooperation among various financial institutions with complementary functions and equal competition. On the other hand, joint-stock commercial banks make full use of the vigorous new mechanism to choose customers in accordance with the market and efficiency principles, strengthen the role of market mechanisms in resource allocation, improve the efficiency of capital use, and greatly promote the expansion of the market economy and optimization of industrial structure. The establishment of joint-stock commercial banks has provided useful experience for the establishment of modern commercial banks in China. It has also achieved positive results in exploring new business operations and development methods of commercial banks in China and has made tremendous efforts to promote the healthy and orderly development of commercial banks in China.

Meanwhile, joint-stock commercial banks are also facing some problems in the rapid development: First, because the risk control and management mechanism is still not sound, internal control effectiveness and operational compliance are insufficient,

---

[1] In June, Hainan Development Bank was administratively closed by the People's Bank of China because it could not pay its due debts in time, becoming the first commercial bank to be closed in China, 1998.

resulting in higher banking risk; second, due to the lack of related professional talents, the staffs in joint-stock commercial banks were unqualified for the rapid development of joint-stock commercial banks; third, the self-development mechanism and self-restraint mechanism that meet the needs of joint-stock commercial banks have not yet been established. The operating mechanism is still relatively extensive. These problems were gradually emerging in the development process of joint-stock commercial banks and would certainly be gradually resolved in further development. The continuous development of China's economy and the continuous deepening of the financial system reform have shown good development prospects for China's joint-stock commercial banks and provided an expandable market space and external environmental protection for the development of joint-stock commercial banks.

(2) *City commercial banks*

The city commercial bank was formed on the basis of the former city credit cooperatives. Although it has a short set-up time, it has become an important part of China's commercial banking system and played an important role in supporting local economic construction and deepening financial system reform.

Since the mid-1980s, urban credit cooperatives that provide financial services to urban private and individual economies have developed rapidly, and satisfied the financial needs of urban collective enterprises, private enterprises and self-employed entrepreneurs to a considerable extent. However, because the credit cooperation system and related legal basis were at an early stage, the organization system and operation mechanism of most urban credit cooperatives departed from the principle of credit cooperatives and became the small commercial banks to the public.

Since 1993, according to the "Decision of the Central Committee on Economic Structural Reform", which required to give full play to the central role of the city, gradually form an economic zone of different scale, openness, and network based on cities, especially large and medium-sized cities",[1] and in order to further strengthen financial supervision, prevent financial risks, improve China's commercial banking system and promote urban economic development, the PBOC began to actively plan a pilot program for the formation of urban commercial banks. In 1995, the State Council issued the "Notice on the Establishment of City Cooperative Banks" and decided to form a city cooperative bank in batches in large and medium-sized cities on the basis

[1] *Decision of the Central Committee of the Communist Party of China on Economic Structural Reform*, Beijing: People's Publishing House, 1984.

of the withdrawal of urban credit cooperatives. In Jul. 1995, Shenzhen City Commercial Bank, the first local joint-stock banking institution in China, officially opened. In the same year, Beijing and Shanghai City Commercial Banks were also established. Subsequently, after piloting the establishment of city commercial banks in 16 cities across the country, it was gradually implemented in major cities and prefecture-level cities across the country, as shown in Table 4–1.

The establishment of city commercial bank was a major achievement in China's financial system reform and a major measure to prevent financial risks. City commercial banks have become an important part of China's banking system and a new force in terms of the number of institutions and assets. They have played an important role in resolving the financial risks of urban credit cooperatives, supporting local economic construction, and promoting the development of China's financial industry.[1]

Table 4–1 Number of institutions and assets of city commercial banks and their deposits and loans

Year	Numbers	Assets (RMB billion)	Deposit (RMB billion)	Loan (RMB billion)
1995	3	64.648	50.618	20.217
1996	18	214.193	147.057	77.981
1997	63	371.163	274.586	165.762
1998	88	355.852	283.898	173.983

Source: Shang Ming, *New China finance 50 years*, Beijing: China Financial & Economic Publishing House, 2000, p.139.

These new type commercial banks, together with the previously established national commercial banks, constitute a commercial banking system in addition to the four-major state-owned commercial banks. They are an important part of China's financial system and have effectively promoted the development of China's commercial banking system.

4.2.3 Foreign banks

Foreign banks have entered China for more than 100 years. After the founding of the People's Republic of China in 1949, four foreign banks, including HSBC, Bank of East Asia, OCBC Bank and Standard Chartered Bank, have continued to operate in

[1] Shang Ming, *50 Years of Finance in New China*, Beijing: China Financial & Economic Publishing House, 2000, p.139.

Shanghai. Since the reform and opening up, China has gradually expanded the geographical and business scope of the financial industry to open to abroad. By the end of 1993, foreign banks had established 76 business institutions in 13 cities in China, operating foreign exchange business for foreign-invested enterprises and foreign residents, with total assets of US$8.9 billion.[1]

In 1994, on the basis of the revision and improvement of the "Regulations on the Administration of Foreign-funded Banks and Sino-foreign Joint Venture Banks of the People's Republic of China on Special Economic Zones" issued in 1985, the State Council promulgated the "Regulations on the Administration of Foreign-funded Financial Institutions of the People's Republic of China". The regulations of foreign-funded banks have stipulated the market access conditions and supervision standards for foreign-funded banks operating, and gradually legalized and standardized the operation of foreign-funded banks in China.

With the promulgation and implementation of the "Regulations on the Administration of Foreign-funded Financial Institutions of the People's Republic of China", the number of foreign-funded banking institutions in China and their business scope have been continuously expanded. The opening-up areas of the banking industry were opened from the coastal and central cities on the basis of the first phase of opening up. The city has expanded nationwide, and foreign banks can set up branches in all cities in China. In Aug. 1994, 11 cities, including Beijing, Shenyang, Shijiazhuang, Xi'an, Chengdu, Chongqing, Wuhan, Hefei, Suzhou, Hangzhou and Kunming, allowed foreign banks to establish business branches. Since 1996, the promulgation and implementation of a series of regulations, such as the "Provisional Regulations on the Establishment of Branches of Foreign-funded Banks in China", the "Interim Administrative Measures for the Pilot Operation of Foreign-funded Financial Institutions in Shanghai", the "Measures for the Administration of Representative Offices of Foreign Financial Institutions in China", and the "Implementation Rules of the Regulations on the Administration of Foreign-funded Financial Institutions", provided legal support for the pilot operation of Chinese currency business of foreign banks. At the end of 1996, the PBOC reviewed and approved nine eligible foreign banks to conduct Chinese currency business pilots in Shanghai and Shenzhen. By the end of 1997, the number of foreign-funded banking institutions in China had reached

---

[1] Li Yang, Wang Guogang and Liu Yuhui, *The Path of Development of China's Financial System*, Beijing: Economy & Management Publishing House, 2013, p.345.

175, which increased 99 in four years, and the total assets had been more than tripled.[1]

After the outbreak of the Asian financial crisis, in order to promote the development of foreign banks in China, China has adopted a series of policy measures in a timely manner by approving Shenzhen as the second pilot city after allowing Shanghai to allow foreign banks to operate renminbi business, allowing foreign banks to join the national interbank lending market to solve the problem of the source of funds for its renminbi business, relaxing the geographical restrictions on the operation of renminbi business by foreign banks, allowing Shanghai foreign banks to expand their renminbi business to Jiangsu and Zhejiang, and allowing foreign banks in Shenzhen to expand their renminbi business to Guangdong, Guangxi and Hunan. The above measures have effectively promoted the development of the establishment and operation scale of foreign banks in China. By the end of 2001, there were 177 foreign-funded banks operating in China with a total asset of US$34.6 billion.[2]

With the formal participation of China into the WTO on Dec.11, 2001, China's financial industry has gradually increased its openness to the world.

4.3 Establishment of the policy bank

Since the reform and opening up, the four state-owned professional banks established in China have played an important role in financing economic development, but there were still many issues in the meantime. One of the important reasons was that policy finance and commercial finance are not separated. State-owned professional banks must handle both commercial finance and policy-based financial services. They are also the dual tasks of commercial credit business and policy credit business. As a result, professional banks can neither faithfully fulfill the obligations of policy banks, nor fully assume the responsibility of commercial banks for their own profits and losses. It was difficult to fundamentally solve the problem of non-discrimination between government and enterprises and provide opportunities for the government to directly intervene in finance. The healthy development of the market and the professional banks are very unfavorable. Therefore, the establishment of a special policy-based financial institution to separate policy finance from commercial finance

---

[1] Li Yang, Wang Guogang and Liu Yuhui, *The Path of Development of China's Financial System*, Beijing: Economy & Management Publishing House, 2013, p.346.

[2] Jiang Shiyin, *Rational Thinking on China's Financial System Reform*, Beijing: China Financial & Economic Publishing House, 2009, p.143.

has become one of the important tasks of China's financial system reform and was the basic premise of fundamental changes in the entire financial system. It was the condition that the state-owned professional bank transformed into the state-owned commercial bank and established the powerful central bank macro-control system.[1]

A policy bank is a non-profitable financial institution with special financing principles created or guaranteed by the government to implement national industrial policies and regional development policies. In Dec. 1993, the State Council officially decided to establish a policy bank under the "Decision on Financial System Reform". In 1994, three policy banks were established in China: The China Development Bank, Agricultural Development Bank of China and the Exim Bank of China are all policy financial institutions directly under the leadership of the State Council, which undertake the tasks of national key construction project financing, agricultural policy loans and support for import and export trade financing respectively. The establishment of the above three policy banks not only laid the foundation for the solution of the policy-oriented capital supply in the three major areas of the country's key construction investment, international trade, and support for "issues of agriculture, farmer and rural area", but also represented a new stage of the reform of China's financial system.

4.3.1 The main task of policy banks

(1) *China Development Bank*

The China Development Bank was formally established in Mar. 1994 with the approval of the State Council. The main tasks of the China Development Bank are to raise and guide domestic and foreign funds in accordance with national laws, regulations, policies and guidelines, to provide loans to policy projects and auxiliary projects for large and medium-sized infrastructure and technological transformation of national infrastructure, basic industries and pillar industries, which would control and adjust the total amount of fixed assets from the source of funds, optimize the investment structure, and improve investment returns.

The China Development Bank handles policy-based financial business with independent accounting and operates independently in a capital-guaranteed manner. Responsibility and rights are unified, and investment constraints and risk responsibility mechanisms

---

[1] Jiang Shiyin, *Rational Thinking on China's Financial System Reform*, Beijing: China Financial & Economic Publishing House, 2009, p.176.

are established. And it's under the guidance and supervision of the PBOC in business operation. The registered capital is RMB50 billion, which is approved and allocated by the Ministry of Finance. Its headquarter is in Beijing, and in May 1996, with the approval of the PBOC, Wuhan Branch and Chengdu, Xi'an and Shenzhen Representative office were established. In 1998, China Investment Bank[1] was merged into the China Development Bank. Based on these, the China Development Bank established 27 branches and a relatively sound branches system.

(2) *Agricultural Development Bank of China*

Agricultural Development Bank of China was established on Nov.18, 1994. It is the only agricultural policy bank in China with a registered capital of RMB20 billion. It is mainly to raise agricultural policy credit funds, undertake the agricultural policy finance business stipulated by the state, and act as the agent for the financial support of agriculture, and serve the agricultural and rural economic development.

The Agricultural Development Bank of China is institutional organized by the head office, tier-1 branches, second-level branches and sub-branches; it's operated with the first-level legal entity system of the head office in management, and the president of the head office is the legal representative; the vertical leadership is implemented in the system. Branches carry out business operations legally within the scope of authorization of the head office.

(3) *The Exim Bank of China*

The Exim Bank of China was established on Apr.26, 1994. It is an important component of China's international trade supporting system and financial system. It is the primary policy financing channel for China's export of mechanical and electrical products, complete sets of equipment and high-tech products, and foreign contracted projects and various overseas investment, the sub-loan bank for foreign government loans, and the accepting bank for Chinese government concessional loans of foreign aid.

---

[1] China Investment Bank is a national professional bank that raises construction funds to handle investment credits abroad. It is a state-owned enterprise that is operated in independent accounting and in responsible for its own profits and losses. It was established in Dec. 1981. Being approved by the PBOC in 1994. it was merged into China Construction Bank. As a wholly-owned subsidiary of a commercial bank, it set up branches in accordance with economic zones and accepted the leadership of the People's Bank of China in its business. In 1998, with the approval of the PBOC, the China Investment Bank was merged into the National Development Bank, and all its debts were borne by the China Development Bank. In Mar. 1999, with the approval of the PBOC, China Everbright Bank took over the assets, liabilities and owner's equity of the former China Investment Bank as well as its business subsidiaries established in various places.

The registered capital of the Exim Bank of China is RMB3.38 billion and is operated with the business policy of independent, capital preservation and enterprise management. The financial business is subject to the supervision and guidance of the PBOC.

The main way of using funds in policy banks is to provide various types of policy loans. Since 1998, the three policy banks have annually added about RMB300 billion of credit investment, which has become an important driving force for promoting China's stable GDP growth. Through reforms, the three policy banks have raised funds through the appropriation from Ministry of Finance, financial bonds issuance, overseas financing, central bank refinancing and interbank lending, providing a financial basis for ensuring the implementation of national policy loans.

4.3.2 Policy banks play the important roles

Since the establishment of policy banks in 1994, in the past 10 years, in accordance with national industrial policies and regional economic development policies, efforts have been made to raise funds, strengthen basic management, and increase policy-oriented policies in key industries, infrastructure, import and export enterprises, and agricultural products circulation. Credit support has made great contributions to China's economic development. In addition, it has made considerable progress in business norms and establishment of rules, business development and institution building, business management and talent development. The scale of policy banks has been rapidly expanded, and their own strength and management level have been greatly improved. It plays an increasingly important role in the national economy.

(1) *The China Development Bank has made tremendous contributions to major infrastructure construction*

As an outcome of China's investment and financing system reform, the China Development Bank shoulders the responsibility of macro-controlling the total amount of funds and the allocation of capital structure of national key infrastructure projects. In the past few years, the China Development Bank has conscientiously carried out the national industrial policies and regional development policies, providing large financial support for the construction and development of national infrastructure, basic industries and pillar industries, and has effectively matched the macroeconomic regulation and control on national total investment and structure of fixed assets. It also has played an active role in optimizing investment structure, improving investment efficiency and supporting economic development in the central and western regions. By 2001, the China Development Bank had loaned nearly RMB600 billion to more than 3,000 projects and realized a total profit of about RMB2.5 billion, basically achieving the business goal of meager profit.

The use of funds by the China Development Bank mainly focused on medium and long-term project loans, and loans to national key projects and policy projects that are supported by national industrial policies and regional economic policies. In the transportation industry, the China Development Bank supported the new expansion of railways and highways, the construction of coastal and inland river ports, the construction of airports and supporting facilities, including Shanghai Pudong Airport, Capital International Airport, Beijing-Kowloon Railway, etc. In the coal and petroleum industry, it has supported the national key projects such as Hebei Handan Mining Area, Daqing Oilfield Development, and Shengli Oilfield Development. In the electric power industry, the China Development Bank raised huge sums of money to support a number of national major projects such as the Yangtze Three Gorges Hydropower-complex Project and the Qinshan Nuclear Power Phase II Project. The medium and long-term loans issued by the China Development Bank have strongly supported the national capital construction, and the economic development of the central and western regions, and ensured the rapid, sustained, stable and healthy development of China's economy.

(2) *The Agricultural Development Bank of China has grown stronger in support of "agriculture, farmer and rural area"*

Since the establishment of the China Agricultural Development Bank, it has fully utilized the powerful lever of agricultural policy finance, conscientiously implemented the national industrial policies and regional development policies, rationally and effectively allocated rural resources, strengthened the basic position of agriculture, and the stamina of agricultural development, consummated the agricultural financial service system, and promoted the comprehensive and healthy development of agriculture and the rural economy.

The Agricultural Development Bank of China is responsible for policy loans such as China's grain and cotton oil reserves, agricultural and sideline products purchases, and comprehensive agricultural development. For a long time, due to the large losses of China's grain, cotton and oil storage enterprises, the purchase and sales reserve funds of grain, cotton, and oil have been heavily misappropriated and lost. In order to achieve a virtuous circle of agricultural policy credit funds, to fully play the functional role of agricultural policy finance, and to ensure the banks' operating continuous and healthy, the Agricultural Development Bank of China actively strives for national policy support, increases state financial capital investment, strengthens its financial strength, strengthens internal management, and improves its operating mechanism to meet the needs of rapid business development.

In terms of institutional building, the Agricultural Development Bank of China was initially lacking the necessary branches, and its main business was entrusted to the Agricultural Bank of China. However, agricultural policy finance business has the characteristics of small single business, large business volume and wide geographical distribution. Comprehensive agency will inevitably lead to higher operating costs, and it is also difficult to achieve closed operation of policy funds. To this end, The Agricultural Development Bank of China has gradually established branches since 1995, and its business operations have gradually moved from principal to self-operating, gradually establishing a relatively integrated branch system and an independently management system and improving the business mechanism. At the same time, the Agricultural Development Bank of China is also actively participating in major reforms such as the national grain and cotton circulation system, insisting on the closed operation of purchase and sales funds, focusing on improving the use efficiency of credit funds and the bank's operating efficiency, gradually improving the quality of credit assets, and striving to do a good job in agricultural policy finance business. The Agricultural Development Bank of China has made matching contributions to China's economic construction and social development.

(3) *The Export-Import Bank of China has become an important window for opening up*

Since its establishment, the Exim Bank of China has conscientiously implemented the country's industrial policy, foreign trade policy and financial policy, and fully exerted the unique role of policy finance in supporting the export of mechanical and electrical products, promoting the restructuring of export commodities and diversifying the export market with both economic and social benefits. In addition, the Exim Bank of China also closely focuses on the needs of China's diplomatic work, and strives to accelerate the implementation of foreign preferential loans, help recipient countries to develop their economies, increase taxes, expand employment, and promote domestic enterprises to make most of "two resources, two markets", and to carry out transnational operations and enhance competitiveness.

In accordance with the country's foreign trade policy and credit policy, the

Export-Import Bank of China has strengthened its support for exporting enterprises by providing services such as export buyer's credit and export seller's credit, and effectively promoted complete sets of equipment such as ships, aircrafts, power stations and other electromechanical product export and satellite launch services. In addition, the Exim Bank of China is also actively engaged in export credit insurance and external guarantee business, providing risk protection for Chinese enterprises to expand the export of electromechanical products and achieve the diversification strategy of the export market.

Since 1995, the Exim Bank of China has undertaken foreign government on-lending business. In accordance with the requirements of bank management, it has continuously standardized business operations and management procedures to improve project management. Since foreign government on-lending projects are mainly concentrated in infrastructure such as energy, transportation, post and telecommunications, and public welfare projects such as heating, water supply, and environmental protection, and agricultural projects, the Exim Bank of China has strongly supported national priorities through foreign government on-lending business, and increased investment in the central and western regions. The Exim Bank of China has also actively strengthened the international exchanges by actively hosting the foreign aid loans of the Chinese government, which has effectively promoted the rapid development of China's foreign trade and the overall situation of China's diplomatic work.

4.3.3 Issues with policy banks

With several years of operation and development since the establishment of the policy bank in 1994, it has made considerable progress, the scale of assets and liabilities has expanded rapidly, the operating mechanism has been gradually improved, and the ability to resist and mitigate risks has been enhanced. However, some issues have also been raised up in actual operations.

(1) *The unclear functional positioning of policy banks*

Although policy banks have made great progress since their establishment, from the perspective of actual operation, the profit targets of policy banks are not consistent with their national interest targets, and sometimes even contradictory. Due to the unclear function positioning of policy banks, their own profit targets of policy financing operations and policy banks themselves such as investment in public or quasi-public areas, development investment in poverty-stricken areas, and credit availability for small and medium-sized enterprises, are inconsistent. Policy banks tend to deviate from national interests and pursue their own interests. This leads to excessive concentration of policy funds in for-profit industries and the squeeze out of commercial financial funds. Therefore, policy banks have not been able to generate the greatest economic and social benefits.

(2) *Insufficient fund and solo financing channel*

Policy banks must operate with certain amount deposits and low-cost funds in order to issue low-interest loans, support strategic industrial structure and balance regional economic development. Therefore, the sources of funding for policy banks are important. When the China Development Bank was set up, the registered capital was RMB50 billion, but more than 80% of them were directly loaned to the project as "soft loans". When the Agricultural Development Bank of China was established, its registered capital was RMB20 billion. A considerable part of it was the assets transferred by the Agricultural Bank of China and Industrial and Commercial Bank of China in the form of loans and the capital of the financial tax rebate, and the actual assigned capital was very small. When the Exim Bank of China was established, its registered capital was RMB3. 38 billion, which was difficult to meet the needs of its rapid development.

In terms of fund raising, policy banks generally have the problem of solo financing channels. The sources of funds of the China Development Bank and the Exim Bank of China mainly include capital transfered by the Ministry of Finance, financial bonds issued to financial institutions, fiscal discount subsidies arranged by the state, and funds raised by issuing bonds on the international market. Except of the principle capital, other sources of funds account for a relatively small proportion, and the duration of funds' holdings does not match the term of the loans. This long-term loans from the short-term funds increase the financing burden of banks. Since the credit means used by policy banks are only loans, there are no other credit and investment methods such as guarantee, investment and credit-linked notes, and it is difficult to make full use of the financial resources of policy banks, which is likely to cause shortages and insufficients of policy loans.

(3) *The imperfect operating mechanism and the large potential risks*

After several years of development, policy banks have gradually explored a business management model suitable for China's national conditions, providing important financing support for national key construction, purchase and sale of agricultural and sideline products, and import and export trade, and effectively implemented the national industrial policy and regional economic policies. However, on the one hand, the state requires policy banks to implement about break-even operations, which are slightly profitable and reflect policy functions; on the other hand, it also requires that the source and use of funds should be compensated and self-circulation. This contradiction has led to the imperfect internal management mechanism of policy banks and raised potential operational risks.

(4) *The absence of laws and regulations for policy banks' operating*

In 1994, the State Council stipulated the main tasks and business scope of the three policy banks in the form of policy bank regulations, and passed the "Regulations on Financial Management of Policy Banks" in 1997. These secured to regulate the operation of policy banks. However, China does not currently have a specialized law to regulate policy-based banking operation, which not only leads to insufficient legal foundation for the supervision and management of policy-based financial institutions, but also restricts the self-development and partial business activities of policy-based financial institutions.

In addition, policy banks generally have problems in management, risk awareness and management concepts. The management of the relevant national economic departments and local governments needs to be further rationalized.

4.3.4 Reforming clues of policy banks

The goal of deepening the reform of policy-oriented banks is to rationally adjust the functional positioning of policy-based banks, establish an independent operational system, and corresponding capital supplements and state subsidy mechanisms. In order to achieve this goal, it is necessary to further deepen policy bank reform in many aspects.

(1) *Correctly handle the relationship between policy banks and the external environment*

In the process of further deepening economic system reform and financial system reform, we correctly handle the relationship between policy banks and governments, state finance, central banks, and commercial banks, and play the appropriate role of the policy-based financial system. According to the different situations of each bank, we chose different reform models and formulated corresponding reform plans, implemented an one-line policy, separately formulated reform plans, and gradually solved the problem of unclear positioning of policy-based banking functions. An open and transparent tendering system for policy-oriented businesses is carried out with purpose, steps and phases.

(2) *Establish a modern enterprise system to achieve sustainable development*

Policy banks should establish a modern enterprise system to achieve their own sustainable development, so that policy banks can better serve the implementation of national economic policies and structural adjustment tasks, and become financial institutions that implement the strategic intentions of national economic development. Only the sustainable policy-based finance can play its role effectively.

(3) *Establish and improve internal management mechanisms to resolve potential risks*

On the basis of clarifying the responsibilities of each policy bank and defining the scope of business, we will further establish and improve the internal operation mechanism of policy banks, including incentive and restraint mechanisms, risk prevention and control mechanisms, etc., through the establishment and improvement of internal management mechanisms, the policy banks can improve efficiency of operating assets to prevent and resolve potential risks effectively.

(4) *Accelerate policy bank legislation*

Policy banks, as well as central bank and commercial banks, should be regulated their operations under the laws. Specialized regulations should be enacted as soon as possible to regulate the business behavior of policy banks.

4.4 Reforming the non–bank financial institution system

Since the reform and opening up, China has developed many types of multi-level non-bank financial institutions. Since 1994, while the reform of commercial banks has been deepened, along with the rapid development of China's securities and insurance market, the reform of non-bank financial institutions represented by securities companies, insurance companies and securities investment funds have continued to move forward in China with great development. The rise of non-bank financial institutions is of great significance to the development of the market economy. It can be said that the emergence and rapid development of non-bank financial institutions has created a new situation in financial competition and has also created a new stage in the development of the financial industry.[1]

[1] Meng Xiaosu, *Modern enterprise system practice book*, Beijing: People's Publishing House, 1995, p.719.

4.4.1 Stock brokerage firms

Since the establishment of China's first professional securities company, Shenzhen Special Economic Zone Securities Co., Ltd. in 1987, with the deepening of China's economic reform and development, the number of securities companies has also increased significantly, and assets have also expanded rapidly. The first climax in the history of the development of China's securities companies thus happened. Since 1996, with the improvement of the securities business environment, the business operations of securities companies have grown rapidly, and the competition among securities companies has intensified. Through mergers and acquisitions and integration within the system, the number and size of securities companies have been greatly improved, and getting profitable, the ability to withstand risks has been greatly enhanced.

"The Securities Law of the People's Republic of China" (hereinafter referred to as the "Securities Law"), which was promulgated in December 1998 and officially implemented on Jul.1, 1999, is China's first law to regulate the issuance and trading of securities, marking China securities industry moving towards a higher level of regulation. According to the provisions of the Securities Law, the state implements classified management of securities companies, which were classified into comprehensive securities companies and brokerage securities companies, and the securities regulatory authorities under the State Council issue business licenses according to their classification. After 1999, securities companies increased their capital and shares on a large scale, and implemented mergers and acquisitions based on internal expansion. The overall strength of securities companies has grown. From 1999 to 2002, there were 106 brokerage companies involving in capital increase and share expansion in the country. Many local brokers with the same strength were ranked as national comprehensive brokers.[1] In addition, from time to time, new brokerages were established. At the end of 2003, there were 131 brokerages with total assets of nearly RMB600 billion, and the overall strength was enhanced. Contrast to these of in 1998, there were only 90 securities companies in China, with total assets of about RMB160 billion, an average of RMB1.78 billion per household.[2] See Table 4–2.

---

1 Wang Jian, *Legal Construction of Asset Securitization*, Beijing: China Fangzheng Press, 2006, p.349.

2 Xin Chengsheng, *Ten Years Development and Review of China's Securities Market*, Beijing: China Yan Shi Press, 2001, p.76.

Table 4–2 Development of Chinese securities companies

Items	1998	1999	2000	2001	2002	2003	2004	2005	2006
Numbers of securities companies	90	90	100	109	127	131	133	133	116
Number of branches	2,412	2,142	2,680	2,700	2,936	2,985	3,020	3,075	3,090

Source: *China Securities and Futures Statistic Yearbook, 2007.*

Although there are differences in the scale, strength and characteristics of more than 130 securities companies in China, there are some common problems. First, the small scale and weak funds have seriously restricted the company's development. The ordinary amount of registered capital of a securities company is too small, and its own funds can hardly be used as a securities business with a large amount of capital demand, and it is definitely unable to withstand large system risks. Second, the types of business operations are single, the business is too narrow, concentrated, and the competition is fierce. Third, management is imperfect, and the laws and regulations are often serious violated. In China, the securities brokers integrated act as the securities dealers, trading dealers, fund custodians and fund liquidators, this "all-round" securities firm system will facilitate securities firms to misappropriate customer deposits for proprietary trading, and can violate the customer intends to carry out operations, etc., causing great harm to the market. The fourth is the lack of talents. The securities industry is a talent-intensive industry with a high degree of specialization. Qualified securities talents must have both financial theoretical knowledge and practical experience, they must understand enterprise management and have a strong international vision. At present, the high-quality talents in China's securities industry are still quite scarce, and it is difficult to compete with foreign brokers, which seriously restricts the further development of China's capital market.

The stock exchange center was cleaned up. Before and after the establishment of the Shanghai and Shenzhen Stock Exchanges, some regions did not have the approval of the State Council, and set up institutions such as property rights exchanges, securities trading centers and securities trading automatic quotation systems, and engaged in illegal off-exchange of equity securities such as stocks and share certificates of non-listed companies. Some stock exchanges were doing the real time trading together with the Shanghai and Shenzhen stock exchanges, and in fact, became the off-site trading hall of the them. Thus a lot of financial risks were under-evaluated in these activities. In March 1998, the State Council forwarded the China Securities Regulatory Commission's "Scheme to Clean Up and Rectify Illegal Stock Trading", and cleaned up and corrected the stock exchanges and other stock trading activities illegally carried out by various securities trading centers and quotation systems, and prohibited disguising stock listing of property rights trading institutions. In September 1998, the State Council forwarded the China Securities Regulatory Commission's "Scheme to Clean and Reorganize Securities Trading Center" to clean up and rectify all these unauthorized exchange centers and securities registration company. According to this, the China Securities Regulatory Commission has carried out the clean-up and rectification of 41 illegal off-exchange and securities trading centers in accordance with the steps of "stopping expansion first, re-cleaning business after, and finally closing the venue".

Securities investment fund management company. Since 1991, a number of funds have been invested in securities, futures, real estate and other markets. They rely on local governments or bank branches to raise funds from the public. By the end of 1996, there were 78 closed-end funds. The total scale of these funds is about RMB6.6 billion, and the investment scope covers securities, real estate and capital borrowing. Among them, real estate investment accounts for a large proportion and has low liquidity. At the same time, some funds listed on the exchange, often become speculative objectives, causing a certain confusion to the market.[1] In order to regulate the development of securities investment funds, the "Interim Measures for the Administration of Securities Investment Funds" was promulgated in November 1997. In March 1998, Guotai Fund Management Company and Southern Fund Management Company were formally established with registered capital of RMB0.11 billion and RMB0.15 billion respectively. In the following nine years, from 1998 to 2006, the number of Chinese fund management companies grew steadily, reaching 58 in 2006.[2]

4.4.2 Insurance companies

In June 1995, the "Insurance Law of the People's Republic of China" was promulgated and implemented, and the principle of separate production and life insurance business was established in the form of law. The basic rules were established for the development of China's insurance industry and the reform of insurance institutions, marking the Chinese insurance industry to be managed in legal

[1] Chen Yulu, *The Megatrends of China's Financial System*, Beijing: China Financial Publishing House, 2011, p.38.

[2] Wang Guangqian, Ying Zhanyu and Jiang Shiyin, *China Financial Reform: Historical Experience and Transformation Model*, Beijing: China Financial Publishing House, 2008, p.53.

basis. In 1996, according to the "Notice of the People's Bank of China on Reforming the Institutional System of the People's Insurance Company of China", the People's Insurance Company of China carried out a comprehensive reform of the institutional system and reformed it into the People's Insurance (Group) Company of China with three sub-companies, PICC Property and Casualty Company Limited, PICC Life Insurance Co., Ltd, PICC Reinsurance Co., Ltd. The property and life insurance businesses in China Pacific Insurance Company and China Ping An Insurance Company were recorded, accounted and managed separately. At the same time, in 1996, Taikang Life Insurance Co., Ltd., Xinhua Life Insurance Co., Ltd., and Huatai Property Insurance Co., Ltd., three national insurance companies and Huaan Property Insurance Co., Ltd. (Shenzhen), and Yongan Property Insurance Co., Ltd. (Xi'an), two regional insurance companies, have established, which promoted the formation of insurance competition and injected new vitality into insurance competition. From 1992 to the end of 1998, with the approval of the State Council, the People's Bank of China approved 12 foreign insurance company branches or Sino-foreign joint venture insurance companies. The national insurance market showed unprecedented prosperity. See Table 4–3.

Table 4–3 Basic information of local insurance companies (before 1998)

Company name	Time to set up	Property	Business scale
PICC	Jan. 1949	State-owned	Property
PICC Life Insurance Co., Ltd.	Mar. 1999	State-owned	Life
PICC Reinsurance Co., Ltd.	Mar. 1999	State-owned	Reinsurance Property and Life
Xinjiang Production and Construction Corps	Aug. 1986	State-owned	Property and Life
China Pacific Insurance Company	Apr. 1991	Joint shares	Property and Life
China Ping An Insurance Company	Mar. 1988	Joint shares	Property and Life
Tianan Insurance Co., Ltd.	Oct. 1994	Joint shares	Property
Dazhong Insurance Co., Ltd.	Jan. 1995	Joint shares	Property
Huatai Property Insurance Co., Ltd.	Aug. 1996	Joint shares	Property
Xinhua Life Insurance Co., Ltd.	Aug. 1996	Joint shares	Life
Taikang Life Insurance Co., Ltd.	Aug. 1996	Joint shares	Life
Yongan Property Insurance Co., Ltd.	Aug. 1996	Joint shares	Property
Huaan Property Insurance Co., Ltd.	Oct. 1996	Joint shares	Property

Source: PBOC.

The modern insurance supervision system began to be established. In accordance with the banking, insurance, and securities separation supervision principles, on Nov.18, 1998, the China Insurance Regulatory Commission was established to unify the supervision of the insurance industry and centrally manage the national insurance market, marking the new stage of the insurance regulatory system in China.

The insurance intermediary market has also begun to develop. Before 1988, China's insurance market was exclusively operated by PICC, and there was no professional insurance brokerage institution in China. With the increase of foreign-invested enterprises and the entry of foreign insurance companies into the insurance market, to expand the business through the insurance brokers has become a new attempt in the insurance industry. In March 1993, Huatai Insurance Consulting Co., Ltd., the predecessor of Huatai Insurance Brokerage Co., was established as the first Chinese-funded company engaged in insurance brokerage business. In June 1993, PBOC Shenzhen Branch and Shenzhen Industrial and Commercial Bureau have separately approved 16 insurance brokerage companies to set up. At the same time, some well-known insurance brokers in the world were attracted by the Chinese insurance market, and have opened representative offices in China, such as Marsh & McLennan Companies and Aon Corporation. In 1995, the "Insurance Law" was promulgated, and for the first time, the status of insurance brokers in the Chinese insurance market was recognized in legal form. With the development of the insurance brokerage industry, the society has had high motivation for applying for the establishment of insurance brokerage companies. The China Insurance Regulatory Commission has begun to implement stricter market access control for insurance brokerage companies, and has gradually established a regulatory framework for insurance brokerage companies.

The reform of the policy insurance system has made a breakthrough. In order to give full play to the positive role of export credit insurance in supporting foreign trade and investment, China Export Credit Insurance Corporation was formally established in December 2001. This is China's first policy insurance company, marking the significant progress of reforming China's policy insurance system.

The insurance industry has further expanded its opening to the outside world. In order to meet the needs of joining the World Trade Organization, in 2001, the China Insurance Regulatory Commission completely cleared 8 regulations and departmental regulations that were inconsistent with the rules of the World Trade Organization and business commitments, involving 22 articles, and promulgated the "Regulations on the Administration of Foreign-funded Insurance Companies" to strengthen management of foreign insurance companies. A number of Sino-foreign joint venture insurance companies and foreign insurance companies have been established, as shown in Table 4–4.

Table 4–4 Foreign insurance companies in China (before 1998)

Company name	Business scale	Location	Fund resource	Time to set up
Min An Insurance (HK) Company Shenzhen Branch	Property insurance	Shenzhen	Hong Kong, China	Oct. 1982
Min An Insurance (HK) Company Haikou Branch	Property Insurance	Haikou	Hong Kong, China	Jan. 1986
AIA Shanghai Branch	Life Insurance	Shanghai	the US	Sep. 1992
The Tokio Marine and Fire Insurance (SH)Co., Ltd.	Property Insurance	Guangzhou	Japan	Jul. 1994
AIG Guangzhou Branch	Property Insurance	Guangzhou	the US	Sep. 1995
AIA Guangzhou Branch	Life Insurance	Guangzhou	the US	Sep. 1995
Winterthur Swiss Insurance Shanghai Branch	Property Insurance	Shanghai	Swiss	Nov. 1996
Manulife-Sinochem	Life Insurance	Shanghai	Sino-Canada	Nov. 1996
AIG Shanghai Branch	Property Insurance	Shanghai	the US	Jun. 1997
Allianz China Life Insurance Co., Ltd.	Life Insurance	Shanghai	Sino-Germany	May 1997
AXA-Minmetals Assurance Co., Ltd.	Life Insurance	Shanghai	Sino-France	May 1997
Pacific-Antna Life Insurance Company Ltd.	Life Insurance	Shanghai	Sino-US	Oct. 1997
China CMG Life Insurance Company Ltd.	Life Insurance	Shanghai	Sino-Australia	Apr. 1998
RSA Shanghai Branch	Property Insurance	Shanghai	the UK	Apr. 1998

Source: Shang Ming, *50 Years of Finance in New China*, Beijing: China Financial & Economic Publishing House, 2000, p.234.

4.4.3 Trust companies

From 1991 to 1993, the Chinese economy showed a tendency to excessively pursue rapid development. While the trust investment company developed rapidly, a large amount of borrowing funds was used to issue loans and invest in real estate and stocks. In order to prevent and resolve financial risks, the State Council decided to start cleaning up and rectifying trust and investment companies in Jul., 1993.

Firstly, the PBOC decided to stop all banks' borrowing funds from various non-bank financial institutions to bound the ability of trust and investment companies to expand loans from the source of funds. In 1995, the promulgation of the "Law of the People's Republic of China on the People's Bank of China" cut off the channels for trust and investment companies to obtain loans from the PBOC. Secondly, the trust investment company is required to be decoupled from its bank, and it has made clear opinions on the business scope of the trust and investment company and the relationship between the bank and the securities industry. In addition, PBOC uncompromisingly cleaned up trust and investment institutions that have violated regulations and leapfrogs, and strictly enforced market access. In 1995, 150 trust-invested companies were revoked, and the number and thus the assets of trust and investment companies decreased significantly.

In 1999, according to the "Notice of the General Office of the State Council on Forwarding the Plan of the People's Bank of China to Reorganize the Trust and Investment Company", the PBOC began to comprehensively clean up the trust and investment company. There were four basic principles for this reorganization: Firstly, the trust investment company is clearly defined. The positioning of "trusted by principles and asset management" is an intermediary service organization that is benefited from fees and commissions. It is strictly forbidden to handle bank deposits and loans. Secondly, the trust industry and the securities industry were separated from operations, establishments, and regulation. For the existing stock trading business of the trust and investment company, it should be separated by establishing or jointly form a securities company or a securities brokerage company. The separated trust and investment companies, securities companies and securities brokerage companies shall be verified by the PBOC and the China Securities Regulatory Commission respectively, and shall be subject to separate management. The third is to operate on a large scale. In accordance with the requirements for risk prevention and scale operation, the trust and investment company will be re-established with strict conditions for establishment and rectification within a time limit. The fourth is classified disposal, which is handled differently according to the asset quality, capital size and risk status of different companies: either reserved, closed, bankrupt, or merged. By the end of 1999, among the 239 trust and investment companies in the country, the PBOC officially instructed the withdrawal of 8 trust companies from the market, of which 4 were rescinded, 2 were restructured, and 2 were merged into commercial banks.[1]

In 2001, the "Trust Law of the People's Republic of China", "Administrative Measures for Trust and Investment Companies" and "Interim Measures for the Management of Trust and Investment Companies' Fund Trust Businesses" were successively promulgated. The regulatory framework for trust industry in China was basically established, and the trust industry began to operate and develop under the law. In 2002, the PBOC formulated and issued a number of trust company business systems and regulations. In 2004, the China Banking Regulatory Commission issued a regulatory policy on trust industry, and China's trust institutions began a new development.

Since the establishment during the reform and opening up, China's trust and investment companies have always been in the cycle of "development-reorganization-redevelopment-re-reorganization". The reason was that there are some irregularities in the operation of trust and investment companies and unfavorable macroeconomic environment. The problem, but in the final analysis, was because the state has not had a clear positioning of the trust and investment company in long-term, and did not turn the trust and investment company into a financial institution that is truly "trusted by principles and asset management", but was treated as a banking institution to regulate. With the implementation of separate management, trust companies had to compete with the banks. And due to their own capabilities, coupled with the lack of necessary legal norms and guarantees, trust companies would certainly move beyond the business scope and in a mess. Therefore, the reform of trust and investment companies must be comprehensively carried out in terms of clarifying their functional positioning, improving laws and regulations, and improving their own operational ability.

4.4.4 Rural cooperative financial reform

(1) *Rural cooperative reform*

In 1996, the State Council convened a "national financial system reform" work conference to promote a new round of rural financial system reform. The "Decision of the State Council on Rural Financial System Reform" promulgated on Aug.22, 1996 clearly pointed out that the guiding ideology of rural financial system reform is to establish and improve rural areas based on cooperative finance, commercial finance,

---

[1] Wang Guangqian, Ying Zhanyu and Jiang Shiyin, *China Financial Reform: Historical Experience and Transformation Model*, Beijing: China Financial Publishing House, 2008, p.53.

and policy-based financial division of labor. The financial system will further improve the level of rural financial services, increase investment in agriculture, promote the comprehensive operation of trade, industry and agriculture, and promote the development of urban and rural integration, the development of agriculture and rural economy and opening up to the outside world. The focus of rural financial system reform is to restore the cooperative nature of rural cooperatives, further enhance the service function of policy finance, and give full play to the leading role of state-owned commercial banks. The reform of the management system of rural credit cooperatives is the focal point of the reform of rural financial management system. The core objective of the reform is to gradually change the rural credit cooperatives into cooperative financial organizations that are invested by farmers, democratically managed by members, and mainly serve members. The rural credit cooperatives and the Agricultural Bank of China were formally decoupled from each other to restore the nature of cooperative financial organizations with independent legal status. In accordance with the spirit of the "Decision of the State Council on the Reform of Rural Financial System", the rural credit cooperatives and the Agricultural Bank of China were separated from the administrative subordination in 1996. Their business management and financial supervision were undertaken by the Rural Credit Cooperative County Association and the PBOC respectively and regulated by the principle of cooperation.

In order to strengthen the leadership of rural financial system reform, the State Council decided to set up a rural financial system reform coordination mechanism at the State Council, the province, the prefecture, and the county level, and set up an office accordingly, requiring that the reform task be completed within two years. By the end of 1996, rural credit cooperatives in 30 provinces, municipalities and autonomous regions had been decoupled from the Agricultural Bank, and the credit cooperatives had strengthened their business management and were directly supervised by the People's Bank of China. So far, from the perspective of the organizational structure of formal finance, China's rural areas have initially formed the rural formal financial system structure and organizational system with agricultural banks, agricultural development banks and rural credit cooperatives as the main body. Since then, the reform on the rural financial system has been carried out with the focus on rural credit cooperatives.

Since 1997, the key points of rural credit cooperative reform have been shifted to its equity setting, democratic management, service orientation, financial management and other aspects of regulation based on the "Regulations on the Management of Rural Credit Cooperatives" and the "Financial System of Financial Insurance Enterprises" issued by the People's Bank of China, to make it a true cooperative financial organization, and playing a greater role in the rural economy.

(2) *Clean up and rectify the rural cooperative foundation*

In the duration of rural financial system reform, private finance and its financing were in a suppressive status, and the cleanup and rectification of the rural cooperative foundation was also an important part of the reform of the rural financial system. In 1996, the CPC Central Committee and the State Council issued the "Decision of the State Council on the Reform of the Rural Financial System" (hereinafter referred to as the "Decision"), Which fully affirmed the positive role of the Rural Cooperative Foundation in increasing agricultural input and alleviating the shortage of farmers' production and living funds. However, the Decision proposed to rectify the rural cooperative foundation for a large number of cooperative foundations to absorb large amounts of resident deposits in the name of floating shares without the shareholders' participation and risk management, and were operated illegally with huge risks. Firstly, the Agricultural Cooperation Foundation can no longer absorb resident deposits in the form of shares floating. Secondly, any deposit and loan business that have already become financial institutions can be incorporated into the existing rural credit cooperatives after they have been cleared, or set up a rural credit cooperative separately. Thirdly, without a deposit and loan business, or with a deposit and loan business but could not be switched to a rural credit cooperative, it must be operated as a real functional cooperative foundation.

After the Asian Financial Crisis, in order to prevent financial risks, the central government decided to comprehensively rectify the rural cooperative foundation in November 1997. Due to the sudden tightening of policies and the contradictions within the Rural Cooperative Foundation, there were the bank runs on a national scale in 1998. Large-scale bank runs have emerged in Sichuan and Hebei, endangering the stability of rural society. In July 1998, the PBOC issued the "Measures for the Banning of Illegal Financial Institutions and Illegal Financial Business Activities". Except for some microfinance and non-interest-bearing lendings to relatives and friends, other informal financial organizations or activities are illegal. In Jan. 1999, the State Council issued a document to ban the Rural Cooperative Foundation. Although private finance and its financing are basically in an illegal state, due to the large gap between rural capital supply and demand, private financing is more common in rural

China, and it is the main channel for rural financing. This is an indisputable fact.

(3) *Problems in the reform of rural financial system*

The rural financial system reform has initially formed a rural formal financial system structure based on rural credit cooperatives, agricultural banks and agricultural development banks. However, there are still many problems.

First, rural financial services are seriously inadequate, and the development of rural credit cooperatives lags behind. The commercialization reform of the Agricultural Bank of China, and the following deepening of non-agriculturalization, has lost its main position in rural finance. Due to commercial motives, the Agricultural Bank of China shifted its focus to cities, and the trend of "non-agriculturalization" intensified. As a policy bank, the Agricultural Development Bank of China has a narrow scope of policy financial services and weak functions. It was limited to a single state-owned grain, cotton, and oil circulation credit service. As the marketization of grain, cotton, and oil purchases and sales accelerates, the policy operation space was getting smaller in this business scale, and public goods such as agricultural development, agricultural technology advancement, and rural infrastructure that were urgently needed for policy support had not received sufficient policy financial support. The rural credit cooperatives have a relatively simple organizational form, weak financing ability, poor quality of credit assets, and relatively serious losses. They are far from being a community-based cooperative financial organization. In addition, rural credit cooperatives had having problems such as unclear property rights, serious insider control issue, and poor resistance to risks, which are far from meeting the needs of rural finance.

Second, rural finance was in a state of suppression. For rural financing, the serious problem is that the supply of funds is insufficient, and the situation of "excessive funds outflow" in rural areas was continuing and intensifying. In considering the prevention of risks and profitability, the four state-owned commercial banks have gradually withdrawn the business from the countryside since 1999, basically canceling the lending rights of county-level branches, and successively closed more than 3,100 financial institutions below the county level. As a policy bank, the Agricultural Development Bank of China has less connection with farmers. The reform of rural credit cooperatives emphasized on risk prevention and commercialization, and was not willing to lend more money to farmers. According to the statistics of the Central Bank, at the end of Jun. 2002, among the various loans of the National Rural Credit Cooperatives, agricultural loans accounted for only 40.5%, and the supply of rural funds was seriously insufficient. Meanwhile, the amount of money that financial institutions have withdrawn from the countryside was increasing. It was estimated that in 2001, the state-owned commercial banks withdrawn funds from the rural areas by means of deposits were estimated to reach RMB300 billion[1]. The diversion of postal savings, which only operated money saving business, exacerbates the scarcity of rural financial resources.

The third is informal finance. Due to the serious shortage of rural capital supply and the huge demand for rural funds, in response to the huge gap between supply and demand, private illegal fund-raising and usury loans were spread unchecked in rural areas with huge capital shortages. In the absence of formal financial arrangements to effectively address rural financial needs, traditional private informal finance had spaces for development and expanding. Although this kind of financial activity has alleviated the contradiction between rural financial supply and demand to some extent, its defects were also obvious. It was not based on pure credit relations, but on social relations based on blood, kinship, and geography. It increased financial risks, and the borrowing rate is higher, which increased the debt burden of farmers.

4.4.5 Problems in the reform and development of non-bank financial institutions

In the process of rapid development of non-bank financial institutions, due to the small scale and limited business volume, the overall operation and management standardization is low, the management confusion and over-range operation are more prominent, and the operation is inefficiency.

(1) *The unclear responsibilities of non-bank financial institutions*

The emergence and development of non-bank financial institutions was a product of economic and financial institutional reform, which in turn strongly promotes the reform of the economic and financial system. The emergence of non-bank financial institutions has broken the mono-business model of banking financial institutions in the past. However, the development of non-bank financial institutions has not fully and correctly reflected its due status. For a long time, the state has not formally treated them as the property management institutions, and supplements of the banking financial institutions. And they were affiliated as "small banks", and relied on banking financial institutions, thus losing their independent character in the financial industry

[1] Yang Shaojun, "Deepen rural financial reform and improve rural financial services", *Wen Gao*, 2002(3).

and without equally competing.

(2) *Non-bank financial institutions irregularly operated*

Since the non-bank financial institutions have developed in short period, there were no ready-made experience for reference. In addition, for their respective economic interests, they had too intensive competition, so there were many irregularities in operation, and even illegal operations.

(3) *Non-bank financial institutions management chaos and out of range operations*

Non-bank financial institutions are complex and diverse. In the absence of sound regulatory mechanisms and inadequate supply of laws and regulations, some non-bank financial institutions operate in violation of regulations and even become fraudulent institutions. Because of the ambiguous boundaries between banks and non-bank financial institutions, many non-bank financial institutions have direct or indirect relationships with banks, sharing personnel, funds and information with their controlling banks to jointly make decisions to achieve common under the current management system. Maximizing profits, non-bank financial institutions have serious moral hazard problems.

(4) *The operational efficiency of non-bank financial institutions needs to be improved*

Due to the limited development environment and stage, China's non-bank financial institutions only act as the supplements, and they are still less specialized with higher operating costs and low operational efficiency.

In view of the various problems in the operation of non-bank financial institutions, we must further deepen the reform of non-bank financial institutions, clarify the responsibilities of non-bank financial institutions, further develop and improve relevant laws and regulations, strengthen financial supervision, and try best to improve the operational efficiency of non-bank financial institutions, so that non-bank financial institutions can be lead to the development path of legalization, standardization and specialization, and thus make contributions to the entire economic and financial development.

4.5 Capital market transformation and development

Since the reform and opening up, China's economy has continuously transformed from a planned system to a socialist market economic system. In the process of transformation, the reform of state-owned enterprises has gradually deepened and China's economy has sustainable developed. Then the financial market, financial system and capital market that are compatible with it have emerged as the consequence, and become an important force to promote ownership reform and improve the resource allocation. With the gradual establishment of the market economic system in China, the demand for market-oriented resource allocation was increasing, and the Chinese capital market was gradually growing. With the development of the capital market, the interbank lending market, the bill market, and the bond market have all developed rapidly, and various problems have emerged in the meantime. Clearing and regulating the capital market and strengthening the supervision of the capital market have become an important part of the reform in this period.

4.5.1 Interbank lending market

The "Provisional Regulations on Bank Administration of the People's Republic of China" promulgated by the State Council on Jan.7, 1986 made provisions for professional banks funds can be borrowed from each other, and interest rates for mutual lending between professional banks are negotiated by both borrowers and lenders. In the same year, the first capital lending market between the urban credit cooperatives since the reform of China's economic system was officially opened in Wuhan, Hubei. Since then, the interbank borrowing market has developed rapidly.

By 1992, the macroeconomic environment and financial situation had improved, and a new round of investment was launched across the country. The trading activities of the interbank borrowing market have also become active, and the transaction volume has been rising steadily. At the same time, the problems of messy borrowing units, excessive borrowing periods, improper use, and illegal trades have become increasingly serious. In Jul. 1993, in response to the illegal borrowing of the lending market and serious disruption of the order of financial market, the PBOC issued a series of policies and regulations to rectify and standardize the interest rates, maturities, capital use, and intermediary agencies of the interbank borrowing market, and limited the borrowing and lending scale of financial institutions. After more than a year of rectification, China's interbank borrowing market has entered a stage of more standardized management, and formed a loose, intangible lending market dominated by the PBOC financing center.

In 1995, to consolidate the results of the rectified inter-bank lending market, the PBOC further strengthened the management of the inter-bank lending market, requiring cross-regional and cross-system interbank lending to be handled by the

PBOC financing center, and non-financial institutions and individuals are not allowed entering the inter-bank lending market, thus the inter-bank lending market has been further regulated and developed. In Nov. 1995, the PBOC issued a notice requesting commercial banks to revoke their lending market before Apr.1, 1996. This measure has laid a solid foundation for the establishment of a unified domestic interbank market.[1]

In 1996, the PBOC carried out a major reform of the inter-bank lending operation mechanism, and built a national unified inter-bank lending market based on the original foreign exchange trading system. The establishment and operation of the national interbank lending market has promoted the management of the assets and liabilities ratio of financial institutions, and has become an important market for commercial banks to effectively allocate funds and conduct liquidity management, creating conditions for the deepening of the interest rate system reform.

On Apr.3, 1998, the PBOC issued a document allowing the head office of a commercial bank to authorize its branches to enter the interbank market; on Apr.28, 1998, it approved the Shanghai Branch of Industrial Bank of Japan and Dai-Ichi Kangyo Bank Shanghai Branch, Citibank Shanghai Branch, Standard Chartered Bank Shanghai Branch, HSBC Bank Shanghai Branch, Crédit Agricole Shanghai Branch, Sanwa Bank Shanghai Branch, and Tokyo Mitsubishi Bank Shanghai Branch to join the national interbank borrowing market, engaged in renminbi interbank lending, bond repurchase and spot bonds Trading; in Aug. 1999, qualified fund management companies and securities companies were allowed to enter the interbank lending market; in Jun. 2000, eligible corporate group finance companies were allowed to enter the interbank borrowing market; starting from Apr.15, 2002, the entry of memberships to the inter-market was changed from the examining system to the approval system, and the rate of increase in the number of market members was significantly accelerated.

In Jul. 2007, the PBOC promulgated a new "Interbank Lending Management Measures", which comprehensively adjusted the access management, term management, quota management, filing management, transparency management, and supervision and management authority of the interbank borrowing market.

[1] Gan Chunhui, *30 Years for Chinese Economic System Reform*, Shanghai: Shanghai University of Finance & Economics Press, 2008, p.451.

4.5.2 Bill market

Due to the serious problem of violations and fictitious bills in the bill market, China has basically suspended the bill business since 1988. In May 1993, the PBOC issued the "Measures of Commercial Drafts". On May 10, 1995, the Third Session of the Standing Committee of the Eighth National People's Congress passed the "Law of Bills of the People's Republic of China" and was officially implemented on Jan.1, 1996. The Act on bills and related laws responsibility has made a principled provision, providing an institutional basis for the redevelopment of the Chinese bill market on a normative basis. In 1997, in line with the transformation of financial macro-control methods, the PBOC further strengthened the macro management and system construction of commercial bills business, and issued the "Interim Measures of the People's Bank of China for the Rediscounting of State-owned Commercial Banks" and "Interim Measures of Bills", and set up a re-discounting window of the head office to improve the rediscounting operation system; PBOC officially approved the pilot branch of the PBOC in Jiangsu Province to carry out the transfer of discounted business in order to promote the circulation of commercial paper between banks; the PBOC promulgated and implemented the "Interim Measures for the Administration of Commercial Bills of Exchange and Discount and Rediscount" to regulate and improve the management and operation of commercial bills business. After 1995, the Chinese bill market, which was dominated by commercial bills, achieved steady development on the basis of norms. Commercial bills of exchange not only became an important financing channel for enterprises, but also became an important tool in credit and monetary policy operation for the PBOC to regulate the economic structure. The rapid development of commercial bills effectively regulates corporate credit behavior, prevents enterprises from defaulting on payment, improves the quality of bank credit assets, and strengthens the macro-control role of the central bank.

4.5.3 Bond repo market

Bond repurchase refers to the transaction when the bond holder (the repurchasing party) sell the bond to the bond purchaser (reverse repurchase party), the buyer and the seller agree to repurchase an equal number of bonds of the same type with the agreed price at a specified date in the future, from the repurchasing party direction to reverse repurchasing party,[1] which is essentially a securities mortgage or pledge loan.

On Sep.14, 1991, the first repurchase transaction in the history of China's financial market development was completed between the two member companies of the national Securities Trading Automated Quotations System (STAQ). Since then, in 1992, Wuhan Securities Exchange Center also launched the government bond repurchase business. Later, with the expansion of the issuance of treasury bonds, the launch of the treasury bond futures pilot, and the increasingly active stock market of treasury bonds, other major securities exchanges, including the Shanghai Stock Exchange, the Shenzhen Stock Exchange, and the Tianjin Stock Exchange centre, have successively opened treasury bonds repo business, and the transaction volume has grown rapidly. Only the Wuhan Securities Exchange Center's government bond repurchases transactions in 1995 exceeded RMB150 billion.[2]

However, due to the lack of necessary regulations, along with the rapid expansion of the turnover of government bonds, the extension of the repurchase period, the lack of collateral and debt defaults have repeatedly occurred. Therefore, in order to strengthen management and regulate market development, in Aug. 1995, the PBOC, the Ministry of Finance, and the China Securities Regulatory Commission (CSRC) jointly issued the "Notice on Reaffirming the Relevant Issues Concerning Further Regulating Securities Repurchase Business". It is strictly forbidden to deal the short contract in securities repurchase. The financier is required to own 100% amount of treasury bills or financial debentures.

From the perspective of the expansion of market scale, the biggest development opportunity for China's national debt repurchase occurred after the establishment of the national unified lending market in Jan. 1996. Due to the eligibility issue for admission, a considerable number of entities cannot enter the lending market to obtain funds through lending, and they can only turn to the alternative market of government bond repurchase. Therefore, the repurchase transaction of government bonds after 1996 has experienced explosive growth. The annual volume of transactions exceeded RMB1 trillion. Under this circumstance, in Jun. 1997, in order to standardize the development of the borrowing market and prevent short-term lending funds from flowing into the long-term market to stabilize and develop the capital market, the

[1] Wang Guangqian, *30 Years of China's Economic Reform, Financial Reform Volume, 1978-2008*, Chongqing: Chongqing University Press, 2008, p.144.

[2] Wang Guangqian, Ying Zhanyu and Jiang Shiyin, *China Financial Reform: Historical Experience and Transformation Model*, Beijing: China Financial Publishing House, 2008, p.60.

PBOC decided that commercial banks should stop repurchasing and spot transactions at the Shenzhen and Shanghai Stock Exchange and all bond transactions should be transferred to the national inter-bank lending market, and must not be carried out off-site, and the bond custody should be transferred from the two major stock exchanges to the China Central Depository & Clearing limited company (CCDC) for centralized custody. Since then, in order to ensure the development of inter-bank bond transactions, the PBOC has successively formulated the "Interim Provisions on Inter-bank Bond Repurchase Business", "Inter-bank Bond Trading Rules", "Inter-bank Bond Settlement Rules", and "Inter-bank Bond Repurchase". Therefore, since Jun. 1997, China's national debt repo market has been divided into two parts: the interbank market and the exchange market.

In view of the fact that the inter-bank bond market has gathered the most well-funded state-owned commercial banks from the beginning, and the scope of participation in the market has been relaxed, the scale of government bond repurchases in the inter-bank bond market since 2000 has been enlarged. It has been getting bigger and bigger, and the exchange of government bond repo transactions is gradually shrinking, as shown in Table 4–5.

Table 4–5 Volume changes of bond repo market

Year	Interbank market (RMB billion)	Ratio (%)	Exchange market (RMB billion)	Ratio (%)
1997	30.7	2.49	1,202.9	97.51
1998	102.1	6.28	1,523.1	93.72
1999	394.9	24.46	1,219.5	75.54
2000	1,578.2	53.38	1,378.4	46.62
2001	4,013.3	71.72	1,582.2	28.28
2002	10,188.5	79.16	2,682.0	20.84
2003	11,720.3	67.72	5,585.6	32.28
2004	9,965.3	68.13	4,660.6	31.87
2005	16,507.0	86.88	2,491.9	13.12
2006	27,351.3	94.37	1,630.1	5.62
2007	46,286.8	96.13	1,861.5	3.87

Source: https://www.chinabond.com.cn/, www.csrc.gov.cn/: Wu Xiaoling, *Review and Prospect of China's Financial System Reform in the Past 30 Years*, Beijing: People's Publishing House, 2008, p.169.

4.5.4 Stock market

In 1991, at the beginning of the establishment of the Shanghai and Shenzhen Stock Exchanges, a model of "scale control + substantive approval" with a strong planned economy was adopted for the qualification of stock issuance and listing. That is, to ensure the smooth and orderly progress of the stock listing process as well as weakening the supply shock, the central government determines an annual quota in advance, and then distributes it in different departments, provinces and cities according to the principle of administrative distribution. This policy did not change until 2001. During the past 10 years, due to changes in related supporting policies, the issuance of the Chinese stock market has experienced two periods of changes.

From 1992 to 1996, the local government examined and approved the application for issuance of local enterprises within the scale of issuance determined by the state. The competent department of the central enterprises examined and approved the application for issuance of the central enterprises after consultation with the local government where the applicant is located. Local governments and the competent authority of central enterprises shall copy to the securities commission after making the approval decision. In the process of implementation, local governments and central enterprises have adopted the "sprinkle-and-paste" quota allocation method for the idea of distributing the limited issuance scale to as many enterprises as possible, which has caused the IPO enterprises increasing rapidly to some extent. But the size of the companies is small. Among the allocation of RMB5 billion (actually RMB4.525 billion) determined in 1993, the number of companies that have obtained listing qualifications was 127, and the average size of each company was only RMB35.6 million.

From 1997 to 2000, under the constraint of "capacity control, centralized mastery, and limited numbers", the China Securities Regulatory Commission (CSRC) reviewed the proposed listed companies under the total amount control. From a practical point of view, the number of companies allocated in the amount of RMB15 billion in 1996 was 207, and the number of companies allocated in the amount of RMB30 billion approved in 1997 was 279. The average size of IPO companies was significantly multiplied higher than before[1], see Table 4–6.

Strictly perform the "distribution control + substantive approval" issuance mode, which made the enterprises from the petroleum, chemical, machinery and other manufacturing industries in mainland China from 1991 to 2000 occupy an absolute advantage, while the financial industry companies, although small in number, were

[1] Wu Xiaoqiu, *China's Capital Market: From Institutional Reform to Strategic Transformation*, Beijing: Renmin University of China Press, 2007, p.106.

special. The nature of the enterprise has made it the second place in the distribution of assets. The number and proportion of enterprises in traditional industries such as wholesale and retail, transportation, and electric water are also high. The number of new industrial enterprises such as information technology and cultural communication and the proportion of assets occupied by them were all lower.

Table 4–6 Changes in the number of domestic listed companies (1990-2001)

Year	Domestic listed companies (A, B shares)	Listed companies in Shanghai Exchange (A, B shares)	Listed companies in Shenzhen Exchange (A, B shares)
1990	10	8	2
1991	14	8	6
1992	53	29	24
1993	183	106	77
1994	291	171	120
1995	323	188	135
1996	530	293	237
1997	745	383	362
1998	851	438	413
1999	949	484	465
2000	1,088	572	516
2001	1,160	646	514

Source: National Bureau of Statistics.

In 1993, the CSRC and the Hong Kong Stock Exchange signed a memorandum of cooperation to remove legal barriers for direct listing of China's mainland companies in overseas. Nearly 50 China's mainland companies were allowed to list in Hong Kong through the issuance of H-share, including 19 companies adopted the "A+H" listing model and raised a total of HK$137.201 billion in Hong Kong.

4.6 Reform of foreign exchange management system

With the deepening of China's economic system reform and the continuous expansion of opening up, the demand for foreign exchange transactions has become increasingly prominent. In 1979, the state reformed the foreign exchange distribution system and implemented the foreign exchange retention method. In Dec. 1985, the state set up the first foreign exchange swap center in Shenzhen to officially open the foreign exchange swap business. In 1993, the 14th National Congress of the CPC made a major decision to transform from a planned economic system to a socialist market economic system. In Nov. 1993, the "Decision of the Central Committee on Some Issues Concerning the Establishment of a Socialist Market Economic System" adopted by the Third Plenary Session of the 14th CPC Central Committee clearly stated: "Reform the foreign exchange management system and establish a market-based, managed float regime exchange rate system and the unified foreign exchange market and gradually make the renminbi a convertible currency".[1]

4.6.1 Main contents of foreign exchange management system reform

Since 1994, in accordance with the predetermined reform steps, China's foreign exchange management system has undergone major reforms, mainly including the following points.

4.6.1.1 Implement a bank settlement and sale system to establish and improve the foreign exchange market

(1) *Cancel the foreign exchange share cropping system and implement the foreign exchange settlement system*

All types of foreign exchange earnings of all domestic enterprises, institutions and social organizations must be transferred back to China in a timely manner; except for foreign-invested enterprises, foreign exchange income within the specified range must be sold to the designated foreign exchange bank at the listed exchange rate of the bank; foreign exchange retention, foreign exchange and foreign exchange quota management system were cancelled. On Mar.1, 1996, with the approval of the State Council, the PBOC authorized the State Administration of Foreign Exchange (SAFE) to organize pilot projects for forex settlement of foreign-invested enterprises in Shanghai, Jiangsu, Dalian and Shenzhen. Meanwhile, since Jan.1, 1994, the issuance of foreign exchange certificates has ceased, but can be continually circulated and used; they will be officially suspended on Jan.1, 1995, and will be exchanged by the bank at the official exchange rate before the unification; on the Jun.30, 1995, the exchange was stopped and the foreign exchange certificates were officially withdrawn from the historical stage.

---

[1] *Decision of the Central Committee of the Communist Party of China on Some Issues Concerning the Establishment of a Socialist Market Economic System*, Beijing: People's Publishing House, 1993.

(2) *Establish an interbank foreign exchange market*

In 1979, China reformed the foreign exchange distribution system and implemented the foreign exchange retention method, which objectively promoted the emergence of the foreign exchange adjustment market. Since 1980-1990, the open market for foreign exchange adjustment has been established, which has promoted the opening up and revitalizing domestic economy in China. On Apr.4, 1994, the China Foreign Exchange Trade System was established in Shanghai, and the inter-bank foreign exchange market was officially launched. On Jun.20, 1996, after the foreign-invested enterprises were included in the foreign exchange settlement system, all the adjustment centers in China were successively transformed into sub-centers of the Foreign Exchange Trade System. The foreign exchange adjustment market finally completed its historical mission and withdrew.[1]

The establishment of the national inter-bank foreign exchange market has greatly promoted the reform of China's exchange rate system and foreign trade. First, the nationwide inter-bank foreign exchange market was implemented in a network operation, which changed the situation in which the exchange rate of the renminbi market was not unified due to the decentralized market in the past, thus unifying the exchange rate of the renminbi market and laying a good foundation for realizing the exchange rate. Second, Through foreign exchange trade system, foreign exchange funds can be reasonably flowed between different regions and banks, effectively ensured the normal development of bank and enterprises' foreign exchange settlement business; third, further improved the macro-control of the central bank. As the China's central bank, the PBOC can realize the cooperation and implementation of monetary policy and foreign exchange policy through public operations in the foreign exchange market, and change the macro-control of financial regulation from direct to indirect.

As it should be, there is still a certain gap between China's foreign exchange market and the internationally standardized foreign exchange market during this period. For example, the currency of foreign exchange transactions and trading instruments were single, the regulations on foreign exchange transactions and operations were still imperfect and unsound, and the foreign exchange intervention mechanism needs to be further improved. In the meantime, China's inter-bank foreign exchange market adopts mandatory foreign exchange on-exchange transactions, that is, all transactions must be

[1] Hu Hai'ou, *Reform and Development of China's Financial System*, Shanghai: Fudan University Press, 2004, p.236.

conducted through exchanges, and the exchanges will collectively call auction and concentrate on liquidation. In practice, this kind of trading system has problems on high transaction costs, low efficiency, etc. This was the place where the reform of the foreign exchange system needs to continue be improved.

4.6.1.2 Implementing renminbi convertible under current account

Renminbi current account convertibility refers to the cancellation of exchange restrictions on current account foreign exchange payments and transfers. In 1994, the foreign exchange management system became the conditional exchange under the renminbi current account. In order to smoothly realize the convertibility of the renminbi current account as soon as possible, the SAFE began a new round of reforms in 1996. On Jan.29, 1996, the State Council promulgated the "Regulations on the Administration of Foreign Exchange of the People's Republic of China", which was officially implemented from Apr. 1 to eliminate certain exchange restrictions on non-operating transactions in current accounts. On May 13, 1996, the SAFE issued the "Measures for the Foreign Exchanges transaction by Domestic Residents", which was officially implemented from Jul. 1, eliminating the exchange restrictions on private use of foreign currency, expanding the scope of foreign exchange, and improving the standard of foreign exchange. The foreign exchange purchase requirements exceeding the standard can be purchased after the authenticity of the SAFE. On Jun.20, 1996, Dai Xianglong, former Governor of the PBOC, announced at the meeting of the National Directors of the SAFE branches that since Jul.1, 1996, foreign-invested enterprises have implemented the bank exchange settlement system, and promulgated the "Regulation of Foreign Exchange Settlement, Remittance and Payment Management", which cancelled the remaining exchange restrictions of other current accounts, and met the requirements of article 8 of the "Agreement of the International Monetary Fund" in advance.

On Jan.14, 1997, the State Council revised the "Regulations on the Administration of Foreign Exchanges of the People's Republic of China", and adopted the form of legislation to determine the implementation of renminbi current account convertibility in China and cancelled the exchange restrictions on international payments and transfers under the current items such as import and export of goods and service trade, but still subject to authenticity review under the international practice.

4.6.1.3 Realize the unification of exchange rates and establish a managed floating exchange rate system

After the reform and opening up, the renminbi was implemented a dual official exchange rate in 1981, that is, a dual exchange rate system between the internal settlement price of trade and the non-trade open price. In 1988, the foreign tradings were implemented the contract responsibility system, the proportion of foreign exchange retention continued to expand, and the foreign exchange adjustment market was established in various places, thus forming a dual exchange rate system in which the official exchange rate and the exchange rate of the foreign exchange adjustment market coexisted, and because the foreign exchange rates of the various exchange adjustment markets were not the same, the market exchange rates were priced in different places, forming multiple exchange rates.

From Jan.1, 1994, China stopped issuing official exchange rates, and the exchange rate of the foreign exchange adjustment center was the sole renminbi exchange rate. A single, managed floating exchange rate system based on market supply and demand was implemented. The renminbi exchange rate at the time of the unification is US$1 to RMB8.7, as shown in Table 4–7.

Table 4–7 Exchange rate from renminbi to US dollar (1993-1994)

Year	Official rate (US$ / RMB)	Market exchange rate (US$ / RMB)	Weighted average exchange rate (US$ / RMB)
Jan. 1993	5.22	7.00	6.64
Feb. 1993	5.22	8.34	7.72
Mar. 1993	5.22	8.20	7.60
Apr. 1993	5.70	8.20	7.70
May 1993	5.70	8.20	7.70
Jun. 1993	5.70	10.07	9.20
Jul. 1993	5.70	11.20	10.10
Aug. 1993	5.70	10.70	9.70
Sep. 1993	5.70	10.00	9.14
Oct. 1993	5.70	9.00	8.34
Nov. 1993	5.80	8.90	8.28
Dec. 1993	5.80	8.70	8.12
Average in 1993	5.60	9.04	8.35
Unification in 1994	8.70		
Depreciation range (%)	3.98		

Note: The weight of the official exchange rate in the weighted average exchange rate is 0.2, and the weight of the market exchange rate is 0.8.

Source: Yi Gang, *On the Financial Reform of China*, Beijing: The Commercial Press, 2009, p.219.

After the exchange rate reform, the long-term overvaluation of the renminbi exchange rate has been changed, the exchange rate level has become more reasonable, and the trend of long-term small decline has changed, entering a relatively flexible floating status. During the Asian financial crisis, in order to curb the outflow of foreign exchange funds and prevent the further spread of the crisis, the Chinese government promised that the renminbi will not depreciate and narrow the floating range of the renminbi exchange rate, which objectively caused the limited and nearly fixed exchange rate fluctuation of the renminbi against the US dollar since 1998, which can not truly reflect changes in market supply and demand, it is difficult to adapt to the needs of China's rapid economic development and structural adjustment, and it is urgent to further improve and reform the renminbi exchange rate formation mechanism.

4.6.1.4 Reform of foreign exchange reserve management

For a long time, China has implemented a policy of basic balance of foreign exchange receipts and payments and a slight surplus. The amount of foreign exchange reserves is not large and is managed by the Bank of China. The Bank of China used the reserve funds together with its own funds and did not establish a complete foreign exchange reserve management system. With the in-depth development of reforms, China's foreign exchange reserves have increased substantially. In 1982, China's foreign exchange reserves stood at US$6.986 billion, and in 1994 it increased to US$51.62 billion. By 1996, it had doubled to US$105.029 billion. See Table 4–8.

Table 4–8 China's forex reserve (1982-1996)

Year	Forex reserve (US$ billion)	Year on year increase (%)
1982	6.986	—
1983	8.901	27.41
1984	8.220	-7.65
1985	2.644	-67.83
1986	2.072	-21.63
1987	2.923	41.07
1988	3.372	15.36
1989	5.550	64.59
1990	11.093	99.87
1991	21.712	95.73
1992	19.443	-10.45

(continued)

Year	Forex reserve (US$ billion)	Year on year increase (%)
1993	21.199	9.03
1994	51.620	143.50
1995	73.597	42.57
1996	105.029	42.71

Source: National Bureau of Statistics.

In order to meet the need for sustained and rapid growth of foreign exchange reserves, the State Council officially authorized the SAFE to operate foreign exchange reserves in 1994. The Foreign Exchange Department of the SAFE changed its name to the Foreign Exchange Reserve Division, which is integrated responsible for the operation and management of the national foreign exchange reserves in accordance with the management objectives on "safety, liquidity and profitability".

With the deepening of reforms, the Forex reserve management has been continuously improved, and various basic constructions have been made great progress, including systematic and programmed tracking and analyzing the economic situation of different markets and countries, and response timely and rapidly; real-time monitoring and timely reporting asset risk status, strictly managing and tracking reports of counterparties; strengthening support systems for clearing, accounting, and technology, and beginning to establish multi-level and rigorous middle-and-back office business frameworks.

4.6.2 The significance of the reform of foreign exchange management system

After the major reform of the foreign exchange management system in 1994, China established a new system of foreign exchange management, which is an important indicator for China to expand its opening up and improve its openness. It would improve the investment environment of China, establish a good investment image and promote the development of an export-oriented economy. It is of great significance to accelerate the pace of integration of China's economy with the international economy and to establish a financial system that meets the requirements of the socialist market economic system.[1]

First, in the realm of foreign exchange, the market mechanism under the state's

[1] Shang Ming, *50 Years of Finance in New China*, Beijing: China Financial & Economic Publishing House, 2000, P.519.

macroeconomic regulation and control was initially formed. The renminbi exchange rate system based on market supply and demand was established, and the plan and approve was cancelled in the foreign exchange distribution, giving full play to the role of the market in resource allocation and laying the foundation for the free exchange of renminbi.

The second is to create a good environment for China's foreign economic and trade development. The new foreign exchange management system has gradually moved closer together with international rules, improving China's investment environment, accelerating the pace of attracting foreign investment, and raising the enthusiasm of foreign-invested enterprises in production and operation. It thus promoted international exchange of goods and services, expanded economic and technological cooperation between China and the rest of the world, and promoted the development of foreign economic relations and trade.

The third is to further promote the rapid development of China's national economy. After the reform of the foreign exchange management system, the domestic market and the international market will be more integrated, and enterprises will be encouraged to invest in accordance with comparative advantages, develop production, make production and investment decisions more in line with their comparative advantages, and promote China's economy in terms of product prices, operating mechanisms, technical levels, and industrial structure, which would accelerate its integration with the international community and accelerate the development of domestic industries toward modernization.

The foreign exchange management system reform fully exerted the role of market mechanism in the allocation of foreign exchange resources, improved the operation mechanism of the foreign exchange market and the renminbi exchange rate, improved the macro-control ability of the central bank, and accelerated the establishment and improvement of the socialist market economic system, which will be in favor of promoting the entire national economy to develope continuously, quickly and healthily.

4.6.3 Problems in the reform of foreign exchange management system

The reform of foreign exchange management system in 1994 was a milestone in the reform of China's foreign exchange management system. Its success promoted the rapid development of China's import and export trade, greatly improved the international balance of payments, basically stabilized the renminbi exchange rate, and rapidly increased the country's foreign exchange reserves. However, there are still some shortages and problems in the reform of the foreign exchange system.

(1) *There is a big gap between the renminbi exchange rate formation mechanism and the predetermined reform target*

The reform goal of the renminbi exchange rate formation mechanism determined by the reform of the foreign exchange system in 1994 was to abolish the original dual-track system of the renminbi exchange rate and implement a single, managed floating exchange rate system based on market supply and demand. Such a reform direction was correct and is in line with the needs of China's economic reform and development. However, in practice, the PBOC had strictly controlled over the foreign exchange market and only allows foreign exchange transactions between a small number of designated foreign exchange banks, resulting in the "excessive demand" in the foreign exchange market. In order to stabilize the renminbi exchange rate, especially during the Asian financial crisis, the PBOC directly intervened in the market and bought a large amount of surplus foreign exchange from the foreign exchange market, strictly controlling the formation and fluctuation of the renminbi exchange rate. "The management floating" was practically shrinked and in turn the renminbi exchange rate could not accurately reflect market signals, which was unfavorable to the development of foreign trade. In such an environment, once the convertibility under the capital account is released, it may lead to the imbalance of China's foreign exchange supply and demand and the confusion of the foreign exchange market. Together with the actual situation of the country's overall economic situation and management capacity, it is predestined that the renminbi can only preliminarily be convertible under the recurrent projects, and could not fully liberalize capital projects.

(2) *The bank's foreign exchange settlement system lacks the necessary flexibility, which is not conducive to giving full play to the subjective initiative of enterprises*

In 1994, the foreign exchange system reform abolished the foreign exchange retention and payment of domestic enterprises, and replaced it with the foreign exchange settlement system of designated banks, instead of the central bank's foreign exchange settlement and distribution system, which is a historical progress. It enabled enterprises to get enough local currency funds for production and operation in time after selling foreign exchange, which changes the situation that some of the retained funds were slowly distributed after the payments of foreign exchanges, and the simplified procedures for purchasing foreign exchanges also facilitate the external payment of enterprises. In practice, the bank's foreign exchange settlement system strictly stipulated the cancellation of all foreign exchange accounts of domestic enterprises, and their foreign exchange income must be fully sold to designated banks of foreign exchange. If the enterprise needs foreign exchange to pay externally, it will be purchased from the designated bank of foreign exchange with the relevant documents. Due to the lack of necessary flexibility, this system has hampered the production and operation activities of domestic enterprises, which is not conducive to giving full play to the subjective initiative of enterprises.

(3) *The unstandardized foreign exchange market is not conducive to the country's macroeconomic regulation and control*

The sound foreign exchange market organizational system consists of a central bank, a foreign exchange bank, a client (enterprise) and a foreign exchange broker. These four units cooperate with each other and constrain each other to ensure that the foreign exchange market trading activities are carried out in a reasonable and orderly manner.[1] The participants of the China Foreign Exchange Trade System were only the central bank and the designated foreign exchange banks. The enterprises had no right to participate in the foreign exchange market trading activities, and there were almost no foreign exchange brokers. Such an foreign exchange market organizational system is obviously not conducive to the development of China's foreign exchange market. At the same time, China's Foreign Exchange Trade System had fewer currencies, and the trading methods were mainly for spot exchange trading, and lack of other trading methods, and the foreign exchange market operation was basically in a closed operation status. This is not conducive to the development of China's foreign exchange market, nor can it create a more favorable local and foreign currency conversion environment for the further integration of China's economy and the international economy.

The reform of the foreign exchange management system since 1994, especially the realization of the convertibility of the renminbi current account in 1996, initially established a foreign exchange management system framework suitable for the national conditions and compatible with the socialist market economic system, which is an important historical milestone in the reform of China's foreign exchange management system. Through a series of reforms, the basic position of the market in the allocation of foreign exchange resources was initially established, which greatly facilitated the economic development of foreign trade and actively supported the rapid development of exports in China's foreign trade.

---

[1] Cao Fengqi, *China's Financial Reform, Development and Internationalization*, Beijing: Economic Science Press, 1999, p.322.

Chapter 5
A New Era of China's Financial System Reform

With China's participation in the World Trade Organization (WTO) and the opening up of financial markets, China's financial industry needs to adopt a new round of financial system reform in response to financial globalization under the conditions of an open economy, and establish an orderly competitive financial market to cope with international economic changes and continually to adjust and improve financial policies, further promote the development of financial markets and the improvement of financial market system, promote financial marketization and internationalization, and make it suitable for the needs of economic development in the new stage.

In Feb. 2002, the central government held a national financial work conference, which clarified that the main tasks of the financial system reform in the new era were: further improve the modern financial institution system, market system, supervision system and regulation system, and strive to achieve effective financial supervision and regulation, sound operating mechanism of the financial enterprises, significantly improve asset quality and operating efficiency, basically improve financial market order, significantly increase level of financial services and the quality of the financial team, and comprehensively enhance competitiveness of China's financial industry.[1]

The characteristics of the financial system reform in the new era are the simultaneous development of commercial banking reform, foreign exchange management reform, rural financial system reform, financial market reform, and financial opening up. The results of financial reforms during this period were striking. China's foreign exchange reserves grew rapidly, and foreign exchange reserves ranked first in the world. The listing of state-owned commercial banks, the reform of the shareholding structure of the capital market, the reform of the renminbi exchange rate formation mechanism, and the issuance of short-term financing bonds were the symbols for China's financial

[1] Xinhua News Agency, "National Financial Work Conference Held in Beijing", *People's Daily*, Feb.8, 2002.

system reform further moving towards marketization and internationalization.

5.1 Deepen the reform of the central bank system

With the establishment and improvement of the socialist market economic system, the role of the PBOC as a central bank in the macro-control system will become more prominent. In order to further strengthen the supervision of the banking industry and enable the PBOC to better exercise the functions of the central bank, the PBOC had conducted the third functional adjustment.

5.1.1 Issues in the central bank system

After years of reform of the central bank system, as the central Bank of China, the PBOC is now a state agency that implements monetary policy and conducts macroeconomic regulation and control. Although the central bank system reform in the 1980s and the gradual improvement by the turn of the century, the characteristics of the original old system of the PBOC are still obvious, and there are still some problems to be solved, especially in the financial system, there is still large gap from the requirements of a mature market economy system. As far as the current central bank system is concerned, there are still many outstanding problems.

(1) *It is difficult for the central bank to implement monetary policy and carry out macroeconomic regulation and control independently according to law*

The independence of the central bank is mainly manifested in its monetary policy autonomy, and its independence from the Ministry of Finance, other government ministries, and local governments. According to the "Law of People's Republic of China on the People's Bank of China", the PBOC exercises monetary policy independently under the leadership of the State Council. However, since the head office is still under the direct control of the central government, some major decisions of financial issues are not made by the Monetary Policy Committee but by the State Council. In this way, the use of monetary policy is often passively followed by the government's claims, it is difficult to fully and effectively reflect the objective laws of the currency movement, and it is more difficult to ensure the continuity and effectiveness of monetary policy implementation. In terms of macroeconomic regulation and control, it is also a subsidiary body of the government and cannot relatively perform its duties independently.

(2) *The central bank still undertakes part of the financial supervision function*

In the process of reform and opening up, China's financial supervision function was performed by the PBOC. After years of reform, the central bank is no longer regulating the banking, securities and insurance industries. The supervision function of the policy banks, commercial banks, trust and investment companies, rural credit cooperatives, and other deposit-type financial institutions conducted by the central bank in past era have been transfered to the China Banking Regulatory Commission (CBRC), but the PBOC still has to undertake some kinds of financial supervision functions. These functions mainly include financial supervision related to compliance regulation such as monetary policy, prevention and resolution of financial risks, regulation of financial markets, and anti-money laundering. Such heavy regulatory tasks and excessive regulatory scope not only seriously affect the effectiveness of central bank supervision, but also affect the implementation of the main duties of the central bank in formulating and implementing monetary policy.

In short, after years of reform, China has established a central bank system that meets the requirements for the development of the socialist market economic system. However, due to the influence of the traditional system, China's current central bank system still has many problems, and further reforms are needed. In particular, there is still a long way to go to establish a central bank system that is compatible with economic and financial globalization and in line with international practices.

5.1.2 Establishment of the CBRC

In Mar. 2003, according to the "Opinions on Deepening the Administrative System and Institutional Reform" adopted by the Second Plenary Session of the 16th CPC Central Committee and the "Organizational Reform Plan of the State Council" adopted by the National People's Congress, the PBOC transferred the functions of financial supervision to the newly established CBRC to strip the banking supervision operation off from the PBOC.

The "Opinions on Deepening the Administrative Management System and Institutional Reform" clearly states that the PBOC no longer assumes the market access and operational supervision functions for banks, asset management companies, trust and investment companies and other deposit-type institutions. The PBOC is mainly responsible for strengthening monetary policy, monitoring financial market, formulating financial institution operation rules, macro-controlling financial industry, preventing and mitigating systemic risks, and continually performing the functions on good foreign exchange management, currency issuance, managerial treasury, payment and liquidation, legal system construction and statistical investigation.

In Dec. 2003, the state revised the "Law of the People's Republic of China on the People's Bank of China" in accordance with the needs of the development of the situation. The revised "Law of the People's Republic of China on the People's Bank of China" further stipulates the functions of the Central Bank. At this moment, the modern central bank system has been gradually improved.

5.1.3 Further deepen the reform of the central bank system

In order to meet the needs of a mature market system, we should further deepen the reform of the central bank system.

(1) *Further strengthen the independence of the central bank in implementing monetary policy*

The independence of the central bank actually involves the relationship between the central bank and the government. It is related to whether the monetary policy can be scientifically formulated, whether it can maintain the stability of the currency, and ultimately to the stability of the national economy. The more the market economy develops, the more it needs to play the role of finance. To play the role of finance in promoting economic development, it is objectively necessary for the central bank to have independent power to implement monetary policy. The stability of the value of the currency is closely related to the independence of the central bank. According to the economic development situation, the central bank can tighten or loosen monetary policy at any time to provide a moderate growth rate of money supply for economic development. Since the reform and opening up, the success of China's financial system reform has fully proved this point. In order to ensure the relative independence of the central bank, it is necessary to further regulate the relationship between the government and the central bank and reduce the intervention from subjective factors in the formulation and implementation of monetary policy.[1]

(2) *Further transformation of the financial supervision function of the central bank*

Since the establishment of the financial supervision system of separate operations and separate supervision, how the central bank handle the relationship with the China

[1] Jiang Shiyin, *Rational Thinking on China's Financial System Reform in 30 Years*, Beijing: Jinghua Press, 2009, pp.176-177.

Banking Regulatory Commission, the China Securities Regulatory Commission and the China Insurance Regulatory Commission, especially how to coordinate and cooperate between them is a question worth pondering. The central government's future regulatory point should be on standardized management. Therefore, to further deepen the reform of the central bank system, the focus should be on establishing financial risk prevention mechanisms and standardized management. With the formation of the financial division supervision system, the financial supervision functions undertaken by the central bank should be continuously transformed, so that it mainly implements monetary policy and conducts macroeconomic regulation and control. Financial macro-control is an important part of macroeconomic regulation and control. Its focus is to stabilize the currency and create a good financial environment for the sustained, rapid and healthy development of the national economy. Financial macro-control is an important function of the central bank and how well it performs has a direct impact and influence on economic development. Since the indirect regulation means have high requirements on market conditions, the indirectization of financial macro-control needs to be coordinated with the further development of the financial market.

(3) *Further improve the central bank's financial macro-control methods*

The macroeconomic regulation and control is the main regulation and control method of the market economy. The development of the market economy requires the establishment and improvement of a macro-control system mainly using financial means and indirect regulation. Since the reform and opening up, the macroeconomic regulation and control methods have undergone significant changes. In 1984, the deposit reserve system was established; in 1986, the rediscounting business was launched; in 1996, the open market business was launched, and in 1998, the loan quota control was abolished, and the financial macro-control measures gradually changed from direct means to indirect means.[1] With the deepening of economic system reform and financial system reform, the central bank is more indirectly regulating the economy by means of statutory reserve ratio, rediscount rate, open market business, interest rates, exchange rates, etc, that is, using economic means to conduct macroeconomic regulation and control. This kind of macro-control aims to stabilize the currency value and promote the rapid development of the economy. To deepen the

[1] Jiang Shiyin, *Rational Thinking on China's Financial System Reform*, Beijing: China Financial & Economic Publishing House, 2009, p.166.

reform of the financial system, it is necessary to further improve the financial macro-control methods carried out by the central bank.

5.2 Joint–stock system reform and interest rate marketization of state–owned commercial banks

Facing the threats of competition from foreign financial institutions after joining the World Trade Organization, in order to establish a more complete Chinese financial system, and an effective micro-subject of the financial market and cooperate with the macro-level of the economic system reform, China began to carry out joint-stock reform of commercial banks trying to make it a real market player. At the same time, as the most important factor affecting the banking business, interest rates are gradually becoming market-oriented.

5.2.1 The background of the shareholding system reform of state-owned commercial banks

After entering the 21st century, the tremendous changes in the economic situation at home and abroad have prompted the comprehensive reform of China's state-owned commercial banks. Around 2000, the non-performing assets of China's state-owned commercial banks were too high, corporate governance was poor, and risks increased.

The National Financial Work Conference held in Feb. 2002 clearly stated that the joint-stock reform of state-owned commercial banks is an important exploration of various forms of public ownership and is the top priority of China's financial industry reform. The reform direction is to carry out the shareholding system reform according to the requirements of the modern financial enterprise system. The qualified state-owned commercial banks can be reorganized into state-controlled joint-stock commercial banks and perfected the corporate governance structure. The good condition ones can be listed.

The "Decision of the Central Committee on Some Issues Concerning the Improvement of the Socialist Market Economy" adopted by the Third Plenary Session of the 16th CPC Central Committee once again clearly stated that state-owned commercial banks must be modern financial enterprises with capital-rich, tightly controlled internally, safe in operation, good in service and good efficiency, selecting state-owned commercial banks with conditions to implement shareholding system reform, speed up the disposal of non-performing assets, enrich capital, and create condition for listing.[1]

In 2003, the State Council established the Leading Group for the Reform of the Shareholding System of State-owned Commercial Banks and decided to select Bank of China (BOC) and China Construction Bank (CCB) to carry out the pilot reform of the shareholding system. The overall goal of the reform is to focus on the reforming management system, improving the governance structure, transforming the operation mechanism, and promoting high performance, and in the transitional period of China's accession to the WTO, most of the state-owned commercial banks would be transformed into modern joint-stock commercial banks with sufficient capital, strict internal control, safe operation, good service and efficiency, and international competitiveness. The reform of the shareholding system has modified the property rights structure and thus broke the soft budget constraint, which will fundamentally improve the operation of state-owned commercial banks and realize the historic transformation of state-owned commercial banks from the traditional system to the modern enterprise system.

5.2.2 The process of state-owned commercial bank shareholding system reform

The shareholding system reform of state-owned commercial banks has experienced three processes of "financial restructuring-corporate governance reform-public listing".

(1) *Financial restructuring*

Financial restructuring is the premise and basis for the reform of the shareholding system of state-owned commercial banks, because only the replacement of credit capital with real capital and the capitalization of the country's credit can break the single state-owned property rights structure. Through financial restructuring, the problem of capital shortage and soft budget constraint, also called the property rights issue, can be solved with mainly two financial restructuring methods. The first is through the injection of foreign exchange by Huijin Company to enrich the capital. In order to transform CCB and BOC into joint-stock commercial banks before the transition period of the WTO accession in 2006, the CPC Central Committee and the State Council decided to use state foreign exchange reserves and some national gold reserves to inject capital into state-owned commercial banks. On Dec.16, 2003, the

[1] Decision of the Central Committee of the Communist Party of China on Some Issues Concerning the Improvement of the Socialist Market Economy, *People's Daily*, Oct. 14, 2003.

Central Huijin Investment Co., Ltd (Huijin) was established as a wholly state-owned investment holding company, which was authorized by the state to make equity investments in state-owned major financial enterprises. On Dec.30, 2003, the central government gave the CCB and BOC a capital injection of US$22.5 billion through Huijin. In Apr. 2005, ICBC accepted Huijin's US$15 billion capital injection, while the Ministry of Finance retained its original capital of ICBC of RMB124 billion to transfer doubtful loans and assets of the loss. On Oct.29, 2008, Huijin Company[1] injected RMB130 billion worth of foreign exchange assets into the Agricultural Bank of China (ABC). The Ministry of Finance will retain the original capital of ABC of RMB130 billion as the base date for the restructuring.

The second is to supplement the subsidiary capital by issuing renminbi subordinated bonds. From July to December 2004, CCB issued a total of RMB40 billion of 10-year subordinated bonds within three times. With the approval of the CBRC, the above subordinated bonds can be counted in the subsidiary capital of the bank. In 2004 and 2005, BOC issued a series of subordinated bonds totaling RMB60 billion. On Aug.19, 2005, with the approval of the PBOC and the CBRC, ICBC issued a total of RMB35 billion in the first phase of the subordinated bonds in the inter-bank bond market to supplement the capital.

During the financial restructuring, the state also wrote off and stripped off the non-performing assets of state-owned commercial banks. The two pilot banks, CCB and BOC, firstly wrote off all loss loans and non-credit assets losses with capital, reserves and profits for the year, and then stripped all doubtful loans off to financial asset management companies, then RMB280 billion of non-performing assets were also striped off in 2004. ICBC also stripped off non-performing assets by transferring assets of the loss and doubtful loans. As of the end of 2005, the non-performing loan ratios of BOC, CCB and ICBC fell to 4.62%, 3.84% and 4. 69%, respectively, and the provision coverage ratios were 80.55%, 66.78% and 54.20% respectively. On Nov.21, 2008, with the approval of the Ministry of Finance, the Agricultural Bank of China, based on Dec.31, 2007, stripped off non-performing assets of RMB815.695 billion on the book value.[2]

---

[1] On Sep. 29, 2007, China Investment Co., Ltd. was established. Huijin Company was incorporated as a subsidiary and continued to operate. On behalf of the state as a funder, it held long-term state-owned shares of state-owned commercial banks.

[2] Sun Xiaoyi, "Research on property rights reform of state-owned holding commercial banks", *Times finance*, 2014(9), pp. 81-82.

After the financial restructuring, Bank of China was reorganized as Bank of China Co., Ltd. on Aug.26, 2004. On Sep.17, 2004, China Construction Bank was respectively reorganized into China Construction Bank Investment Co., Ltd. and China Construction Bank Corporation. On Oct.28, 2005, Industrial and Commercial Bank of China was reorganized as Industrial and Commercial Bank of China Co., Ltd. On Jan.16, 2009, the Agricultural Bank of China Co., Ltd. was established, marking the completion of the shareholding system transformation of the four state-owned commercial banks of China. They were transformed from state-owned commercial banks into state-controlled joint-stock commercial banks.

(2) *Corporate governance reform*

Corporate governance reform is the core and key to the shareholding reform of state-owned commercial banks. In order to strengthen the corporate governance reform of state-owned commercial banks and ensure the real effects of the shareholding system reform, the CBRC promulgated the "Guidelines for Corporate Governance and Relevant Supervision of State-owned Commercial Banks" on Apr.18, 2006, stipulated that state-owned commercial banks shall be based on the "Company Laws of the People's Republic of China" to establish a general meeting of shareholders, the board of directors, the board of supervisors and senior management, formulate the bank charter that reflects the requirements of the modern financial enterprise system, and clarify the duties and responsibilities of the general meeting of shareholders, the board of directors, the board of supervisors and senior management, as well as directors, supervisors, senior managers, to combine the rights, responsibilities and benefits together, and to establish the mechanisms of scientific and efficient decision-making, implementation and supervision to ensure the independent operation of the parties, effective checks and balances.

The premise of corporate governance reform is to solve the soft budget constraint, that is, the property rights issue, and the diversification of property rights is the premise to solve the problem of soft budget constraint. The introduction of strategic investors is an effective way to realize the diversification of property rights. Therefore, a notable feature of this shareholding system reform is the reform of the state-owned bank property rights system. The introduction of institutional investors, strategic investors and public investors, broke the state-owned sole proprietorship structure and truly turning state-owned commercial banks into modern commercial bank. After the introduction of strategic investors by state-owned commercial banks, in the case of diversification of investment subjects and stakeholders, it is impossible for state finances to unlimitedly be responsible to the operating losses of commercial banks. This not only eliminates the moral hazard for commercial banks' counting on national assistance, but also legally rules out the possibility of the country's "blood transfusion" any more, and lays a solid foundation for the listing. In Dec. 2003, the "Measures for the Administration of Chinese Financial Institutions Invested by Overseas Financial Institutions" issued by the CBRC increased the maximum proportion of investment by a single foreign financial institution to Chinese-funded financial institutions from 15% to 20%.

BOC, CCB and ICBC signed strategic investment and cooperation agreements with overseas strategic investors in mid-August, mid-June and early July, and Jan.27, 2006. The strategic cooperation projects mainly involved corporate governance, risk management, asset management, non-performing loan management, treasury operations, corporate and investment banking, and employee training. See Table 5–1 for the introduction of overseas strategic investors by domestic banks.

Table 5–1 List of overseas strategic investors introduced by domestic banks

Category	Time	Domestic banks	Foreign institutions	Shares (%)
State-owned commercial bank	Aug. 2005	CCB	American Bank	8.52
State-owned commercial bank	Aug. 2005	CCB	Fullerton Financial Holdings Pte. Ltd.	5.88
State-owned commercial bank	Aug. 2005	BOC	The Royal Bank of Scotland	10.00
State-owned commercial bank	Oct. 2005	BOC	United Bank of Switzerland	1.61
State-owned commercial bank	Oct. 2005	BOC	Asian Development Bank	0.24
State-owned commercial bank	Dec. 2005	BOC	Fullerton Financial Holdings Pte. Ltd.	5.00
State-owned commercial bank	Dec. 2005	ICBC	Group investment of Goldman Sachs, Allianz Group, American Express	10.00
Joint-stock bank	Sep. 2003	Shanghai Pudong Development Bank	Citi Bank	4.65
Joint-stock bank	Sep. 2003	China Minsheng Bank	International Finance Corporation	1.22
Joint-stock bank	Mar. 2004	Industrial Bank	Hang Seng Bank	15.98
Joint-stock bank	Mar. 2004	Industrial Bank	Government of Singapore Investment Corp	5.00

(continued)

Category	Time	Domestic banks	Foreign institutions	Shares (%)
Joint-stock bank	Mar. 2004	Industrial Bank	International Finance Corporation	4.00
Joint-stock bank	Aug. 2004	Bank of Communications	HSBC	19.90
Joint-stock bank	Sep. 2004	Shenzhen Development Bank	Newbridge Capital	17.89
Joint-stock bank	Nov. 2004	China Minsheng Bank	Temasek Holdings Private Limited	4.55
Joint-stock bank	Oct. 2005	Huaxia Bank	Deutsche Bank, Sal. Oppenheim	14.00
Joint-stock bank	Dec. 2005	China Bohai Bank	Standard Chartered Bank	19.99

Source: Wang Guangqian, Ying Zhanyu and Jiang Shiyin, *China Financial Reform: Historical Experience and Transformation Model*, Beijing: China Financial Publishing House, 2008, p.50.

In 2006, the three pilot banks further improved corporate governance, perfected the internal control system, changed the operating mechanism, implemented comprehensive risk management, increased internal integration, reformed the organizational structure and business processes of the branches, implemented agreements with strategic investors, and strengthened strategic cooperation in innovation and risk management. After the reform, the financial indicators such as capital adequacy ratio, asset quality and profitability of the three banks improved significantly before the restructuring, so did the financial situation.

(3) *Public listing*

Financial restructuring and the introduction of strategic investors laid the foundation for the final realization of the listing of state-owned commercial banks. Public listing is an important means to consolidate the reform results and enhance market constraints, and is the deepening and sublimation of the shareholding system reform of state-owned commercial banks.

After completing financial restructuring and establishing a joint-stock company, China Construction Bank, Bank of China and Industrial and Commercial Bank of China continued to improve corporate governance, strengthen internal control and risk management, and steadily promote strategic investment and listing. In Oct. 2005, CCB successfully listed in Hong Kong. In June and July 2006, BOC successfully issued H shares and A shares in Hong Kong and China's mainland respectively, raising funds of HK$86.7 billion and RMB20 billion respectively. On Oct.27, 2006, ICBC successfully listed in Hong Kong and Shanghai simultaneously with the simultaneous issuance and simultaneous listing of A+H shares, raising funds of HK$124.9 billion and RMB46.4 billion respectively, becoming the world's largest IPO of the time.

Listing on domestic and overseas capital markets, the state-holding commercial banks have had following benefits: first, they expand the financing channels, and further improve their shareholding structure; second, they increase the core capital and capital adequacy ratio in consequence; third, they maintain the status of state-owned nature of state-owned commercial banks. On the basis of widening social capital, they expand the control scope of state-owned capital, reduce the risk of state-owned capital, and maximize the operational efficiency of state-owned capital; fourth, the market constraints and external supervision, as well as the dual regulation of the banking industry and the securities industry, have prompted the listed banks to increase transparency, operate in accordance with market-based benefits, promote separation of government and enterprises, and improve corporate governance.

5.2.3 The result of the joint-stock system reform of state-owned commercial banks

(1) *Significant progress in corporate governance reform of state-owned banks*

First, the boundaries of responsibilities between the shareholders' meeting, the board of directors, the board of supervisors and the senior management are becoming clearer, and a working mechanism that is fully coordinated and effective checks and balances is gradually being established. The distribution of power at all levels is more scientific and reasonable. Second, the construction of the board of directors has been strengthened, and the board's major strategic decision-making role has been effectively played. Third, the supervisory role of the board of supervisors and the senior management has been continuously brought into play.

(2) *The fundamental transformation of the development strategy and business philosophy of state-owned banks*

State-owned banks no longer use the traditional model of deposit growth rate, loan growth rate, market share, etc. as performance indicators, but fully consider the provisions and bad debt write-off in performance appraisal, pay attention to the calculation of credit costs, and gradually take the risk-adjusted return on capital as the benchmark for the assessment of branches and departments. The bank value and the interests of shareholders are maximized as the business objectives.

(3) *State-owned banks' main performance benchmarks have improved significantly*

In terms of capital adequacy, asset quality and profitability, they have greatly improved than that of before the joint-stock system reform. As of the end of Dec. 2006, the average return on assets (ROA) and average return on equity (ROE) of the share reform banks reached 0.7% and 15%, respectively, while the average of these two major indicators in international banks was around 1% and 14% respectively.[1]. Through the joint-stock system reform, the bank's operating performance has improved significantly.

(4) *The transparency of information disclosure by state-owned banks continues to increase*

After the banks joint-stock system reform, information disclosure of commercial banks should be reviewed by the Board of Directors and the Board of Supervisors of the Bank, and must meet all the requirements of the Hong Kong Stock Exchange (HKSE) and the CBRC and the China Securities Regulatory Commission (CSRC), as well as the audit of external auditors and the legal assessment of external lawyers. The information disclosure of the joint-stock reform bank has reached all the standards of overseas listed companies. Its authenticity and timeliness have been recognized by international investors, and the external binding force formed by information disclosure has been further enhanced.

5.2.4 Issues of the joint-stock system reform of state-owned commercial banks

It must be recognized that the reform of the joint-stock system of China's state-owned commercial banks is far from over, and the joint-stock reform cannot resolve all the problems. Compared with some advanced international banks, state-owned commercial banks still have many shortcomings in terms of system and mechanism. In particular, many deep-level problems reflected by higher non-performing loan ratios have not been completely resolved. The success of the reform of state-owned commercial banks will be further improved by the bank's governance structure, internal management and financial ecological environment.

(1) *Low quality of credit assets*

At present, the non-performing assets of state-owned commercial banks account for too high proportion of loan ratio, which has always been a hidden danger for the stable operation of financial enterprises and the national economy. In order to reduce

---

[1] Deng Zhiyi, "Present opportunity and challenge of large banks during reform and development", *China Finance*, 2007 (10), pp. 34-37.

the proportion of non-performing assets of state-owned commercial banks, the state not only directly finances the capital of state-owned commercial banks through the issuance of special treasury bonds by the Ministry of Finance, but also establishes financial asset management companies through financial capital injection to strip off the bank's non-performing assets. The state has successively established four asset management companies: Cinda, Huarong, Dongfang and Great Wall. However, it often happened that the asset management company has not completely sold out the old non-performing assets, and the new non-performing assets of the state-owned commercial banks have been generated already. This also reflects the problems existing in the asset management of state-owned commercial banks to some extent.

(2) *Corporate governance system needs to be further improved*

Although the joint-stock reform can solve the problem of property rights falsification and clarify the main body of property rights, changing property rights is only a means to change competition, and the problem of corporate governance structure cannot be solved. After the state-owned commercial banks in China implemented the joint-stock system reform, the corporate governance structure of the corporate system was initially established, effectively separating the ownership and management rights. However, from the actual results, the governance structure still faces some important defects and problems: the ownership structure is unreasonable, and the organizational structure needs to be further improved. The number of shares outstanding in the shareholding ratio is very small, and the legal person shares account for the majority in non-tradable shares, while the majority of legal person holding companies are state-owned companies. The problem of lack of principals and agents is serious, and the internal motivation for effective supervision of banks has been lost. None of these problems have been completely resolved.

(3) *The severe risks of the capital market raise new demands on financial supervision*

The reform and development of state-owned commercial banks will also bring new problems to financial supervision. Financial supervision must obviously be consistent with the reform of financial institutions, otherwise the financial market will be exposed to greater risks. China's capital market supervision has repeatedly caused many problems. For example, the shady funds, the Monkey King Group bankruptcy, and the Yinguangxia incident all reflect the chaotic state of China's stock market. It is urgent to establish a complete, standardized and comprehensive supervision system through the use of a series of effective policy instruments and open and transparent market regulation and enforcement measures to implement supervision and management of listed banks.

In addition, in terms of the regulatory mechanism, the regulatory level and regulatory efficiency of the regulatory authorities have yet to be further improved. A regulatory system that is regulated by the external supervision of the regulatory authorities, internal control of commercial banks, and the intermediary market is not yet formed. In terms of the market environment, the construction of faith and credit system of the whole society has just started, and the construction of the financial legal system has yet to be improved.

The reform of the joint-stock system of state-owned commercial banks is a complex systematic project that won't be overnight successful, thus determining that it is an arduous and lengthy process. We believe that to become a dominant market player and to build a first-rank commercial bank comparable to the international advanced banks, we also need to make great efforts.[1]

First, via effective means, the joint-stock system is implemented step by step, and the government and enterprises are separated. Following the principle of separation of powers in decision-making, execution, and supervision, the corporate governance structure of state-owned commercial banks will be constructed in accordance with the three levels of shareholders' meeting, board of directors and CEO.

The second is to accelerate the improvement of their own profitability and enhance the endogenous capacity of the expansion of core capital. Through the government's capital injection, the introduction of overseas strategic investors, and public listing, the core capital scale has been greatly improved, but the amount of capital retained and transferred to the capital is reduced. Therefore, state-owned commercial banks should increase the amount of their own capital accumulation as soon as possible.

The third is to improve asset quality and reduce the ratio of non-performing loans. In order to maintain the current good capital position, state-owned commercial banks must pay more attention to the control of non-performing loans and accelerate the collection and disposal of non-performing loans, further strengthen the concept of capital constraints, control the growth of asset scale, diversify assets, and strive to find lower risk weights. The business with relatively stable income will further reduce the

---

[1] Liu Mingkang, *30 Years for China's Banking Sector Reform and Opening Up*, Beijing: China Financial Publishing House, 2009, p.167.

ratio of non-performing loans.

The fourth is to improve the business evaluation system. The new assessment system must include both quantifiable financial indicators and non-quantitative non-financial indicators. The administrative ranks of branches and managers at all levels actually existing in long-term should be cancelled, and the performance compensation system for bank employees should be constructed according to the value of positions and individual performance.

5.3 Capital market development

The "Securities Law" promulgated in 1998 confirmed the status of the capital market in legal form. The revision of the "Securities Law" in Nov. 2005 marked a higher level of capital market development. At this stage, China has carried out continuous reforms around the improvement of the socialist market economic system and the comprehensive construction of a moderately prosperous society in all-round. The Chinese economy has been fully open, and state-owned and non-state-owned joint-stock companies have continuously entered the capital market, and the depth and breadth of the capital market have been expanded.

5.3.1 Further regulation and development of the capital market

(1) *Capital market law improved gradually*

The "Company Law" and the "Securities Law" are two important laws regulating the capital market. With the continuous deepening of economic and financial system reform and the sustainable development of the socialist market economy, China's capital market is changing from a government-led to a market-oriented one. Some basic market mechanisms and systems have gradually formed and are widely accepted. The level of marketization is also constantly improving. Great changes have taken place in all aspects of the market, and many new situations have emerged. These two laws were no longer fully suitable to the objective needs of the development of the new situation and need to be revised. In Oct. 2005, the National People's Congress revised the Company Law and the Securities Law and implemented it on Jan.1, 2006.

In line with the revision of the "Company Law" and the "Securities Law", the National People's Congress and various ministries and commissions of the State Council have sorted out and adjusted relevant laws, regulations and rules. The National People's Congress passed the "Criminal Law Amendment (6)", which further clarified the criminal responsibility of serious violations by listed companies and securities and futures institutions, and increased the punishment for market manipulation. At the same time, the "Bankruptcy Law" was amended to standardize the bankruptcy behavior of enterprises and comprehensively protect the interests of all parties. The CBRC has sorted out and integrated relevant regulations and institutional documents in accordance with the provisions of the revised "Company Law" and the "Securities Law", and successively promulgated the "Measures for the Implementation of the Freezing and Sealing of the China Securities Regulatory Commission" and the "Guidelines of Listed Companies Governance", "Rules for the Shareholders' Meeting of Listed Companies", "Guidelines for the Articles of Association of Listed Companies" (revised in 2006), "Rules for the Implementation of Non-public Issuance of Stocks by Listed Companies", "Measures for the Supervision of the Qualifications of Directors, Supervisors and Senior Management of Securities Companies", and "Measures for the Administration of Securities Settlement Risk Funds", a number of regulations and normative documents, which have basically formed a regulatory system that is compatible with the "Company Law" and the "Securities Law".

The revision of the "Company Law" and the "Securities Law" and the improvement of relevant laws and regulations in the capital market further rationalized the legal relationship of the capital market, improved the operating mechanism of the capital market, and adapted to the requirements of the market economy for the development factor market, and comprehensively improved the status of the capital market in the socialist market system. These would have a far-reaching impact on comprehensively improving the rule of law in the capital market and accelerating the reform and development of the capital market[1].

(2) *The bond market has been initially developed*

In recent years, the scale of China's bond market has continued to increase, market trading rules have gradually improved, and infrastructure such as bond custody systems and trading systems have been accelerating.

The bond varieties and market size of the exchange bond market continued to grow, and the trading methods continued to improve. The institutional construction of the inter-bank bond market was gradually improved, and the market variety continued to expand. In Oct. 2005, IFC and the Asian Development Bank issued RMB1.13 billion and RMB1 billion respectively in the national inter-bank bond market. This is

---

[1] CSRC, *China Capital Markets Development Report*, Beijing: China Financial Publishing House, 2008, p.76.

the first time that the Chinese bond market has introduced the institutions of foreign-funded issuance. It is an important measure and a useful attempt to open up the Chinese bond market. It has set up a commercial bank counter market and is engaged in the retail business of government bonds for individual investors and small and medium-sized enterprises.

(3) *Futures market begins to recover*

In 1990, China's Zhengzhou grain wholesale market was approved by the State Council. Based on spot trading, the futures trading mechanism was introduced. As the first commodity futures market in China, it took the first step in the development of China's futures market. By 1993, driven by departmental and local interests, in the absence of unified management, the Chinese futures market developed blindly and fell into disorder. After twice clean-ups and rectifications in 1993 and 1998, the chaotic and disorderly situation of the futures market was reversed, and great achievements were made in the construction of laws and regulations, and the Chinese futures market entered a stage of standard development.

In Mar. 2001, the 10th Five-year Plan approved by the National People's Congress first proposed "steadily develop the futures market", which ended the seven-year clean-up and rectification of China's futures market. In mid-Oct. 2003, the 3rd Plenary Session of the 16th CPC Central Committee wrote "steady development of the futures market" in the "Decision of the Central Committee of the Communist Party of China on Some Issues Concerning the Improvement of the Socialist Market Economy". On Feb.1, 2004, the State Council issued the "Several Opinions on Promoting the Reform, Opening, and Stable Development of the Capital Market", and further elaborated and deployed the "steadily develop the futures market" and became the program to guide the development of the futures market. Since then, relevant measures to promote the reform, opening up, and stable development of the futures market have been introduced.

On Mar.16, 2007, the State Council promulgated the "Regulations on the Administration of Futures Trading", extending the scope of application from the commodity futures trading of the "Provisional Regulations on the Administration of Futures Trading" to the trading of commodities, financial futures and options contracts; positioning futures companies as financial enterprises and deleting the prohibitive provisions that the financial institutions in the original regulations were not allowed to engage in futures trading, could not finance futures transactions, and provided guarantees. The futures brokerage company also changed to a futures company. In view of the risk characteristics of the futures market, the futures market is required to strengthen the basic system construction and continuously improve the market risk control system, such as setting up a futures investor protection fund and establishing an investor protection mechanism. Meanwhile, it has also made specific provisions on improving the supervision system of the futures market, strengthening and improving the supervision of futures companies and other market entities, and the participation of state-owned enterprises in futures trading. The turnover of the domestic futures market reached a high point of RMB10.06 trillion in 1995, and then fell for five consecutive years. In 2000, it fell to a low point of RMB1.6 trillion. In 2001 and 2002, the market resumed growth, with RMB3.01 trillion and RMB3.95 trillion respectively. After that, it has grown year by year and has achieved rapid development[1], as shown in Figure 5-1.

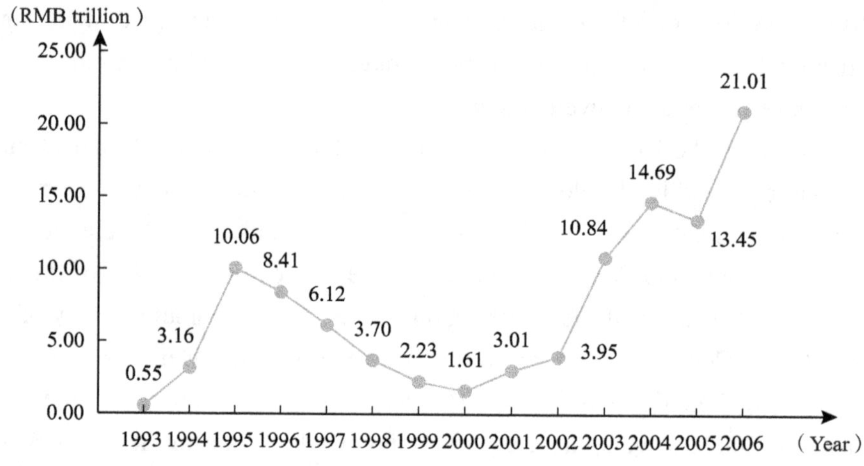

Figure 5-1 1993-2006 Trend of total futures turnover

Source: National bureau of statistics.

On May 18, 2006, with the approval of the State Council, the China Securities Regulatory Commission established the China Futures Market Monitoring Center as a futures margin depository institution, funded by the Shanghai Futures Exchange, the Dalian Commodity Exchange, and the Zhengzhou Commodity Exchange, acting as the non-profit company legal entity. It is responsible for timely discovering and reporting the risk of misappropriation of futures deposits, and cooperating with futures regulatory authorities to deal with margin risk events. The establishment of China

[1] Gan Chunhui, *30 Years for Chinese Economic System Reform*, Shanghai: Shanghai University of Finance & Economics Press, 2008, p.127.

Futures Market Monitoring Center is of great significance for ensuring the security of futures trading funds and safeguarding the interests of investors.

On Sep.8, 2006, the China Financial Futures Exchange was established in Shanghai. It was jointly established by Shanghai Futures Exchange, Zhengzhou Commodity Exchange, Dalian Commodity Exchange, Shanghai Stock Exchange and Shenzhen Stock Exchange. After the establishment of China Financial Futures Exchange, it began to prepare for the launch of financial derivatives such as stock index futures.

(4) *The capital market is open to the outside world*

With the in-depth development of economic globalization, the links and mutual influences between China's economy and the world economy are deepening, and the domestic and the international market are firmly connected. Objectively, it is required to further improve the level of opening up and better promote the sustained and stable development of China's economy. Actively and steadily implementing the opening up of the capital market will help optimize the market structure, improve the quality of the capital market, and enhance the overall competitiveness and risk resistance of China's capital market.

The Joint venture securities futures business were approved to be established. In 2002, the China Securities Regulatory Commission issued the "Rules for the Establishment of Foreign-Shared Securities Companies" and the "Rules for the Establishment of Foreign-invested Fund Management Companies". In the same year, the Shanghai and Shenzhen Exchanges also issued the "Interim Provisions on the Administration of Special Overseas Members". Chinese-foreign joint venture securities companies, Sino-foreign joint venture fund companies, and foreign-funded securities institutions' representative offices in China have settled in the Shanghai and Shenzhen stock exchanges and are engaged in B-share business. In addition, in 2006, Galaxy Futures Brokerage Co., Ltd. and ABN Amro jointly established the first joint venture futures company in China, marking the formal entry of foreign institutions into the Chinese futures market.

The Qualified Foreign Institutional Investors (QFII) and Qualified Domestic Institutional Investor (QDII) mechanisms were established. In the absence of full convertibility under renminbi capital, China implemented a QFII system in Dec. 2002 that allows approved foreign institutional investors to invest in the Chinese securities market. After entering the capital market in China, QFII realized the initial docking of domestic and overseas capital markets, improved the international influence of

China's capital market, increased the medium and long-term capital supply of the market, and promoted the maturity of investment ideas in China's capital market and advanced investment risk management. The application of technology has improved the overall level of the industry. In May 2006, China implemented a QDII system that allows approved domestic institutions to invest in overseas securities markets. The introduction of QDII not only helps to rationalize the supply and demand relationship in the foreign exchange market, but also gives Chinese investors the opportunity to invest in a broader international capital market, which is of great significance for promoting Chinese enterprises to "go global".

Foreign-invested joint-stock company issued domestically listed and foreign-funded strategic investment listed companies. In Nov. 2001, China issued "Several Opinions on Issues Related to Foreign Investment in Listed Companies", allowing eligible foreign-invested joint-stock companies to apply for listing in China. In Nov. 2002, the China Securities Regulatory Commission, the Ministry of Finance, and the State Economic and Trade Commission issued the "Notice on Issues Concerning the Transfer of State-Owned Shares and Legal Person Shares of Listed Companies to Foreign Countries", allowing foreign capital to transfer state-owned shares and corporate shares of listed companies. In Feb. 2006, the "Measures for the Administration of Strategic Investment by Listed Companies by Foreign Investors" was issued to allow foreign investors to obtain A shares of the company through a long-term strategic M&A investment of a certain size for listed companies that have completed the share-trading reform.

Since 2006, on the basis of the proper settlement of the historical problems of China's capital market and the gradual improvement of the legal system, there have been a series of positive and profound changes in the Chinese capital market. The market scale has expanded rapidly and transactions have become increasingly active. The Chinese capital market developed rapidly in recent years. Practice has proved that to promote the reform and development of China's capital market, capital market must be regarded as an important strategic task. It must closely serve the needs of China's economic development, accelerate the pace of market-oriented reforms and mobilize the enthusiasm of market participants to achieve the goal of market development and innovation, further improve the legal and regulatory system, and continuously improve the level of market standardization. We must actively promote the orderly opening of the capital market, increase its degree of internationalization, and continuously enhance the comprehensive competitiveness of China's capital market in the future international financial system.

5.3.2 Major reform of the capital market

For more than a decade, China's capital market has gone through a mature market for decades or even hundreds of years, and has achieved great success. However, on the whole, it is still in the initial stage of development. In the meantime, China's capital market cannot be separated from the overall level of social and economic development and institutional reform, and it has gradually accumulated some deep-seated issues in its development. Since 2001, the stock market has continued to be in a downturn, and some structural contradictions have become increasingly apparent. In order to promote the resolution of these problems, on Jan.31, 2004, the State Council issued "A Number of Opinions on Promoting the Reform and Opening up, and Stable Development of the Capital Market", raising the development of China's capital market to the height of national strategic tasks, and further reforming the capital market. It has laid a solid foundation for development, and the Chinese capital market has been reformed in many ways.

(1) *Share-trading reform*

Share-trading refers to the fact that the shares of listed companies in the A-share market are classified as tradable shares and non-tradable shares according to whether they can be listed on the stock exchange. Before the public offering of a listed company, the shares held by the shareholders can only be transferred through agreement, which is called non-tradable shares; publicly-issued shares purchased by the public can be listed on the stock exchange, which is called a tradable share.

The existence of share-trading originated from the early development of the market. The understanding of the Joint-stock system and the function and positioning of the capital market was not uniform. At the same time, the reform of the state-owned asset management system was still in its earlier stage, and the concept of state-owned capital operation was not fully established. As an institutional defect left over from history, share-trading has restricted the standard development of China's capital market and the reform of state-owned asset management system in many aspects. With the continuous accumulation of new shares and listings, it is unfavorable to the reform and opening up and stable development of the capital market. The negative impact is also growing[1].

---

[1] CSRC, *China Capital Markets Development Report*, Beijing: China Financial Publishing House, 2008, p.50.

First, it has distorted the pricing mechanism of the capital market. Price discovery is the basic function of the capital market and the premise of optimizing resource allocation. The share-trading affects the pricing efficiency to a large extent: under the share-trading structure, the stock price includes both the company's fundamental factors and the expectation that 2/3 shares will temporarily not be listed for trading affects normal stock pricing expectations; 2/3 shares cannot be listed for circulation, which objectively leads to a relatively small scale of single listed share, and public share price is easy to be manipulated, resulting in large stock price fluctuation and distortion of pricing mechanism. These two factors make stock pricing relatively higher than the company's intrinsic value.

Second, it leads to a lack of common interests in corporate governance. Due to the existence of share-trading, the interests of non-tradable shareholders are mainly due to the increase or decrease of net asset value, while the interests of tradable shareholders are mainly due to stock price fluctuations in the secondary market, objectively forming non-tradable shareholders and tradable shareholders "separated interests".

Third, it is not conducive to the market capital operation of listed companies. In the international capital market, market-oriented capital operation is an important way for listed companies to achieve rapid development. The capital circulation of listed companies in China is divided into two markets: agreement transfer and trading in stock exchange, which forms two kinds of prices, which makes the market capitalization of listed companies such as mergers and acquisitions lack operation basis; the interests of shareholders are not integrated, and the financing costs of listed companies are high. It is difficult and it affects the long-term development of the company.

Fourth, it restricts the internationalization process of capital markets and product innovation. Due to the existence of institutional differences in share-trading, the introduction of important measures related to the internationalization of capital markets, such as QFII, large-scale enterprises and domestic and overseas simultaneous issuance and listing of banks, may lead to distortions in domestic and foreign market stock prices, thus affecting the interests of public investors in domestic markets. At the same time, the innovation of financial derivation based on stock prices will also have greater uncertainty due to the unresolved issue of share-trading.

Fifth, it is not conducive to the management of state-owned capital operations. Under the share-trading structure, the non-tradable shares transfer market dominated by state-owned shares is a limited negotiated pricing market for participants. The trading mechanism is non-transparent and the price discovery is insufficient, which seriously affects the smooth flow and valuation of state-owned assets. At the same time, the state-owned equity value cannot be reflected by the dynamic valuation of marketization. It can only conduct maintenance of value and value-added management with static indicators such as net assets, and it cannot form an incentive mechanism and market-oriented assessment standards for enterprises to strengthen internal management and enhance asset value-adding capabilities.

With the development of the capital market, the resolution of the share-trading issue has begun to be put on the agenda. In the latter half of 1998 and 2001, there were two exploratory attempts to reduce state-owned shares. However, due to unsatisfactory results, they were quickly stopped. In Apr. 2005, under the leadership of the CPC and the State Council, the China Securities Regulatory Commission issued the "Notice on Relevant Issues Concerning the Pilot Reform of the Share Separation Reform of Listed Companies", and launched the pilot program of share-trading restructuring. The share-trading reform was promoted in accordance with the principle of "pilot first, coordinated advancement, and step-by-step implementation".

The purpose of resolving the issue of share-trading is to restore the proper function of the capital market, rather than focusing on the realization of the circulation of state-owned shares. Solving the problem of share-trading will inevitably break the existing interest pattern of the market. The dynamic balance between the shareholders of tradable shares and the shareholders of non-tradable shares is the key to the smooth progress of reform and the maintenance of market stability. Therefore, in the reform, the non-tradable shareholders and the tradable shareholders adopted a consideration arrangement to balance the mutual interests, and the non-tradable shareholders transferred to the tradable shareholders a portion of the interests from the listing and circulation of their shares. The consideration arrangement is determined by the relevant shareholders of each listed company in a market-based manner on the basis of equal consultation, mutual understanding and independent decision-making. The process includes the non-tradable shareholders moving, the parties negotiating and revising the reform plan, and classified voted of all shareholders and the shareholders of tradable shares. The reform plan must be approved by both more than 2/3 of the voting shares held by the voting shareholders and more than 2/3 of the voting rights held by the voting shareholders. This ensures that the interests of small and medium investors in the participating entities are fully protected.

In Aug. 2005, the CSRC, the State-owned Assets Supervision and Administration

Commission, the Ministry of Finance, the PBOC and the Ministry of Commerce jointly issued the "Guiding Opinions on the Share-trading Reform of Listed Companies", and the CSRC promulgated the "Administrative Measures on the Reform of the Share Separation Reform of Listed Companies". The share-trading reform was comprehensively promoted. On Dec.31, 2007, the market capitalization of listed companies that had completed or entered the share-trading reform process accounted for 98% of the total market capitalization of listed companies, and the share-trading reform was basically completed.[1] By 2015, all stocks listed on the Shanghai and Shenzhen stock exchanges have completed the share-trading reform.

The smooth progress of the share-trading reform has resolved the problems of separation of state-owned shares, legal person shares, and tradable shares, and the separation of prices. All types of shareholders enjoy the same rights to list shares and share prices, and all types of stocks are priced according to the unified market mechanism, and become the common interest base of all kinds of shareholders. The basic completion of the share-trading reform, and the combination of the share-trading reform and the stable development of the market, a series of policy measures, have eliminated the biggest uncertain factors affecting the expected stability of the market, and laid the market for further optimizing the resource allocation function of China's capital market. The basis of the marketization makes the Chinese capital market no longer fundamentally differ from the international market at the market-based institutional level,[2] and it has epoch-making significance.

(2) *Improve the quality of listed companies in an all-round way*

Listed companies are the cornerstones of the development of the capital market. For more than 20 years, China's listed companies have continued to grow and develop, and have become the backbone of promoting corporate reform and driving industry growth. However, due to influences of some factors such as the receptor system, mechanism, and environment, a considerable number of listed companies have inadequate corporate governance structures, unregulated operations, and low quality, which seriously affect investors' confidence and restrict the healthy and stable development of the capital market. The CSRC has successively promoted a series of

---

[1] Li Qiang and Yang Yuanyuan, "Empirical analysis on effects of ownership structure on earnings management in Chinese new-material listed companies", *Journal of Chongqing University of Technology* (*Social Science*), 2015 (6), pp. 61-67.

[2] Zhang Lei, *The Credit Expansion and Financial Distortions in the Era of China's High Economic Growth*, Beijing: Social Sciences Academic Press (China), 2013, p.141.

reform measures that are conducive to improving the quality of listed companies, effectively protecting the legitimate rights and interests of investors and promoting the sustainable and healthy development of the capital market.

The supervision system of listed companies was improved. The regulatory responsibility system for listed companies that began to be implemented in 2004 is a major reform in the regulatory system of listed companies. This reform puts forward the requirements of "local supervision, clear rights and responsibilities, responsibility to people, and mutual cooperation", further clarifies the job responsibilities and positioning of the dispatched institutions of the CSRC, effectively exerts the first-line supervision advantages of the dispatched institutions and improves. the timeliness, relevance and effectiveness of supervision. It also has integrated the system supervision force and enhanced the depth and intensity of supervision. On the basis of implementing the supervisory responsibility system of the jurisdiction, the CSRC has accelerated the construction and improvement of the comprehensive supervision system of listed companies jointly participated by various departments and local governments, and enhanced the authority and effectiveness of supervision.

Information disclosure was strengthened. After 1999, the supervision of listed companies gradually shifted from administrative examination and approval to enhance information disclosure. The CSRC, in conjunction with capital market development practices, continued to comprehensively regulate the information disclosure of listed companies. In order to meet the higher requirements of the new "Company Law" and "Securities Law" for information disclosure of listed companies, improve the transparency of the operation of listed companies, and adapt to the requirements of the new situation after the share-trading reform on the supervision of listed companies, in Feb. 2007, the "Measures for the Administration of Information Disclosure of Listed Companies" was issued, which further improved the information disclosure rules and regulatory procedures, and improved the quality of information disclosure and the effectiveness of supervision of listed companies. Since 2014, the content and frequency of voluntary disclosure of information have been piloted in state-controlled listed companies, especially to increase the number of soft information related to the company's internal institutional mechanisms and important personnel changes. The regulatory agencies have helped to reduce the cost of information disclosure and take measures to improve the consciousness of the listed company to disclose information voluntarily.

Corporate governance was Standardized. In order to improve corporate governance, the CSRC has successively issued a series of related regulations, including the "Guidelines for the Companies Listing", "Special Opinions of the General Meeting of Shareholders", "Guidelines for the Governance of Listed Companies", etc., and introduced the independent director system. After the start of the share-trading reform, the CSRC revised the "Rules of the General Meeting of Listed Companies", "Guidelines for the Companies Listing" and other regulations, so that the framework and principles of the governance structure of listed companies are basically established, and the governance of listed companies has embarked on the track of standardized development.

The equity incentive mechanism was established. Under the circumstances of the revision of the "Company Law", "Securities Law" and the the share-trading reform, the legal environment and market environment for the implementation of equity incentives in China have been continuously improved, and the timing of the introduction of the equity incentive mechanism has gradually matured. To this end, the CSRC issued the "Measures for the Administration of Equity Incentives for Listed Companies (Trial)" in Jan 2006, stipulating that the main methods of equity incentives are restricted stocks and stock options, and rule the equity incentives mechanism from the perspective of implementation procedures and information disclosure. This has had a profound impact on the standardized operation and sustainable development of listed companies. As of the end of 2015, there were a total of 808 listed companies that launched the equity incentive plan, involving 1,110 equity incentive plans, of which 229 companies launched two or more equity incentive plans, which obviously promoted technology-based and innovative companies.[1] On Jul.13, 2016, the CSRC officially promulgated the "Measures for the Administration of Equity Incentives for Listed Companies", focusing on information disclosure, deregulating and strengthening supervision according to the regulatory concept of lenient enrollment and strict management, and gradually forming an independent decision-making and market-constrained equity incentive system effectively for listed companies.

Market-oriented mergers and acquisitions was promoted. By amending the "Measures for the Administration of the Acquisition of Listed Companies and the Information Disclosure Guidelines", the pilot of issuing shares to subscribe for assets to specific targets was launched, which promoted the improvement of listed companies

[1] CSRC, "The China Securities Regulatory Commission issued the 'Management Measures for Equity Incentives of Listed Companies'", Jul.15, 2016, http: //www.csrc.gov.cn.

and encouraged the controlling shareholders of listed companies to concentrate high-quality assets and advantageous projects on listed companies. The market-oriented listed companies' mergers and acquisitions and corporate listings have increased significantly. In Sep. 2007, the CSRC set up a merger and acquisition audit committee for listed companies, which was responsible for reviewing the application for mergers and acquisitions of listed companies, thereby further standardizing the audit system, enhancing the transparency of the audit work and improving the efficiency of the audit. The capital market has become the main venue for Chinese corporate restructuring and industrial integration. In 2014, the CSRC revised the "Measures for the Administration of Major Assets Restructuring of Listed Companies" and the "Measures for the Administration of the Acquisition of Listed Companies", and canceled the approval report for the listed company's acquisition report beforehand; all the approvals of the purchasing, selling and replacement of major assets of listed companies, except for the possibility of the backdoor listing, were cancelled; the approval of the tender offer obligation was simplified; the pricing mechanism for mergers and acquisitions was improved; the M&A and payment instruments were enriched, and the listed companies were allowed to issue preferred shares and convertible bonds to implement mergers and acquisitions.

Listed companies are groups with development advantages in China's economic operation and are the source of investment value in the capital market. Improving the quality of listed companies is an inherent requirement for strengthening the competitive advantages of listed companies and achieving sustainable development; it is the foundation for consolidating the foundation of the capital market and promoting the healthy and stable development of the capital market; it is the key for enhancing the attractiveness and vitality of the capital market and giving full play to the optimization of resources allocation in the capital market. To improve the quality of listed companies, we must base ourselves on maximizing the interests of all shareholders, and continuously improve corporate governance and management, credibility and transparency, and the company's profitability and sustainable development capabilities.

(3) *Comprehensive management of securities companies*

Securities companies are important intermediaries in the capital market and play a pivotal role in the healthy development of the capital market. Due to defects in the system and mechanism, securities companies have accumulated many contradictions and problems in the development process. Some securities companies have arbitrarily misappropriated customer transaction settlement funds and securities, illegal financial management, and the illegal use of funds by shareholders and related parties. Around 2004, the problems accumulated by securities companies for a long time were fully exposed, the risks were concentrated, and the survival and development of the whole industry encountered severe challenges. In order to solve the problem fundamentally, the CSRC, in accordance with the deployment of the State Council, based on three approaches of the risk disposal, daily supervision and promotion of industry development, implemented comprehensive governance on the securities company.

Since 2004, the CSRC has established the evaluation criteria for innovative and regulated securities companies; the census finds out the risk base of securities companies, clears misappropriation of customer deposits, misappropriation of customer bonds, capital occupied by shareholders and related parties, illegal entrusted wealth management and off-balance sheet business; while maintaining market and social stability, the CSRC actively and steadily disposed of 31 high-risk securities companies with risk exposure, self-help hopeless or serious violations, and explored the diversified restructuring merger and acquisition model, developed 3rd party depository system for settlement funds, reformed the basic business system of government bond repurchase, asset management, and self-operated business, established financial information disclosure and basic information disclosure system for securities companies, and improved risk monitoring and early warning system with net capital as the core. Also CSRC strengthened the supervision of senior executives and shareholders of securities companies, regulated the behavior of senior executives and shareholders. In order to improve the investor protection mechanism, and change the market exit mode of securities companies, by introducing international experience, China Securities Investor Protection Fund Co., Ltd. was established. During the comprehensive management, according to the principle of "pilot first, and gradually release", in the premise of risks can be measured, controlled and endured, CRSC support high-quality companies to introduce the new products, pilot new business, expand their business space, and improve the profit model. A good demonstration effect has been achieved. In Jul. 2007, the CRSC reclassified securities companies based on the risk management capabilities of securities companies, and combined with the market influence of the company to support high-quality securities companies to become stronger and bigger.

In 2009, the CSRC issued the "Regulations on the Classification of Securities Companies", which simplified the risk management capability evaluation indicators from 6 categories and 69 indicators to capital adequacy, corporate governance and compliance management, dynamic risk monitoring, information system security, customer rights protection, and information disclosure, totally 6 categories of 27 indicators. This highlights the comprehensive evaluation of corporate risks, and promotes industry to enhance competitiveness, encourage innovation, and become better and stronger.

After comprehensive management, the long-term accumulation of risks and historical issues of securities companies have been resolved smoothly. The financial information that has seriously plagued the healthy development of the securities industry has been solved, such as false financial information, off-balance-sheet operations, misappropriation of customer assets, and occupation of shareholders and related parties. However, since the innovative business of brokerages flourished in 2012, various brokerages have devoted themselves to the innovation of the business. The innovative business has broken through the original department and market boundaries. At this time, the risk control has become the biggest challenge for brokers. According to statistics, in 2015, the CSRC issued 29 tickets to 23 brokers, from business warnings to deadlines for rectification, from suspension of qualifications to executive bans. Brokers were penalized include not only CITIC Securities, Haitong Securities, Guoxin Securities, but also include small and medium-sized brokers such as Founder Securities and Minsheng Securities.

Practice has proved that mitigating risks and institutional construction must be promoted simultaneously, strengthening industry supervision and encouraging innovation and development must be associated combined; reform of the securities market must address both the symptoms and the root causes; risk disposal must ensure industry, market and social stability; to maintain the long-term healthy development of the securities industry, the basic institutions for the operation and supervision of securities companies must be improved.

(4) *Stock issuance system reform*

From 1990 to 2000, China's capital market was in the early stage of establishment and development. In the early stage of market establishment, the issuers, intermediaries and investors were all lack experience, and the understanding of the rules, rights and obligations of the capital market was insufficient. The securities issuance management system was implemented as the approval system for quota distribution and government-recommended enterprises. This kind of approval system was the choice in the market and social environment at that time. However, due to the limitation of quota and the vicious competition of local governments, there were many problems in stock issuance.

The "Securities Law" implemented in 1999 clearly stipulated: "The securities regulatory authority under the State Council shall be responsible for approving applications for stock issuance in accordance with statutory conditions." On Mar.16, 2000, the "China Securities Regulatory Commission's Stock Issuance Approval Procedure" was promulgated and implemented, the quota approval system was abolished, and the lead underwriter recommendation system and the stock issuance approval system were implemented. The concept of the approval system is to strengthen the responsibilities of intermediaries, enforce information disclosure, and play the independent audit function of the issuance audit committee. The issue and pricing are determined by the issuer and the underwriter. Since Mar. 2001, the approval system for the issuance of new shares has established. The responsibility mechanism for pre-existing accountability, legal disclosure and post-accident investigation with mandatory information disclosure as the core were also established. The legal system for securities issuance supervision was initially set up. The level of procedural and standardization of the audit work was improved. At the same time, the stock issuance pricing system has changed from executive-led to market-led. In Dec. 2003, the CSRC issued the "Interim Measures for the Sponsorship System for Securities Issuance and Listing", and implemented the sponsor system, which requires the company's initial public offering of shares and the issuance of new shares and convertible corporate bonds by listed companies should be sponsored by sponsors and sponsor representative. The sponsorship system is a major measure to make the approval system a reality. It has made clear requirements for intermediaries, abolished the "channel system" in the meantime, and introduced institutional qualifications and management systems, and the first licensee system.

In Dec. 2003, the CSRC promulgated the "Interim Measures for the Stock Issuance Review Committee" to reform the system of issuing audit committees. Established in 1993, the Issuance Review Committee is a professional organization that audits the qualifications of companies applying for stock issuance. It aims to solve the problem of excessive concentration of issuing auditing power. The members of the issuance audit committee are composed of 80 members. Each of the audit committees selects 9 people to participate in the issuance review. The audit opinions are formed by secret ballot. The number of votes is 2/3. Since the operation of the audit committee has been in a state of non-publicity and opacity, it is also prone to corruption, and it has been repeatedly questioned by the market. In Dec. 2003, the CSRC reformed the system of the audit committee: the number of members was reduced from 80 to 25, and each meeting was attended by 7 members, 5 votes to agree will be approved, and the voting method was changed from anonymous to registered. The accountability mechanism and supervision mechanism for the members of the audit committee to strengthen the audit responsibility of the members, were set up. The improvement and reform of the IEC system is an important measure to continuously improve the degree of specialization and transparency of the issuance of audits, increase social supervision and improve the efficiency of issuance.

The market mechanism for securities issuance has been strengthened. In 2006, the "Measures for the Administration of Securities Issuance of Listed Companies", the "Measures for the Administration of Initial Public Offerings and Listings", the "Measures for the Administration of Securities Issuance and Underwriting" and the corresponding supporting rules were successively launched, forming a new share issuance system under the full circulation model, including introduce the market price increase mechanism of the listed company and the failure mechanism of the share allotment; strictly guarantee the responsibility, cancel the mandatory requirement of the one-year counseling period; promote the financing method and tool innovation, and introduce the convertible corporate bond of the separable transaction; institutional arrangements such as strategic investors' targeted placement, simultaneous issuance and listing of domestic and overseas markets, and pilots of over-allotment options have further strengthened market constraints and improved distribution efficiency.

The pricing mechanism is gradually marketized. With the increasing pricing power of institutional investors, the CSRC issued the "Notice on Several Issues Concerning the Trial Inquiry System for Initial Public Offerings" at the end of 2004, approving the issue price of stocks and implementing an inquiry system. The implementation of the inquiry system has strengthened the market's constraints on issuers. The "Measures for the Administration of Securities Issuance and Underwriting" issued in Sep. 2006 further focused on the inquiry, pricing and stock placement of initial public offerings, improved the inquiry system, and strengthened the regulation to issuers, securities companies, securities service institutions and investors involving in the securities issuance.

In 2013, the CSRC issued the "Opinions of the China Securities Regulatory Commission on Further Promoting the Reform of the New Share Issuance System", promoted the market-based issuance mechanism of new shares, strengthened the fiduciary duty of the issuers and their controlling shareholders, and further improved the marketization of new stock pricing. Also it reform the way in which new shares are placed, increase supervision and enforcement, and practically safeguard the principles of openness, fairness, and justice. In 2016, the CSRC also revised the "Measures for the Administration of Securities Issuance and Underwriting", the "Measures for the Administration of Initial Public Offerings and Listing", and the "Measures for the Administration of Initial Public Offerings and Listing on the Growth Enterprise Market", and formulated the "IPO and Refinancing Guiding Opinions on Matters Related to Diluted Spot Reward for Major Asset Restructuring", which is problem-oriented and has a strong pertinence, is conducive to solving the negative impact of huge funds on the secondary market, and is conducive to highlighting the audit focus. These in turn reflect the supervision concept centered on information disclosure and will help to further strengthen the supervision of intermediaries, effectively protect the legitimate rights and interests of investors, and reflect the reform orientation of marketization and rule of law. It is an important step based on the concept and direction of the reform of the registration system.

The practice of stock issuance system reform shows that the institutional arrangement of capital market should gradually change from "government-led" to "market-oriented", strengthen market restraint mechanism, improve the transparency of market operation, and give more pricing power to the market, which not only enhances the accuracy of pricing, but also enables the development of the market to proceed smoothly. It also enables market participants to bear corresponding responsibilities and risks while obtaining their own interests, and is conducive for securities institutions to enhance risk prevention capabilities and improve core competitiveness in the market.

5.4 Rural credit cooperative reform

China's financial reforms began in the cities, and urban financial reforms were faster than rural areas. In the first 20 years of financial reform, rural financial reforms have been slow, and they are far from meeting the requirements for supporting the development of agriculture, farmer and rural area. Since the country's vigorous development of the "agriculture, farmer and rural area" policy, the pace of rural financial reform has gradually accelerated.

Rural credit cooperatives have always been an important part of the rural financial system and have played a key role in supporting the development of rural economy. However, the development path of rural credit cooperatives is also tortuous.

Over the years, after several changes, it has undergone several major reforms until today. The reform is still going on. Since the founding of the People's Republic of China, China's rural credit cooperatives have experienced many reforms from the management of the people's communes and production brigades, to the management of middle and lower peasants, and to the management of agricultural banks. After the Agricultural Bank of China resumed in 1979, the rural credit cooperatives became its subordinate institutions. In 1984, the State Council approved the "Report on the Reform of the Management System of Credit Union Cooperatives" by the Agricultural Bank of China(ABC). This reform emphasized the "three characteristics" of rural credit cooperatives, namely, organizational cooperation, management democracy and management of flexibility[1]. However, the restoration of the "three characteristics" reform has not achieved significant results, and the operation of rural credit cooperatives is still carried out in accordance with the top-down command plan. After the 1990s, the State Council required rural credit cooperatives to gradually separate from the agricultural banks. In 1993, the State Council issued the "Decision of the State Council on Financial System Reform"; in 1994, the ABC and the Rural Credit Cooperatives began to work independently; in 1996, the State Council issued the "Decision on Rural Financial System Reform", the rural credit cooperatives and the ABC were officially decoupled and started to be hosted by the PBOC.

In 2002, the "Central Committee of the Communist Party of China and the State Council Opinion on Further Strengthening Financial Supervision, Deepening Financial Enterprise Reform, and Promoting the Healthy Development of the Financial Industry" firstly proposed that "the focus of rural credit cooperative reform is to clarify property rights relations and management responsibilities, strengthen internal management and self-restraint mechanism, further enhance the function of serving the 'issues of agriculture, farmer and rural area', and give full play to the role of the rural credit cooperatives in supporting the agricultural and rural economic development of the main financial forces and the financial links of the peasants."[2]

In June 2003, the "Notice of the State Council on Printing and Distributing the Pilot Program for Deepening the Reform of Rural Credit Cooperatives" required that the management and property rights institutional reform of rural credit cooperatives

---

[1] Li Lili, "Reform and institutional change of rural credit cooperatives", *China Agricultural Economic Review*, 2006,4(1), pp. 86-93.

[2] *Selected Works of Important Literature Since the 15th National Congress, Vol.2*, Beijing: Central Literature Publishing House, 2011, p.461.

should be accelerated in accordance with the overall requirements of "clear property rights relations, strengthen restraint mechanisms, enhance service functions, appropriate state support, and local government responsibility". And rural credit cooperatives should be gradually established as community-based local financial institutions that are invested by farmers, rural industrial and commercial households and various economic organizations to serve farmers, and agriculture and rural economic development. The rural credit cooperatives should fully play as the main force and the financial ties of the peasants that will better support the structural adjustment of the rural economy and promote the coordinated development of urban and rural economy. This reform mainly includes three aspects.

First was to reform the management system of rural credit cooperatives, mobilize the enthusiasm of local governments, and transfer management and risk responsibilities to provincial governments. After the decoupling of rural credit cooperatives and agricultural banks, business management and financial supervision were undertaken by the Rural Credit Cooperative County Union and the PBOC respectively. After the establishment of the CBRC, the supervisory responsibilities will be borne by the CBRC. Under this management system, the enthusiasm of local governments has not been fully exerted. It is often that local governments intervened in the operation of rural credit cooperatives, and the risks were borne by the central regulatory authorities, and the powers and responsibilities are not equal. This reform requires the provincial government to assume the management responsibility for the rural credit cooperatives, and at the same time bear the responsibility for risk disposal. To this end, the provinces have set up provincial rural credit cooperatives unions without carrying out specific business, and carry out the guidance and management functions of rural credit cooperatives. This new management system has mobilized the enthusiasm of local governments to participate in the management of rural credit cooperatives to a certain extent, and also strengthened the responsibility of local governments to undertake the risk control of rural credit cooperatives.

The second was to reform the property rights system of rural credit cooperatives and establish a diversified property rights reform direction guided by joint-stock reform. Since the establishment of the rural credit cooperatives, the property rights structure has always been a cooperative system. The stocks were relatively scattered and there were many members holding shares. However, due to external interventions and serious insiders' control, the legal rights of the ordinary members to participate in democratic management were not guaranteed, enthusiasm could not be mobilized.

This reform required that the property rights system should be guided by the joint-stock reform, adapt to local conditions, explore multiple property rights models, and strengthen incentive and restraint mechanisms. In practice, it is mainly the reform of three property rights models: the governance structure of a joint-stock rural commercial bank in an economically developed region, was completely regulated in accordance with the joint-stock commercial bank; the rural cooperative banks in the economically developed regions, were introduced two forms of investment shares and qualification shares. The governance structure adopted a combination of joint-stock system and cooperative system; the cooperative system was continued in underdeveloped areas, and the county union and township rural credit cooperatives were unified into county-level legal persons, and strengthened internal management. After the reform, the enthusiasm of all parties to buy shares and participate in rural credit cooperatives was very high, the scale of capital was greatly expanded, the management of rural credit cooperatives was strengthened, and the profitability was greatly improved.

The third was to comprehensively use fiscal, taxation and monetary means to resolve historical burdens. For the reformed rural credit cooperatives, the comprehensive application of fiscal policy, taxation policy and monetary policy means to help rural credit cooperatives to resolve historical burdens, including: the loss of rural credit cooperatives from implementing the national macro-policy to do the value-preserved savings business and pay more subsidy interests as government subsidies; from 2003 to 2005, the rural credit cooperatives piloted in the western region will be temporarily exempted from corporate income tax. From 2004, the business tax of all rural credit cooperatives in the pilot area will be levied at a rate of 3%[1]; for 50% of the amount of the insolvent amount of the rural credit union's actual assets in the end of 2002, the PBOC arranged special re-loans or special central bank bills to replace non-performing assets and recorded losses. These policies and measures have improved the financial status of rural credit cooperatives to a certain extent, especially the form of support for special bills, and require rural credit cooperatives to meet certain requirements before they can apply for redemption to the PBOC. This policy had a positive incentive effect.

The fourth was to strengthen financial supervision and implement the modern

[1] Guo Lihua, *Research on Anti-monopoly Control of China's Rural Financial Market*, Beijing: Intellectual Property Publishing House, 2008, p.202.

supervision concept of "managing legal persons, managing risks, controlling internal control, and improving transparency". In 5 to 10 years, the rural credit cooperatives would be divided into batches into modern financial enterprises with clear property rights and distinctive business functions, and the requirements for unified supervision standards based on the regulatory requirements of commercial banks will be fully implemented. In 2006, the five-category classification of loans was fully implemented, and the core regulatory requirements such as capital adequacy ratio and non-performing loan ratio were achieved in line with commercial banks. In accordance with the requirements of classified supervision and delivery standards, the rural credit cooperatives supervision rating system was established, the supervision progress assessment was organized, the differential regulatory requirements were set according to the regulatory rating, and differentiated supervision measures were adopted to improve the effectiveness of supervision.

After this reform, the rural credit cooperatives have undergone profound changes in the management system and property rights system. They have fully mobilized the enthusiasm of all parties in the management system, established the reform direction of the joint-stock system, and strengthened the incentive and restraint mechanism. The overall reform work has advanced rapidly. In 2003, 8 provinces began piloting. In 2004, the "Opinions on Further Deepening the Pilot Reform of Rural Credit Cooperatives" expanded the scope of reform pilots, and 21 provinces except Hainan were included in the pilot scope. After the reform, the rural credit cooperatives completely got rid of the operational difficulties, and the loss situation in successive years, and entered into the fastest development period in history.

The next step was to continue to deepen the reform of rural credit cooperatives. First, we must standardize the operation and give play to the role of the main force of rural finance. In accordance with the general principle of "separation of government and enterprise, standard management; service-oriented, stable county; adapting to local conditions, diversified forms; market operation, gradual and orderly progress", we should steadily promote the reform of the rural credit cooperatives' provincial unions; the process of promoting joint-stock system should focus on property right transformation, reform the property rights system, and optimize the shareholding structure. The formation of a unified corporate structure should be accelerated, and support qualified institutions to introduce strategic investors and timely listing and financing. Rural credit cooperatives should adhere to the principle of serving the "issues of agriculture, farmer and rural area" and consolidating the counties' border, continue to promote deepening reforms, strengthen county financial power, improve county financial services, and continue to play a leading role in supporting agriculture. The second is to relax market access and increase policy support. In order to effectively solve the problems of heavy regional institutions, low competitiveness, and insufficient support for "agriculture, farmer and rural area", the regulatory authorities will further relax the market access policy. First is to relax the investment ratio limit, and appropriately liberalize the shareholding ratio of rural financial institutions, such as mergers, acquisitions, and strategic investment in rural financial institutions and non-bank financial institutions. Second is to relax the geographical restrictions on investment and allow eligible capital to cross-regional merger, reorganize or invest in rural small and medium-sized financial institutions. Third is to relax the risk financing channels, allowing voluntary investment, corresponding capital contribution according to the proportion of equity, replacement of non-performing assets with high-quality assets, and commitment to replace non-performing assets with income from shares by local governments, sponsors or members (shareholders), to help rural small and medium-sized financial institutions that have been merged, restructured, and strategically invested to dispose the historical burdens and resolve stocking risks.

5.5 Financial regulatory system reform

Financial supervision is the supervision and examination, and control of various types of banks and other financial institutions by financial regulatory agencies to ensure the security and stability of the financial system and to ensure the interests of financial actors. The choice of financial supervision system is not only closely related to a country's economic and financial development level, but also closely related to politics, social system and management system.[1]

5.5.1 The development of China's financial regulatory system

Before the reform and opening up, China had only one financial institution of the PBOC, and there was no financial supervision system. Since the reform and opening up, with the continuous development of China's financial system, the financial supervision function of the PBOC has also been adjusted and improved accordingly.

[1] Jiang Shiyin, *Rational Thinking on China's Financial System Reform*, Beijing: China Financial & Economic Publishing House, 2009, p.221.

Three changes have taken place in China's financial regulatory system. In 1984, the ICBC was separated from the PBOC, and the PBOC specialized in the functions of the Central Bank. In 1998, the CSRC and the China Insurance Regulatory Commission (CISC) were established. The regulatory functions of securities and insurance were immediately separated from the PBOC, and initially formed a separate supervision system; in 2003, the CBRC was established and the banking supervision function was separated from the PBOC. The PBOC still undertakes part of the financial supervision functions including compliance regulation related to monetary policy, prevention and resolution of financial risks, supervision of financial markets and anti-money laundering. So far, the financial supervision system of the PBOC, the CBRC, the CSBC, and the CIBC under the leadership of the State Council has been formed to separate and supervise related institutions independently.

5.5.2 Financial industry mixed operation trend and separate supervision

The mixed operation of the financial industry usually refers to the financial business model in which commercial banking, investment banking, insurance company business and other financial businesses with investment nature are integrated in different degrees and in different scopes.[1] With the deepening of China's financial market opening to the outside world, facing the competition of foreign financial institutions with all-round operations, China's financial industry has shown a trend from separate operations to mixed operations.

Under the background of weak financial foundation, lack of financial supervision experience, poor self-discipline ability and risk control ability, the supervision of "one bank and three commissions" effectively realized the supervision of China's financial industry, which played a significant role. Its role has laid a solid foundation for the safe and efficient development of China's financial industry. However, with the development of the era, under the impetus of market competition and financial innovation, cross-market financial cooperation has been deepening, cross-market financial products are increasing, and cross-holding of equity between financial institutions has been constantly emerging. Various types of the financial holdings company have become an important force in the financial market. In contrast, financial institutions that operate in a mixed manner can adopt and manipulate financial

---

1 Qin Yuhuan, "Construct the environment for the development of mixed business in China's financial industry". *Reformation & Strategy*, 2006(S1), pp. 96-98.

instruments more flexibly, so that can better avoid risks and obtain profits than institutions that are only involved in a single industry. Mixed operation has become an inevitable trend in the development of financial institutions.

China's current financial supervision model is the supervision of separate institutions under the separate business model. Specifically, the CBRC has specifically exercised supervision over the banking industry, while the CSRC and the CIRC are responsible for the supervision of the securities industry and the insurance industry respectively, forming a typical pattern of separate supervision. This arrangement of financial supervision mode is compatible with the separate operation system that has been implemented since 1993. The financial structure at that time was characterized by a simple financial structure, a large proportion of bank assets in the entire financial assets, a relatively weak securities market and insurance market, and strict separation of business controls. However, in recent years, with the advancement of financial deepening, the cooperation and innovation of marginal business between silver, securities and insurance has emerged, and to some extent, it has broken through the industry limits. China's financial structure has undergone great changes, showing the diversification of financial structure and the complexity of financial risks. The current separate supervision model is also increasingly difficult to meet the practical needs of the development of the financial industry.

However, under the current national conditions in China, it is not advisable to implement unified supervision too fast, but to maintain the pattern of separate supervision. However, by setting coordination methods, including coordination of information exchange, coordination of regulations, coordination of daily supervision, and handling coordination, etc. the existing regulatory conflicts and regulatory omissions can be solved. This is because, at present, China is still a separate operation pattern, and it is difficult to change in the short term. In this circumstance, it is obviously impossible to obtain an economic scale of supervision under the unified supervision, and it is easy to lead to the monopoly of power and the emergence of extreme bureaucracy. Fundamentally speaking, China's current financial industry's poor supervision and poor performance are not only due to the unreasonable setting of the regulatory agencies, but also the unclear financial supervision concept, the backward operation mechanism, the immature legislative enforcement environment, and the monopoly of state-owned banks.

5.5.3 Problems in the financial regulatory system

(1) *The financial division supervision system does not meet the reality of mixed operation in the financial industry*

With China's accession to the WTO, the trend of China's financial industry mixed operation is more obvious, and the financial product structure and organizational structure are undergoing fundamental changes. At the structural level of financial products, the integration of banking, securities, and insurance businesses allows different financial institutions to provide alternative compound financial products, such as insurance agents, pledged securities, margin accounts, and investment-linked insurance. When the business of different financial institutions is increasingly crossed, if the business supervision involves multiple supervisory departments, it usually needs to be coordinated by multiple departments for a long time to complete. For these new businesses, it is easy to lead to the drawbacks of duplication of supervision and lack of supervision. Moreover, China's current separate supervision system characterized by institutional supervision implements the business approval system for management, which also limits the space for financial business development and innovation to a certain extent. At the organizational level of the financial industry, the trend of China's financial grouping has been accelerating. The funds and business communications between banks, trusts, securities and insurance institutions under the control of financial holding groups, bank holding groups and enterprise group companies have become increasingly frequent, forming a defacto mixed operation. Under the financial separate supervision system, it is difficult for regulators to comprehensively examine the risks of these financial groups, and the transparency of financial group supervision is not high. The issue of transparency is not only due to the financial status of individual members of the holding group, but also to the financial status of the entire holding group, as well as to the governance structure of the holding group. The complex organizational structure and internal transactions of financial holding companies make it difficult for supervisory authorities to understand and accurately determine the real risks faced by a group member. For such companies, under the financial separate supervision system, it is difficult for China's supervisory authorities to reach an effective cooperation to supervise them.

(2) *Difficulties in coordination between monetary policy and financial regulatory policies*

In order to solve the role conflict between the central bank's monetary policy function and financial supervision function, in 2003, China separated the banking supervision function from the PBOC and established the China Banking Regulatory Commission, which is responsible for banking supervision. At this point, it can be said that the monetary policy function and the financial supervision function have basically been separated. However, this did not completely eliminate the conflict between them. Since there is a very important relationship between monetary policy and financial supervision, effective financial supervision is a strong support for the implementation of monetary policy, and financial supervision also needs to take monetary policy as a starting point. Therefore, an accurate positioning is needed in the relationship between these two functions, especially in developing countries, where financial supervision and monetary policy are highly consistent at the specific implementation and operational levels, while the current regulatory system is almost completely separated from the central bank's monetary policy. It is not conducive to the effective implementation of them.

(3) *The financial supervision information sharing mechanism is not perfect*

Whether it is unified supervision or separate supervision, coordination between different regulatory areas is important. The exchange and sharing of regulatory data and regulatory information between financial regulatory authorities is the basis for strengthening effective supervision and coordination between different regulatory authorities. "One bank and three commissions" have certain powers of collecting regulatory information according to law, established their own regulatory information systems, and collected regulatory information from multiple sources to increase the burden of regulatory objects. Meanwhile, the various regulatory authorities, from their respective perspectives, after analyzing, processing and forming financial institution risk assessment reports, cannot provide reference to other regulatory authorities through effective and smooth information sharing channels, resulting in serious waste of regulatory resources. It is not helpful to the supervision department to find out the cross-market supervision issues that need to be coordinated and solved on the basis of mastering comprehensive information.

(4) *Lack of regulatory coordination between regulators*

At present, under the separate supervision system of China, there is a lack of necessary coordination among various financial regulatory agencies. In 2003, the

CBRC, the CSRC, and the CIRC signed the "Memorandum on the Share Out the Work and Cooperate with One Another in Financial Supervision with the China Banking Regulatory Commission, China Securities Regulatory Commission and the China Insurance Regulatory Commission", and established a working mechanism for holding joint meetings, and a regular contact mechanism for discussing and negotiating specific professional regulatory issues on a quarterly basis. However, so far the number of supervisory joint meetings has been limited, and the "regulatory joint meeting" system is only forum-style and has no decision-making process. In the context of mixed operations, the coordination content of today's regulators remains at the general and regular regulatory exchanges and cooperation. The financial regulatory coordination mechanism in the cross-market financial product supervision and coordination and the prevention of the risk-contagion caused by the cross-shareholding of financial institutions are seriously absent. Especially for many financial holding companies that have actually formed in the past, there is not only a legislative gap in financial law, but also lack of substantive institutional arrangements in the coordination of financial supervision, resulting in potential evolution of the systemic risks of financial markets, which affect the long-term healthy development of China's financial system.

In view of the problems existing in China's financial supervision system, China's financial regulatory system reform should promote the balanced development of financial reform and financial innovation to significantly improve the ability of financial services to the real economy. Comprehensive supervision of banks, securities, insurance and other industries should be conducted, and finally establish a unified financial supervision system. A macro-prudential financial management system framework should be established to maintain financial stability and ensure financial security.

5.6 Reform of foreign exchange management system and internationalization of renminbi

Before the reform and opening up, China implemented a highly centralized planned economic system. The state has always implemented the unified management, distribution and use of foreign exchange, and different foreign exchange earning management. Due to the shortage of foreign exchange resources, strict foreign exchange controls have been implemented. Since the reform and opening up, China has carried out a series of reforms to the foreign exchange management system. Since the beginning of the 21st century, with the continuous expansion of China's foreign exchange reserves, the foreign exchange management system has undergone comprehensive and profound reforms, which has further promoted the development of China's foreign trade and investment.

5.6.1 Foreign exchange management system reform

In 2001, after China joined the WTO, it accelerated its integration into economic and financial globalization, further improved the socialist market economic system, expanded foreign trade, maintained a high level of foreign investment, maintained a double surplus in the international balance of payments, and continued to increase foreign exchange reserves. In 2006, China's foreign exchange reserves exceeded Japan, and ranked first in the world.[1] Under the new institutional environment and foreign exchange income and expenditure situation, China's foreign exchange management has undergone fundamental changes in its concepts, methods and means, which are embodied in the following aspects.

(1) *Further increase the degree of trade facilitation*

In 2001, the opening standards for foreign exchange settlement accounts of Chinese-funded enterprises were relaxed, and the scope of opening accounts was expanded. In 2002, the conditions for the opening of foreign exchange accounts for current-income enterprises by Chinese-funded enterprises were removed, and the original foreign exchange settlement accounts and special foreign exchange accounts were merged into current accounts of Forex account; in 2003, the Forex account limit in current account under the temporary collection and payment of international underwriting projects was released; from May 2004 to Aug. 2007, it was relaxed in four times until the opening account conditions and limit management of current account were cancelled. The opening, change and closure of the current account Forex account shall be adjusted by prior approval to be handled directly by the bank in accordance with foreign exchange management requirements and commercial practices. The cancellation of the current account Forex account limit management has enabled domestic institutions to retain their current account foreign exchange income

[1] Wang Yuanhong, "A Research on Internal and External Balance of China Economy", Beijing: Renmin University of China, 2009.

as needed, and to meet the reasonable current account remittance needs of enterprises and individuals.

(2) *Steadily promote the convertibility of capital projects and broaden the flow channels of funds*

In Dec. 1996, after China accepted the eighth clause of the "International Monetary Fund Agreement" and realized the full convertibility of the renminbi in the current account, the focus of foreign exchange management began to shift to the foreign exchange management of capital account. The goal of foreign exchange management of capital account has undergone phase changes. Maintaining the independence of monetary policy, maintaining the stability of the nominal exchange rate of the renminbi, maintaining the balance of international payments, and preventing the spread of the financial crisis have become the main objectives of foreign exchange management of capital account. After 2001, in order to comply with the objective needs of economic development and opening up, the reform of foreign exchange management of capital account began to deepen. The foreign exchange management of capital account gradually changed from "wide-in and strict-out" to balanced management, and a series policy measures of enhancing capital inflow management and encouraging capital outflows were introduced.

First is to steadily promote the opening up of capital projects, relax restrictions on foreign exchange purchases, implement pilot reforms of foreign exchange management for overseas investment, gradually expand capital outflow channels, and support the implementation of the "go global" strategy. Banks are allowed to collect domestic foreign exchange or renminbi to purchase foreign exchange to invest in overseas financial markets, and to support securities institutions to collect domestic institutions and individuals to invest in overseas securities markets, and to encourage insurance institutions to make financial investments in foreign countries with their own foreign exchange or foreign exchange purchases within a certain percentage.

The second is to strengthen and improve the management of capital inflows and foreign exchange settlements. The classification and management of foreign exchange receipts and settlements of trade shall be fully facilitated by legitimate operating agencies. The state also strengthened the management of foreign debts and foreign exchange settlements of real estate enterprises, implemented the principle of real demand and self-use for foreign investment in domestic real estate, and continued to strengthen the management of short-term foreign debts. The limit on the foreign exchange purchase of foreign investment was also cancelled, and to pay the upfront fee in advance for the purchasing of foreign exchange is allowed. The state also should improve the relevant management policies of the Qualified Foreign Institutional Investor System and actively guide them to promote the development of the domestic capital market.

(3) *Strengthen the management of capital inflows and actively prevent financial risks*

The implementation of the "Regulations on Foreign Exchange Control" was revised, which improved the long-standing weak links in foreign exchange management, highlighted the balanced and standardized management of foreign exchange capital outflows, and provided strong legal protection to better maintain the balance of payments, prevent international economic and financial risks, and further expand reform and opening up. The State Administration of Foreign Exchange (SAFE) focused on strengthening the management of foreign exchange collection and settlement of "concerned enterprises" which is obviously inconsistent with trade collection and foreign trade exports. In 2008, it implemented a joint export verification and settlement verification policy with the General Administration of Customs and the Ministry of Commerce, and implemented the bond and debt registration management system for trade in goods in the mean time, to strengthen the authenticity and consistency of trade capital inflows and goods exports, and effectively prevent abnormal funds from flowing through trade channels. Through the information network for export collection and settlement network verification, the efficiency is greatly improved and the procedures are more convenient.

5.6.2 Reform of renminbi exchange rate formation mechanism

After more than 10 years of practice in the reform of the foreign exchange system in 1994, the managed floating exchange rate system based on market supply and demand is compatible with China's economic development stage, financial supervision level and corporate affordability, and is in line with the selection of China's national institutions. After the exchange rate was consolidated in 1994, the renminbi exchange rate remained basically stable and slightly appreciated, which enhanced the confidence of all sectors in the stability of the renminbi value. After the outbreak of the Asian financial crisis, China promised that the renminbi will not depreciate, and narrowed the exchange rate fluctuation range. Objectively, the volatility of the renminbi against the US dollar since 1998 has been limited and almost fixed, and could not truly reflect the changes in market supply and demand. The renminbi exchange rate formation mechanism was difficult to adapt to the needs of China's rapid economic development and structural adjustment, which was not suitable to the economic response to the challenges of economic globalization. The changes in the situation and the long-term development of China's economy required it to be improved.

On Jul.21, 2005, the Chinese government carried out drastic reforms in the renminbi exchange rate formation mechanism and began to implement a "floating exchange rate system based on market supply and demand with reference to a basket of currencies". The renminbi exchange rate is no longer solely peg US dollar, but referring to a basket of currencies, floating according to market supply and demand. In accordance with the principle of initiative, controllability and gradualism, the role of market supply and demand in the formation of exchange rates has been exerted, exchange rate flexibility has been enhanced, and the renminbi exchange rate has remained basically stable at a reasonable and balanced level (see Table 5–2).

Table 5–2 Changes in the foreign exchange rate system since the reform and opening up

Timeline	Institution of exchange rate	Exchange rate level
1979-1980	Managing a floating exchange rate system	The exchange rate is stable in the international market, the exchange rate of the countries is above the middle level, and it is stable and rising.
1981-1984	Peg a basket of monetary system	The internal trade settlement price was introduced, and the dual exchange rate system in which the official exchange rate and the market exchange rate coexisted that is, the crawling and pegged exchange rate system.
1985-1993	Manage exchange rate system and floating exchange rate system	The official exchange rate and the foreign exchange adjustment price coexist, floating exchange rate system implemented after 1991.
1994-2005	Managing a floating exchange rate system	Implement a fixed exchange rate system pegged to the US dollar, and the exchange rate will remain unchanged for a long time.
2005 to present	Peg a basket of monetary system	Implement a managed floating exchange rate system, increase the exchange rate fluctuation range, increase the frequency.

Source: Jiang Shiyin, *Rational Thinking on China's Financial System Reform*, Beijing: China Financial & Economic Publishing House, 2009, p.202.

In 2006, we deepened the reform of the renminbi exchange rate formation mechanism, improved the managed floating exchange rate system, and successively introduced a series of exchange rate formation mechanism reform supporting measures to further improve the managed floating exchange rate system. First is to improve the foreign exchange market system, introduce the market maker system and over-the-counter method (OTC) in the inter-bank foreign exchange market, and improve the formation method of the renminbi exchange rate intermediate price. The second is to expand the scope of forward foreign exchange settlement, and facilitate market entities to avoid exchange rate risks, launch the renminbi swap transactions, and enrich products in the foreign exchange market. The third is to expand market makers and members of the foreign exchange market and increase the level of activity in the foreign exchange market.

In June 2010, the reform of the exchange rate formation mechanism was further promoted. The core is to adhere to the market supply and demand, adjust with reference to a basket of currencies, and continue to dynamically manage and adjust the renminbi exchange rate fluctuations according to the published exchange rate fluctuation range of the foreign exchange market. In 2007 and 2012, the PBOC expanded the exchange rate of renminbi against the US dollar in the inter-bank spot foreign exchange market twice, and gradually enhanced the flexibility of the renminbi exchange rate. It should be emphasized that the reform of the renminbi exchange rate system cannot be separated from the reform of the interest rate formation mechanism. In an environment of open economy and capital flows, any difference in the interest rates of local and foreign currencies will theoretically induce international capital flows and affect the exchange rate of a country. In other words, any interest rate adjustment must be accompanied by exchange rate fluctuations. Therefore, the rigid interest rate system will inevitably bring a huge impact on the renminbi exchange rate, which in turn will affect the normal operation of the entire exchange rate system.

5.6.3 Renminbi internationalization

When the Asian financial crisis broke out in 1997, an important revelation of reflecting on this financial crisis was the issue of the monetary system. After joining the WTO, China has paid more attention to comprehensive, multi-level, flexible and pragmatic foreign financial cooperation, and has made important progress in strengthening regional financial cooperation and steadily promoting financial cooperation with Hong Kong and Macao. In particular, in line with the development requirements of the international and domestic situations, the cross-border use of renminbi has achieved remarkable results, and the cross-border renminbi business has expanded from current account to part of capital account.

(1) *The impact of the internationalization of renminbi*

Currency internationalization refers to the function of a currency in the international accounting unit, trading intermediary and storage currency. The internationalization of renminbi refers to the wide recognition and acceptance of renminbi in the international market, and the function of the pricing unit, exchange medium and value storage, that is, the international settlement currency, investment currency and reserve currency. The path selection of renminbi internationalization is shown in Table 5–3.

Table 5–3 International monetary function and the path choice of renminbi internationalization

International monetary function	Renminbi internationalization path		
	Current path	**Medium-term goal**	**Long-term outlook**
Medium of transaction	Cross-border trade settlement	Foreign Direct Investment	Non-residents capital of each country
Value scale	Offshore market in Hong Kong and other places	Onshore market, multinational industry, wealth and useful resources pricing	
Value storage	Bilateral currency swap	Join the Special Drawing Rights (SDR) basket	

Source: Zhen Feng, "The Internationalization of renminbi: Development", Prospects and Orientation. *Economic Theory and Business Management*, 2014(5), pp.22-31.

What impact does the internationalization of renminbi have on China? From a positive perspective, the impact of renminbi internationalization on China mainly includes: first, it is conducive to improving China's position in the international economic system and the distribution of international interests; second, it helps to reduce exchange rate risks and promote the development of China's international trade and investment; third, it is helpful for the development of China's banking industry. Of course, the internationalization of the renminbi is also costly. First of all, the output of the renminbi will bring many unforeseen problems and constraints to the formulation and implementation of domestic monetary policy. Second, as an international currency medium, the international movement of renminbi funds will affect China's interest rate, exchange rate and price level. Third, after the internationalization of the renminbi, it will assume the task of international financial stability. The formulation of its macroeconomic policies will cause great externalities to other countries, and coordination with other countries in macroeconomic policies will become necessary. Finally, a sustained capital account deficit or current account deficit must be accepted to allow the national currency to be exported. But in general, the internationalization of the renminbi is more beneficial than the disadvantages.[1] Therefore, gradually promoting the internationalization of the renminbi is one of the directions of China's financial development.

(2) *The inevitability of the internationalization of the renminbi*

Currency internationalization should generally have the following preconditions: currency issuing countries have large scale economies and trades; stable currency values; political stability; convertible under capital account; financial markets are generally open, with extensive financial instruments, deep secondary markets, and completely functional institution; a strong central bank. Although China does not fully satisfy all the preconditions of currency internationalization, based on the analysis of China's economic aggregate, openness and economic stability, the internationalization of renminbi has its inevitability.

First of all, as the basis of renminbi credit, China's economic aggregate has expanded rapidly, and its role in pulling the world economy has increased. From the international experience, the greater the impact of the economic aggregate of a country's economy on the world economy, the more likely its currency will become an international trading intermediary and reserve currency. In the 19th and 20th centuries, the British pound and the US dollar became the international core currencies respectively. After the 1970s, the degree of internationalization of the Japanese Yen and the Deutsche Mark continued to increase, all of which were closely related to the entry of the countries into the world's most developed economies. Among the world's major currency issuers, China's total economic output accounted for 14.86% of the world's total economy in 2012, which is equivalent to the size of the Euro zone's economy. The gap with the United States is less than 4% points, much higher than Japan and the UK. The huge wealth accumulated by China has consolidated the credit foundation for the internationalization of the renminbi.[2]

Secondly, the openness of China's finance has been continuously improved, laying the institutional foundation for the internationalization of the renminbi. Since the reform and opening up, in order to meet the needs of the internationalization of economic development, the pace of China's financial internationalization has accelerated.

---

[1] Chen Jiangsheng and Chen Zhaoming, "The reform of world monetary system and renminbi internationalization", *Journal of the Party School of the Central Committee of the CPC*, 2010 (1), pp. 56-61.

[2] Chen Jiangsheng, "The time has come to raise the renminbi's, profile in the international monetary system", *Paper of Shenzhen Special Zone*, Oct. 21, 2014.

Especially in recent years, China's financial industry has developed rapidly. A number of financial laws and regulations involving banks, securities and insurance have been introduced or revised one after another, initially forming a relatively complete financial law support system; financial institutions are diversified development pattern, state-owned Banks, joint-stock commercial banks, local commercial banks, private banks, and foreign banks compete for each other; financial rules are constantly in line with international standards, a number of domestic financial institutions are on the international stage, and a number of international financial institutions enter the domestic market; financial markets are steadily improving, the control system of central banks is sound and powerful. A good financial market and a complete financial system will not only improve the international competitiveness of China's financial industry, but also help the renminbi to play its international monetary function. On Jul.21, 2005, China reformed the renminbi exchange rate formation mechanism and began to implement a managed floating exchange rate system based on market supply and demand with reference to a basket of currencies. The renminbi is no longer pegged to the US dollar, creating a more flexible exchange rate mechanism, which has created favorable conditions for the further internationalization of the renminbi.

Finally, the stable development of domestic economic and financial development has laid an environmental foundation for the internationalization of renminbi. The important basis of the international currency is the stable development of the domestic economy and finance, the fluctuation of the exchange rate is not large, and the inflation rate is low, so the assets invested in the currency can be preserved and value-added. Judging from China's situation, China's economy has continued to grow rapidly since reform and opening up. Despite the impact of the global financial crisis 2008, China's economy has maintained an average growth rate of 8%, while high economic growth has not brought high inflation. Since 2008, China's annual average inflation rate is about 4.7%, which is equivalent to the world inflation level, far lower than the inflation of more than 8% in emerging countries in the same period.[1] The stable operation of China's economy has brought a steady increase in the renminbi exchange rate for many years.

(3) *Progress has been made in the internationalization of renminbi*

In recent years, the attractiveness of renminbi has increased, and the abroad

[1] Chen Jiangsheng, "The time has come to raise the renminbi's profile in the international monetary system", *Paper of Shenzhen Special Zone*, Oct. 21, 2014.

circulation and use have continued to expand, and the process of internationalization of renminbi has made tremendous progress.

First, border trade settlement has accelerated the regionalization of the renminbi. The circulation of renminbi was mainly developed along with the development of border trade, private trade and border tourism. The renminbi as a settlement currency and payment currency has been widely used in the border areas of Sino-Vietnam, Sino-Russia, Sino-North Korea, and Sino-Laos, and can be freely exchanged with the currencies of these countries. To some extent, the renminbi has become a defacto regional currency. The scope of regionalization of renminbi will also be further expanded, and the status of regional currencies will be increasingly consolidated, thereby promoting the internationalization of the renminbi.

Second, tourism consumption promotes the internationalization of renminbi. With the rise of tourism, the circulation of renminbi has continued to develop in Singapore, Malaysia, Thailand, South Korea and other countries. Since Jan.10, 2005, the "UnionPay Card" has been opened in South Korea, Thailand, and Singapore, enabling cardholders to use the "UnionPay Card" for shopping in these countries. It can also be used at ATMs in these countries. A certain amount of national currency can be withdrawn for day-to-day consumption. Since Dec. 2005, it has opened the China UnionPay card ATM acceptance business in Germany, France, Spain, Belgium and Luxembourg. All of this shows that the international status of the renminbi has further improved, and the internationalization of the renminbi has been further advanced.

The third is currency swap and economic exchanges to promote the internationalization of the renminbi. In China's bilateral currency swap agreements with Japan, South Korea, Malaysia, Belarus, Indonesia, Argentina and other countries, the exchange of renminbi and the other country's currency is allowed. It can be seen that the renminbi has been widely accepted by China's neighboring countries or regions to a certain extent, and the internationalization of the renminbi is at a stage of gradual development.

In addition, according to a report released by the Society for Worldwide Interbank Financial Telecommunication (SWIFT), since Oct. 2013, the renminbi has replaced the Euro, becoming the second most commonly used international trade financing currency, second only to the US dollar[1].

Promoting the internationalization of the renminbi is in line with China's

---

[1] Zhang Xiujuan, *Powerful Finance*, Beijing: Economy & Management Publishing House, 2016, p.102.

long-term interests. At present, China also has certain favorable conditions. We should take the favorable opportunity in time, eliminate unnecessary policy obstacles, and steadily advance as market needs. However, we must also see that it is not true to realize the internationalization of renminbi in the short term. Man-made forced promotion of the internationalization of renminbi is not only unbenefit to the stable development of economic and financial development, but also not suitable to the law of international financial development. We must judge the situation and be cautious.

5.7 Open financial industry to the outside world

From the history of more than 40 years of reform and opening up, opening up is accompanied by the entire reform process. As early as the beginning of the reform, Deng Xiaoping was very aware of the need to engage in Sino-foreign cooperation and opening up. In 1979, China drafted the first "Sino-foreign Joint Venture Enterprise Law", and established China International Trust and Investment Corporation as a window for attracting foreign investment and international economic and financial cooperation, and successfully issued the first foreign debt. Some foreign banks have also begun to set up representative offices and business offices in China. The outbreak of the Asian financial crisis in 1997 highlighted the profound impact of economic and financial globalization on China. Since China's accession to the World Trade Organization in 2001, with the in-depth development of globalization and the sustained and rapid growth of China's economy and the increasing integration of domestic and foreign markets, the voice for international cooperation with China to strengthen financial policy coordination and enhance mutual cooperation has been growing.

5.7.1 Fulfilling WTO commitments and opening up financial markets

After China's accession to the WTO, it fulfilled a series of commitments to open up the banking, securities, and insurance industries, and increased the opening up of the financial industry in a planned and step-by-step manner.

First, in order to meet the needs of opening up and economic development, strengthen and improve the management of foreign financial institutions, and promote the steady operation of the banking industry, the "Regulations on the Administration of Foreign Financial Institutions of the People's Republic of China", which was revised on Feb.1, 2002, was officially implemented. It actively supports and encourages foreign banks to develop in the central and western regions, and opens renminbi businesses in cities such as Xi'an, Shenyang, Harbin, Changchun, Lanzhou and Xining to foreign banks in advance, and relaxes the qualifications for their renminbi business in these regions. It has opened up a green channel for foreign banks to set up institutions and start businesses in the central and western regions, and prioritizes the approval of their establishment and business start-up applications under the same conditions.[1]

Second is to timely adjust the working capital policy of foreign banks, gradually reduce the working capital level of operating the local and foreign currency business, and reduce the working capital requirements. The Chinese banking industry fully liberalized its foreign exchange business in 2001. In Dec. 2003, it extended the client objects of the foreign bank's renminbi business to Chinese-funded enterprises. On Oct. 27, 2005, China Construction Bank Corporation listed on the Hong Kong Stock Exchange. It marks the beginning of the move of Chinese state-owned commercial banks to the international capital market.

Third, in Dec. 2002, the "Interim Measures for the Administration of Domestic Securities Investment by Qualified Foreign Institutional Investors" was promulgated. The implementation of the QFII system has had a profound impact on the size, structure and investment concept of the Chinese securities market. As another arrangement for opening up to the outside world, on Feb.1, 2006, the "Measures for the Administration of Strategic Investment by Listed Companies by Foreign Investors" was officially implemented, allowing foreign investors to make strategic investments in listed companies that have completed the share-trading reform. Foreign banks and Chinese banks are allowed to simultaneously set up derivative trading business, domestic securities investment custody business of qualified foreign institutional investors, overseas financial management and custody business on behalf of customers, and allow foreign banks to open agency insurance business.

5.7.2 Actively participate in international economic organizations

With the acceleration of the reform and opening up process and the continuous improvement of economic strength, China has shifted from passive adaptation to active participation in relevant organizations in global multilateral organizations, gradually began to participate in formulating international rules, and actively

[1] Zhang Chenghui, "The overall opening up policies and basic conditions of the Chinese mainland's financial industry", *Foreign Investment in China*, 2007 (10), pp. 25-26.

contributed to promote the fair and rational development of the world economy.

First, since China officially resumed its legal seat in the International Monetary Fund (IMF) in 1980, representatives of the Chinese government have exchanged views with representatives of various countries on the world economy and the international financial situation, international currencies system, and the views of the member states' macroeconomic policies in the IMF's committees and executive boards. In exploring ways to promote the stable development of the world economy and enhance international financial cooperation, the positions and policy propositions published by China have gradually attracted the attention of the world. Meanwhile, China has long been a creditor country of the IMF, providing funds for the IMF's various loan arrangements, and able to support the IMF's preferential loan programs for poor countries. After the outbreak of the Asian financial crisis, China has increased financial support for crisis countries and other countries with economic difficulties. It has invested US$2.5 billion through the IMF and provided nearly US$1 billion in bilateral loans.

Second, the Bank for International Settlements, known as the central bank of the central banks, is also the birthplace of important regulatory concepts and international regulatory rules. In recent years, the cooperation between China's financial management department and the Bank for International Settlements has continued to deepen. Each year, China sends representatives to attend the central bank governors meeting organized by the bank to publicize domestic economic policies and become familiar with and participate in the formulation of international rules. China was invited to participate in the activities of the professional committees such as the Market Committee of the Group of Ten, the Global Financial System Committee, and was appointed as the chairman of the Asian Advisory Committee of the Bank for International Settlements. It established the channel of communication between members of the Asia Pacific region and the board of directors and management. On Jul.1, 2006, China officially joined the board of directors of the Bank for International Settlements, which enabled China to participate more deeply and comprehensively in the formulation of international standards and norms, and was conducive to promoting effective cooperation with the international community at a higher level.

Third is to actively participate in the international economic and financial high-level forum and strengthen dialogue with relevant major powers. The Chinese government has actively participated in the international economic and financial high-level forum, effectively publicized the policies and achievements of China's economic reform and opening up, enhanced the consensus with the international community, and created a favorable external environment for China's economic development. Bilateral financial cooperation is also an important channel for China to strengthen financial openness and cooperation. Since the launch of the China-US Strategic Economic Dialogue in 2006, China and the US have continuously strengthened dialogue and consultation in the core areas of international financial system reform, financial cooperation, monetary policy, anti-money laundering, and financial supervision through this platform, and continuously deepened bilateral economic and financial cooperation. At the same time, China strengthens financial cooperation with central banks such as Russia, Kazakhstan, South Korea, and Japan, and jointly promote the continued development of bilateral financial cooperation through various cooperation mechanisms.

5.7.3 Strengthen international financial supervision and cooperation

China's financial industry attaches great importance to regulatory cooperation with international counterparts, attaches importance to the construction of international regulatory cooperation mechanisms, continuously develops and deepens exchanges and cooperation with international regulatory agencies, strengthens regulatory dialogue and communication at different levels, and continuously improves cross-border supervision. At the same time, it has deepened the understanding of the international community on financial reform and the regulatory process.

First, strengthen international coordination and cooperation in banking supervision. Since 2007, the CBRC has signed bilateral memorandums of understanding or regulatory cooperation agreements with financial regulatory authorities with the US, the UK, Australia, Russia, Japan and other countries and regions, and has established bilateral or multilateral periodic consultation agreements and meeting mechanism with many countries and regions, and participate in multilateral regulatory agencies and actively participate in the construction of international regulatory cooperation mechanisms. In addition to participating in the regulatory exchanges and cooperation between the International Monetary Fund and the Bank for International Settlements, China's financial regulatory authorities also actively participate in the activities of multilateral regulatory organizations such as the World Bank, the Central Bank of the Pacific Rim, and the SENZA. Especially in recent years, China has joined a number of international or regional multilateral regulatory agencies, and the breadth and depth of foreign cooperation in the field of financial supervision has increased.

Second, strengthen international coordination and cooperation in securities supervision. In Jul. 1995, at the 21st annual meeting organized by the International Securities Regulatory Commission, the China Securities Regulatory Commission became a full member. The exchanges and cooperation between the CSRC and overseas securities and futures regulators, the International Securities Regulatory Commission and other international organizations have been continuously strengthened. As of Jun. 2015, the CSRC has signed 62 bilateral memorandums of cooperation with securities and futures regulators in 60 countries or regions.[1] The signing of these memorandums enables Chinese and foreign regulators to exchange regulatory information, provide mutual cross-border investigation assistance, and conduct personnel exchanges and research cooperation.

Third, strengthen international coordination and cooperation in insurance supervision. In 2000, the China Insurance Regulatory Commission officially joined the International Association of Insurance Supervisors (IAIS). In Dec. 2005, the CIRC joined the International Pension Supervisors Association and was elected a member of the Executive Committee. In Oct. 2006, the 13th annual meeting of the IAIS was held in Beijing. Nearly 700 representatives from 94 countries and regions attended the meeting. At the same time, the CIRC has continuously strengthened bilateral and multilateral insurance regulatory cooperation of Sino-US, Sino-Europe, and Sino-Asia, and established a bilateral insurance regulatory dialogue mechanism between China and the US. In 2005, the CIRC organized the insurance regulatory authorities of 14 countries and regions in Asia to jointly publish the "Beijing Declaration on Asian Regional Insurance Supervision and Cooperation", and initiated the establishment of the "Asia Insurance Supervisor Forum", marking the Asian regional insurance regulatory cooperation from conception to reality.

5.7.4 The positive role of China's financial opening up

First, promoting financial reform. The opening up of the financial industry has exerted tremendous impetus to China's economic and financial reforms, and has formed the institutional reform effect of opening up and promoting reform. On the whole, the opening of China's financial industry reflects the obvious characteristics of "promote reforms through opening up". Before the accession to the World Trade

[1] CSRC, "List of memorandums signed by the China Securities Regulatory Commission and overseas securities (futures) regulators (Jun 2015)", http://www.csrc.gov.cn.

Organization, China's state-owned financial institutions operated at high risk. Under the competitive pressure of foreign financial institutions, domestic financial institutions have significantly accelerated the pace of reform. With the gradual opening up of foreign financial institutions, the structure of China's financial market has undergone profound changes. The monopoly structure of state-owned financial institutions has been gradually broken. The structure of financial markets has been transformed from a highly concentrated pattern of oligopoly to a moderate concentration pattern of monopolistic competition. The financial market organization structure has been continuously optimized, and the diversification trend of financial market property rights has become increasingly obvious. The degree of concentration has been reduced while the degree of competition has been increasing, and the efficiency of resource allocation has tended to increase. The deepening of financial openness has broken the inefficient balance of China's financial industry and accelerated the pace of reform of the domestic financial industry.

Second, establishing a modern financial system. The most prominent feature or basic requirement of the modern financial enterprise system is the clear financial property structure and the perfect corporate governance structure. With the gradual advancement of the financial industry, through cooperation with foreign financial institutions, Chinese-funded financial institutions improve the corporate governance structure through the participation of foreign shareholders, restructure the governance structure and business processes, improve risk management capabilities, and regulate the company's market behavior. The continuous expansion of the financial sector to the outside world has not only attracted capital, but more importantly, it has introduced advanced foreign financial management experience and technology, and promoted the process of establishing a modern financial enterprise system in China's financial industry.

Third, improving the level of financial supervision. With the continuous expansion of China's financial industry in the field of opening up, the level of supervision of China's financial regulatory authorities is gradually increasing. The opening of China's financial industry is bound to be accompanied by strict supervision and deepening reforms. Most of the foreign-funded financial institutions entering China's financial market are international first-class multinational financial institutions. They are highly active and have rich experience in playing games with financial regulatory authorities. They often use the fuzzy areas of regulatory regulations to conduct financial innovation and evade supervision. This situation will inevitably require

China's financial regulatory authorities to raise the level of supervision, implement strict access examinations and daily supervision of foreign financial institutions in line with international standards, timely discover and make up for loopholes in the financial regulatory framework, and make the regulatory system more reasonable. These will help to form a more active and effective legal system and regulatory framework.

Fourth, improving the competitiveness of financial institutions. The entry of foreign financial institutions into the Chinese financial market has brought about demonstration effects, learning effects and competitive effects. Under the influence of these effects, Chinese-funded financial institutions continue to accelerate the pace of innovation, and by learning from the mature products and service models of foreign financial institutions, they can improve the high value-added business capabilities beyond traditional businesses. The rich management and management experience of foreign-funded financial institutions has produced a large spillover effect, which has continuously increased the competitiveness of Chinese-funded financial institutions.

In order to adapt to the urgent need of China's financial industry to open up new situations and effectively cope with the pressure of China's financial further opening up, China needs to formulate and implement a clear financial opening-up strategy. In fact, after years of exploration, the basic framework of China's overall financial opening-up strategy has been formed, that is, keeping the initiative in our own hands, step by step, safe and controllable, competitive and cooperative, and mutually beneficial and win-win.[1] In the process of expanding financial opening up, we will further optimize the structure of financial opening up, improve the quality of financial opening up, focus on the benefits of financial opening up, upgrade the financial opening-up strategy, effectively improve financial efficiency and efficiency, and achieve overall planning and development. Through establishment of internal and external linkage, mutual benefit and "win-win", secured and efficient open financial system, China financial industry form a new advantage in international financial cooperation and competition under the conditions of economic and financial globalization, promote the sound and rapid development of China's economy under the conditions of expanding openness, and gradually promote China from an open financial power to a great financial power.

---

[1] Wen Jiabao, "Deepening financial reform in an all-round way to promote the sustainable and healthy development of the financial industry", *Gazette of the State Council of the People's Republic of China*, 2007(3).

Chapter 6
New Measures for China's Financial Reform

In his speech on the 40th group study of the Political Bureau of the CPC Central Committee, General Secretary Xi Jinping pointed out: "Finance is the core of the modern economy. To maintain a stable and healthy economic development, we must do a good job of finance. Since the reform and opening up, we have been emphasizing on finance work, and financial security which are always highly valued. China's financial industry has made tremendous achievements. Finance has become an important tool for resource allocation and macroeconomic regulation and control, and has become an important force in promoting economic and social development."

Since the 18th National Congress of the CPC, in accordance with the strategic arrangements of the party and the state, especially the spirit of the 3rd Plenary Session of the 18th Central Committee, a new round of comprehensive and deep reforms has been launched. The core of comprehensive deepening reform is marketization, and the core of market-oriented reform is the marketization of factor prices. The report of the 18th CPC National Congress clearly stated: "Deepen the reform of the financial system, improve the modern financial system that promotes macroeconomic stability, support the development of the real economy, develop multi-level capital markets, steadily promote the reform of interest rate and exchange rate marketization, and gradually realize renminbi exchangeable under capital account. Accelerate the development of private financial institutions, improve financial supervision, promote financial innovation, and maintain financial stability". From the transition of economic development model, modern economic system construction and internal and external economics, the interest rate marketization, the improvement of bond market, the marketization of exchange rate formation mechanism, the improvement of multi-level capital market system and the deepening reform of banking system are core tasks of financial market systems. And the development and regulation of innovative financial services is also an important issue for the marketization of financial factors.

6.1 Interest rate marketization reform enters a new stage

Interest rates are important economic levers for banks to play a role in promoting and regulating the national economy. Interest rate liberalization is one of the core reforms in China's financial sector. The interest rate management system at the beginning of China's reform is a strict planned economic management system. Under this system, the interest rate is set by the State Council, and the interest rate management right is completely concentrated in the head office of the PBOC. The major adjustment of interest rates must be reported to the State Council for approval, and all branches and professional banks have no right to change interest rates. Over the past 40 years of reform and opening up, China has gradually established the basic role of the market in resource allocation, and has realized the transformation of macroeconomic regulation from direct mode to mainly relying on indirect mode. After the introduction of commodity relations into the financial resource allocation system, the scarcity of financial resources also requires the use of price mechanisms to identify demand and improve allocation efficiency. Therefore, interest rate marketization reform and interest rate regulation have gradually entered the vision of policy makers.

In recent years, according to the strategic arrangements of the Central Committee of CPC and the State Council, China's interest rate liberalization reform has accelerated and made key progress. At present, interest rate control has been basically liberalized, and market-based interest rate formation and regulation mechanisms have been continuously improved, creating favorable conditions for giving full play to the decisive role of the market in resource allocation. In 2012, the 18th CPC National Congress report stated that it is necessary to "steadily advance the market-based reform of interest rates and exchange rates". The 3rd Plenary Session of the 18th CPC Central Committee also proposed that "it is necessary to accelerate the marketization of interest rates". The goal of this market-oriented reform is to establish an interest rate formation mechanism that determines the deposit and loan interest rates of financial institutions by market supply and demand. The central monetary policy tools regulate and guide market interest rates, so that market mechanisms play a decisive role in the allocation of financial resources.

6.1.1 Stage of interest rate marketization reform

Since the reform and opening up, China's interest rate marketization reform can be roughly divided into four stages.

The first phase is the formation of interest rate mechanisms among national financial institutions. In 1996, the national inter-bank lending market was networked, and the national unified interbank lending market interest rate was formed. In Sep. 1998, the state liberalized the issuance rate of policy financial bonds. At this stage, interest rate liberalization between financial institutions has been achieved.

In the second stage, the upper limit of the loan interest rate of financial institutions was gradually liberalized, and the marketization of loan interest rates was promoted. From 1998 to 1999, the PBOC expanded the loan interest rate twice. In Sep. 2000, during the reform of the foreign exchange interest rate management system, the foreign exchange loan interest rate was liberalized. In the first half of 2002, the financial institutions raised the loan interest rate of all enterprises by 30%. In 2002, the scope of the pilot reform of the interest rate reform of rural credit cooperatives was expanded, the floating rate of interest rates of rural credit cooperatives was further expanded, and the foreign currency interest rate management policy of Chinese-funded and foreign-funded enterprises was unified. In 2003, the floating range of loan interest rates was expanded, and the loan interest rate of financial institutions to all enterprises fluctuated to 50%; in early 2004, the loan interest rate ceiling was extended to 70%. On Oct.28, 2004, the central bank completely abolished the restriction on the interest rate of commercial banks, and commercial banks could independently price the rate according to the risk situation of enterprises and specific businesses. At this point, the domestic commercial bank's renminbi loan interest rate has basically transitioned to the stage where the upper limit is liberalized and the lower limit management is implemented. This stage is mainly an attempt to market-based reform of loan interest rates. After more than six years, the market-oriented reform of loan interest rates has achieved initial success.

In the 3rd stage, the lower limit of the loan interest rate gradually tried to realize the marketization of the loan interest rate. In Jan. 2005, the PBOC issued the "Steady Promotion of Interest Rate Marketization Report", stating that it is necessary to strengthen the construction of interest rate pricing mechanism for financial institutions, and establish a sound scientific pricing system in accordance with the principle of symmetry of risks and benefits. Subsequently, the PBOC adjusted the mortgage interest rate. In this interest rate adjustment, the central bank decided not to impose a preferential interest rate on real estate mortgage loans, and the mortgage interest rate returned to the level consistent with the commercial loan interest rate over the same period, allowing 10% floating of the benchmark interest rate set by the PBOC. This thoroughly changed the history that China's loan interest rate has not been able to float in a long time. Opening the interbank deposit interest rate of financial institutions provides a broader space for commercial banks to independent price, and promote the improvement of capital use efficiency and liquidity management level of commercial banks. In addition, starting from Sep.21, 2005, various commercial banks can determine the interest-bearing method of deposits, and the marketization of deposit interest rates has finally taken a historic step.

In 2006, the interest rate marketization reform was further advanced. First, the construction of the benchmark interest rate system in China's money market was initiated. The Shanghai Interbank Offered Rate was commissioned from October to December 2006 and officially launched on Jan.4, 2007, attempting to provide financial markets with pricing benchmarks for products within one year. Second, on Aug.19, 2006, the lower limit of the commercial personal housing loan interest rate was expanded from 0.9 times the official loan interest rate to 0.85 times, which expanded the pricing space for personal housing loans. These measures help to provide financial institutions with independent pricing capabilities and improve the transmission mechanism of monetary policy. In 2007, the Shanghai interbank market offered interest rate was officially launched and gradually established its benchmark position in the money market interest rate system. In 2012, the PBOC adjusted the upper limit of the floating range of deposit interest rates of financial institutions to 1.1 times the benchmark interest rate, and the lower limit of the floating range of the loan interest rate was adjusted to 0.7 times the benchmark interest rate. In Jul. 2013, the lower limit of the lending rate of financial institutions was 0.7 times of the benchmark interest rate, and the financial institutions independently determined the loan interest rate according to commercial principles. The bill discount rate control will be abolished, and the discount rate will be changed based on the rediscount rate. The financial institution will determine it by itself and fully liberalize the loan interest rate control of financial institutions. The previous interest rate adjustments since the reform and opening up are shown in Table 6–1.

Table 6-1 Interest rate adjustment since 1978

Cycle	Time line	Interest rate regulation time	Annual benchmark interest rate (%)	Increase rate (%)	Decline rate (%)	Increase frequency	Decrease frequncy
1	1979-1982	Apr. 1979 -Apr. 1982	3.24-5.76	2.52	—	3	—
2	1982-1986	Apr. 1985-Aug. 1985	5.76-7.20	1.44	—	2	—
3	1987-1991	Sep. 1988-Feb. 1989-Mar. 1990-Apr. 1991	7.20-11.34-7.56	4.14	3.78	2	3
4	1992-1998	May 1993-Jul. 1993-Apr. 1996-Dec. 1998	7.56-10.98-3.78	3.42	7.20	2	6
5	1999-2002	Jun. 1999-Feb. 2002	3.78-1.98	—	1.80	—	2
6	2003-2008	Sep. 2004-Dec. 2007-Sep. 2008-Sep. 2008	1.98-4.14-2.25	2.16	1.89	8	4

Source: Yi Gang, "On the market-based interest rate reform", *Journal of Financial Research*, 2019(1).

In the fourth stage, the floating range of deposit interest rates will be gradually expanded to realize the marketization of deposit interest rates. On Nov.22, 2014, the PBOC decided to combine the promotion of interest rate liberalization reform to adjust the upper limit of the floating range of deposit interest rates of financial institutions from 1.1 times the deposit benchmark interest rate to 1.2 times; adjustment on Mar.1, 2015 was 1.3 times; it was adjusted to 1.5 times on May 11, 2015. On Aug.26, 2015, the PBOC decided to release the interest rate floating ceiling for time deposits of one year or longer (excluding one-year period), the interest rate floating limit for demand deposits and time deposits below one year (1.5 times) were unchanged. Beginning on Oct.24, 2015, the PBOC decided not to set a floating ceiling for deposit interest rates for commercial banks and rural cooperative financial institutions, and basically realized the marketization of deposit interest rates.

After the administrative control of interest rates was abolished, the funds could be fully independently priced in theory, and the traditional profit model dominated by banks' deposit-loan spreads was seriously challenged. China's interest rate marketization reform has entered a new stage, and the core has turned to accelerating the construction of interest rate formation and regulation mechanisms that are compatible with the market.

6.1.2 Establish interest rate self-regulation mechanism

On Sep.24, 2013, financial institutions established a self-discipline mechanism for market interest rate pricing. Under the premise of complying with relevant state interest rate management regulations, they will conduct self-discipline management of financial market interest rates such as money market and credit market independently determined by financial institutions, and maintain market competition order, and promote the healthy development of market regulation. The membership of the self-regulatory mechanism has continued to expand. As of the end of 2016, the membership of the self-regulatory mechanism has expanded to 1,556, including 12 core members, 873 basic members and 671 observers. The self-discipline mechanism has played an important role in self-discipline management of financial institutions' independent pricing, maintaining market interest rate pricing order, and orderly promoting interest rate marketization.

6.1.3 Establish a deposit insurance system

On Feb.17, 2015, Premier Li Keqiang signed the State Council Order and announced the "Deposit Insurance Regulations" on Mar. 31. The implementation of the China Deposit Insurance System was officially established on May 1, 2015. More than 3,000 banking financial institutions that have absorbed deposits in the country have all gone through the formalities for insurance, and the implementation of the system has been carried out in an orderly manner. As an important basic institutional arrangement of the financial industry, the deposit insurance system has a very good mechanism for improving the financial safety net, strengthening depositor protection, promoting the formation of market-oriented financial risk prevention and disposal mechanisms, and establishing a long-term mechanism for maintaining financial stability.

In the next stage, the PBOC will continue to deepen the reform of interest rate marketization, supervise the sound internal control of financial institutions, enhance the independent and reasonable pricing power and risk management level, focus on cultivating the market benchmark interest rate and yield curve, and continuously improve the market-based interest rate formation mechanism; improve the central bank's policy interest rate system, enhance the ability of interest rate regulation, and rationalize the mechanism of the central bank's policy interest rate transmission to the financial market and even the real economy; play a good role in the three "defense lines" of financial institutions, self-discipline mechanisms, and central banks, strengthen the supervision and management of irrational pricing behavior of financial institutions, adopt an effective way to encourage and restrict interest rate pricing behavior, and maintain a fair and reasonable pricing order.

The acceleration of the interest rate marketization reform has not only injected new impetus to the transformation and development of financial institutions, but also promoted financial institutions to further enhance their independent pricing power, effectively improve the level of financial services, and enhance the capacity for sustainable development. It also transformed the monetary policy framework. The creation of conditions is conducive to the real interest rate to reflect the market supply and demand situation, provide an important reference for the central bank's interest rate regulation, improve the efficiency of macro-control, and also play a significant role in giving full play to the decisive role of the market in resource allocation.

6.2 Multi-level capital market initial establishment

The multi-level capital market system is an important part of perfecting the modern financial market system and a strategic task to promote China's economic transformation and upgrading. The 13th Five-year Plan outlines to improve the financial market system, actively cultivate open, transparent and healthy development of the capital market, increase the proportion of direct financing, and reduce the leverage ratio. It also creates conditions to implement the stock issuance registration system, develops a multi-level equity financing market, deepens the reform of the GEM and the National Equities Exchange and Quotations (NEEQ), standardizes the development of regional equity markets, and establishes a sound transfer mechanism and exit mechanism. With the deepening of reform and opening up, China's capital market basic system construction has been continuously improved, especially in the past five years, that is, during the 12th Five-year Plan period, China's capital market has ushered in a period of rapid development. The multi-level market system has gradually improved, the institutional investor team has grown stronger, the service level of intermediaries has improved significantly, the market innovation vitality has been stimulated, the level of opening up has been significantly expanded, market supervision has been continuously strengthened, and the capital market has played an important role in promoting the transformation of the national economic development mode.

6.2.1 Innovative industry development, institutional competitiveness is significantly enhanced

First, the stock market resource allocation function has been significantly enhanced. As of Jun. 2015, there were 2,797 listed companies in Shanghai and Shenzhen stock markets, including 1,550 main board companies, 767 SME board companies, and 480 GEM companies. The total market value was RMB62.7 trillion, an increase of 136.4% compared with the end of 2010 and second only to the US in the world. As of Aug. 2015, the total number of listed companies in the NEEQ reached 3,359, covering 31 provinces (autonomous regions and municipalities directly under the Central Government) and 82 industry categories, of which private enterprises accounted for more than 95%, high-tech enterprises accounted for 77%; the total market value of listed companies reached RMB1.41 trillion, and the cumulative transaction volume of the market was RMB141.98 billion. The total number of investor accounts reached 0.1729 million, of which institutional investors were 15,500. During the 12th Five-year Plan period, the accumulated financing amount of the listed companies of the NEEQ reached RMB78.067 billion, and the total amount of mergers and acquisitions transactions was RMB10.504 billion.

The second is to vigorously expand the business scope of securities companies, turn the margin financing and securities lending business from a pilot to a routine operation, and support securities companies to conduct asset management business and foreign exchange business in compliance with laws and regulations. It also vigorously promotes product innovation, supports securities companies to carry out private fund comprehensive custody, OTC derivatives, equity investment in direct investment subsidiaries, equity incentives pledge financing, asset securitization and other innovative businesses, enriching the types of services. The financing channels of securities and futures operating institutions are broadened and the compliance control of securities companies is improved. As of Jun. 2015, 125 securities companies had total assets of RMB7.81 trillion, net assets of RMB1.18 trillion, and net capital of RMB976.5 billion, and increased 290%, 110% and 130% respectively from the end of 2010. As of Jun. 2015, 34 regional equity markets have been established nationwide, with a total of 2,742 listed companies and 30,200 exhibiting companies, with a total of RMB281.8 billion of financing for enterprises. A total of 3.5856 million investor accounts were opened in the counter market of securities companies. A total of 8,692 private equity products of 21 counter market pilot companies were issued through the counter market. The issued amount reached RMB620.343 billion, and 1,022 transfer transactions were realized. The transfer amount was RMB13.304 billion.

The third is to promote the reform of the public fund management company and the public offering business license approval system, and explore the implementation of the public fund product registration system; construct a private equity fund rules system and a regulatory system framework; strengthen the supervision and inspection of auditing and evaluation agencies, and strengthen the development and supervision of credit rating agencies. In-depth special on-site inspections were carried out to strengthen the supervision of securities ranking information disclosure. As of Jun. 2015, 104 publicly-funded asset management institutions managed public funds of RMB7.36 trillion, an increase of 192% from the end of 2010 (RMB2.52 trillion). In 2014, the industry achieved operating income of RMB49.62 billion, a 39% increase over 2010, and a net profit of RMB12.37 billion, an increase of 9.5% over 2010.

Private funds are an important part of a multi-level capital market system. The development of private funds can not only improve the multi-level capital market system, enrich the trading pattern of capital markets, expand the scope of market services, enhance the service capabilities for emerging industries, small and medium-sized enterprises, but also effectively expand the investment channels of residents, stimulate the vitality of private investment, and improve social capital use efficiency. As of the end of Jul. 2015, there were 16,604 private fund managers registered with the Asset Management Association of China, and 17,415 private funds were filed, with a subscription scale of RMB4.11 trillion, a paid-up scale of RMB3.34 trillion, and private funds practitioners 0.2614 million.

The fourth is to support the strength of futures companies. The CSRC promotes the innovation and development of the futures industry and enhances the ability to serve the real economy; supports futures companies to fund the establishment of OTC derivatives service platforms, explores off-exchange business, provides personalized risk management services for entities; and supports futures companies to list through domestic and overseas markets, list through NEEQ, and issue subordinated debts and corporate bonds to raise funds in multi-level; support the development of new formats such as private futures funds, OTC traders and Commodity Trading Advisors (CTA); improve the basic supervision of the futures market. The system consolidates the compliance foundation of the futures industry. As of Jun. 2015, the total assets of 150 normally operating futures companies reached RMB81.3 billion, net assets reached RMB67.6 billion, net capital reached RMB49.8 billion, and customer equity reached RMB418.7 billion, up 167%, 151%, 98% and 159% respectively from the end of 2010. In 2014, the industry achieved operating income of RMB19 billion, a 34% increase from 2010; net profit reached RMB4.1 billion, an increase of 61% over 2010.

In addition, it has further promoted the development of securities intermediary service institutions. During the 12th Five-year Plan period, the CSRC strengthened supervision and inspection of auditing and evaluation institutions, strengthened the development and supervision of credit ranking agencies, conducted in-depth on-site inspections, strengthened supervision of securities ranking information disclosure, and further simplified the administrative licensing approval process. It also broke the division of the consulting business sub-licensing, promoted the transformation and development of the securities and futures investment consulting business, and encouraged consulting institutions to carry out privately offered asset management business.

6.2.2 Deepen international cooperation, and promote bidirectional open and steady progress

During the 12th Five-year Plan period, the CSRC increased the bidirectional opening up of the capital market and the securities and futures industry, deepened international cooperation in supervision and law enforcement, strengthened cooperation and exchanges with the international market, and achieved fruitful results in opening up to the outside world.

China has successfully opened the Shanghai-Hong Kong Stock Connect pilot and actively supported qualified domestic enterprises to go listings abroad. As of Jun. 2015, a total of 113 Hong Kong brokers and 94 mainland brokers participated in the Shanghai-Hong Kong Stock Connect transaction. The mainland investors opened nearly 700,000 accounts with Hong Kong stock exchange trading rights; the transaction volume of Shanghai-Hong Kong Stock Connect and Hong Kong Stock Through reached RMB1,005.299 billion and RMB413.986 billion respectively.

China has continued to expand the bidirectional opening of the securities and futures industry, implement the RQFII system, improve the QFII and RQFII tax policy, and continually expand the participation of foreign capital in the industry. By the end of 2014, a total of 205 domestic companies had been listed overseas, with a total financing of US$244.443 billion; 11 foreign-invested securities companies, 46 fund management companies and 3 futures companies. From 2011 to the end of Jun. 2015, the CSRC approved a total of 185 QFIIs and 165 RQFIIs. The foreign exchange bureau newly approved QFII quotas of US$55.8 billion and RQFII quotas of RMB390.9 billion. In the long run, QFII has always been full of confidence in the A-share market. One of the important performances is that it has opened a new A-share account for 45 consecutive months, and the total number of accounts opened has reached 950.

In terms of further improving the level of opening up of the capital market, the regulatory authorities actively support qualified domestic enterprises to go listing abroad; support institutions register and establish professional subsidiaries and branches in the Shanghai Free Trade Zone; continue to expand the bidirectional opening of the securities and futures industry; the listing of crude oil futures is a breakthrough, actively introduces foreign traders and brokerage institutions to participate in the domestic futures market, and builds an international trading settlement platform.

China has strengthened international cooperation in regulatory enforcement. As of Jun. 2015, the CSRC has signed 62 bilateral memorandums of cooperation with securities and futures regulators in 60 countries or regions.

At the same time, new progress has been made in cross-border regulatory cooperation, specifically including actively participating in the work of the International Organization of Securities Commissions (IOSCO), acting as the vice chairman of the IOSCO Multilateral Memorandum Supervision Group since May 2012, and joining IOSCO all eight policy committees responsible for the development of securities and futures regulatory standards in 2013, and serving as the vice chairman of the Investment Management Committee, joining the long-term financing special working group, and hosting the 37th annual meeting of IOSCO.

China also has joined the Financial Stability Board (FSB) OTC Derivatives Working Group and OTC Derivatives Data Summary Method Research Group, participated in drafting the "7th OTC Derivatives Market Regulatory Reform Progress Report", and the "OTC Derivative Data Summary Method Feasibility Study Report".

6.2.3 Strengthen the foundation of the law and increase the intensity of regulatory transformation

During the 12th Five-year Plan period, the CSRC promoted regulatory transformation from multiple levels, including deepening the reform of the administrative examination and approval system; strengthening the construction of market-based systems; strengthening the integrity of the capital market; enriching regulatory measures, strengthening inspection and enforcement; strengthening investor education; protecting the legitimate rights and interests of investors; preventing and controlling the systemic risks of the capital market; and building an information disclosure system.

China also pushed on regulatory transformation, further deepened the reform of the administrative examination and approval system, relaxed pre-existing control, focused on strengthening post-event supervision, promoted the market to play a decisive role in resource allocation, continuously enriched the power of inspection and law enforcement, effectively strengthened inspection and law enforcement, and consolidated the foundation of the rule and law in the capital market. The improvement of market infrastructure, the strengthening of risk prevention, and the monitoring work have achieved new results.

In terms of the reform of the administrative examination and approval system, since the reform of the administrative examination and approval system from 2001 to the end of 2014, the CSRC has cancelled 151 administrative examination and approval items.

In terms of market-based system construction, the CSRC promoted the revision of the "Securities Law" and the formulation of the "Futures Law" into the legislative work plan of the 12th National People's Congress Standing Committee. On Jun.1, 2013, the revision of the "Securities Investment Fund Law" was completed and implemented. In the name of the General Office of the State Council, the "Opinions on Further Strengthening the Protection of the Legal Rights and Interests of Small and Medium-sized Investors in the Capital Market" was issued.

China had strictly cracked down on illegal and irregular behaviors in various securities and futures markets, such as market manipulation, fraudulent issuance, insider trading, and the use of undisclosed information transactions, and effectively and fairly handled a series of major cases with remarkable social impacts. As of Jun. 2015, during the 12th Five-year Plan period, the CSRC and the dispatched agencies had concluded a total of 483 cases, and a total of 406 administrative penalty decisions were made. A total of 107 individuals were banned to enter into the secutirty market. The total amount of fines was RMB2.183 billion.

It should be said that this series of regulatory transformations have effectively promoted the market's decisive role in resource allocation, solidified the market rule and law, and played an important role in promoting market development.

6.2.4 Problems in the development of China's capital market

Although China's capital market has developed rapidly in recent years and initially established a multi-level capital market, there are still some problems in China's capital market.

Firstly, China's capital market is not large enough and its structure is irrational. It has not fully played its role in the allocation of social resources and corporate resources in the capital market. At present, the stock market is developing slowly, the scale is small, and the corporate bond market is smaller. It is difficult to play the role of deploying corporate resources and social resources. From the perspective of China's financing scale and financing effect, it still relies on indirect financing and bank financing, and the financing scale of the capital market is small. In the entire financial system, the capital market accounts for a relatively small proportion; the market development level needs to be improved, and the ability of serving real economy is relatively weak; the stock market is in the form of "inverted pyramids", which has less coverage for small and micro enterprises, and the fund-raising function is not prominent. In the first half of 2015, the GEM was even observed more cash-out than fund raised. The futures and derivatives markets need to be further developed, and there is still much room for the pricing mechanism and the construction of its internal stability mechanism. The competitiveness of market players needs to be improved, especially the long-term development capability of institutional investors and their role in the financial system.

Secondly, the securities issuance and tradings tend to be administration, planning, and approval. For a long time, China's securities issuance and trading have the characteristics of administration, planning and approval, which is the biggest obstacle to the development of China's capital market. At present, although the quota and scale are not controlled, a strict audit system is also applied to the listed company, and the company's profitability is mainly reviewed, resulting in the company being unable to go public for a long time. When the stock market is not good, the suspension of new shares in order to stabilize the market has not only failed to stabilize the market, but has caused the number of companies to be listed to accumulate.

Thirdly, the interests of the majority of small and medium-sized investors have not been well protected and they have not enjoyed the wealth effect of the capital market. Up to 90% of Chinese capital market investors are retail investors, and they have given money to enterprises, but they have not received corresponding returns. The Chinese capital market is a typical fund-raising market, a typical speculative market. To further develop and expand the capital market, the core issue is to turn the financing market into a real investment market and turn the speculative market into a long-term investment market. The capital market can only develop healthily if it is built into a market that protects investors, especially the legitimate rights and interests of small and medium-sized investors, and is a market that can invest, get return, and make money.

Fourthly, there is a long way to go to build a unified bond market system and management mechanism. The bond market supervision system has the drawbacks of multiple management and relatively divided. The bond market is dominated by the government and the public sector, and there are major structural problems. The bond market operates mainly for the financial system itself, not for the real economy. There is a relatively obvious division in the domestic bond market. The market yield curve and pricing mechanism are unreasonable. In particular, the bond yield curve duration and interest rate structure are unreasonable, and the basic functions of risk-free interest rates cannot be realized. The infrastructure of the bond market is relatively weak, and market-based defaults and disposal mechanisms are lacking.

6.2.5 Advance the market-oriented reform of the capital market

China's overall financial structure is still dominated by indirect financing of banks. The capital market system is still not perfect. The proportion of direct financing is still low. The macro leverage ratio is high while the economic and financial risks are concentrated in the banking system. During the 13th Five-year Plan period, efforts should be made to strengthen the multi-level capital market investment function, optimize corporate debt and equity financing structure, and significantly increase the proportion of direct financing, especially equity financing. It is estimated that from 2014 to 2020, the proportion of direct financing of non-financial enterprises in social financing will increase from 17.2% to 25%, and the balance of bond market to GDP will increase to about 100%. We will promote the reform of the stock and bond issuance trading system, with the full disclosure of information as the core, reduce the substantive review and value judgment of the securities regulatory authorities on the issuer qualification; strengthen the supervision of the matter and afterwards, improve the delisting system, and effectively protect the legitimate rights and interests of investors. We'll also deepen the reform of the GEM and the NEEQ, improve the multi-level equity financing market, develop the bond market mainly by qualified institutional investors and the OTC market, and form a layered and orderly, full-range, complementary functional and unified multi-level capital market system both in the market in the field and the OTC market.

The first is to promote the reform of the stock issuance registration system. With sufficient information disclosure as the core, in the process of stock issuance, we shall reduce the substantive review and value judgment of the securities regulatory authorities on the issuer qualification, weaken the administrative examination and approval, enhance the flexibility of the issuance system, reduce the cost of stock issuance, and improve the efficiency of financing. The regulatory authorities need to strengthen the supervision of matters in and after the event, improve various civil and criminal liability investigation systems, and effectively curb fraudulent listings, further improve the delisting system of listed companies, and improve the quality of listed companies through the survival of the fittest. In addition, they shall increase the crackdown on securities violations such as false statements, market manipulation and insider trading, strengthen the market constraints and integrity constraints of market participants such as listed companies and intermediaries, and promote market participants to perform their duties, protect investors' legitimate rights and interests, and safeguard the principle of "equality, fairness and openness" of the securities market.

The second is to promote equity financing through multiple channels. While continuing to improve the main board, SME board and GEM, we will continue to promote the construction of the NEEQ market. Also we shall accelerate the improvement of the equity market for small and medium-sized enterprises that are institutions-oriented and openly transferred, establish and improve institutional arrangements such as market makers, targeted issuance, mergers and acquisitions, enrich financing tools and trading varieties, and enhance the ability to serve small and medium-sized enterprises. All provinces (autonomous regions, municipalities) can establish regional equity markets in accordance with the needs of regional economic development under a unified institutional framework. They shall actively guide the healthy development of private equity investment funds and venture capital funds, and support equity financing for innovative and growth companies. They also should establish and improve the differential institutional arrangements between different levels of markets and a unified registration and settlement platform to promote the formation of an associated linked equity market system.

The third is to develop and standardize the bond market. We will steadily expand the size of the bond market, promote the innovation and diversification of financial products, and increase the intensity of asset securitization. We'll explore municipal bonds and improve the financing mechanism for urbanization. And we'll develop financing tools such as set bonds and private placement bonds for SMEs, broaden corporate financing channels, and increase support for the real economy. In addition, we need to give play to the role of the inter-ministerial coordination mechanism of the company's credit bonds, strengthen coordination and cooperation of bond management departments, improve information disclosure standards, implement regulatory responsibilities, strengthen the infrastructure construction of the bond market, and further promote the coordinated development of the interbank market and the exchange market. We will steadily push the bond market to open to the outside world.

6.3 Banking market reforms are gradually deepening

Over the past 40 years of reform and opening up, China's economy has continued to grow at a high speed, creating a rare economic miracle in the world. Along with the rapid development of China's economy, the Chinese banking industry has intensified its reforms and its strength has been continuously enhanced. Especially in the past ten years, the corporate governance of large commercial banks, which has been stripped off non-performing assets and reformed by joint-stock system, has gradually improved, and the asset scale and profitability have increased significantly. The ranking of the world's top 1,000 banks published by the UK's *Banker* magazine shows that among the top 10 banks ranked by Tier 1 capital, ICBC, CCB, BOC and ABC ranked 1st, 2nd, 7th and 9th respectively. According to the statistics of the CBRC, from 2003 to 2016, the total assets of China's banking financial institutions increased from RMB27.66 trillion to RMB226.3 trillion, a 7.2 times increase; after-tax profits increased from RMB32.28 billion to RMB2 trillion, a 61 times increase. In addition to large banks, other joint-stock banks and small and medium-sized banks have also grown rapidly in the context of China's rapid economic development. The importance of private capital in small and medium-sized banking institutions has gradually emerged. In 2014, private capital entered an important breakthrough in the banking industry. The first batch of five private banks completed the approval, 14 privately-held non-bank financial institutions were newly established, and 108 private-capital-dominant rural banks were added. In 2015, the development of private banks once again ushered in major policy breakthroughs. Premier Li Keqiang said in his government work report that "promote the qualified private capital to initiate the establishment of financial institutions such as small and medium-sized banks, once ready once approve, no quota". At present, China's first "virtual bank" Qianhai WeBank has officially opened in Jan. 2015, and the development of private banks will further accelerate. The deposit insurance system was introduced, and a major breakthrough was made in the construction of the market-based exit mechanism of the banking industry. The pace of opening up the banking industry will be accelerated, and the conditions for foreign banks to enter and operate the renminbi business will be relaxed. Overall, the past ten years have been the golden period for the rapid development of China's banking industry.

6.3.1 Banking services to the real economy have achieved new results

The banking industry takes the better service of the real economy as the basic starting point, constantly innovating ideas, methods and business products, and achieving a steady improvement in service quality and efficiency, mainly as follows. First, loans in the key areas of the national economy have grown rapidly. As of the end of 2015, the balance of infrastructure industry loans was RMB19 trillion, an increase of 51.1% from the end of 2010; the balance of affordable housing projects was RMB1.8 trillion, an increase of 276.6% over the end of 2011. Second, the support in the livelihood consumption is increasing. The balance of various loans and personal loans for service enterprises was RMB43.4 trillion and RMB18.2 trillion respectively, an increase of 88.5% and 128.7% respectively from the end of 2010. Third, the satisfaction of inclusive finance has further improved. China's banking industry has a total of 4,091 legal entities and 0.216 million domestic outlets, which basically achieve full coverage of urban and rural financial services. And the provision of inclusive finance credit continues to increase. At present, the balance of small and micro enterprise loans is RMB22.5 trillion, which is 83% higher than the end of 2011; the balance of agriculture-related loans was RMB25.6 trillion, an increase of 117.5% over the end of 2010. The fourth one is that progress was made in cutting overcapacity and developing green credit. Banking financial institutions adhere to the principle of differential treatment and safeguards, promote the elimination of excess capacity and the transformation and upgrading of traditional industries, develop green credit, and support the construction of energy-saving and environmental protection projects. The current green credit balance is nearly RMB7 trillion. The fifth is to reduce the cost of social financing. The social financing costs have been further reduced by strengthening deposit and loan pricing management, clearing charged items, shortening the financing chain, and improving loan approval and distribution efficiency. At the end of 2015, the weighted average interest rate of non-financial enterprises and other sectors was 5.7%, of which the weighted average interest rate of general loans was 6%, and the weighted average interest rate of bill financing was 4.3%, falled by 0.5%, 0.3% and 1.2% respectively from Dec. 2010.

6.3.2 Risk management capability of banking industry has improved

Focusing on the core of institutional reform, the banking industry has continuously strengthened the construction of a long-term mechanism for risk prevention and control, which has achieved initial success. First, corporate governance is constantly being improved. The rules of corporate governance and internal control systems of commercial banks have been further improved, and the organizational structure, incentive and restraint mechanism and internal control mechanism of corporate governance have been gradually improved. Second, the comprehensive risk management framework was initially established, which guide banking financial institutions to scientifically formulate and implement risk appetite, management and control strategies and disposal mechanisms in combination with their own characteristics, and comprehensive risk management capabilities have been significantly improved. Third, risks in key areas have been effectively prevented and controlled. The banking institutions actively guard against platform loan default risks, strictly prevent risks in real estate loans, overcapacity loans, interbank and wealth management businesses, and off-balance sheet business, and prevent external risks from being transmitted. The current risks are generally controllable. Fourth, the advanced method of capital measurement was officially implemented. Since Apr. 2014, six banks have officially implemented advanced methods of capital management, which have improved the bank's quantitative risk management capabilities and refined management levels, and promoted the transformation of bank development methods.

6.3.3 Banking industry made new progress on deepening reform and opening up

We attach great importance to the role of the driving force behind reform and opening up, promote the sound development of the banking industry, and make positive progress in many aspects. First, the reform of banking institutions has been carried out in an orderly manner. The reform of policy banks, large banks, and postal and banking institutions has been comprehensively promoted; the transformation of unified creditors in rural credit cooperatives in counties and cities has been basically completed. Second, private capital has steadily entered the banking industry. By the end of 2015, five private banks, six private financial leasing companies and two private consumption finance companies had been opened; private capital also accounted for large proportion among banking institutions such as city commercial banks, rural commercial banks, rural banks and trust companies. Third, the pilot effect of the comprehensive operation of the financial industry has emerged. As of the end of Mar. 2016, 12 of the 16 listed commercial banks were allowed to set up fund management companies, 7 of these were allowed to join the insurance company, 15 of these were allowed to establish or participate in financial leasing companies, 5 of these were allowed to participate in the trust company, and 4 of these were allowed to set up consumption financial companies, 9 of these were approved securities companies, a certain synergy between banking institutions and non-bank financial institutions has occurred, which further developed business structure integration, customer structure balancing and income structure diversification[1]. Fourth, the level of opening up of the banking industry has continued to increase. By the end of 2015, Chinese banks had established more than 1,200 branches in 55 countries and regions, and 40 foreign-funded legal entities, 109 branches and 174 representative offices in China had established by 52 abroad banks, the ability of "go global" strategy has been improved significantly.

6.3.4 Banking industry upgrades its regulatory capabilities to a new level

China persists in improving the effectiveness of supervision as the top priority, and always upholds the concept of legal supervision, supervision for the people, and scientific supervision, and promotes the continuous improvement of supervision efficiency. First, the regulatory system is more complete. A prudential regulatory system covering all types of institutions, business and corporate governance, risk management, capital, and provision has been formed. Second, the regulatory tools are more abundant. Basically, a regulatory "toolbox" including non-performing asset ratio, liquidity ratio, and provision coverage ratio has been created. Third, the regulatory structure is more scientific. In accordance with the separation of regulatory rules from implementation, separation of prudential supervision from behavioral supervision, separation of administrative affairs from regulatory matters, separation of on-site inspections from regulatory penalties, reconfiguration of the regulatory organization system has performed, strengthening the supervision of the main business, and reducing and decentralizing the administrative power. Fourth, the regulatory focus is

[1] China Bank Association, "China Banking Industry Development Report (2016)", Website of CBA.

more prominent. China continues to strengthen systemic risk analysis and monitoring; vigorously promotes macro-prudential supervision; actively strengthens supervision of systemically important banks; and constantly regulates the development of shadow banking. Fifth, regulatory coordination is more effective. In the areas of unified regulatory standards, prevention of regulatory arbitrage, prevention of systemic financial risks, and enhanced coordination of monetary, fiscal, industrial, and regulatory policies; supporting local development, preventing financial risks, handling illegal fundraising, and communication and coordination with local governments has also been widely recognized. Sixth, the regulatory cooperation is deeper. As of February 2017, the CBRC has signed bilateral memorandums of understanding or cooperation agreements with financial regulatory authorities in 67 countries and regions; deeply participated in international financial regulatory reforms, and actively participated in high-level bilateral and multilateral meetings;[1] the 18th International Banking Supervisors Conference (ICBS), the International Monetary Fund and the World Bank fully affirmed China's banking supervision in relevant assessments.

6.3.5 Opportunities and challenges in front of current banking reform and development

At present, the internal and external environment of China's banking industry is undergoing profound changes. It is necessary to use a clearer mind to clearly judge and accurately grasp the situation, to grasp new opportunities and meet new challenges with greater wisdom and confidence, and to be more persevering and persistent patience and courage to solve problems and conflicts.

(1) *Opportunities and challenges brought about by the new normal of economy*

At present, China's economy is entering a new normal of growth rate adjustment, structural optimization, and power conversion. Although the economic growth rate is adjusted, the actual increase is still considerable, the growth trend will be more stable, the growth momentum will be more diversified, the development prospects will be more stable, and market vitality will be further released. For the banking industry, on the one hand, new technologies, new products, new formats, and new business models will emerge rapidly, which will certainly provide a broader market space for the development of the banking industry; economic structure optimization, industrial

---

1 CBRC, "List of Memorandums of Understanding and Regulatory Cooperation Agreements for Bilateral Regulatory Cooperation signed by the China Banking Regulatory Commission", CBRC website.

transformation and upgrading, and local government debt swaps, etc., and will create more favorable conditions for the banking industry to revitalize the stock. On the other hand, the slowdown in economic growth and de-capacity, destocking and de-leveraging may accelerate risk exposure and increase the difficulty of risk management.

(2) *Opportunities and challenges brought about by market-oriented reforms*

China's financial market factors and the reform of the participating entities will have a profound impact on the development of the banking industry. Interest rate marketization reform is conducive to commercial banks to expand their autonomy management and accelerate financial innovation, but it will also challenge the profitability of commercial banks; exchange rate market reform may increase the operational space of commercial bank's foreign exchange business products, but it will also bring challenges for the innovation of renminbi foreign exchange financial instruments and the ability of independent pricing of commercial banks; the entry of private capital into the banking industry will help to innovate institutional mechanisms and stimulate business vitality, but its strong profit-seeking motives may also lead to excessive risk-taking.

(3) *Opportunities and challenges brought by Internet finance*

At present, China's banking industry has realized the accumulation of big data including customers information, accounts information, products information, transactions information, management information, etc., and established information technology service system including online banking, telephone banking, mobile banking and self-service banking. The banking industry has taken solid steps to use the internet. The rapid rise of Internet finance will further promote scientific decision making, fine services and cost savings in the banking industry. And third-party payment represented by internet payment has brought challenges to the banking industry's payment business; the network financing model represented by small loans, P2P and crowdfunding has already challenged the banking industry's financing business; The Internet financial industry represented by funds and balance management has already put pressure on the deposits of the banking industry. In addition, some institutions are under the guise of internet finance, unauthorized conducting business or even illegally raising funds, which may have an impact on the entire financial market order.

(4) *Opportunities and challenges brought about by economic and financial globalization*

The globalization of economy and finance provides a good opportunity for

China's banking industry to expand its overseas business, achieve asset allocation on a global scale, and enhance international competitiveness. Meanwhile, the cross-border settlement and use of renminbi, the "go global" strategy of Chinese enterprises to carry out mergers and acquisitions, and the strong financial services demand of countries and regions with financial and trade relations with China have also provided new growth points for China's banking industry. However, the rapid growth of international trade and foreign investment will test the cross-border financial service capability of the banking industry; the international political and economic structure is complex and changeable, and some regions are turbulent, which will test the cross-border risk management and control capabilities of the banking industry; the reform of international regulatory rules will test the adaptability of bank capital, liquidity, leverage and other aspects.

On the whole, China's banking industry is still in an important period of strategic opportunities for sustainable development. The fundamentals of long-term economic development have not changed. The basic trend of sustained and healthy development of the banking industry has not changed. The development space is broad, the development potential is huge, and the challenges are flexible. These key traits have not changed, and the momentum of reform and innovation with strong vitality has not changed. China's banking industry has been reforming and developing for many years, and it has accumulated a solid material foundation for coping with risk challenges. We have full confidence and firm determination to push our country's banking industry to a new level.

6.3.6 The direction of banking reform and development

The 13th Five-year Plan period was the stage of decisive completion of a well-off society in an all-round way, and various reform undertakings entered a "critical period". The banking industry should continue to fully implement the spirit of the 18th National Congress of CPC and the 3rd, 4th and 5th Central Committees, and the Central Economic Work Conference, insist to the fundamental purpose of serving the people, insist to the fundamental direction of serving the real economy, and stick to the basic bottom line of prevention of systemic and regional financial risks. The banking industry has been continuously promoted to achieve higher quality, more efficient, fairer and more sustainable development, and strive to form a multi-level, wide-coverage and differentiated banking institution by 2020.

(1) *Adhere to innovative ideas and improve service quality*

Innovation is the first driving force for development. The banking industry relies on business innovation, product innovation and technological innovation to explore new ways to support the development of the real economy. The first is to support mass entrepreneurship and innovation. The banking industry should improve the working mechanism of supporting mass entrepreneurship and innovation, explore investment and loan linkages, and meet the characteristics of the life cycle of innovative and entrepreneurial enterprises, and conform to China's actual technology financial service model; continue to promote the establishment of science and technology credit franchises to promote the effective transformation of scientific and technological achievements, push innovation to drive strategy implementation. The second is to accelerate the integration of information technology and financial services. The banking industry actively develop the "Internet + Finance" business model, strengthen the collection, development and application of big data, introduce modern information technology in risk prevention and control, precision marketing, intensive management, etc., realize the associated combination of online and offline, and improve the efficiency of financial services.

(2) *Adhere to risk-based management and enhance competitiveness*

Adhering to the risk-based concept, banking institutions accelerate transformation and development in accordance with the requirements of the "new normal", continue to deepen reforms, expand openness, enhance risk management and control capabilities, and improve service entity economic efficiency. The first is to further deepen institutional reforms. We need to improve corporate governance, further optimize the shareholding structure and governance structure, formulate scientific and reasonable remuneration policies, avoid short-term behaviors that simply pursue profits and blindly pursue scale; optimize organizational structure, continue to deepen the reform of the departments' system, actively promote the reform of the franchise system, and explore some of the business sectors and the implementation of the subsidiary system. The second is to further expand the opening to the outside world. We continue to promote the entry of private capital into the banking industry, promote the establishment of private banks in accordance with the law, and promote the establishment of new consumption finance companies and financial leasing companies, expand the scope of private shares of rural banks, and encourage private capital to participate in the restructuring and transformation of high-risk banking institutions. The third is to further optimize the development strategy and market positioning.

Guide banking financial institutions to formulate scientific development strategies, clarify market positioning, and seek sustainable development paths in line with their own resource conditions, functional advantages and regional environment according to target markets, regions and customers; promote characteristic management around market positioning and comparative advantages forming a distinctive brand, and provide targeted financial products and differentiated financial services according to market demand. The fourth is to further establish and improve a comprehensive risk management system. We should continuously improve the risk management framework that matches the risk status and system importance; implement sound risk appetite and risk management policies and procedures to form a risk culture that is compatible with its development strategy; effectively use various risk management tools to continuously strengthen internal control, and improve the management information system to ensure the effective identification, measurement, monitoring and control of various traditional risks and new risks faced by the banking industry.

(3) *Adhere to administration according to law and strengthen financial supervision*

International experience has repeatedly proved that the more finance develops, the more it needs to strengthen supervision. In order to lead China's banking industry to go smoothly in a complicated and grim situation, we must strengthen supervision in all aspects. The first is to comprehensively promote the rule of law in the banking industry. In accordance with the strategy of governing the country according to law, we should insist the rule of law, improve the banking industry regulatory system; promote the reform of the regulatory law enforcement structure, improve the law enforcement procedures, strictly perform the law enforcement responsibilities, improve the regulatory and credibility of regulatory enforcement, and promote the banking industry's legal compliance. Second is to continue to streamline government administration and delegate powers. We shall reasonably divide the supervisory responsibilities and powers, further decentralize the examination and approval authority to the grassroots, improve the transparency of supervision, and ensure the efficiency of legal supervision being continuously improved. The third is to improve the regulatory framework of macro-prudential and micro-prudential associated integration. We have to promote the implementation of new regulatory standards such as capital and liquidity; improve the macro-prudential supervision system, promote the construction of systemically important banks and countercyclical capital supervision systems, and improve the early warning, assessment and response capabilities of systemic risks. The fourth is to continuously improve the supervision techniques and methods. We continue to promote the reform of the regulatory framework; strengthen the supervision of things in and after the event; improve on-site inspection; continue to improve and use the regulatory toolbox; use modern information technology to ease the contradiction between regulatory resources and regulatory tasks. The fifth is to improve the market-based exit mechanism of financial institutions, which needs to establish a legal system for the disposal and bankruptcy of banking institutions suitable for China's national conditions, strengthen the effective connection between administrative exit and judicial bankruptcy, and promote the normalization and standardization of the financial market exit mechanism. The sixth is to further strengthen the coordination of financial supervision. We shall strengthen overall coordination, reform and improve the financial regulatory framework that adapts to the development of modern financial markets, improve the regulatory rules in line with China's national conditions and international standards, achieve full coverage of financial risk supervision, and continuously improve the ability to monitor and control for the country to contribute to a well-off society.

6.4 The reform of the renminbi exchange rate formation mechanism has been effective

The renminbi exchange rate formation mechanism is actually the choice of the renminbi exchange rate system. From Jan.1, 1994, China began to implement a single, managed floating exchange rate system based on market supply and demand. From this point, the renminbi exchange rate generation gradually became market-oriented.

6.4.1 The stage of reform of the renminbi exchange rate formation mechanism

In Dec. 1993, the Chinese government consolidated the official foreign exchange market with the foreign exchange adjustment market and announced the implementation of a single, managed floating exchange rate system based on market supply and demand. The main steps in the reform of the renminbi exchange rate formation mechanism are shown in Table 6–2.

Table 6–2 The main steps in the reform of the renminbi exchange rate formation mechanism

Time	Events
Dec. 1993	The official foreign exchange market is in line with the foreign exchange adjustment market, implementing a single, managed floating exchange rate system based on market supply and demand.
Jul. 2005	The exchange rate of renminbi against the US dollar rose by 2% at a time; a single, managed floating exchange rate system based on market supply and demand; the daily fluctuation of the renminbi against the US dollar was around 3‰; the daily exchange rate was the next day middle price of exchange rate.
Jan. 2006	The central bank authorized the China Foreign Exchange Trading System to announce the central parity of the renminbi against the major currencies on the same day at 9:15 am on each working day as the median price of the exchange rate on the day.
May. 2007	The daily fluctuation of the exchange rate of renminbi against the US dollar has been expanded from about 3‰ to 5‰.
Jun. 2010.	Enhance the flexibility of the renminbi exchange rate formation mechanism.
Apr. 2012	The daily fluctuation of the exchange rate of renminbi against the US dollar has been expanded from around 5‰ to 1%.
Mar. 2014	The daily fluctuation of the exchange rate of renminbi against the US dollar has been expanded from around 1% to 2%.
Aug. 2015	The daily price of renminbi against the US dollar refers to the previous day's closing price to a greater extent.
Nov. 2015	Renminbi joins SDR currency basket, effective in Oct. 2016.

Source: Zhang Ming, "Reform of renminbi exchange rate formation system: achievements, current situation and future direction", *International Economic Review*, 2016(3).

Since the PBOC announced the reform of the renminbi exchange rate formation mechanism on Jul.21, 2005, the changes in the exchange rate formation mechanism can be roughly divided into three stages.

The first phase is from Jul. 2005 to Apr. 2012. In the situation of the continuous oversupply of the US dollar in the foreign exchange market, the monetary authorities chose the exchange rate policy of the gradual appreciation of the renminbi against the US dollar. From the perspective of the exchange rate formation mechanism, whether it is pegged to the US dollar or let the renminbi gradually appreciate against the US dollar, market supply and demand had no direct decisive effect on exchange rate formation. During this period, the renminbi exchange rate significantly fluctuated twice which are the 2008 subprime mortgage crisis and the sharp deterioration of the European debt crisis in the fourth quarter of 2011. The former forced the renminbi to re-peg the dollar from Oct. 2008 to Jun. 2010, the latter depreciated renminbi in 11 consecutive days.

The second phase is from Apr. 2012 to Aug.11, 2015. In Apr. 2012, the fluctuation of the renminbi-to-US dollar trading price on the spot foreign exchange market expanded from 0.5% to 1%; on Mar.17, 2014, the daily fluctuation range was further expanded from 1% to 2%. The daily volatility of the renminbi exchange rate has been apparently enlarged. Although the monetary authorities are still the dominant force in the exchange rate formation mechanism, the role of market forces has begun to emerge in the formation of the renminbi exchange rate. Year 2014 is a turning point in the trend of the renminbi exchange rate. Before 2014, due to the sustained rapid growth of China's economy, the long-term "double surplus" of current accounts and capital accounts, the renminbi exchange rate was under tremendous pressure of appreciation for most of the time. After the 3rd quarter of 2014, due to changes in fundamentals at home and abroad, China experienced a balance of payments deficit and renminbi depreciation pressure.

The third stage is after the exchange reform on Aug.11, 2015 to present. On Aug.11, 2015, the PBOC announced the further reform of the renminbi exchange rate formation mechanism, so that the median exchange price of the daily renminbi against the US dollar refers to the previous day's closing price to a greater extent.

The core of the "8·11" exchange rate reform is to refer to the closing price of the previous day of the commercial bank, and comprehensively consider the foreign exchange supply and demand situation and the changes of the international major currency exchange rate, give the quoted price of the day according to the given rules, and then the central bank determines the median price of the renminbi against the US dollar on the day the given price with the formula. The market exchange rate can fluctuate within 2% of the middle price. The purpose of this reform is obviously to enhance the role of market supply and demand in the renminbi exchange rate formation mechanism. Before the exchange reform on Aug.11, most people expected the renminbi exchange rate to depreciate by 2% or 3% during the year. Unexpectedly, the exchange reform itself has stimulated the expectation of depreciation. The market's expectation of renminbi depreciation has generally soared to 7% to 8%, and individual depreciation is expected to be as high as 10% to 20%. Depreciation expectations have led to a sharp increase in capital outflows, which in turn have exacerbated the pressure of depreciation. On Aug.11, the renminbi exchange rate quickly depreciated after the opening bell, and soon approached the 2% lower limit. The opening of the market fell again on Aug.12, but the renminbi suddenly rose sharply near the market closing. Obviously, this is because the central bank worried that the closing price is too low, so the intervention in the market has raised the renminbi exchange rate. After Aug.13, the central bank basically implemented the "crawling and pinning" exchange rate policy.

By vigorously intervening in the foreign exchange market, it is trying to re-enter the exchange rate depreciation expectation into "Pandora's box". The central bank does not want to intervene in the foreign exchange market endlessly, but once the central bank stops or reduces intervention, the exchange rate will fall rapidly. In Aug. 2015, the PBOC issued the China Foreign Exchange Trading System (CFETS) renminbi exchange rate index and the renminbi exchange rate index of the Bank for International Settlements (BIS) currency basket and the SDR currency basket, guiding the market to observe the renminbi exchange rate through a basket of currencies, reflecting the renminbi more comprehensively change of the value[1]. We also further improve the quotation mechanism of the renminbi exchange rate in the middle price, the benchmark role of the middle price is obviously improved, the renminbi exchange rate is bidirectional floating, the flexibility is obviously enhanced, and the exchange rate is closer to a reasonable and balanced level.

In Feb. 2016, the central bank further clarified that the quotes of market makers should refer to the closing price of the previous day plus the change of the 24-hour basket exchange rate. The central bank's "closing price + basket currency" pricing mechanism has been well received by the market. The expected renminbi exchange rate is relatively stable, the pressure on the depreciation of the renminbi is declining, and the sharp decline in foreign exchange reserves has been curbed. However, whether this new exchange rate formation mechanism can truly achieve the independent stability of the exchange rate, that is, the exchange rate stability under the market supply and demand, will be further tested by time.

6.4.2 Historical achievements in the reform of renminbi exchange rate formation mechanism

Since the reform of the renminbi exchange rate formation mechanism, the market exchange rate has been able to give full play to the resource allocation function, the international payments imbalance has been greatly eased, the renminbi exchange rate undervaluation has been significantly corrected, the exchange rate fluctuation flexibility has increased significantly, and the exchange rate has initially presented a

[1] PBOC, "People's Bank of China Annual Report 2015", PBOC website.

two-way wave dynamic potential. The administrative intervention in the foreign exchange market is gradually weakening, and the impact of the balance of payments on the independence of domestic monetary policy is decreasing.[1]

(1) *The undervaluation of the renminbi exchange rate was corrected and the exchange rate flexibility was significantly enhanced*

Since the renminbi exchange rate formation mechanism was restarted on Jul.21, 2005, the exchange rate of the renminbi against the major international currencies has appreciated significantly. From 2005 to 2017, the appreciation of the renminbi against the US dollar, the euro, and the Japanese yen was around 20%. In contrast, the effective exchange rate of the renminbi against a global basket of currencies has appreciated more. This has significantly improved the past state of the undervalued renminbi exchange rate. In addition to the significant appreciation of the renminbi exchange rate, the flexibility of the renminbi exchange rate has also increased significantly over the past 10 years. In May 2007, Apr. 2012 and Mar. 2014, the PBOC expanded the daily fluctuation range of the renminbi against the US dollar three times, which has been expanded from ±3‰ to ±2%.

(2) *The internal and external balance of the Chinese economy has improved*

In the past, due to the continued undervaluation of the renminbi exchange rate, the Chinese economy faced significant internal and external imbalances. The so-called external imbalance refers to the ratio of China's current account balance to GDP is too high (up to 10% in 2007, significantly higher than the internationally recognized reasonable range of 3% to 4%); the so-called internal imbalance means that the undervaluated renminbi exchange rate continues to underestimate the price of domestic service products compared to manufactured goods, which has caused resources to flow from the service industry to the manufacturing industry, which has led to a situation in which the manufacturing industry is over-developed and the service industry is underdeveloped.

With the significant appreciation of the renminbi exchange rate over the past 10 years, the internal and external imbalances facing the Chinese economy have improved significantly. With the global foreign demand weakened from the global financial crisis and the strong appreciation of the effective exchange rate of the renminbi, the ratio of China's current account surplus to GDP has continued to fall below 3% during

[1] Zheng Liansheng, "Current situation, problems and suggestions of financial reform since the 18th Central Committee of CPC", *The Chinese Banker*, 2015(11).

the five years from 2011 to 2015. This aspect shows that China's external imbalance has improved significantly. On the other hand, it also indicates that the current renminbi exchange rate level is close to the equilibrium exchange rate. Since the significant appreciation of the renminbi exchange rate has largely corrected the undervaluation of the prices of services relative to manufactured goods, the pace of development of China's service industry has significantly exceeded that of manufacturing in recent years. In fact, since 2012, the proportion of China's tertiary industry's output value to GDP has continued to exceed the GDP share of the secondary industry's output value, which means that China's internal industrial structure imbalance has also been corrected to some extent.

6.4.3 The internationalization of renminbi has achieved rapid development

Since 2009, the PBOC has begun to promote the internationalization of renminbi with a "three-pronged" strategy: first is to promote renminbi pricing and settlement of cross-border trade and investment; second is to develop offshore renminbi financial markets; third is to make bilateral currency swap with the central bank of other economies. So far, the internationalization of the renminbi has made significant progress on the above three levels. The use of the renminbi in cross-border trade and direct investment continues to rise. In 2015, the amount of renminbi receipts and payments for the current account was RMB7.23 trillion, a year-on-year increase of 10.4%. The amount of foreign direct investment (ODI) renminbi receipts and payments was RMB736.17 billion, an increase of 228.1% year-on-year; foreign direct investment (FDI) renminbi was RMB1.59 trillion, an increase of 65.2% year-on-year.[1]

The renminbi liquidity of the offshore financial center of the renminbi, represented by the Hong Kong, has grown significantly in recent years, and the international use of the renminbi has developed steadily. As of the end of 2015, the balance of non-resident renminbi deposits in China (excluding Hong Kong, Macao and Taiwan region) was RMB1.54 trillion, the balance of renminbi deposits in the main offshore market was approximately RMB1.45 trillion, and the outstanding balance of renminbi international bonds was RMB590 billion. According to incomplete statistics, as of the end of 2015, the balance of renminbi assets held by foreign central banks and monetary authorities in domestic and overseas markets, such as bonds, stocks and

[1] PBOC, "Renminbi Internationalization Report (2016)", PBOC website.

deposits, was approximately RMB864.7 billion.[1] On Nov.30, 2015, the executive board of the IMF decided to include the renminbi in the International Monetary Fund's Special Drawing Rights (SDR). This is a milestone on the road to internationalization of the renminbi. It marks the recognition of China's economic development and the achievements of reform and opening up, especially the recognition of the internationalization of the renminbi. After the renminbi joins the SDR, with the continuous opening of the domestic financial market and the continual enrichment of renminbi financial products in the international financial market, the confidence of foreign investors in the renminbi will continue to increase, and the willingness to hold renminbi assets will continue to strengthen.

By the end of 2016, the PBOC had signed bilateral currency swap agreements with central banks or monetary authorities in 36 countries and regions. The total size of the agreement exceeded RMB3.32 trillion;[2] renminbi clearing arrangements were established in 20 countries and regions. Southeast Asia, Western Europe, Central Europe, the Middle East, North America, South America, Oceania and Africa support the renminbi as a regional pricing currency.

6.5 Accelerate the reform of financial supervision system

In 2008, the global financial crisis hit the global economy, and challenged the excessive financial liberalization and financial supervision mode. Countries began to fully consider their financial supervision. China has also accelerated the reform of the financial supervision system, and introduced corresponding laws and regulations for the supervision of various fields such as commercial banks, capital markets, and insurance. However, the development of China's financial practice shows that China's financial supervision system is not perfect, and there are still many unsuitable places. General Secretary Xi Jinping stressed at the 2016 Central Economic Work Conference: "At present, financial risks are prone to high incidence. Although systemic risks are generally controllable, non-performing assets risks, liquidity risks, bond default risks, shadow banking risks, external shock risks, real estate bubble risks, government debt risks, Internet financial risks, etc., are accumulating, and financial

[1] PBOC, "Renminbi Internationalization Report (2016)", PBOC website.

[2] PBOC, "Bilateral currency exchange list between the People's Bank of China and other central banks or monetary authorities (as of Jun. 2016), Central and Chinese Central Banks Sign Bilateral Currency Exchange Agreement", PBOC website.

markets are also chaotic".

6.5.1 The motivation of China's financial supervision system reform

Finance is the facility of funds. The goal is to improve the efficiency of capital service to real economy development. Financial efficiency has an important impact on economic development. Although the issue of whether financial services can effectively serve the development of the real economy is very complicated, strengthening financial supervision has become an important means to promote the economic development of financial services. In recent years, although China's financial regulatory system has caused widespread concern in the society, the relevant system has not yet undergone in-depth adjustments. Currently, the PBOC, the CBRC, the CSRC, the CIRC and the Foreign Exchange Bureau continue to have a system of "one bank, three commissions, one bureau". In order to strengthen coordination among various regulatory authorities, the inter-ministerial joint conference system of financial supervision and coordination led by the PBOC established in Aug. 2013 plays an important role in promoting the healthy operation of China's financial system and serving the real economy.

However, with the growth of China's economic volume and the continued expansion of the currency, the problems of low financial efficiency has become increasingly prominent. As of 2016, China's money supply has reached nearly RMB160 trillion, ranking first in the world, and the money supply accounted for more than 200% of GDP. At present, China's money supply is twice that of the US, but GDP is only 2/3 of that of the US, which indicates that China's monetary and financial efficiency is low. In addition, 70% of China's social financing is realized through credit, and more than 10% is realized through bonds. Since loans and bonds are social debts, more than 80% of China's currency enters society through debts and loans, resulting in high social debt operation, the problem of high leverage of enterprises is outstanding, and the micro-entities, such as enterprises, are under pressure to pay interest and principle, and the return on investment of enterprises is low[1].

China's financial inefficiency has an important relationship with the financial supervision system. At present, China's financial industry accounts for more than 8% of GDP, which is higher than the average level of the world's major developed

[1]Zhang Yuan and Chen Jianqi, "Motivation, challenge and countermeasure of Chinese financial supervision system reform", *Chinese Cadres Tribune*, 2017(4).

countries. The financial reality is considered to be an important performance of financial inefficiency. It is considered to be an important issue for financial regulation. In recent years, the financial industry has continued to innovate, financial business has continued to expand, and a large number of funds have formed a financial closed loop through the extracorporeal circulation, which has promoted the continuous expansion of the financial industry. At the same time, a large number of financial resources also promoted the financial sector in the real economy through speculation, especially in some cities, a large amount of funds poured into the real estate market, causing real estate prices to soar, causing real estate growth expectations to increase, and a large amount of funds self-circulating in the real estate sector, which in turn increased the risk of financial transformation form real economy to fictitious economy.

The problem of financial inefficiency caused by the financial transformation from real economy to fictitious economy not only constitutes an escalation of financial risks caused by the financial extracorporeal circulation, but also causes the real economy to lack effective financial support. How to strengthen financial supervision to promote financial mismatching has become an important task at present. On the one hand, by strengthening financial supervision, it will help to avoid further flow of financial resources into the fictitious economy, provide more financial support for the real economy, and reduce the risk of capital extracorporeal circulation. On the other hand, by strengthening financial supervision, it will help to activate the stock funds, allow idle funds to enter the real economy, and improve the efficiency of capital use. On the basis of strengthening financial supervision, China has accelerated the reform of other financial market systems, especially actively promoting capital market reforms, prompting more enterprises to conduct equity financing through capital markets, thereby promoting a steady decline in leverage ratio, and funding service entities. The strength of economic development is expected to be enhanced. On the whole, financial inefficiency breeds financial risks and downward pressure on the economy. Strengthening financial supervision has become an important driving force for the development of the real economy. Financial inefficiency has become an important driver of the reform of the financial regulatory system.

6.5.2 The challenges faced by China's financial regulatory system reform

The failure of financial services to effectively serve the development of the real economy constitutes the direct cause of the reform of China's financial regulatory system. However, there is no perfect experience in the world for the reform of the financial regulatory system. Even the most developed financial system in the US is still exploring. After the reform of the financial regulatory system, Trump was preparing to amend the "Dodd Frank Act" passed by the Obama administration after he was elected president of the US. The reform of China's financial regulatory system must also be analyzed in light of China's actual situation. From the perspective of China's financial and economic development level, the current financial regulatory system reform still faces the following challenges.

The first is the question of "who is going to supervise". The construction of a comprehensive regulatory department or a model of coexistence of multiple regulatory agencies with separate supervision is still lacking scientific basis and experience. At present, China implements a "one bank, three commissions, one bureau" and inter-ministerial joint meeting. If the UK's financial regulatory centralization model is adopted, it will face the challenge of institutional integration. If China wants to follow the current model of separate supervision, then with the rapid advancement of financial innovation and the rapid deepening of the derivatives market, such a system will gradually expose the drawbacks of weakly dealing with the systemic financial risks.

The second is the issue of regulation target. The blurring of business boundaries of financial institutions constitutes the unclear objects of supervision, making it difficult for regulators to clarify the objects of supervision, and it is easy to create challenges such as regulatory vacuum or regulatory crossover. Some financial groups cover a full range of financial services such as banking, securities, trusts, insurance, funding, asset management, and futures. Traditional commercial banks will participate in other asset management services through financial management, etc., which all indicate that financial management system of the division related to the separate supervision system will undergo a huge adjustment. Under this background, if the financial institutions are still supervised according to the traditional methods, there may be a situation of regulatory confusion. In addition, in the subject of financial supervision, due to the emergence of new formats such as the internet, financial business has also been innovating, resulting in some businesses failing to be included in the scope of supervision. In particular, internet finance has developed rapidly in recent years, and the regulatory authorities are not familiar with the new financial form. The relevant regulatory laws have a large lag, and the issues that are more difficult to clarify are prominent. In the future, as the influence of digital currencies such as Bitcoin expands, the global monetary system may become more vulnerable, and the financial risks arise from these may be more subtle.

The third is the issue of "how to supervise". Financial regulation faces the problem of how to weigh efficiency and risk. If the goal of minimizing financial risks is to be achieved, then over-regulation of financial institutions may result, resulting in a lack of vitality in the financial system, and the efficiency of the financial services to real economy may be affected. Similarly, if the dynamism of the financial system is over-emphasized, it may lead to excessive financial liberalization, which may lead to problems of rapid financial risk rise and even systemic financial risks. The core challenge in solving this problem is how to clarify the relationship between the government and the market in the financial sector. In order to effectively prevent risks and protect financial vitality, it is necessary to closely integrate domestic and international market changes, market players, market structure, investor behavior and financial infrastructure, etc., to constantly adjust on various aspects of regulatory concepts, regulatory tools, regulatory methods, regulatory agencies and regulatory coordination. However, these adjustments involve not only different financial institutions, but also different regulatory authorities, and thus face greater challenges in how to coordinate.

In the process of implementing financial supervision, the issue of how macro regulation and micro-regulation are coordinated is also more prominent. The slowdown in macroeconomic growth will gradually expose the unstable factors accumulated in the early stage of the financial system, and thus increase the pressure on financial supervision. Coupled with the need for market-oriented reforms and the service of the real economy, both financial market operators and financial regulators need to pay more attention to innovation and balance in the future. On the one hand, strengthening macro-prudential supervision is the main content of global financial regulatory reform after the financial crisis. China also needs to strengthen the construction of a macro-prudential regulatory framework to ensure that regional and systemic financial risks do not occur. On the other hand, information asymmetry is an important cause of market failure, and if the regulatory agency cannot grasp the corresponding market information, it will undoubtedly greatly reduce the effectiveness of supervision.

6.5.3 Suggestions on deepening the reform of China's financial supervision system

At present, the central government has put the reform of the financial supervision system in a prominent position. General Secretary Xi Jinping emphasized at the fifteenth meeting of the Central Financial and Economic Leading Group on Feb.28, 2017 that "to prevent and control financial risks, it is necessary to speed up the establishment of a regulatory coordination mechanism and strengthen macro prudential supervision, strengthen overall coordination, prevent and resolve systemic risks. It is necessary to promptly make up for the shortcomings of supervision, do a good job in the investigation of loopholes in system supervision, and make clear requirements in light of international standards. We must resolutely control market chaos and resolutely crack down on illegal activities. It is necessary to reform and innovate through institutional mechanisms to improve the ability and level of financial services to the real economy". This not only shows the central government's emphasis on the reform of the financial regulatory system, but also points to the overall direction of the future financial regulatory system reform. Based on the current domestic and international situation and the deployment of the central government, China's financial regulatory system reform should be comprehensively promoted in the following aspects.

First, it will promote the development of financial services to real economy as the starting point and the foothold of the financial regulatory system reform. The focus is to broaden the financial regulatory objectives and further extend the compliance and risk supervision emphasized by traditional financial theory to the scope of serving the real economy. It is not limited to the financial industry of the financial supervision. This model is not only too narrow, but also breeds the self-circulation of the financial industry, which is contrary to the ultimate goal of the financial service to real economy development. All previous financial crises have shown that financial regulation that is separated from the development of the real economy is inefficient. A financial regulatory system that serves the economic development of the real economy should be established, and the efficiency of financial supervision should be evaluated through the development of the real economy. In light of China's actual situation, the current focus should be on reducing or avoiding the problem of extracorporeal circulation of funds through financial supervision. We should focus on studying the prominent institutional problems such as "barbarians" in the capital market, and strengthen the institutional construction of financial supervision, which exclude the unfavorable financial behavior from the development of the real economy.

Second, we must promptly establish a regulatory coordination mechanism, strengthen macro-prudential supervision, strengthen overall coordination, and solve the problem of the lack of supervision that is currently plagued by separated supervision. The combination of internet technology and financial innovation will accelerate the transformation of the financial market system, from the traditional separated business model to the mixed business model. If there is no coordination mechanism, then the "one bank, three commissions, one bureau" separated supervision mode will be difficult to keep up with changes in the financial market system. At present, the pressure on the reform of the existing separated supervision mode in China is increasing. On how to deal with the volatility of the stock market in recent years and the continuous bids of insurance funds, the coordination mechanism should be strengthened in the future by strengthening inter-ministerial joint meetings, and more coordination agencies should be given functions. With a more macro-scale framework, we shall coordinate various regulatory bodies and regulatory resources to achieve the purpose of prudent supervision of systemic risks, and finally solve the problem of "who supervises".

The third is to speed up the study of new financial formats, improve the policy measures to promote financial innovation, establish relevant financial supervision systems in a timely manner, achieve full coverage of financial supervision, and solve the problem of targets of financial supervision. On the one hand, in view of the financial innovation of traditional financial institutions, the supervisory body should study the supervision method in a timely manner according to the innovative format, avoid the lack of supervision of innovative business such as commercial banks and other traditional financial institutions, and strengthen the full coverage of financial supervision in traditional financial institutions. On the other hand, in view of new financial formats such as internet financial innovation, digital currency, and blockchain, we will timely study the development model, development trend and development orientation of new formats, clarify the regulatory bodies of new financial formats, and avoid the arbitrage between traditional finance and new formats, to truly achieves full coverage of financial supervision.

The fourth is to deepen the innovation of financial supervision methods, actively promote the construction of "financial supervision + internet", improve the level of supervision through modern information technology and other means, and solve the problem of "how to supervise". The important reason for the current low efficiency of supervision is information asymmetry. There is incomplete information between the regulatory authorities and the regulated entities, and the behavior of financial institutions cannot be effectively monitored. In the future, we should pay more attention to the application of information technology in financial supervision. When the internet brings new impetus to financial innovation, it also provides important support for financial regulatory innovation. By improving the application of Internet technology in financial supervision, it will have a more comprehensive understanding of financial institutions' information, which can promote the sharing of financial regulatory information in financial institutions, public security departments and other departments, forming before, during, and after-the-event supervision chain, consolidate promote the efficiency of financial supervision.

6.6 Accelerate the opening up of the financial industry

Opening up is the only way for the country to prosper and develop. All-round opening up is an inevitable requirement of financial development. Promoting the bidirectional opening of the financial industry, promoting the orderly flow of domestic and international factors, the efficient allocation of financial resources, and the deep integration of financial markets are the only way to deepen financial reform. Since the 18th CPC National Congress, the pace of China's financial opening up has been significantly accelerated, and its effectiveness has been remarkable. The opening up of the financial industry has effectively promoted the deepening of financial reforms, enhanced the sense of competition among financial market players, improved financial innovation capabilities, and promoted China's financial stability, efficiency and safe operation, which strongly support the national economic growth.

6.6.1 Actively participate in global financial and economic governance

China has participated in international multilateral development financial institutions and jointly set up investment and financing platforms. In 2015, Pan American Investment Co., Ltd., a subsidiary of the Inter-American Development Bank Group, increased its shareholding, and its shareholding ratio will rank first among the member states outside the region. In Jan. 2016, China officially joined the European Bank for Reconstruction and Development (EBRD), further strengthening exchanges and cooperation with Central and Eastern Europe, the Eastern Mediterranean and the South and Central Asia, which is another engine to promote Chinese companies and financial institutions to "go global". In order to further enrich the foreign investment and financing platform and deepen cooperation with international multilateral development institutions, the People's Bank of China and the Inter-American

Development Bank jointly established a US$2 billion joint venture fund for Latin America and the Caribbean in 2013, and the World Bank in the same year. The Group's affiliated international finance company jointly established a US$3 billion co-financing fund. In 2014, it established a US$2 billion African Common Growth Fund with the African Development Bank.[1]

China continues to participate in the work of the Financial Stability Council (FSB), the Basel Committee on Banking Supervision (BCBS), the East Asia and Pacific Central Bank Governors Meeting (EMEAP) and other international organizations and working groups, and deeply participates in the rules-making of Total Loss-Absorbing Capacity (TLAC) in global systemically important banks (G-SIBs).

By promoting the implementation of the International Monetary Fund (IMF) share and governance reform program, China's IMF share ranking rose to third place, and the representation and voice of emerging markets and developing countries in the IMF were further enhanced. Since Oct.1, 2016, the renminbi has joined the International Monetary Fund (IMF) Special Drawing Rights (SDR). The participation of renminbi to the SDR is both the recognition of the IMF's internationalization process and the promise of continued promotion of the financial reform such as capital account opening.

By actively using platforms such as the G20, China deeply participates in and guides the global economic governance process. China became the chairman of the G20 in 2016 and officially became one of the G20 "Troika". Taking this as an opportunity, the PBOC has deeply participated in and guided the global economic governance process and macroeconomic policy coordination. PBOC also actively participates in the G20 financial channel series meeting, promotes all concerned parties to discuss key issues such as the global economic situation and growth framework, fully safeguards national interests, and actively exerts China's influence in global affairs.

China in-depth participates in the financial cooperation between the "BRIC" countries, continuously improves the BRICS emergency reserve arrangements, and promotes the "Central Bank Inter-bank Agreement for the BRICS Emergency Reserve Arrangement", which will complement the global financial safety network. China also actively participates in the "BRIC" finance ministers and central bank governors meeting, strengthens communication, enhances mutual trust, and coordinates positions

---

1 PBOC, "People's Bank of China Annual Report 2015", PBOC website.

with the "BRIC" parties on issues such as IMF reform and seeks support.

6.6.2 Strive to strengthen regional financial cooperation

Under the Executives' meetings of East Asia-Pacific Central Banks (EMEAP) mechanism, the Asian Bond Fund will play its role in promoting the development of the Asian bond market, continuously improve the regional crisis management framework, and strengthen the monitoring and exchange of regional economic and financial situations. Under the financial cooperation mechanism between ASEAN and China, Japan and Republic of Korea (10+3), we further improve the operability of the "Chiang Mai Initiative Multilateralization" (CMIM) mechanism, continuously improve operational guidelines and conduct rescue drills, and do a good job of upgrading "ASEAN+3" Macroeconomic Research Office (AMRO) to international organizations and improve its governance structure.

China actively promotes the Belt and Road Initiative (BRI) to cooperate and play the role of financial support to BRI. We will improve the financial policy framework that supports the BRI and increase financial support to enterprises for "going global" strategy of to expand the use of renminbi in countries along the route. We hosted the 7th China-Japan-Republic of Korea Central Bank Governors Meeting, actively participated in relevant work under the Boao Forum for Asia and the Asia-Pacific Economic Cooperation (APEC), and strengthened exchanges and cooperation with all parties.

6.6.3 Continuously deepen bilateral financial coordination and cooperation

China-US economic and financial cooperation has made pragmatic progress. The 7th round of the China-US Strategic and Economic Dialogue reached 77 results in strengthening economic and policy cooperation, supporting financial stability and reform, enhancing global cooperation and improving international rules.

China has the progress to promote China-EU financial cooperation. Positive progress has been made in the development of the offshore renminbi market in Paris and the promotion of mutual recognition and approval of qualified central counterparties between China and Europe. It has taken the lead in setting up a Sino-European joint investment fund with a scale of EUR10 billion to make a good connection between the Belt and Road and the European investment plan; extending the RQFⅡ pilot to Luxembourg and Hungary, and actively considering the establishment of renminbi clearing arrangements with Belgium; the successful issuance of RMB5 billion central bank bills in London and the establishment of branches of the China Foreign Exchange Trading System in London to create a "golden age" for Sino-British financial cooperation.

In order to better promote the international capacity cooperation among China, Africa and Latin America, and the innovative cooperation model, the PBOC and the SAFE respectively established the US$10 billion Central Africa Capacity Cooperation Fund and the US$10 billion Sino-Latin Production Cooperation Investment Fund in 2015 together with the China Development Bank and the Export-Import Bank of China to strongly support the production capacity cooperation for Chinese-funded enterprises in these regions.

Financial cooperation with neighboring countries is closely increasing. China has successfully held the China-Russia Financial Cooperation Sub-Committee and the China-Kazakhstan Cooperation Committee; China and Kazakhstan reached cooperation consensus on implementing local currency swaps, expanding local currency settlements, and strengthening financial cooperation in the Horgos International Border Cooperation Center. We also give or increase the RQFII quota for South Korea, Singapore, Malaysia and Thailand. The China-Vietnam Financial Cooperation Working Group was established and China reached an agreement on the expansion of the size of local currency swaps with Indonesia. China also hosted the 33rd Central Bank Governors' Club of Central Asia, Black Sea Region and Balkan Region, and created a friendly atmosphere for deepening cooperation with the Central Asia, Black Sea Region and Balkan Region, especially the Central and Eastern European countries, and improved the coordinated investment and financing framework between China and Central and Eastern Europe, and strengthened financial cooperation with 16 countries in Central and Eastern Europe.

General Secretary Xi Jinping pointed out at the symposium on promoting the construction of the Belt and Road that "financial power is an important manifestation of national competitiveness". At a time when international trade protectionism is on the rise and the anti-globalization trend is rising, China firmly adheres to the principle of comprehensive opening up and financial expansion and opening up. This reflects China's role as the world's second largest economy in promoting economic globalization and more sustainable development responsibility of the great power. China also takes the open policy measures that are practicable and welcomed by the international community, and strives to promote win-win cooperation between the Chinese economy and the world economy. There are good reasons to believe that China's financial expansion and opening up to the outside world will not only provide strong momentum for China's sustained and stable economic development and transformation and upgrading, but also inject new impetus into the accelerated recovery and balanced development of the world economy.

Chapter 7
Summary and Prospect of China's Financial System Reform

For thousands of years, China's finance has experienced countless twists and turns, basically showing a spiraling upward trend. China has experienced from the exchange of goods in barter economy, to the fixed general equivalent in value of shellfish, from the physical currency to coins, and then to banknotes and electronic money; from the pawn activities of the longevity library to the mortgage shop in the Song Dynasty, the pawnshops and banks in the Ming Dynasty, the finance companies of the Qing Dynasty, etc., to modern banks, securities companies, insurance companies, internet finance companies; from the "dual financial" pattern of the traditional financial sector and modern financial institutions in the Republic of China, to the financial system of "great unity" in early days of the People's Republic of China, to reform and opening up, especially since the financial system has diversified since the 18th National Congress of CPC. The development and reform of China's financial system has experienced too many twists and turns. The historical process of the establishment and development of the financial system in the past millennium has proved that advance or lag in the reform of the financial system relative to the reform of the economic system will bring losses to the reform and economic development. Only to proceed in parallel of both of these can achieve the coordinating, and accelerate the reform of the economic system and promote the development of economy.

7.1 Summary of China's financial system reform

Over the past 40 years of reform and opening up, especially since the 18th CPC National Congress of China, China's financial industry has played an important role in creating an independent monetary system, maintaining financial stability, supporting economic development and economic restructuring, and has become an indispensable and important channel of macroeconomic management and regulation process.

7.1.1 Achievements in China's financial system reform

To sum up, the achievements of China's financial reform and opening up are mainly reflected in the following six aspects.

(1) *A unified and sound monetary system has been established to stabilize the value of the renminbi*

Money is an inevitable condition for the existence of finance, and thus the most basic element of the financial system. In the modern monetary economy, the exchange of goods and the flow of production factors are carried out through money. Therefore, the stability of the currency value in the domestic and international market is directly related to the willingness of investment and the efficiency of resource allocation, which in turn affects the security of the financial system and the financial functions. At the beginning of the establishment of the People's Bank of China, the establishment of a unified monetary system and stabilization of market prices were the primary duties. In the past few decades, after the PBOC established a relatively complete monetary system through a series of reforms, the renminbi has become a relatively stable currency in the world. After the reform and opening up, through the continuous reform of the foreign exchange system, a single, managed floating exchange rate generation mechanism based on market supply and demand, which is basically in line with China's national conditions, has formed a common market basis for the renminbi's domestic and foreign currency values. In the international economic trade, the stability of the renminbi exchange rate has also gained a good international reputation. After the outbreak of the Southeast Asian financial crisis in 1997, the PBOC cautiously responded to changes in the situation, moderately adjusted the operation and adjustment methods of monetary policy, and ensured the stability of the renminbi exchange rate, which was widely endorsed and highly evaluated at home and abroad. Also, with the assistance of the relevant ministries and commissions of the State Council, the PBOC, through flexible monetary and credit policies, has basically kept domestic prices stable, ensuring that there is no large fluctuation in the value of the renminbi against the domestic currency, and providing a good financial environment for economic development and social progress.

(2) *Formed a fully functional financial organization system to enhance financial strength*

In the modern market economy, monetary circulation must be completed by means of specialized financial institutions (media). Various financial institutions play different roles in the allocation of capital resources. For example, commercial banks mainly absorb deposits and issue loans. Securities companies (or investment banks) mainly provide intermediary services to convert some funds directly into long-term capital; insurance companies, via transfering and spreading risks, and reducing losses, provide economic security for all aspects of social reproduction. It can be seen that finance must play a central role in the modern economy. Its most important micro-foundation is the financial organization system with complete functions, reasonable division of labor and fair competition. In China, from a single national banking system, the financial organization system has initially established a multiple financing channels coexisting, complementary functions and coordinated development financial system regulated and supervised by the "one bank and three commissions". In this system, the state-controlled commercial banks act as the main body, with the separated policy finance and commercial finance, and various institutional division of labor and cooperation. Via this financial system, China has built a good monetary and financial environment for the sustained, healthy and stable development of the national economy.[1]

(3) *A competitive and orderly financial market has been constructed*

The orderly operation of the financial market is an important condition for promoting the optimal allocation of resources and the effective functioning of the financial system. The financial market mainly consists of two parts: the money market and the capital market. The former is mainly to adjust the surplus of funds, while the latter is responsible for providing long-term capital and permanent capital. The balanced development of the money market and the capital market can make a reasonable proportion between direct financing and indirect financing, and help to improve the social financing structure. China has established a relatively complete currency market including interbank lending market, inter-bank bond market, negotiable certificates of deposit market and commercial paper market. The smooth flow of funds in the money market has strengthened the bank's loan capacity and

---

[1] Wang Chaoyang, *Research on Financial Service Industry Cluster: also on the Construction of China's Regional Financial Center*, Beijing: Social Sciences Academic Press (China), 2013.

improved the efficiency and intensity of monetary policy transmission. The money market interest rate can more sensitively reflect the changes in the position of financial institutions and the monetary policy of the central bank, and gradually become the important operational objectives and major economic indicators of monetary policy of the central bank, laying a good foundation for interest rate liberalization. In the capital market, the rapid development of the bond market, stock market, fund market and futures market over the years has provided a good foundation for establishing a multi-level capital market system, improving the capital market structure and enriching capital market products.

(4) *A flexible and efficient financial macro-control system has been formed*

A sound financial macro-control system will help to achieve a basic balance between aggregate supply and demand, and promote the healthy, coordinated and sustainable development of the national economy. Generally speaking, a sound financial macro-control system requires a relatively independent central bank, a fully functional monetary policy tool and a smooth channel for the transmission of monetary policy. The purpose of this system is to maintain the stability of the currency's internal and external stability and to promote economic development. After the financial reform began in 1979, the macroeconomic management gradually shifted from physical management to value management, and the guiding plan and market regulation gradually replaced the mandatory plan. Banks began to replace the fiscal sector in the centralization and distribution of social funds, and the scope of bank loans gradually expanded. After the Asian financial crisis broke out in 1997, the options, use, timing and intensity of monetary policy tools and the transmission mechanism of monetary policy have undergone significant changes. In recent years, through policy adjustment and implementation, financial macro-control has produced good results in promoting economic development.

(5) *Clearly regulated financial regulatory system*

Due to the inherent fragility of the financial system, especially the banking system, in order to maintain the stable operation of the financial institution and the full play of the financial system, it is necessary to strengthen supervision of the financial industry, promote financial institutions to strengthen internal risk control, and fully protect the interests of depositors and investors. A necessary condition for improving the efficiency of financial supervision is to establish a financial supervision system that is compatible with the development level of the financial industry. Since the reform and opening up, China has successively promulgated a series of financial laws and regulations, and established and improved the legal framework for financial supervision by conducting a series of bank and non-bank, securities, and insurance industry regulatory legislation. In order to adapt to the diversification of financial institutions and the cross-over and competition of financial services, a financial system with separate operations and supervision has been established. Through reforming the central bank's regulatory system, establishing and improving the securities, insurance, and banking regulatory systems, and gradually enriching the regulatory tools in the process of reforming financial supervision, the financial regulatory system has been further developed and improved. It has played an important role in maintaining the financial order, implementing the national economic and financial policies, and promoting the development of the national economy.

(6) *Financial openness is remarkable*

In the era of economic and financial globalization, only by continuously improving the level of opening up of the financial industry can we better play the central role of finance in the modern economy. Since the reform and opening up, China's financial industry has implemented a policy of opening to the outside world, and its external exchanges have been continuously expanded. The content of international financial cooperation has become increasingly rich. In accordance with the principle of domestic economic development and international cooperation, since 1979, China has opened up domestic financial markets in a planned and step-by-step manner. With China's accession to the WTO and the implementation of the strategy of combining the "go global" with the country, China's financial industry has accelerated its opening up to the outside world, and the level of financial opening up has been continuously improved. The central bank has strictly fulfilled its commitment to join the WTO. Banks can handle foreign exchange business without geographical and customer restrictions, and further increase the number of foreign banks engaged in renminbi business. In international financial affairs, the PBOC, on behalf of the government, participates in international financial activities of various countries, safeguards China's sovereign interests, and also fulfills its corresponding international obligations. The People's Republic of China is a member of international financial institutions such as the International Monetary Fund, the Bank for International Settlements, and the Asian Development Bank. In these organizations, the PBOC has played the role of the member states on behalf of the government.

However, it must also be noted that the financial industry is also facing greater risks while opening up to the outside world. Therefore, to actively participate in international competition, actively integrate into the process of financial globalization, and effectively prevent the risks that financial openness may bring, it is necessary to establish a sound financial opening mechanism. According to the overall strategic needs of economic system reform, China has adopted a gradual improvement strategy in the process of financial opening up to ensure the stable operation and development of the financial system.[1]

7.1.2 Characteristics of China's financial system reform

(1) *China's financial system reform is a progressive reform*

China's economic system reform, including financial system reform, is gradual improvement, unlike Russia's one-stop shock therapy. Progressive reform is a process of institutional change from partial to overall. China's overall economic reforms have chosen a gradual approach to reform. Based on the limitations and constraints of this institutional change model, the financial system reform has also adopted a progressive reform logic. China's financial system reform has no ready-made model and can only be explored. This process should be sound and progressive. The reform should ultimately be based on the principle of not interrupting the financial relationship in the course of economic operations, and not causing economic operations and huge social fluctuations.

China's financial reform has also adopted a gradual approach in financial market reform. First, the interbank lending market interest rate was liberalized, and the main players in the interbank borrowing market were gradually strengthened. Then, the primary market of the national debt market was also marketized, and the floating rate of interest rates on SMEs loans was expanded.

China's foreign exchange market has also adhered to the principle of gradual and orderly control from strict control to gradual opening. The first step is the conditional convertibility of the renminbi current account in China in 1994. The second step is that in 1996, according to the requirements of Article 8 of the "Agreement of the International Monetary Fund", China basically implemented the convertibility of renminbi current account, which is a major measure to further relax foreign exchange control and expand foreign financial opening, and thus effectively promote development of China's import and export trade. The third step is the exchange of

[1] He Dexu and Zhang Junzhou, *Innovation, Risk and Safeguard: Financial Safety in China's Financial Development*, Beijing: Social Sciences Academic Press (China), 2012, p.13.

some items of the renminbi capital account. Finally, the foreign exchange control of capital account is gradually liberalized when the financial order and financial supervision capabilities are available.

The opening up of finance is also a principle of gradual and orderly progress. According to the extent of China's financial system reform and China's own economic strength, it is a major feature of China's financial system reform to gradually promote China's financial opening up. In the Asian financial crisis that began in 1997, one of the most important reasons why China can avoid direct shocks is that we adhere to the principle of gradual and progressive financial openness. In the opening up of the financial services industry, China has always adopted some effective control measures to avoid the impact of an over-opening on the domestic economy and finance. For example, China has adopted a combination of restricting access, strict business scope and providing preferential policies for foreign banks, which can avoid the impact on domestic banks and financial markets, and can also exert the enthusiasm of foreign banks.

(2) *China's financial system reform is a reform that coordinates the relationship between the government and the market*

Every step of China's financial system change is in top-down order. From the establishment of a two-tier banking system, the diversification of financial institutions to the development of financial markets, from the integrated operation of commercial banks to the division of business, from the unified supervision of the PBOC to the division of the "three-legged" of the China Banking Regulatory Commission, the China Securities Regulatory Commission and the China Insurance Regulatory Commission, etc., China's financial system has adopted a government-led mandatory system change approach. Although this method reduces the time cost and friction cost of institutional change, the institutional supply is largely difficult to meet the institutional needs of the micro-banking entities. As the "first action group" that promotes the change of the banking system, the government not only promotes the motives of the micro-banking main body and the overall financial efficiency, but also maintains the public ownership when deciding the form, speed, breakthrough and time path of the change of the banking system. Banks' property rights remain unchanged, fulfilling part of the financial functions and tax functions through the financial system, ensuring the continuous growth of national economic output, and maximizing the government's own interests.[1]

Giving full play to the fundamental role of market mechanisms in the financial sector is a prerequisite for the healthy development of finance. Finance is the product of the development of commodity monetary economy. It is inherently market-oriented. Practice has proved that finance can play a huge role in the national economy when it recognizes the market nature of finance, respects the objective laws of currency credit, and gives full play to the role of the market mechanism of currency credit. During the recovery of the national economy, we stopped the hyperinflation; in the 1960s, we overcame economic difficulties and stabilized financial prices; after reform and opening up, we continued to rectify and maintain the sustained and steady development of the national economy, all of which were realized under the influence of giving full play to the market mechanism of monetary credit. After the reform and opening up, there has been a gradual understanding of the development of financial markets. However, as the system is still in transition, especially in the financial sector, the system transition is relatively slow, and the role of the market mechanism is still subject to many restrictions. It was not until 1994 that the goal of establishing a socialist market economic system was clearly stated. After the role of the market mechanism must be exerted in economic construction, the pace of market-oriented reform of finance will be accelerated. In the future, the focus of financial reform will still be to change concepts, liberate the mind, reform those systems and methods left over from the planned economic system to undermine financial marketability, and truly play the fundamental role of market mechanisms in financial operations. This is the premise of adapting to the financial system of the socialist market economy. Without doubt, while giving full play to the fundamental role of the market mechanism, we must not neglect the necessary macroeconomic regulation and control and financial supervision.

(3) *China's financial system reform cannot be separated from a strong central bank*

China's financial system reform is carried out under the leadership of the government. As the government's financial management organ, the central bank plays an important role in the development of finance. The effective supervision of financial institutions by the central bank is an important aspect of the financial system and the

[1] Cui Hongyan and Chen Yuhe, "The path choice and government action of Chinese financial system change", *Foreign Investment in China*, 2011 (20), pp. 65-66.

main content of financial management. Before the reform and opening up, China's financial institutions were relatively simple. The PBOC was a central bank and a commercial bank. It was both a regulator and an operator. It was both a referee and an athlete. Its management function is mainly implemented by direct administrative orders and directive plans, and thus no real regulation exists. Since the reform, with the transformation of the functions of the PBOC and the continuous development of financial institutions, specific credit management methods such as "difference responsibility, real deposit and loan, proportional management, risk control" have been implemented in the management of financial services. In terms of financial supervision, it has gradually embarked on the path of "separate management and separate supervision". At present, breakthroughs have been made in the reform and construction of China's financial regulatory system. The pattern of supervision of banks, securities and insurance has been basically formed, and the financial system of vertical management across administrative regions has been in operation. These are inseparable from the positive role played by the central bank in financial management activities. It can be said that a strong central bank is an important guarantee for the smooth progress of China's financial system reform.

(4) *Financial stability is the core of China's financial system reform*

The financial industry is a sunrise industry. As a comprehensive department of social resource allocation and macroeconomic management, financial institutions are responsible for the important task of financing social funds. However, financial development will inevitably breed financial risks, and finance itself is an industry with great risks. The risks it faces are characterized by uncertainty, concealment, suddenness, universality and proliferation. The financial practice of various countries has repeatedly proved that if a country lacks understanding or improper handling on financial security issues, it will threaten its own economic security, administrative security and even national security.[1] In the process of financial system reform, it is a very important and successful experience to always strengthen financial supervision and maintain the security and stability of the financial system as a prerequisite for reform and opening up. In recent years, through all of the rectification and restructuring of trust and investment companies, the closure of the Rural Cooperative Foundation, the use of reforms to regulate the stock market operation, and the steady

[1] Wen Bingxun, *Research on Government Intervention*, Changsha: Hunan People's Publishing House, 2005, p.263.

development of the stock market, we have maintained financial stability in long run. The reform is ultimately to promote financial development. In the past, China began with institutional expansion, focusing on establishing an effective corporate governance structure and operating mechanism, establishing self-restraint and development mechanisms, strengthening internal control construction and strengthening supervision, so that financial efficiency was improved. And in fact, financial development strongly promoted financial stability.

(5) *Learning from the experience of foreign financial system reform, serving the reform of China's financial system*

China has always adhered to the direction of establishing a financial system that is compatible with the socialist market economic system, boldly using the experience of foreign financial system reform, and combining China's national conditions to propose reform plans with Chinese characteristics and implement them in a planned manner to ensure China's financial system reform running smoothly. The goal of China's economic system reform is to establish a socialist market economic system. The socialist market economy is a type of market economy. Naturally, there is a commonality with the general market economy, especially in the microeconomic field. That is to say, many practices of banks in market economy countries can be used for reference. According to the needs of reform, combined with the actual situation in China, the introduction of certain practices of banks in these countries can avoid the exploration from the beginning and achieve twice the result with half the effort. Since the reform and opening up, the reason why China's financial system reform can achieve such great achievements in just 20 or 30 years is to seek truth from facts, attach importance to sum up the experience of China's banking industry, liberate the mind, and boldly innovate. In addition, it has benefited from the creative absorption of many successful practices from the financial reforms of market economies. For example, the central bank system, the financial market system, the participation of banks in macroeconomic regulation, and the formulation of host banks are all the result of drawing on advanced experience.

7.1.3 Problems in China's financial system reform

Since the reform and opening up, although China's financial system reform has made great achievements, it is undeniable that there are still many problems in the current financial system construction. Due to the weak financial base and the imperfect financial system, the irregular capital market and the inefficiency of financial institutions, China's financial system lags behind the reform of the entire market system in the short term. In addition, the asset efficiency and quality of some commercial banks are not high, which seriously damages the financial infrastructure, distorts the reform and development of the financial system, causes the accumulation of financial risks and the inefficient operation of the entire financial system, seriously weakening the competitiveness of Chinese financial system in international competition.

(1) *The supply of rural financial services is seriously lacking*

Financial development has obvious geographical and regional characteristics. One of the main functions of the financial system is to provide economic resource transfer between different time, region and industry. Therefore, the geographical characteristics of the financial system are inherent. This geographical feature, or the cross-regional flow of financial resources, is of great significance to economic and social development. China's financial reforms have shown a tendency of focusing on cities and ignoring rural areas. Financial resources have been concentrated in cities, large and medium-sized enterprises, and emerging industries. The agricultural and rural economies at and below the county level are suffering from extremely severe credit squeeze. At present, the contradiction of rural capital shortage in China is very prominent. Due to the imperfect rural financial organization system, the financial service supply is severely constrained, the rural financial market is underdeveloped, the non-marketization of capital prices, and the poor deposit-to -investment transformation process make the rural financial operation inefficient, and it is difficult to meet the needs of rural economic development. The adjustment of the rural economic structure has been largely suppressed, and it is difficult to provide good financial support for the construction of a new socialist countryside.[1]

First, the rural financial organization system is not perfect, and the supply of financial services is severely constrained. From the perspective of financial service providers, China's rural financial system includes formal finance and private finance. The rural formal financial system mainly includes Agricultural Bank of China, China Agricultural Development Bank, Rural Credit Cooperatives, Rural Commercial Banks, and Post Office Savings banks, rural banks and microfinance companies; private finance mainly includes private free lending and various forms of "underground

[1] Bu Chengliang and Shen Linrong, *China's Path: The Path to Progressive Reform*, Beijing: Central Party School Press, 2009, p.171.

finance" activities. Although this kind of financial system is relatively complicated and seems to be complete, in practice, due to the reform of formal financial institutions and commercialization reforms, the "agricultural color" of rural financial institutions in China is getting weaker and lighter, and the existing rural financial system to support rural economic development is extremely weak.

Second, as far as China's current rural financial market is concerned, a prominent problem is the imbalance between the supply and demand of financial services. On the one hand, the demand for financial services of farmers and rural enterprises is expanding; on the other hand, the financial supply of formal financial institutions in rural areas shows serious insufficient. Of course, the reasons for this imbalance between supply and demand are diverse. On the demand side, from the perspective of default rate, the weak nature of agriculture and the instability of farmers' income determine that there is a high possibility of default in rural financial demand entities. However, it must also be noted that different types of farmers and rural enterprises also show large differences in loan risk, which should be treated differently. On the supply side, there are still some shortcomings in the supply mechanism of rural financial services in China. These are as follows: the risk assessment procedure of rural financial institutions limits the access of farmers to financial resources; even if farmers can access financial resources, they must meet certain additional conditions to really obtain loans; the marketing of formal financial institutions to meet rural areas demand is excluded from the target market; financial institutions also have strong price exclusion for the financial needs of farmers. Therefore, whether at the macro level or at the micro level, it is difficult to reach a consensus between the characteristics of rural financial demand and the current supply of rural financial services in China.

Third, the rural financial structure and economic structure are not coordinated, which has restrained the adjustment of the rural economic structure. At present, the rural economy is no longer a single primary industry, and both the secondary industry and the tertiary industry have developed considerably. At the same time, with the advancement of the reform of township enterprises, the private economy and the joint-stock economy have increased substantially. The adjustment of the rural economic structure has not only raised new requirements for financing, but also has new requirements for other financial businesses. However, the adjustment of the rural financial structure is far behind the changes in the economic structure: on the one hand, from the perspective of both the industrial structure and the ownership structure, loan investment, the loan term, interest rate, and method are not suitable for the optimized rural economy; on the other hand, rural financial institutions with rural credit cooperatives as the main body cannot provide diversified financial products and financial services such as insurance, consulting, agency and settlement.

In addition, the positioning of credit unions in the rural financial system has been alienated. The function of the rural credit cooperatives granted by the state is mainly to serve the "agriculture, farmer and rural area", giving full play to the role of the financial main force supporting the agricultural and rural economic development and the financial link between the farmers. At present, China's rural credit cooperatives basically do not have the characteristics of cooperative finance, and their business objectives have gradually deviated from the original intention of serving the "agriculture, farmer and rural area" and implementing the private credit function. The business object, the commercialization of the business scope, and the urbanization of the operating organization and the resulted reversal capital flow of the profit-oriented from the rural areas to the urban areas have made the support for the "agriculture, farmer and rural area" essentially absent. These are unfavorable to the development of the rural economy, resulting in a large potential financial risks in individual areas.[1]

(2) *The coordination and cooperation of financial supervision is still not in place*

From the perspective of global development trends, financial supervision is undergoing profound changes in four aspects: from separate supervision to mixed supervision, from institutional supervision to functional supervision, from one-way supervision to comprehensive supervision, and from closed regulation to open regulation. In recent years, China has made some new progress in the improvement of financial regulatory institutions and the reform of financial regulatory systems. At the same time, however, it should be noted that China's financial supervision still has obvious defects, such as the lack of a comprehensive regulatory policy framework, strict market access management, lack of continuous supervision, strict regulation, lack of risks management, strict external supervision, lack of internal control, strict personel governance, and lack of rule of law, which are still widespread. These have become factors that can not be ignored in restricting China's financial development. Further, problems in financial regulation may also jeopardize financial stability and the country's economic security.

[1] Ji Heng and Zou Zhi, "Preliminary study on the new pattern of state-owned commercial Banks in China", *Restructuring and Development—Youth Essays of Industrial and Commercial Bank of China*, Beijing: China Financial Publishing House, 2003.

At present, the separate supervision mode implemented in China is gradually difficult to adapt to the fast-growing financial market. Mixed operation has become a new development trend. When faced with cross-sectoral financial innovation products, divisional supervision often leads to regulatory conflicts among various regulatory authorities, which is not only unfavorable to the establishment of a unified financial market, but also to the competitions between different institutions that operate similar products. Competition may also trigger moral hazard in market participants, which will affect financial stability. From the perspective of the interaction between financial innovation and financial supervision, financial innovation is relatively lagging behind in the cross-disciplinary field of supervision. Most of the innovations are caused by external pressure, not by the pursuit of profit; in the field of regulatory authority, due to the relatively fierce competition between the regulatory authorities and their affiliates, financial innovation has become more active. Most financial innovations in recent years belong to this field. In order to avoid these drawbacks, and improve the level of financial supervision under the financial supervision system, it is necessary to establish and improve coordination mechanisms between banks, securities and insurance regulatory agencies and with the central bank and the financial department.

7.2 The development direction of China's financial system reform

The rise of a great power requires great finance. Looking at the relationship between finance and economic development from a long-term perspective, we can always see that the financial rise of great power is almost achieved in parallel with its economic rise. For the future China, the financial development in the global perspective should fully reflect its strategic positioning. By constructing a stable, efficient and unified great power financial system, it can effectively support the country's industrial structure upgrading, economic transformation and social optimization, and fully serve the dual strategic needs of the great power economic and financial rise. For a long period of time in the future, China's economic and social development will still be in an important period of strategic opportunities. By facing both rare development opportunities and many risks and challenges, whether we can seize the opportunity to deepen various reforms and complete the transformation of the economic development mode is related to the overall situation of China's future economic and social development. In this process, China's financial development model and path must fully serve the overall layout of the country's economic and social development, and fully reflect its strategic orientation. The key is to firmly grasp the essential requirements of the financial services to real economy and adhere to the reform market-oriented allocation of finance resources, and the development concept of coordination between innovation and supervision. The financial system should be deployed in accordance with the decision-making of the 3rd Plenary Session of the 18th CPC Central Committee to comprehensively promote financial reform, opening up and development, and accelerate the improvement of a modern financial market system with complete types, reasonable structure, efficient service, and security.

7.2.1 Coexisting of China's financial development opportunities and challenges

The report of the 18th CPC National Congress clearly pointed out: "Overview of the international and domestic trends, China's development is still in an important strategic opportunity period that can make a big difference." Under such overall judgment, the opportunities and challenges of China's financial development coexist.

From the perspective of the international environment, the opportunities for China's financial development are: after the financial crisis, the economic growth prospects of developed countries are not clear. Some developed capitalist countries are deeply falling into debt crisis, and their control and discourse power in international economic governance are somewhat weakening; the rising status of developing and emerging market economies plays an increasingly important role in international economic and financial affairs. Certainly, there are challenges in the opportunity: the world economic situation is more complicated. Either for a developed country or a developing country, the original financial development model needs to be transformed to adapt to the new environment. The coordination between monetary and financial policies among countries is even more difficult; as the financial influence between countries becomes deeper and deeper, how to coordinate domestic interests and international interests and ensure the cooperation of financial strategies rather than exclusivity of that will become a common problem faced by all countries.

From the perspective of the domestic environment, the opportunity for China's financial development lies in the fact that in the past 40 years of reform and opening up, China's financial industry has achieved tremendous development achievements, the comprehensive strength of financial institutions has been significantly improved, the functions of financial markets have been increasingly strengthened, the financial infrastructure has become increasingly developed, financial macroeconomic regulation and control are more perfect, and financial opening up and cooperation is continuously deepening, these factors have laid a good foundation for future reforms. With the new industrialization, informationization, urbanization, and agricultural modernization with Chinese characteristics, the transformation of economic development mode will make the pattern of investment, consumption and import and export more balanced, and the contribution of consumption to economic growth will be greater and greater; the reform of income distribution and the integration of urban and rural areas will further narrow the gap between urban and rural areas, and the income level of residents will be significantly improved. These factors not only provide a more optimized real economic environment for financial development, but also put more demands on financial development, which is conducive to promoting financial system reform and innovation and development of the financial industry.

Meanwhile, financial reforms also face some challenges in China. Firstly, due to the intensification of the downward pressure on economic growth and the relative overcapacity, the potential risks in the financial sector are further aggravated, such as real estate loans, local government financing platforms, shadow banking, etc. The problem needs to be highly concerned. Secondly, when the reform enters the deep-water zone and the tackling stage, whether the existing monopoly and interest pattern can be broken, or whether the financial internal opening can be smoothly advanced, still need further observation; finally, there's still a long way to go on how to formulate the China's policy, present China's voice and assume China's responsibilities on global issues such as international financial standards development and governance.

Finance is at the heart of the modern economy. Financial development and innovation must serve the real economy, whether in past, present and future. Historical experience has proven that excessive financial virtualization, excessive self-service, and excessive separation from the real economy will inevitably lead to different forms of financial crisis. In the face of a new period of strategic opportunities, the report on the 18th CPC National Congress put forward the ambitious goal of ensuring the realization of a comprehensive well-off society by 2020; it is required to achieve a doubling GDP and per capita income of urban and rural residents by 2020 compared to 2010; at the same time, to enter the ranks of innovative countries, the regional coordinated development mechanism has basically taken shape, and international competitiveness has been significantly enhanced[1]. Therefore, the new mission of the future financial system reform is to make full use of the dividends of reform and innovation, play a central role in the allocation of finance in resources, and ensure the smooth realization of the above development goals.

7.2.2 The direction of China's financial system reform

As far as the financial development model is concerned, the two different modes of so-called bank-led and market-oriented do not have the inevitable advantages and disadvantages, but only the external manifestations of different stages of financial development and the characteristics of the domestic economy. However, there is no doubt that regardless of the advancement of interest rate and exchange rate marketization reforms, or the realization of capital account opening and renminbi internationalization, China's rise as a financial power needs a strong financial market. Therefore, it is particularly important to build a rich financial institution system and a diversified financial market system. Due to the innate profitability and inherent vulnerability of the financial industry, a sound prudential management framework and a coordinated financial regulatory system are needed as a guarantee throughout the reform process. In order to track the reform dynamics and grasp the development direction in a timely manner, it is also necessary to strengthen external financial cooperation, and constantly cultivate and improve a sound financial infrastructure and environment to push China's financial reform to a new stage of development.

(1) *Enrich financial institution system*

The number and types of financial institutions in China are still relatively small, and they cannot meet the needs of providing financial services for economic development. Therefore, it is necessary to enrich the financial institution system. It is necessary to improve the financial institution system that is rational and complementary to commercial finance, development finance, policy finance, and cooperative finance.

The first is to strengthen the independence of the central bank. The government's goals in any country are multiple. The single policy goal of "stable currency" of China's central bank and the multiple policy objectives of the government will

---

[1] Hu Jintao, *Firmly March on the Path of Socialism with Chinese Characteristics and Strive to Complete the Building of a Moderately Prosperous Society in All Respects*: *Report to the Eighteenth National Congress of the Communist Party of China*, Beijing: People's Publishing House, 2012.

inevitably contradict each other. Although the "Law of the People's Republic of China on the People's Bank of China" gives the central bank a relatively independent status, as the state financial administration under the leadership of the State Council, the central bank must also obey the leadership of the government. This determines the current macro-control of China's central bank must be under the coexistence of the direct and indirect regulation, administrative, economic, and legal means, not only to regulate the total amount, but also to undertake the task of regulating the structure. This in turn often leads to a decline in the effectiveness of regulation, and a single monetary policy goal is difficult to achieve. The reform of the central bank system in the future should be based on strengthening the independence of the central bank and improving its decision-making level and authority. After the market operation mechanism of the regulated object is truly established, the central bank needs to be independent to effectively eliminate various administrative interferences and separately perform the duties of macro financial regulation and supervision.

The second is to accelerate the institutional innovation of state-owned commercial banks. To make a state-owned bank a commercial bank in a truly modern sense, we must start with clear property rights and clear powers and responsibilities. The joint-stock system or limited liability company system is a form of ownership generally practiced by modern international commercial banks. Reforming state-owned banks into joint-stock or limited liability companies, allowing non-state-owned capital to enter state-owned banks, can fundamentally solve the problem of the lack of ownership of state-owned banks, so that banks can truly become profit-oriented financial enterprises, operating independently, self-financing, at its own risk. For the state-owned commercial banks that have completed the listing reform, the reform focus should be on continuing to improve the corporate governance structure and internal control, strengthen the monitoring and management of loan risks, and establish a scientific, reasonable and effective risk management mechanism covering all businesses.

The third is to introduce and nurture non-state financial institutions. Vigorously developing non-state-owned financial institutions, such as private banks, joint-stock investment companies, fund management companies, investment banks, and insurance companies, etc., have an important role in improving the service capabilities and competitiveness of financial institutions. With the risk prevention mechanism and the soundness of the social supervision and management mechanism, China should establish a large number of small and medium-sized, local and private joint-stock banks suitable for the financial services needs of SMEs, laying the foundation for the establishment of a competitive banking system. Small and medium-sized financial enterprises are more likely to become the source of innovation because they face relatively low risks in innovation. In the future, small and medium-sized financial enterprises with multiple ownership systems in China will develop rapidly. In addition, the corporate governance structure of securities companies and fund management companies needs to be further improved. Trust and investment companies should improve in the direction of standardized development and further deepen the institutional reform of insurance companies. Therefore, these non-bank financial institutions can be built to an appropriate scale financial enterprise with operating characteristics.

The fourth is to increase the supply of rural financial services. In order to promote stable production of agriculture, promote the continuous growth of peasants' income and realize the rapid development of rural economy, it requires a large amount of capital investment and financial support. Therefore, rural finance is the focus of financial reform in the coming period. The current rural financial system arrangement will face the possibility of reshuffling. The measures that should be taken to address the financial needs of building a new socialist countryside include: To further improve the rural financial organization system, the Agricultural Bank of China and the Agricultural Development Bank of China, as the backbone and pillar of the rural financial system, should further deeply reform their internal norms and business development; provide rich and diversified financial products and services for rural economic development, including microfinance, co-guarantee loans, credit loans, agricultural insurance, and agricultural products futures; establish and improve a multi-level, wide-coverage, sustainable financial system that can serve the vast rural and small and medium-sized enterprises, and strengthen the financial system's inclusive character; further liberalize the rural financial market, encourage private capital to enter the rural financial market by means of purchasing share, restructuring rural commercial banks or setting up rural banks, and vigorously developing private financial institutions; foster true rural cooperative finance, continue to deepen the reform of rural credit cooperatives; develop informal rural finance in China, guide private lending with interests, and adopt a standardized approach to meet the financing needs of farmers.

(2) *Diversified financial market system*

In 2016, the second section of Chapter 16 of the "Thirteenth Five-Year Plan for

National Economic and Social Development of the People's Republic of China" adopted by the 4th Session of the 12th CPC National People's Congress proposed to "improve the financial market system and actively cultivate a transparent and healthy development of the capital market, increase the proportion of direct financing and reduce leverage".[1] In terms of financial market development, the next step of reform is to actively promote the construction of a multi-level financial market system, strengthen the registration of basic systems, improve the registration, custody, trading and clearing systems of financial markets, and establish a multi-level market system and sound market competition environment[2].

The first is to establish a multi-level equity market. To improve the existing financial market system, we must firstly define the different functional positioning of diversified capital markets in corporate finance, and promote institutional and market innovation. Secondly, we need to establish a review system suitable for the characteristics of small and medium-sized enterprises and speed up the listing process. It may consider reforming the current issuance review system, formulating the issuance review standards different from traditional enterprises, appropriately relaxing the requirements of financial indicators, and establishing a "green channel" for the issuance and listing of small and medium-sized enterprises with independent innovation capabilities. Thirdly, we should strive to develop the property rights trading market and improve the ways of transferring shares of non-listed enterprises. We can consider all kinds of property rights trading institutions relying on property rights exchanges, actively adopt auctions, bidding, etc., and give full play to the role of market mechanisms. Finally, the transition mechanism and market exit mechanism between the main board, the SME board, the GEM, the NEEQ, and the property rights exchange market should be established to form a market environment for survival of the fittest.

The second is to promote the rapid development of the bond market. As the weak part of China's capital market, the bond market needs to accelerate the development speed. In particular, the issuance scale of corporate bonds should be further expanded. The bond management system, the market-based issuance mechanism and the self-restraint mechanism of the issuer must be further improved to establish a bond

---

[1] *The 13th Five Year Plan for Economic and Social Development of the People's Republic of China*, Beijing: People's Publishing House, 2016.

[2] He Dexu and Zhang Junzhou, *Innovation, Risk and Safeguard: Financial Safety in China's Financial Development*, Beijing: Social Sciences Academic Press (China), 2012.

market with centralized supervision and interconnection. First of all, to expand the size of the bond market, we can consider using local debt as a breakthrough. On the one hand, we will increase the scale of local bonds represented by the central government, and on the other hand, the municipal bond pilots will be further promoted by individual cities such as Shanghai and Shenzhen. China's bond market still mainly implements the system of scale control, centralized management, and grading approval. To overcome the shortcomings of the bond market's long-term supervision and inefficiency, it is necessary to cancel the administrative approval and management system in China, so that the approval and supervision of the bond market will be oriented to the procedural review and changed from the approval system to the registration system. In addition, the development of the bond market is inseparable from efficient and good supervision. To this end, it is necessary to continue to improve the information disclosure mechanism of the bond market, improve the guarantee system, and improve China's credit ranking system. By expanding the current QFII and RQFII pilots, further opening up the bond market to foreign central banks and international organizations, and attracting the participation of the world's top institutional investors will help China to establish a sound bond market supervision system.

In addition to the reform of the stock and bond markets, the money market, insurance market and futures market should also be continuously improved in development, and some new financial products will be introduced to further enrich market trading tools.

The third is to further promote the reform of interest rate marketization. Interest rates as the price of financial commodities are the most active factors in the entire financial market. In developed and mature financial markets, the prices of all financial products are comparable. It is characterized by an endless chain of interest rate structures. For example, if the financial entity changes the price of any financial product, it will cause all commodities, like dominoes, prices change and changes in supply and demand, investors in financial markets can also buy the goods they need at any time based on changes in interest rates. At present, although China's interest rate marketization is basically completed, it is still not perfect, and microfinance entities lack sufficient product pricing power. As the interest rate loses the optimization of the allocation of funds, the financial market itself loses its vitality. Therefore, in order to cultivate market mechanisms and fully activate the financial market, the reform and improvement of interest rate marketization should become the focus of financial market reform in the 21st century.

(3) *Strive to improve financial supervision capabilities*

In order to better and more effectively prevent and resolve financial risks and create suitable conditions for China's financial development, we must improve the level of China's financial supervision as soon as possible. This is also the emphasized point in the 13th Five-year Plan.

The first is to promote the balanced development of financial reform and innovation. To promote financial reform, at the micro level, it is necessary to expand the autonomy of financial institutions' business and product innovation, and to adopt a reporting system for most products; for innovative products and services that must be approved by regulatory agencies, it is necessary to simplify the means of examination and approval and reduce approval time. In view of the fact that China's financial innovation is lagging behind, we should actively promote and encourage product innovation, and develop asset securitization, credit mitigation tools, high-yield bonds and other basic financial products that meet the needs of the real economy, so as to significantly improve the ability of financial services to the real economy. It is also necessary to strengthen the functional supervision of financial innovation, minimize the fuzzy areas and vacuum zones of financial innovation supervision, prevent the loss of financial innovation, and especially guard against excessive derivatization of financial instruments.

Second, it is necessary to update the financial supervision concept in a timely manner, clarify the content of financial supervision, and implement innovations in financial supervision mode, financial supervision means, and financial supervision content, so that China's financial supervision can be changed from traditional compliance supervision to operational risk supervision and functional regulation, from simple maintenance of financial security supervision to balancing financial security and improving the core competitiveness of the financial industry, from external supervision to internal and external combined supervision. In the reform of the financial supervision system, it is necessary to protect the legitimate rights and interests of financial consumers. This is also a shortcoming of the current system. In the process of implementing the 13th Five-year Plan, these must be strengthened, including the protection of the legitimate rights and interests of financial consumers, protection of privacy, and improving the security of financial infrastructure and financial systems, and strengthening education for consumers to better protect their rights.

The third is to improve the ability of financial supervision and coordination, to comprehensively supervise the banks, securities, insurance, etc. At present, China's financial industry has been in the trend of industrial financialization and financial integration, but the separate supervision system often only regulates institutions and businesses in a single field. Considering that China's financial system is still not perfect, the modern financial enterprise system is not sound enough, and the enterprise's risk control awareness and ability need to be further improved, the separated supervision system of banking, securities and insurance will continue to be implemented for some time in the future. In order to identify and manage risks for financial supervisory authorities in financial innovation, the focus of financial regulatory reform should be shifted to the gradual advancement of the regulatory approach to capital adequacy ratios. We also need to establish and complement the effective coordination and communication mechanisms between regulatory agencies of banks, securities, and insurance and of these, central bank and financial department, strengthen risk supervision, and establish a market-oriented positive incentive mechanism and timely risk correction mechanism to reduce the accumulation of systemic financial risks. In addition, in order to effectively prevent risks and maintain financial stability, the financial institution market exit mechanism needs to be further regulated, and the corresponding deposit insurance, investor protection and insurance protection systems must be established.

The fourth is to establish a macro-prudential financial management system framework. Under the financial opening pattern, establishing a macro-prudential management system suited to the national conditions is an inevitable choice for maintaining financial stability and ensuring financial security. Under the current regulatory framework, the central bank has the means of macroeconomic regulation such as currency issuance, interest rates and exchange rates, while the three supervisory authorities only identify and monitor the internal risks of financial institutions such as banks, securities and insurance. Therefore, a macro-prudential regulatory body or group should be established in conjunction with the "one bank and three commissions" to establish and improve a systematic financial risk monitoring and evaluation method and operational framework suitable for the national conditions. On the issue of the stability of the entire financial system, it is necessary to have the regulatory authorities' prudential supervision of individual financial institutions, and to distinguish between cross-market, cross-institutional and cross-industry risks, and pay attention to the implementation of counter-cyclical financial regulation policies.

(4) *Accelerate the opening up of the financial sector and the internationalization of the renminbi*

After joining the World Trade Organization, China has paid more attention to conduct comprehensive, multi-level, flexible and pragmatic foreign financial cooperation, and has made important progress in strengthening regional financial cooperation. In the future, China's financial opening up should not be limited to the implementation of relevant commitments, but concentrate on the improvement of opening quality and level, based on ensuring that the financial opening up is compatible with the overall economic reforms, and that the market development level and supervision level are consistent.

In the coming period, the financial opening up should actively and prudently promote the opening up of the financial sector in the context of the "efficiency-stable" comprehensive balance, comprehensively enhance China's right to speak in the international financial system, overall weigh and balance between the stability and efficiency of the financial industry, promote financial efficiency while ensuring financial stability. We should strengthen regional and international financial cooperation, let more and more domestic financial institutions go abroad to enter the world market, and let the Chinese financial industry integrate into the global financial system with a more active attitude.

In line with the requirements of international and domestic development, orderly promotion of renminbi internationalization is one of the directions of China's financial development. However, it should be recognized that the internationalization of the renminbi is a long-term process of gradual expansion of a region (from regional to global) and functions (from settlement currency to reserve currency), and cannot be rushed for success. The internationalization of renminbi needs to be combined with the cultivation of financial markets, and the improvement of the regulatory and the controlling system, and adapted with the capital flow channels, exchange rate formation mechanisms and transformation of economic growth patterns.[1] In particular, the construction of renminbi outflows and return channels needs to be gradually improved under the conditions that are compatible with the gradual opening up of capital account, including the construction of international boards and the access of international investors.

---

[1] Chen Xuebin and Li Zhong, "Currency internationalization: global experience and enlightenment", *Finance & Trade Economics*, 2012(2), pp. 45-51.

In addition, in the process of building an opened financial system of a great power, we should also actively play the financial guidance function of foreign exchange reserves. Through the strategic use of huge foreign exchange reserve resources, we will lead China to seize strategic, resources and finance commanding heights in the next round of scientific and technological competition in the world: first is aiming at the trending global emerging industries, occupying the high-end position of the industrial chain in the next round of the world economic cycle; second is aiming at the strategic resource industry and laying a solid resource reserve for the economic development in transition; third is actively participating in and leading the establishment of regional and cross-regional financial organizations to enhance China's voice in the international financial system.[1]

(5) *Strengthen infrastructure construction and optimize the financial development environment*

First is continue to strengthen the construction of the financial legal system. In view of the many changes in the current international and domestic environment, on the one hand, it is necessary to amend the current financial laws and regulations such as the "Law of the People's Republic of China on the People's Bank of China" and "Securities Law" to promote the further improvement of the financial legal environment and protect the legitimate rights and interests of various investors in accordance with the law, and prevent and combat all forms of financial crime and illegal financial activities. On the other hand, laws and regulations on bankruptcy of financial institutions, deposit insurance, and protection of financial consumer rights should be established in a timely manner to change the status quo of the long-term failure of financial institutions to be largely repaid by the state, so that depositors, investors and consumers have established a significant sense of risk.

The second is to strengthen the construction of a social credit system. We should speed up the construction of the credit reporting system, vigorously promote the construction of a unified credit information platform for the financial industry, establish and improve credit information files, and expand departmental sharing and publicity in accordance with the law. Meanwhile, we must pay attention to strengthening the protection of personal credit information. We should also vigorously develop various credit intermediary service organizations, build a credit service system, promote the development of the credit rating industry, encourage credit

[1] Chen Yulu, "Financial development under the framework of big finance", *China Finance*, 2014 (19), pp. 71-73.

ranking agencies to adopt advanced ranking techniques and ranking methods, establish a credit information system covering the whole society, and improve the foundamental database of national financial credit information.

The third is to strengthen the construction of the payment and settlement system. On the basis of further improving the payment and settlement laws and regulations, we should continue to improve the relevant infrastructure, effectively improve the security and reliability of the payment system, and provide the public with safer, more convenient and low-cost payment services. The registration, custody, transaction, clearing system and central counterparty mechanism of the financial market should be further improved to unify the existing custody and settlement platforms. In addition, it is necessary to speed up the construction of a new generation of central bank interbank payment system and cross-border renminbi clearing system, coordinate the payment system and foreign exchange settlement system, and promote the connection between securities, foreign exchange settlement systems, and domestic and foreign payment systems.

Bibliography

[1] Ba Shusong, "The focus and direction of China's financial reform", *Business Weekly*, 2012 (21).

[2] Ba Shusong, Yan Min and Wang Yuexiang, "Analysis of the influence of interest rate liberalization on commercial bank", *Journal of Huazhong Normal University* (*Humanities and Social Sciences*), 2013 (4).

[3] Bai Jiawen and Zhu Zhengye, "Research on the transformation of financial industry modernization in the Republic of China", *Seeker*, 2015 (11).

[4] Beijing International Finance Forum Group, "China's financial opening to the outside world: history, challenges and solutions", *Review of Economic Research*, 2009 (4).

[5] Bu Chengliang and Shen Linrong, *China's Path: the Path of Progressive Reform*. Beijing: Central Party School Press, 2009.

[6] Cao Fengqi, *China's Financial Reform, Development and Internationalization*, Beijing: Economic Science Press, 1999.

[7] Cao Fengqi, *Monetary and Financial Management*, Beijing: Peking University Press, 2008.

[8] Chang Jian and Rao Changlin, "Historical investigation and analysis of characteristics of legal system of China's central bank", *Journal of China University of Mining & Technology* (*Social Science*), 2014(3).

[9] Chang Yuan, "The Research on the Issue of renminbi Internationalization", Shenyang: Liaoning University, 2014.

[10] Chen Ganlin, "China's political restructuring since the reform and opening up", *Developing*, 2011 (10).

[11] Chen Huawen, "The vivid interpretation of ancient finance—reading 'China is a financial history' has a feeling", *Property Rights Guide*, 2013 (9).

[12] Chen Jiali, "Policy measures to further open up the financial sector", *China Journal of Commerce*, 2015 (22).

[13] Chen Jiangsheng and Chen Zhaoming. "The reform of world monetary system and renminbi internationalization", *Journal of the Party School of the Central Committee of the CPC*, 2010 (1).

[14] Chen Jiangsheng, "The time has come to raise the renminbi's profile in the international monetary system", *Paper of Shenzhen Special Zone*, Oct.21, 2014.

[15] Chen Jianhua, "The influence and countermeasure of China's financial industry after joining WTO", *Economics Information*, 2000 (10).

[16] Chen Xiaorong. "On commercial bank notes under the financial system of the republic of China", *Lantai World*, 2014 (13).

[17] Chen Xuebin and Li Zhong, "Currency internationalization: global experience and enlightenment", *Finance & Trade Economics*, 2012 (2).

[18] Chen Yufeng and Ye Zhipeng, "Theoretical progress and practical experience of financial system reform—a summary of the first Wenzhou seminar on financial reform and development", *Economic Research Journal*, 2014 (5).

[19] Chen Yulu, "Financial development under the framework of big finance", *China Finance*, 2014 (19).

[20] Chen Yulu, "The choice of optimal financial system structure", *Financial View*, 2015 (4).

[21] Chen Yulu, *The Megatrends of China's Financial System*, Beijing: China Financial Publishing House, 2011.

[22] Chen Zhiwu, "Which finance does China need?", *International Financing*, 2006 (3).

[23] Cheng Shengshu and Jin Zujun, "Inflation during the period of the Republic of China: three changes in the currency system", *Journal of Jiangxi University of Finance and Economics*, 2011 (4).

[24] China Banking Regulatory Commission, http://www.cbrc.gov.cn/index.html.

[25] China Securities Regulatory Commission, *China Capital Markets Development Report*, Beijing: China Financial Publishing House, 2008.

[26] China Securities Regulatory Commission, CSRC issued equity incentive management measures for listed companies, Jul.15, 2016, http://www.csrc.gov.cn/pub/newsite/zjhxwfb/xwdd/201607/t20160715_300783.html.

[27] China Securities Regulatory Commission, List of memoranda signed by CSRC and overseas securities (futures) regulators (June 2015), Aug.7, 2015,

http://www. csrc.gov.cn/pub/newsite/gjb/jghz/201508/t20150807_282485.html.

[28] Cui Hongyan and Chen Yuhe, “The path choice and government action of Chinese financial system change”, *Foreign Investment in China*, 2011 (20).

[29] Cui Huifang and Zhao Wei, “The international experience of interest rate liberalization and China strategies”, *Journal of Huazhong Normal University* (*Humanities and Social Sciences*), 2014 (4).

[30] Cui Huifang, “The Development and Reformation of Financial System in Japan and South Korea Enlighten Our Country as to the Financial System Reformation”, Yanji: Yanbian University, 2003.

[31] Dai Juan, “On the reform and development of the financial system”, *China Science and Technology Review*, 2014 (19).

[32] *Decision of the CPC Central Committee on Several Issues Concerning the Establishment of a Socialist Market Economy System*, Beijing: People’s Publishing House, 1993.

[33] Deng Zhiyi, “Present opportunity and challenge of large banks during reform and development”, *China Finance*, 2007 (10).

[34] Ding Ning, “On the enterprise of specialized banks”, *Studies of International Finance*, 1992 (1).

[35] Ding Yifan, “Reform and development of China’s financial system”, *Marxism & Reality*, 2013 (2).

[36] Editorial Board, *Personnel Management in Financing Institutions*. Beijing: Contemporary China Publishing House, 1999.

[37] Fan Fangzhi, “The forecast and review of our country’s central bank organizational reform to the 30th anniversary of China’s Opening up and reform policy”, *Journal of Central University of Finance & Economics*, 2009 (2).

[38] Fang Chunqin, “Discussion on the ownership of pawn industry in China”, *Theory Research*, 2013 (23).

[39] Gan Chunhui, *30 Years for Chinese Economic System Reform*, Shanghai: Shanghai University of Finance & Economics Press, 2008.

[40] Gan Chunhui, *China Industry Development Report 2008*, Shanghai: Shanghai University of Finance & Economics Press, 2008.

[41] Gao Guangchun and Ji Weibing, “The process, problems and countermeasures of systematic reform of financial institutions”, *Shandong Social Science*, 1998 (4).

[42] Gu Xiaojing and Wang Dingxiang, “China’s financial development and urbanization process”, *Financial Theory & Practice*, 2011 (9).

[43] Guo Jianwei and Zhao Yuanyuan, "Internationalization of Renminbi: ideal vs. reality", *Economic Problems*, 2013 (1).

[44] Guo Lihua, *Research on Anti-monopoly Control of China's Rural Financial Market*, Beijing: Intellectual Property Publishing House, 2008.

[45] Han Jiyun, "An analysis of the defects and effects of the reform of China's new foreign exchange system", *Study & Exploration*, 1998 (1).

[46] Han Jiyun, "The defects and perfection of China's new foreign exchange system reform", *Journal of Hebei University of Economics and Trade*, 1997 (6).

[47] Hao Mingchao, "The Research on the Modernization of China's Financial System Between 1927-1937", Harbin Institute of Technology, 2014.

[48] He Bingmeng, *Financial Reform and Economic Security*, Beijing: Social Sciences Academic Press (China), 2007.

[49] He Dexu and Zhang Junzhou, *Innovation, Risk and Safeguard: Financial Safety in China's Financial Development*, Beijing: Social Sciences Academic Press (China), 2012.

[50] He Dexu, "Retrospect and prospect of 30 years' reform of financial system in China", *Theory Front*, 2008 (9).

[51] He Dexu, *Research on China's financial innovation and development*, Beijing: Economic Science Press, 2001.

[52] He Maochun, *The Liberalization of and the Rules of Trade in Service*, Beijing: World Affairs Press, 2007.

[53] Hong Jiaguan, *Chinese Financial History*, Sichuan: Southwestern University of Finance and Economics Press, 1993.

[54] Hou Jianxin, "Review on the financial industry of the Nanjing National Government from 1927 to 1937", *Journal of Inner Mongolia Normal University (Philosophy and Social Sciences Edition)*, 2014 (3).

[55] Hu Anquan, "The internal logic of the evolution of the CPC reform thought", *Review of Economic Research*, 2012 (72).

[56] Hu Hai'ou and Wu Guoxiang, *Theory and Practice of China's Financial Reform*, Shanghai: Fudan University Press, 2000.

[57] Hu Hai'ou, *Reform and Development of China's Financial System*, Shanghai: Fudan University Press, 2004.

[58] Hu Jintao, *Firmly March on the Path of Socialism with Chinese Characteristics and Strive to Complete the Building of a Moderately Prosperous Society in All Respects: Report to the Eighteenth National Congress of the Communist Party of*

China, Beijing: People's Publishing House, 2012.

[59] Hu Yanlong, *New China's Financial History*, Kunming: Yunnan University Press, 1993.

[60] Huang Da, "China's financial reform in the face of economic globalization", *Chinese Public Administration*, 1999 (11).

[61] Huang Lei, "Analysis on the development process and countermeasures of financial leasing in China", *Market Weekly*, 2011 (6).

[62] Huang Zhenglin, "Dual economy: the local financial system research in social transition period—an example of Henan Province during 1912-1937", *Journal of Historical Science*, 2009 (9).

[63] Huo Jiguang, "Deepen rural financial reform and improve rural financial services", *Huabei Finance*, 2007 (11).

[64] Ji Wei, "New China's financial memorabilia", *China Finance*, 2014 (19).

[65] Jiang Guiqin, "On the Reform of China's Financial System", Hefei: Anhui University, 2004.

[66] Jiang Lichang, "The birth of industrial and commercial bank of China", China Urban Finance, 2012 (1).

[67] Jiang Shiyin, "System reform of central bank and how to deepen the reform", *Journal of Hebei University of Economics and Trade*, 2009 (1).

[68] Jiang Shiyin, *Rational Thinking on China's Financial System Reform in 30 Years*, Beijing: Jinghua Press, 2009.

[69] Jiang Shiyin, *Rational Thinking on China's Financial System Reform*, Beijing: China Financial & Economic Publishing House, 2009.

[70] John King Fairbank, et al., *The Cambridge History of China Vol. 12: Republican China 1912-1949, Part 1 (Chinese Version)*, Beijing: China Social Sciences Press, 1994.

[71] John King Fairbank, et al., *The Cambridge History of China Vol. 13: Republican China 1912-1949, Part 2 (Chinese Version)*, Beijing: China Social Sciences Press. 1994.

[72] Kong Weiyan, "Research on Property Rights Reform of State-owned Holding Commercial Banks", Party School of the Central Committee of the CPC, 2010.

[73] Kuang Jiazai, "Rural finance system reform since 1978: the changes of policy and the path to development", *Researches in Chinese Economic History*, 2007 (1).

[74] Li Bin, "Market-based interest rate reform and monetary policy",

Comparative Economic & Social Systems, 2014 (1).

[75] Li Chunyan, "Explore the history of financial reform in the republic of China", *Lantai World*, 2012 (19).

[76] Li De, "Reform and development of China's securities market", *Financial Perspectives Journal*, 2011 (4).

[77] Li Guoping, *Prosperity and Crisis of Banking Sector in China*, Xiamen: Xiamen University Press, 2014.

[78] Li Hongjiang, "The development and future of Chinese foreign direct investment", *Commercial Research*, 2004 (5).

[79] Li Hongjin, "The challenge and response of interest rate liberalization to commercial banks", *Studies of International Finance*, 2015 (2).

[80] Li Jianjun, Zhen Feng and Cui Xiqiang, "Current situation, degree measurement and prospect evaluation of renminbi internationalization", *Studies of International Finance*, 2013 (10).

[81] Li Li, "1979-2006 China's financial revolution", *Digital Business Era*, 2007 (11).

[82] Li Lili, "Reform and institutional change of rural credit cooperatives", *China Agricultural Economic Review*, 2006(1).

[83] Li Qiang and Yang Yuanyuan, "Empirical analysis on effects of ownership structure on earnings management in Chinese new-material listed companies", *Journal of Chongqing University of Technology* (*Social Science*), 2015(6).

[84] Li Yang, *Research on the 30 Years of China's Financial Reform and Opening up*, Beijing: Economy & Management Publishing House, 2008.

[85] Li Yang, Wang Guogang and Liu Yuhui, *The Path of Development of China's Financial System*, Beijing: Economy & Management Publishing House, 2013.

[86] Li Yuanjun, "Discussion on the impact of China's entry into WTO on financial market", *Manager Journal*, 2011(4).

[87] Li Zheng and Yu Na, "South Korean financial system research and its reform to China's reference", *Oriental Enterprise Culture*, 2010 (5).

[88] Lian Ping, "Try to analyze the new development of foreign exchange system reform", *Shanghai Finance*, 1996 (6).

[89] Liang Ying, "Deng Xiaoping's Financial Theory and the Construction of China's Financial System", Beijing: University of International Business and Economics, 2006.

[90] Lin Hua and Hu Yanxi, "Research on the issue of China's financial security

after its entry into WTO", *Jinan Journal (Philosophy & Social Science Edition)*, 2001 (4).

[91] Lin Yifu, "What is the direction of our country financial system reform", *Forward Position in Economics*, 2004 (8).

[92] Lin Youping and Zhang Shu, "Summary of research on financial risk", *Economic Review*, 1998 (6).

[93] Literature Research Office of the CPC Central Committee, *Selection of Important Documents since the 15th National Congress*, Beijing: Central Party Literature Publishing House, 2011.

[94] Liu Dong, "Developing finance and deepening the reform of China's financial system", *New Thinking*, 2012 (10).

[95] Liu Hongru, "The development and prospect of China's capital market", *Financial Science*, 1999 (2).

[96] Liu Hongru, "The formation of China's central banking system", *China Finance*, 2013 (23).

[97] Liu Hongru, *The Change: The 60-year Development of China's Financial System*, Beijing: China Financial Publishing House, 2009.

[98] Liu Jie and Gao Pan, "China has officially become the third largest shareholder in the IMF", Xinhuanet, http://news.xinhuanet.com/2016-01/28/c_11179 24308.htm.

[99] Liu Jing, "Foreign banks in China: business development and regulatory status", *Contemporary Economics*, 2011 (4).

[100] Liu Mingkang, *30 Years for China's Banking Sector Reform and Opening Up*, Beijing: China Financial Publishing House, 2009.

[101] Liu Rui, "The Process and Development Trend of Financial System Reform in China", Wuhan: Wuhan University of Technology, 2003.

[102] Liu Xiaoping, "Learning Deng Xiaoping's financial theory to speed up the construction of modern financial enterprises", *Financial Resource*, 2004(12).

[103] Liu Xiaoyong, "On the financial reform from the perspective of the supervision", *Comparative Economic & Social Systems*, 2008 (4).

[104] Liu Xin and Liu Gang, *Three Decades of Chinese Economics*, Beijing: China Financial & Economic Publishing House, 2008.

[105] Liu Yingshuang, "The course of Chinese financial reform: based on the recount of financial institution, financial market, financial regulation", *Social Sciences in Nanjing*, 2011 (4).

[106] Lu Qiu'e and Liang Yu, "Some thoughts on the reform of transitional

financial regulation and supervision system under the trend of mixed operation", *Enterprise Science and Technology & Development*, 2009 (10).

[107] Lu Shimin, "Review and prospects for the monetary system reform of new China", *The Study of Finance and Economics*, 1999 (10).

[108] Ma Changlin, *Ancient Chinese Finance*, China International Broadcasting Press, 2011.

[109] Ma Changwei and Yao Huiyuan, "The voucher system in the issuance of banknotes during the republic of China and its enlightenment", *Studies of International Finance*, 2014 (6).

[110] Ma Qingquan and Liu Zhao, *A Brief History of Chinese Securities*, Taiyuan: Shanxi Economic Press, 2015.

[111] Meng Xiaosu, *Modern Enterprise System Practice Book*, Beijing: People's Publishing House,1995.

[112] Mu Desheng. "The impact of China's entry into WTO on China's financial industry", *Finance and Economics*, 2000 (1).

[113] NAES Research Group, "China's financial system reform in new era: target, path, and advice", *Chinese Review of Financial Studies*, 2013(3).

[114] National Bureau of Statistics, http://www.stats.gov.cn/.

[115] National Cadre Training Textbook Compilation and Review Steering Committee, *Financial Development and Risk Prevention*, Beijing: People's Publishing House, 2011.

[116] Pan Liangui, "The four banks in north and the three banks in south", *China Finance*, 2003 (1).

[117] Peng Ziqin, "On the enterprise reform of specialized Banks", *Social Science Front Bimonthly*,1986 (4).

[118] Pi Haizhou, "Three aspects are needed to improve the quality of listed companies", *Financial View* (*Wealth*), 2017 (3).

[119] Qian Shuitu, "Review and evaluation of last three decades' rural financial system reform in China", *Journal of Zhejiang Gongshang University*, 2009 (2).

[120] Qu Yanbin, "The revival of Chinese pawn auction industry", *Encyclopedic Knowledge*, 1996 (12).

[121] Qu Yan-bin, "The situation evaluation and development countermeasure of Chinese pawn industry comeback for ten years", *Social Science Journal*, 1999 (1).

[122] Sha Wenbing and Liu Hongzhong, "Renminbi internationalization, exchange rate change and exchange rate expectation", *Studies of International Finance*, 2014 (8).

[123] Shang Ming, *50 Years of Finance in New China*, Beijing: China Financial & Economic Publishing House, 2000.

[124] Shang Ming, Chen Li and Wang Chengming, *Financial Memorabilia of the People's Republic of China*, Beijing: China Financial Publishing House, 1993.

[125] Sheng Songcheng and Liu Xi, *The Coordinated Advancement of Financial Reform*, Beijing: CITIC Press, 2015.

[126] Su Huaiping, "Review rural finance development from the ABC's history", *The Chinese Banker*, 2012 (11).

[127] *Suggestions of the CPC Central Committee on Formulating the Ten-Year Plan for National Economic and Social Development and the Eighth Five-Year Plan*, Beijing: People's Publishing House, 1991.

[128] Sun Jianhua, "Analysis of fragility of Chinese stock exchanges and its causes in modem times", *Economic Management Journal*, 2014(1).

[129] Sun Naiyan and Jin Xizai, "Overview of the development of China's insurance industry since the reform and opening up", *Modern Management Science*, 2012 (6).

[130] Sun Xiaoyi, "Research on property rights reform of state-owned holding commercial Banks", *Times finance*, 2014 (9).

[131] Tan Yao, "Study on the Development of Chinese Postal Savings Banks", *Journal of Regional Financial Research*, 2012 (2).

[132] Tan Yuhuan, "Construct the environment for the development of mixed business in China's financial industry", *Reformation & Strategy*, 2006 (S1).

[133] Tang Liu and Wang Xuxiang, "Exchange Management: Review and Forecast", *The Chinese Banker*, 2013 (4).

[134] Tao Shigui, *The Internal Logic and Path Choice of China's Banking System Change*, Beijing: People's Publishing House, 2014.

[135] *The Central Committee of the Communist Party of China about the Decision of the Economic System Reform*, Beijing: People's Publishing House, 1984.

[136] The People's Bank of China, http://www.pbc.gov.cn/.

[137] The State Council, "Decision of the State Council on the Reform of the Financial System", Gazette of the State Council of the People's Republic of China, 1993 (31).

[138] Wan Xin, "Consideration about the shareholding system reform of state-owned commercial banks", *Sci-Tech Information Development & Economy*, 2006 (22).

[139] Wang Chaoyang, *Research on Financial Service Industry Cluster: also on the Construction of China's Regional Financial Center*, Beijing: Social Sciences Academic Press (China), 2013.

[140] Wang Guangqian, *30 Years of China's Economic Reform: Financial Reform Volume, 1978-2008*, Chongqing: Chongqing University Press, 2008.

[141] Wang Guangqian, *China's New Stage of Economic Growth and Financial Development*, Beijing: China Development Press, 2004.

[142] Wang Guangqian, Ying Zhanyu and Jiang Shiyin, *China Financial Reform: Historical Experience and Transformation Model*, Beijing: China Financial Publishing House, 2008.

[143] Wang Jian, *Legal Structure of Asset Securitization*, Beijing: China Fangzheng Press, 2006.

[144] Wang Jianhong, Wang Xianming and Zhao Xiaoming, "Three big difficulties for internet finance development in China", *Credit Reference*, 2015 (3).

[145] Wang Quan, "Research on Propelling Interest Rate Marketization in China", Changchun: Jilin University, 2013.

[146] Wang Renfei, "Discussion on the current situation and mode of China's foreign debt management under the new situation", *Journal of Financial Development Research*, 2013 (8).

[147] Wang Sheng, "The Transformation of China's Financial Opening Strategy and the Internationalization of China's Financial Industry", Shanghai Academy of Social Sciences, 2010.

[148] Wang Yuanhong, "A Research on Internal and External Balance of China Economy", Beijing: Renmin University of China, 2009.

[149] Wang Zhen, *Research on China's Foreign Exchange Reserve Management*, Beijing: China Financial Publishing House, 2007.

[150] Wei Bijun and Tang Kai, "From the comparison of the two financial systems, the reform of China's commercial banks", *Legal System and Society*, 2008 (15).

[151] Wen Bingxun, "Historical evolution of the financial system in new China", *CPC History Studies*, 2006 (4).

[152] Wen Bingxun, *Research on Government Intervention*, Changsha: Hunan People's Publishing House, 2005.

[153] Wen Feng, "A brief discussion on the problems and countermeasures faced by China's financial companies in the development process", *Journal of Hunan College of Financial and Economic*, 2005(2).

[154] Wen Jiabao, "Deepen financial reform in all-round way to promote the sustainable healthy development of the financial Industry", Gazette of the State Council of the People's Republic of China, 2007(3).

[155] Wu Cao, "Study on financial legal system of national government in the Anti-Japanese war (1937-1945)", Southwest University of Political Science & Law, 2011.

[156] Wu Cong, *The Historical Experience of English and American Financial Pathways and its Inspiration for China*, Beijing: China Social Sciences Press, 2016.

[157] Wu Fulin, "What extent does Chinese interest rate marketization go to?", *Economist*, 2012 (4).

[158] Wu Pingfan and Chen Yongsheng, "The enlightenment of the subprime crisis to our financial regulation", *Social Science Research*, 2009 (6).

[159] Wu Xiaoling, "The core and significance of bank corporatization", *Journal of Financial Research*, 1986 (10).

[160] Wu Xiaoling, "The progress of China's foreign exchange system reform: the renminbi is convertible from current account to capital account", *Journal of Financial Research*, 1997 (1).

[161] Wu Xiaoling, *Review and Prospect of China's Financial System Reform in the Past 30 Years*, Beijing: Peoples Publishing House, 2008.

[162] Wu Xiaoling, Xie Ping and Shen Bingxi, "A follow-up study on the reform of China's financial system" (Part 1), *Reform*, 1997 (3).

[163] Wu Xiaoling, Xie Ping and Shen Bingxi, "A follow-up study on the reform of China's financial system" (Part 2), *Reform*,1997 (4).

[164] Wu Xiaoqiu, *China's Capital Market: from Institutional Reform to Strategic Transformation*, Beijing: China Renmin University Press, 2007.

[165] Wu Xiaoqiu. "China's 'three-dimensional' financial reform", *Capital Markets*, 2014 (1).

[166] Wu Yongguang, "The Study on the Changes of the Financial Supervising and Managing System during the National Government Time", Guangxi Normal University, 2006.

[167] Wu Yunxian and Li Zhenya, "Current statues and developing trend of China's financial system reform", *Journal of Beijing Union University*, 2000 (4).

[168] Xie Ping and Xu Guoping, *Reform of the Financial Regulatory System and the Functions of Central Banks*, Beijing: China Financial Publishing House, 2004.

[169] Xie Ping and Zou Chuanwei, *How to Reform China's Financial Sector*,

Beijing: China Financial Publishing House, 2013.

[170] Xie Xiaowen, "The Study on Linkage among China's Financial Markets—On the Issue of China's Financial System Reform", Tianjin: Nankai University, 2014.

[171] Xin Chengsheng, *Ten Years Development and Review of Chinese Securities Market*, Beijing: China Yan Shi Press, 2001.

[172] Xu Shiyuan,"The evolution of the livelihood view since China started reform and opening up", *Journal of Zhejiang Ocean University* (*Humanities Sciences*), 2011 (5).

[173] Xu Yinjie, "The difficult exploration of China's financial system reform", *Times Finance*, 2011 (24).

[174] Yan Congshan, "A preliminary study on the coordination mechanism of financial supervision under mixed operation conditions", *Journal of Jiangxi Administration Institute*, 2006 (A2).

[175] Yan Jinping, "The historical experience of new China's financial system evolution", *Journal of Hunan Institute of Socialism*, 2006 (4).

[176] Yan Qingmin and Li Jianhua, *Research on Shadow Banking Regulation in China*, Beijing: China Renmin University Press, 2014.

[177] Yang Peixin, "Review of China's financial system reform", *Research on Financial and Economic Issues*, 1994 (4).

[178] Yang Xitian, *The 6th Volume of China's Financial History: the Period of the People's Republic of China* (*1949-1996*), Beijing: China Financial Publishing House, 2002.

[179] Yao Sui, *History of China Finance*, Beijing: Higher Education Press, 2007.

[180] Ye Chenyi, *Corporate Credit Management*, Shanghai: Fudan University Press, 2011.

[181] Yi Gang, "On the market-based interest rate reform", *Journal of Financial Research*, 2009 (1).

[182] Yi Gang, *On the Financial Reform of China*, Beijing: The Commercial Press, 2009.

[183] Ying Zhanyu, "Is there a 'China model' for financial system reform?", *The Journal of World Economy*, 2008 (2).

[184] Yu Yongding, "Some thoughts on renminbi internationalization", *International Economic Review*, 2011 (5).

[185] Yue Shuping, Wang Aijun and Li Xiaoqin, "An analysis of strengthening financial supervision in new regime", *Huabei Finance*, 2004 (4).

[186] Zhai Binbin, "A brief analysis of the shareholding reform of state-owned commercial banks", *Business China*, 2010 (2).

[187] Zhang Chenghui, "The overall opening-up policies and basic conditions of the Chinese mainland's financial industry", *Foreign Investment in China*, 2007 (10).

[188] Zhang Chenghui, "Thinking on reconstruction of China's financial regulatory framework and recommendations", *Journal of Chongqing University of Technology* (*Social Science*), 2016 (9).

[189] Zhang Fengyou, "An analysis of China's financial system reform", *China Business*, 2010 (8).

[190] Zhang Jieshan, "On renminbi current account convertibility", *Finance and Economy*, 1999 (9).

[191] Zhang Jun, "The Research on the Rural Financial System Reform in China", Kaifeng: Henan University, 2014.

[192] Zhang Lei, *The Credit Expansion and Financial Distortions in the Era of China's High Economic Growth*, Beijing: Social Sciences Academic Press (China), 2013.

[193] Zhang Liansheng, "On China's comprehensive commercial banks", *New Finance*, 1991 (8).

[194] Zhang Minhui and Li Jianchun, "The enhancement of our party's cognition of currency in the bank currency issuance of Shaanxi-Gansu-Ningxia border region", *Journal of Shandong Academy of Governance*, 2012 (1).

[195] Zhang Peng and Li Kechuan, "Research on Chinese commercial banks function evolution", *Journal of Financial Development Research*, 2011 (2).

[196] Zhang Xiaodong, "Exploration on modernization of financial supervision system: origin, logic and prospect", *Financial Theory & Practice*, 2016 (9).

[197] Zhang Xiujuan, *Powerful Finance*, Beijing: Economy & Management Publishing House, 2016.

[198] Zhang Yaguang, "On modern deconstruction of the financial thought of Republic of China (1912-1949)", *Journal of Hebei University of Economics and Business*, 2015 (3).

[199] Zhang Yuyan, "Internationalizing the renminbi: pros and cons", *International Economic Review*, 2010 (1).

[200] Zhao Guojun, "Reflection and prospect on the reform of Chinese financial institutions", *Economic Forum*, 2010 (12).

[201] Zhao Xiaona, "Thought for China's financial supervision system reform

under the new situation", *Journal of Qinghai Normal University (Philosophy and Social Sciences Edition), 2016* (3).

[202] Zhen Feng, "The internationalization of renminbi: development, prospects and orientation", *Economic Theory and Business Management*, 2014 (5).

[203] Zheng Yaodong, "The changes of China's financial system and the transformation of financial regulations (1978-1998)", *Teaching and Research*, 1998 (12).

[204] Zheng Yaodong, "The development of financial industry of new China changes and brilliant achievement", *Journal of the Central Institute of Socialism*, 1999 (Z1).

[205] Zhou Dexiang and Gao Xincai, *The Spirit of Chinese Development: Economics*, Lanzhou: Gansu Culture Press, 2004.

[206] Zhou Xun and Liu Xin, "Problems in the development process of finance company in enterprise group and suggestions for improvement", *Finance & Accounting*, 2011 (10).

[207] Zhou Zhengqing, "A discuss about the enterprise of professional bank", *Journal of Financial Research*, 1986 (11).

[208] Zhou Zhenhai, "Study on the China's Financial System Reform Since the Reform and Opening up", Changchun: Northeast Normal University, 2007.

[209] Zhu Huaxiong and Kong Jie, "Research on insurance thoughts during the period of Republic of China (1912-1949): based on the investigation of national insurance industry", *Economics Information*, 2011 (11).

[210] Zhu Ping and Jiang Hongye, "Soviet currency during the agrarian revolutionary war (Part 3)", *China Finance*, 1982 (1).

[211] Zhu Qing, "Research on the Evolution of China's Commercial Banks' Ownership since the Reform and Opening up", Nanchang: Jiangxi Normal University, 2013.

[212] Zi Xinshuang, "Research on China's financial opening up", *Business Research*, 2012 (22).

This book is the result of a co-publication agreement between Economic Science Press (China) and Paths International Ltd (UK).

Title: China's Financial System Development and Reform
Author: Chen Jiangsheng, Liu Lei, Zhang Tao
Translated by Liu Huaiyu et al.
Proofread by Wang Yanshu
ISBN: 978-1-84464-752-1
Ebook ISBN: 978-1-84464-753-8

Paths International Ltd
Published in the United Kingdom
www.pathsinternational.com

www.ingramcontent.com/pod-product-compliance
Lightning Source LLC
LaVergne TN
LVHW080602031225
826550LV00004B/80